The Holy Spirit and
the Reformation Legacy

The Holy Spirit and the Reformation Legacy

Edited by
MARK J. CARTLEDGE
and
MARK A. JUMPER

PICKWICK *Publications* · Eugene, Oregon

THE HOLY SPIRIT AND THE REFORMATION LEGACY

Pickwick Publications
An Imprint of Wipf and Stock Publishers
199 W. 8th Ave., Suite 3
Eugene, OR 97401

www.wipfandstock.com

PAPERBACK ISBN: 978-1-5326-9543-8
HARDCOVER ISBN: 978-1-5326-9544-5
EBOOK ISBN: 978-1-5326-9545-2

Cataloguing-in-Publication data:

Names: Cartledge, Mark J., editor. | Jumper, Mark A., editor.

Title: The Holy Spirit and the Reformation Legacy / edited by Mark J.Cartledge and Mark A. Jumper.

Description: Eugene, OR: Pickwick Publications, 2020. | Includes bibliographical references and index.

Identifiers: ISBN 978-1-5326-9543-8 (paperback). | ISBN 978-1-5326-9544-5 (hardcover). | ISBN 978-1-5326-9545-2 (ebook).

Subjects: LCSH: Holy Spirit—History of doctrines. | Reformation. | Luther, Martin, 1484–1546. | Calvin, John, 1509–1564. | Church history—16th century. | Theology.

Classification: BT121.3 H65 2020 (print). | BT121.3 (ebook).

Manufactured in the U.S.A.   AUGUST 17, 2020

To the faculty and students of
Regent University School of Divinity

Contents

Acknowledgments

THE EDITORS WOULD LIKE to acknowledge the support given by Regent University for the conference on the theme of "The Holy Spirit and the Reformation Legacy," held in the fall of 2017 with one hundred scholars attending. All the chapters in this volume were presented initially as conference papers. This conference was held under the auspices of the Center for Renewal Studies, directed at the time by Prof. Mark J. Cartledge. The main conference organizer was Dr. Mark A. Jumper. Last but not least, we wish to acknowledge the enthusiastic support of the conference by the Dean of the School of Divinity, Dr. Corné Bekker.

Contributors

Lance Bacon is an ordained bishop in the Church of God who has served sixteen years as a senior pastor. He currently serves in that role at Greater Discipleship Center in Hampton, Virginia. He earned his Master of Divinity from the Regent University School of Divinity in 2016 and is in the PhD dissertation phase at that school. He delights in his role as an adjunct professor of Christian Ministry, Christian Ethics, and Christian History/Thought at the Regent University College of Arts and Sciences. He is the author of *The Scariest Word in the Bible*.

David M. Barbee, PhD, is an Assistant Professor of Christian Thought at Winebrenner Theological Seminary in Findlay, Ohio. His academic research focuses primarily on late medieval scholasticism and early modern Protestantism. He earned his PhD in Religious Studies with a focus in the History of Christianity from the University of Pennsylvania in Philadelphia.

Mark J. Cartledge, PhD, FRSA, is Principal of the London School of Theology and was previously Professor of Practical Theology and Director of the Center for Renewal Studies at Regent University School of Divinity. He is a priest in the Church of England and a practical theologian who also works in the field of constructive theology. His current research interest lies at the intersection of pneumatology, ecclesiology, and public life. He has studied Pentecostal and Charismatic Christianity for many years.

Mara Lief Crabtree, DMin, is an Associate Professor at the Regent University School of Divinity, Virginia Beach, Virginia, where she teaches in the areas of Christian Spirituality and Spiritual Formation. She completed her doctoral studies immersion experience in Poland, visiting and studying the Holocaust areas of Auschwitz, Birkenau, Treblinka, and others. Mara holds ordination with the Communion of Evangelical Episcopal Churches. She served for over twenty years as a Chaplain for the International Order of

St. Luke the Physician (OSL), an ecumenical religious order. She currently serves as Region 2 Representative for OSL Chapters in the Commonwealth of Virginia.

Jan Drayer became a believer in August of 1984 in Taos, New Mexico, and married Leslie Alexander in December that year. He earned the BS in Bible, focusing on World Missions, in 1991 from the University of Valley Forge in Phoenixville, Pennsylvania. He and his family then moved to the Philippines, where they served as missionaries for sixteen years. They returned to the U.S., where in 2008 Jan became the senior pastor of Community Gospel Church in Pasadena, Maryland, affiliated with Elim Fellowship (with which he holds ordination). He earned the MTS from the Regent University School of Divinity in Virginia Beach, Virginia, in 2013. He is an MPhil/PhD student at the London School of Theology under the supervision of Dr. Graham McFarlane. His research focus is toward a pneumatological rendering of James Davison Hunter's "faithful presence" model.

Barbara Elkjer is an Assemblies of God minister who served for eight years at First Assembly of God in Sioux Falls, South Dakota. She is a PhD candidate at the Regent University School of Divinity in Virginia Beach, Virginia, writing on the role of prophecy in the eschatological mission of the Church, and teaching hermeneutics and theology in a local Assemblies of God School of Ministry. She and her husband have four grown children and five grandchildren—and counting!

Daniel Gilbert, PhD, a Presbyterian minister, has ministered the Spirit-empowered Gospel for over thirty-five years in church, para-church, mission, and higher education venues. He is Director of Master's Programs and an Assistant Professor at the Regent University School of Divinity in Virginia Beach, Virginia. He is the founder of EmPowered Living International Ministries, a teaching and humanitarian ministry, and the founder and President of ELIM Theological Institute, a Bible school in Kenya training village pastors in sound theology and humanitarian action, accomplished in the power of the Holy Spirit. He is the author of *The Big 5: Discovering the Five Foundations Every Christian Should Know*, with a foreword by Dr. M. G. "Pat" Robertson. He earned the PhD in Theology from the University of Aberdeen, Scotland; the MDiv from the Regent University School of Divinity; and the BS in Business Administration from Mars Hill University in North Carolina. He and his wife, Mary Beth, share a happy marriage of thirty-four years and a lovely daughter, Maria.

James M. Henderson, PhD, is Assistant Professor of Biblical Studies and Christian Ministry at Regent University's College of Arts and Sciences in Virginia Beach, Virginia. He is also an Ordained Minister with the International Church of the Foursquare Gospel. His work focuses on justification, divine election, and the work of the Holy Spirit in the world.

Mark A. Jumper, PhD, is an Associate Professor and Director of Chaplaincy and Military Affairs at the Regent University School of Divinity in Virginia Beach, Virginia. A third-generation Presbyterian minister, he is ordained by the Evangelical Presbyterian Church, which he has served as Endorser for Chaplains and as moderator of two presbyteries. He is a retired Navy chaplain whose service included the U.S. Marine Corps and the U.S. Coast Guard at sea, on land, and in the air, in peace, war, and storm. He earned the PhD in Humanities from Salve Regina University in Newport, Rhode Island; the MDiv from Columbia Theological Seminary in Decatur, Georgia; and the BA in History from Oral Roberts University in Tulsa, Oklahoma. He is a contributor to several edited collections. He and his wife, Ginger, are parents of seven children.

Don Kammer is a Theology PhD student at the Regent University School of Divinity in Virginia Beach, Virginia, concentrating in the History of Global Christianity. He is a retired United States Army chaplain and combat veteran. He is endorsed by the Assemblies of God as an institutional chaplain and serves in the Washington, DC area. He earned the MDiv from Assemblies of God Theological Seminary in Springfield, Missouri, with emphasis on Theological Studies and Pastoral Counseling, in 1989. He earned the MA in History from Missouri State University in Springfield, Missouri, in 1990; and the MA in American Studies at the College of William and Mary in Williamsburg, Virginia in 2005. Don became interested in Christianity through an encounter with the Invisible Church, a charismatic Jesus Movement community that existed fleetingly in London, the United Kingdom in the 1970s and 80s. He was then a young atheist soldier stationed in West Berlin, West Germany, who encountered God while on leave in London.

Samuel W. Muindi, PhD, is a Lecturer in Biblical and Theological Studies at International Leadership University in Nairobi, Kenya. His areas of teaching and research interest include Old Testament Biblical Studies, Biblical Hermeneutics, Pentecostal Studies, and African Christian Spirituality. His recent publications include: *Pentecostal-Charismatic Prophecy: Empirical-Theological Analysis* (Oxford: Lang, 2107); "Ritual and Spirituality in Kenyan Pentecostalism," in *Scripting Pentecostalism: A Study of Pentecostals,*

Worship and Liturgy (ed. M. Cartledge and A. J. Swoboda; London: Routledge, 2017); and *Ancient Israelite and African Wisdom Traditions: A Comparative-Hermeneutical Analysis* (Nairobi: Christian Academic Publishing, 2015). He earned the PhD from the University of Birmingham, UK. He and his wife, Jane, live in Nairobi, Kenya. They are blessed with four children and four grandchildren and are actively involved in church ministry, particularly among the African Initiated Pentecostal-Charismatic churches.

Michael M. C. Reardon is a PhD student in New Testament and Historical Theology at Wycliffe College of the University of Toronto, Canada. His research explores the role of deification in New Testament soteriology and its reception by Medieval and Early Modern thinkers. He is currently the Professor of Biblical Languages and Christian Thought at Canada Christian College in Toronto. His other research interests include German idealism, Pietism, hermeneutic methodology, and Sino-Christian theology. Outside of academia, Michael enjoys spending time with his wife and two children, playing basketball, and serving in his local church.

Andrew Snyder is a PhD candidate in Theological Studies at the Regent University School of Divinity in Virginia Beach, Virginia, and is writing his dissertation on the qualitative distinction between Kierkegaard's concepts of anxiety and despair. He earned the MA in Christian Thought from Gordon-Conwell Theological Seminary in South Hamilton, Massachusetts, and lives in Williamsburg, Virginia, with his wife, Christabel.

Fitzroy John Willis, PhD, teaches Physical Science and Bible at Landmark Christian School in Fairburn, Georgia, and is the co-founder of The Willis Group, LLC, a consulting firm that supports individuals and organizations to fulfill their talent, learning, and developmental needs. He was previously an Adjunct Professor of Worldviews, Theology, Bible, and Biblical Interpretation at Ohio Christian University. He earned the PhD in Christian Theology from the Regent University School of Divinity in Virginia Beach, Virginia, where he also earned an MA in Biblical Interpretation. He also earned the MS from SUNY Health Science Center in Brooklyn, and the BS in Biochemistry from SUNY Stony Brook, New York. He lives in Metro-Atlanta with his wife and five children.

Christopher J. Wilson holds the PhD in Renewal Studies with a concentration in ChristianTheology from the Regent University School of Divinity in Virginia Beach, Virginia. His dissertation will be published as *Renewal Apologetics: The Argument from Modern Miracles*. His interests include the intersection of medical miracles and Christian prayer as a primary means of apologetics, evangelism, and renewal, developed from a comprehensive theology of the miraculous. He is married with four children, ages eight and down. He enjoys watching sports, playing chess, reading (apologetics, theology, and philosophy), and spending time with his family.

Introduction

MARK A. JUMPER AND MARK J. CARTLEDGE

THE PROTESTANT REFORMATION REPRESENTED a revolution in the religious affairs of the West that reverberates to the present. The East–West Schism in Christendom (1054) between Roman Catholic and Orthodox had reflected formal actions of the bodies, Rome and Constantinople, that had long been recognized as definitive leaders of the Church. The Protestant Reformation (1517), in contrast, sprang from the soil, as it were: if not *ex nihilo* (progenitors included such as Huss and Wycliff, among other persons and movements), certainly not *ex cathedra*. The formation of two leading movements, Lutheran and Reformed, as well as Anglicans, Anabaptists, and others proceeded unplanned and piecemeal with many diversions and dispersions in the process. In the meantime, the Roman Catholic Church experienced many reformations of its own, including the forming of the innovatively modern Society of Jesus.[1] Years of struggle and battle followed -theological, ecclesial, political, and military- that remade not just the face of Europe, but its religious configuration, by the time of Westfalia's peace of 1648.

We note that the European discovery, exploration, and expropriation of the New World predated the Reformation by only twenty-five years, reaching its floodtide even as Reformation conflicts tore the explorers' homelands. The New World's melee of new boundaries and rulers reflected much of Europe's conflicts, eventuating in North America generally aligning Protestant and South America, Roman Catholic. The dynamics occurring in both Europe and the New World were thus not isolated, but mutually interactive in myriads of unpredictable and sometimes unrecognized ways.

---

1. Eire, *Reformations*, 442, 451.

Technical, economic, and social change also claimed roles in the times' convulsions. New technology, most notably the movable type printing press, had a primary role. The Gutenberg Bible was completed by 1455, when the future Pope Pius II spoke of it sixty-two years before Luther's handwritten 95 Theses were posted. However, it was Luther and the Protestants who made mass pamphlet printing and distribution their trademark method of propagation and teaching. That teaching implicitly depended upon the Holy Spirit's illumination of those lesser-trained individuals who read it in private and public. New social developments included travel, trade, infusions of New World gold, spice, and crops, and new uses of capital. These brought significant changes to a continent not so far removed from feudalism. To generalize, Protestant places tended to be more open to these changes, embracing them with enthusiasm in some contexts. Max Weber later named *The Protestant Ethic and the Spirit of Capitalism* as the mutually reinforcing winners of that war.[2]

We also remember that Europe, after centuries of loss to Muslim conquerors from the south, had only recently put a definite close to Christendom's near-death threat at Islam's hands. Spain's 700-year self-deliverance from Islamic rule, the *Reconquista*, was only completed in 1492, with the victorious Ferdinand and Isabella promptly sending Columbus on his momentous voyage (as well as exiling Jews who took their prosperous practices elsewhere).[3] The gates of Vienna only survived the climactic Ottoman assault in 1529, finally leaving central and western Europe to stew in their internecine conflicts rather than have their weakened pieces consumed by Islam's cumulative victories. Islam's retreat from high tide, Spain in 1492 and Vienna in 1529, thus overlapped the Reformation's early years, along with the New World dynamics.

Finally, we note the Renaissance as another of the Reformation's overlays, starting as it did in the 1300s and continuing through the 1700s. This movement of academic and cultural recovery of ancient literature and philosophy combined with an energetic flowering of art and new philosophies, and the rise of humanism and science, to undermine many of the assumptions and underpinnings of Christendom's *ancien regime.*

It may thus be seen that the Reformation does not stand alone in its revolutionary role. If the Renaissance weakened the *ancien regime*, perhaps the Reformation administered a *coup de grace* of sorts. However, the

2. Weber, *The Protestant Ethic,* 67–75.

3. Johnson notes, "Isabella . . . boasted that, from her passionate devotion to the faith, she had caused the ruin of royal towns, emptied them of their inhabitants and desolated whole regions. Ferdinand, too, stressed the losses to the royal revenue . . ." (*A History,* 227).

conjunctions of the New World's opening horizon, Islam's ebbtide, and paradigmatic changes in technological, social, scientific, and economic developments were certainly of momentous import. These factors, each in itself of defining consequence, joined to birth a new world that is yet with us as our formative heritage: "No Westerner can ever hope to know him- or herself, or the world he or she lives in, without first understanding this crucial turning point in history. And the same goes for any non-Westerner who wants to understand Western civilization."[4]

The question then arises: as Christians who affirm the providence and sovereignty of God, do we dare to discern the role of the Holy Spirit amid such momentous events? This question lay at the root of the conference from which these chapters sprang. We should remember that while the above-mentioned movements and influences provided the context for the several reformations that occurred, the center stage of the era was religious.[5] We dare to suggest that church, theology, and faith with its experience were the prime drivers of the era's events. In other words, the living out of belief in God lay at the core of it all. It is this claimed nexus of this definitive era that gives us pause to ask how God's Spirit, who hovered over the earth's waters in Genesis 1:1, was active amid the Reformation's human striving and strife.

Martin Luther linked his revolution, recognizing faith as primary over works, to the Holy Spirit:

> Faith is God's work in us, that changes us and gives new birth from God. (John 1:13). It kills the Old Adam and makes us completely different people. It changes our hearts, our spirits, our thoughts and all our powers. It brings the Holy Spirit with it. Yes, it is a living, creative, active and powerful thing, this faith. Faith is a living, bold trust in God's grace, so certain of God's favor that it would risk death a thousand times trusting in it. Such confidence and knowledge of God's grace makes you happy, joyful and bold in your relationship to God and all creatures. The Holy Spirit makes this happen through faith. Because of it, you freely, willingly and joyfully do good to everyone, serve everyone, suffer all kinds of things, love and praise the God who has shown you such grace.[6]

It is significant, too, that Luther emphasized this infusion of the Spirit's presence and illumination in personal terms, rather than primarily in

---

4. Eire, *Reformations*, viii.

5. Eire, *Reformations*, x-xi.

6. Irmischer, *Dr. Martin Luther's*, 124–25.

corporate (ecclesial) or communitarian (sacramental) terms. This emphasis on the private person's relationship to God through the Holy Spirit became central, for good and ill, in individualized Western society, even if, in our context, we are now recovering the importance of communal approaches to theological reflection.

Calvin, too, attributed high of place to the Holy Spirit. He was even given the sobriquet, "Theologian of the Holy Spirit," [7] by various theologians including B. B. Warfield:

> In the same sense in which we may say that the doctrine of sin and grace dates from Augustine, the doctrine of satisfaction from Anselm, the doctrine of justification by faith from Luther- we must say that the doctrine of the work of the Holy Spirit is a gift from Calvin to the church.
>
> [And] above everything else, it is the sense of the sovereign working of salvation by the almighty power of the Holy Spirit which characterizes all Calvin's thought of God.[8]

Calvin went to great lengths in his *Institutes* to expand upon the Holy Spirit's significant role, in both personal and theological terms:

> The Scriptures obtain full authority among believers only when men regard them as having sprung from heaven, as if there the living words of God were heard . . . The testimony of the Spirit is more excellent than all reason. For as God alone is a fit witness of himself in his Word, so also the Word will not find acceptance in men's hearts before it is sealed by the inward testimony of the Spirit . . . Those whom the Holy Spirit has inwardly taught truly rest upon Scripture, and that Scripture indeed is self-authenti- cated . . . Let us, then, know that the only true faith is that which the Spirit of God seals in our hearts.[9]

It is thus safe to say, of Calvin as well as Luther, that the Reformation represented recovery and reemphasis of the person and work of the Holy Spirit. Indeed neither would have maintained his path apart from "popery," as Calvin called it, were he not convinced that such a drastic move was not only justified but required as a faithful act in response to the move and lead- ing of the Holy Spirit of God.

7. Evans, "John Calvin."

8. Warfield, *Calvin and Augustine*, 484–87.

9. Calvin, *Calvin and Augustine*, I.7.1, 4, 5.

G. W. F. Hegel later sought to explain history in terms of a (capitalized but impersonal) World Spirit[10] that "consists in what is produced by man":[11]

> The realm of Spirit is all-comprehensive; it includes everything that ever has interested or ever will interest man. Man is active in it; whatever he does, he is the creature within which the Spirit works. Hence it is of interest, in the course of history, to learn to know spiritual nature in its existence, that is, the point where Spirit and Nature unite, namely, human nature.[12]

We Christians, while resonating with Hegel's wish to learn the spiritual nature of history, take a different tack that seeks to discern the winds of the person of God's Spirit moving through time, space, place, and people's lives. We believe that God's divine, personal, providential plan and presence, mediated by his Spirit's activity through all time, ultimately achieve his will to bring about his Kingdom, ruled by Christ.

Exploring the degree to which the Reformation represented and reflected that rule is one aim of the conference that we convened on the Reformation's 500th anniversary. We took our specific task from the conference's title, "The Holy Spirit and the Reformation Legacy." This title entailed three emphases that were required of each presentation as we examined but a few of the Reformation's facets: first, the presence and role of the Holy Spirit in a given area of interest; second, awareness and placement of the Spirit's role in the historical locus of the Reformation; and third, ways in which those Reformation beliefs and actions, regarding the Holy Spirit, left lasting legacies that still live today.

Regent University, the host of the conference through its School of Divinity's Center for Renewal Studies, has, from its start, been part of the Holy Spirit renewal movement that swept the world from the twentieth century on. This movement includes Pentecostal, Charismatic, and Third Wave streams, as well as a vigorous stream in the Roman Catholic Church. Our Reformation 500 conference thus sought to take its distinction from other Reformation celebrations and explorations by giving primary attention to the Holy Spirit. We pray that this conference may thus make a unique contribution to the scholarship of those Reformation events that continue to echo through time.

As you consider each conference paper chapter, we also pray that you will find fresh insight, not only into what happened and what has come

10. Hegel, *Reason in History*, 48.

11. Hegel, *Reason in History*, 20.

12. Hegel, *Reason in History*, 20.

about but into the activity of the Holy Spirit in this earthly veil—including in your life.

It now remains to offer a brief outline of the chapters in this book. We have divided the book into three parts. The first part clusters chapters that consider the influence of Martin Luther and includes chapters 1–6. Chapter 1 by Michael M.C. Reardon discusses Luther and his influence on Melanchthon's pneumatology in relation to the doctrines of the Trinity and justification. This legacy is then brought into conversation with the idealism of Hegel and its traces in Rahner, suggesting that Luther's legacy has impacted a wide variety of thought beyond the confessionalism of the Lutheran tradition. Chapter 2 by Samuel W. Muindi takes a hermeneutical turn. It considers the legacy of Luther concerning biblical hermeneutics and in particular canonical criticism. It does this by analyzing Luther's hermeneutical approach before attending to the post-Reformation trajectories from the Enlightenment. He continues by discussing the similarities of Luther's hermeneutics with the canonical criticism of Brevard Childs before concluding with a discussion of pneumatic hermeneutics. Chapter 3 by Donald W. Kammer takes an entirely different approach as it reviews the early Pentecostal devotional literature in America and Britain from 1907 and how these early Pentecostals conceived of themselves as inheritors of the Lutheran legacy through their devotional practices. In particular, they regarded Martin Luther as a spiritual exemplar and incorporated him into their view of church history, thus adding an interesting ecumenical perspective.

Chapter 4 by Mara Lief Crabtree brings the legacy of Martin Luther into conversation with the issue of spirituality and, in particular, the nature of spiritual formation. Crabtree first discusses key elements in Luther's spirituality before tracing his influence via the printing press, *visio divina* and *lectio divina*, and diverse theologies of the Eucharist. Then follows a description of Luther's understanding of suffering in the Christian life, including his view on purgatory, before a brief discussion of joy and priestly formation. The chapter concludes by identifying aspects of the Reformation legacy that can be seen in spiritual "re-formation" today. Lance Bacon writes chapter 5. In this chapter, the author investigates the influence of Luther on the Pentecostal appreciation of the cross and Pentecostals' appropriation of John Wesley's approach to Christian perfection. Having identified the plurality of Pentecostalism, Bacon then considers Luther's theology of the cross in some detail before bringing it into conversation with Wesley's theology. The discussion is then brought back to how American Wesleyan Pentecostalism has appropriated both justification and sanctification in its theology. He then concludes with a discussion of pneumatology and ethics in the light of the legacy of Luther and Wesley. Chapter 6, written by Barbara

Elkjer, concludes the section investigating the legacy of Luther. She takes a look at Luther's theology of marriage and in particular, his marriage to his wife Katharina von Bora. She places this discussion within an historical context, both ancient and medieval, before considering ideas of virginity and marriage that Katharina developed during her marriage to Luther. Thus, this chapter brings an essential perspective on Luther's legacy, often missed, which relates to the Pentecostal empowerment of women through a pneumatic spirituality.

The second part brings together chapters that discuss the legacy of John Calvin and includes chapters 7–10. Chapter 7 by Andrew Snyder investigates Calvin's pneumatology in relation to soteriology and in particular, the believer's union with Christ by means of the Holy Spirit. He traces the influence of Augustine on Calvin's theology more generally before focusing on Calvin's pneumatology and soteriology. He then considers implications of this discussion in relation to sacramental theology, especially Calvin's eucharistic pneumatology. Chapter 8 by David M. Barbee explores the influence of Calvin's pneumatology on Karl Barth. He begins by noting Calvin's pneumatology and its reception by Schleiermacher and via Schleiermacher to Barth. Given this pneumatological trajectory, the author then discusses the theme of revelation in Barth before noting some similarities between Calvin and Barth and the impact of Calvin's pneumatology on Barth. Chapter 9, by Fitzroy John Willis, is a review of Calvin's criteria for the use of the *charismata* and their possible use within contemporary worship. The author begins by elucidating Calvin's understanding of the proper employment of prophecy within a worship service before considering how contemporary theology has considered the application of these criteria to today's worshipping communities. He discusses the relationship between prophecy and preaching and the nature and use of speaking in tongues and interpretation, as well as the issue of the cessation of the *charismata*. Finally, there is a discussion of *charismata*, gender, and the *mulier taceat*. Chapter 10, written by Daniel B. Gilbert, provides a second study of John Calvin and the *charismata*, with a particular emphasis on the gift of prophecy. He begins with a general description of Calvin's view of the *charismata* before a discussion of soteriological gifts, the *charismata*, and the gift of prophecy. He discusses the nature of the temporary-permanent distinction before applying this understanding to its use in the church today.

Part three gathers three papers that reflect on several Reformation themes and are not as focused on a discussion of either Luther or Calvin. It contains chapters 11–13. Chapter 11 picks up the theme of cessationism and addresses it in relation to the Reformation and renewal of the Holy Spirit. It is written by Christopher J. Wilson. It begins with a short historical sketch of cessationism in the Patristic era before considering the Reformation period. He then discusses anti-supernaturalism and the rise of historical criticism. Finally, he addresses the position of David Hume in relation to the Pentecostal and Charismatic Renewal movements from the twentieth century. Chapter 12, by James M. Henderson, investigates the relationship of justification to the idea of the *theōsis*. He begins with an analysis of justification as *theōsis* in recent Pentecostal theology and literature before considering whether *theōsis* could be understood as part of the process of justification. He then develops a discussion engaging the work of Finnish Lutheran theology in particular before considering the critique of this school of thought by German theologian, Eberhard Jüngel. Carl R. Trueman is also brought into the conversation as another critical dialogue partner with regard to the Finnish Lutheran school of thought, before a discussion of justification and transformation in the Reformed theology of Jonathan Edwards. Finally, the essay concludes by addressing the issue of how justification with transformation may be regarded as a better model than *theōsis*. Chapter 13 is the final chapter of the book, and it is written by Jan B. Drayer. It reviews the impact of the Reformation heritage in dialogue with the cultural change theory of James Davidson Hunter. On this account, the social change initiated by the Reformation is seen as still significant for our understanding of the contemporary religious landscape. He notes Hunter's critique of the common understanding of culture in American society, his alternative suggestions for understanding culture, and in particular, his analysis of the Reformation, before providing an overall analysis of the Reformation, social change, and the Holy Spirit. Finally, he observes the limited role that Pentecostals have played in the field of social change, being more concerned with evangelism rather than social transformation.

BIBLIOGRAPHY

Calvin, John. *Institutes of the Christian Religion*. Library of Christian Classics. Philadelphia: Westminster John Knox, 1960.

Eire, Carlos M. N. *Reformations: The Early Modern World, 1450–1650*. New Haven: Yale University Press, 2016.

Hegel, G. W. F. *Reason in History: A General Introduction to the Philosophy of History*. Translated by Robert S. Hartman. Upper Saddle River, NJ: Prentice-Hall, 1997.

Irmischer, Johann, ed., trans. Robert E. Smith. *Dr. Martin Luther's Vermischte Deutsche Schriften*. Vol. 63. Erlangen: Heyder & Zimmer, 1854. https://www.ligonier.org/learn/articles/martin-luthers-definition-faith/.

Johnson, Paul. *A History of the Jews*. New York: HarperPerennial, 1988.

Warfield, Benjamin Breckinridge. *Calvin and Augustine*. Edited by Samuel G. Craig. Phillipsburg, NJ: Presbyterian & Reformed, 1956.

Weber, Max, trans. Stephen Kalberg. *The Protestant Ethic and the Spirit of Capitalism: The Revised 1920 Edition*. Oxford: Oxford University Press, 2010.

PART ONE

The Legacy of Martin Luther

1

Rivers of Living Water

Martin Luther's Pneumatology, German Idealism, and Modern Catholic Theology

MICHAEL M. C. REARDON

INTRODUCTION

THOUGH RIGHTLY CELEBRATED, THE legacy of the Reformation is mixed, being composed of both positive and negative developments that have been augmented over the past five centuries and concretized within Christian theological discourse. Positive results include the "newfound" prominence and interpretative power of the Scriptures to articulate rightlythe Christian faith, a re-examination of soteriology, and the transfer of specific elements of Christian praxis from the clerical elite to the lay masses. Tangible negative outcomes must also be considered when remembering and assessing the events that transpired from 1517. For example, many see ecclesial disunity as the Reformation's greatest scandal. That disunity has accelerated at an unabated pace in modernity, not least because such thoughtful reflection often does *not* occur. Strikingly, this blemish on the heritage of the Reformation indirectly affects every aspect of the Christian faith as it allows for a multitude of theological fads and opinions to be given a near-equal platform to be voiced and accepted. From the nature of Scripture to the efficacy of the sacraments, there exists no single doctrine that can be articulated in a homogenous manner across denominations. Indeed, this lack of doctrinal agreement frequently engenders contentious dialogue *within* denominational persuasions. This chapter explores the presence of this "mixed" legacy within the theology of its most visible progenitor (Martin Luther) and the group that bears his namesake (Lutheranism).

Specifically, this exploration is situated with a growing stream of research that probes the ostensible dissimilarity between Martin Luther's theology and later promulgations of Lutheranism, best embodied (or at least formatively shaped) by the theology of Philipp Melanchthon. Concerning their divergent theological trajectories, research in the past four decades is particularly noteworthy, especially the findings of the Mannermaa school and its posited retrieval of Luther's *true* doctrine of justification, which bears a striking resemblance to the Eastern Orthodox doctrine of *theōsis*.[1] Concerning this exercise, Veli-Matti Kärkkäinen comments that this rereading offers *not only* an alternative view of Luther's soteriology; much rather, it has extensive pneumatological implications as well.[2] These latter ramifications are of particular import to this essay, which argues that a robustly pneumatological stream extends from the theology of Luther—a stream that is altogether absent from the theological lineage of Melanchthon. This posited stream is situated outside of the historical purview of either of these Reformers, and thus, no claim is being made concerning the purposeful intention of either thinker.

Nevertheless, the existence of pneumatological differences in Luther and Melanchthon's theology bore (and continues to bear) influence on countless metaphysical frameworks. Due to the sweeping nature of this claim, the following analysis is at best a cursory exercise that aims to be illustrative, not exhaustive, of the influence of Luther's pneumatology upon later thinkers and their respective philosophical and theological outlooks. Additionally, the doctrinal stream that is being suggested has been conceptually delimited only to *pneumatological concerns*—no assertion is made concerning strict genealogical relations between theologians, nor of orthodox or heterodox theological positions. With this in mind, we may turn to the succeeding remarks, which are structured as follows: first, an overview which delineates significant differences between Luther and Melanchthon in their conceptions of the Trinity and in their conceptions of the doctrine of justification, with an emphasis on their pneumatological implications; second, an examination of the presence and influence of Luther's pneumatology in

---

1. For further reading, see Mannermaa, *Christ Present in Faith*, passim.

2. Kärkkäinen, *Pneumatology*, 85.

the philosophy of German idealist Georg Wilhelm Friedrich Hegel; third, a presentation elucidating how Hegel's reimagining of Luther's pneumatology formatively shaped the theology of twenteith-century Roman Catholic theologian Karl Rahner; and lastly, a brief conclusion which synthesizes these findings both for future research and present reflection.

THE REFORMERS:
MARTIN LUTHER AND PHILIP MELANCHTHON

Luther and Melanchthon formed an unlikely duo in the early days of the Reformation. While Luther was known for his acerbic temperament and unsystematic thinking, Melanchthon has been described as charitable, lucid, and coherent.[3] Moreover, while Luther was trained in monastic theology, Melanchthon was educated in intellectual humanism.[4] Still, "duo"—if carrying the sense of equality in stature—may be a misleading descriptor as their relationship was asymmetrical: Luther was a larger-than-life personality and leader whereas Melanchthon was the spokesperson and devotee. Melanchthon considered Luther "the Elijah" of the present age and stated that he "would rather die than be separated from Luther."[5] But despite both his "junior status" and lack of recognition outside of the academy, it was Melanchthon's systematic presentation of Luther's theology that facilitated its assimilation within sixteenth-century scholarly circles and provided the framework for modern Lutheranism. Though to be clear, this 'systematized presentation' was anything but a regurgitation of Luther's sentiments. Concerning this, Samuel Powell rightly states that "the thoughts of Luther and Melanchthon were capable of leading in several directions."[6] Indeed, the succeeding decades of theological development engendered substantial doctrinal divergences between them, an occurrence Paul Hinlicky brilliantly notes in a humorous assessment of Mark Mattes' "test of genuine Luther-theology"—a metric that Hinlicky claims would exclude Luther himself from "genuine Lutheran theology!"[7]

3. Hinlicky, *Paths not Taken*, 154.

4. Rogness, *Philip Melanchthon*, 2–7.

5. Peterson, *Preaching in the Last Days*, 103; Manschreck, *Melanchthon*, 54.

6. Powell, *The Trinity in German Thought*, 147.

7. Hinlicky, *Paths not Taken*, 156. Here Hinlicky asserts that the items used to describe "genuine Luther-theology" are in fact developments in Melanchthon's theology.

The Trinity

Luther's Trinitarian theology is firmly rooted within the Western Christian tradition,[8] as evidenced by what he considers to be the three symbols of the Christian faith: the Apostles' Creed, the Athanasian Creed, and the hymn *Te Deum Laudamus.*[9] For Luther, this historical tethering of his Trinitarian claims to patristic Christianity was necessary, as he considered the doctrine of the Trinity to be one of "the sublime articles of the divine majesty" that were "not matters of dispute or contention" between Protestant and Catholic churches.[10] However, unlike his scholastic predecessors, Luther did not spend time speculatively explicating the Trinity via logic and philosophy. Rather, he relied upon a scripturally-grounded Trinitarian framework; indeed, it undergirded every one of his doctrinal commitments.[11]

Regin Prenter presses Luther's Trinitarian-oriented framework further, noting that it is not merely the Trinity, but rather "the concept of the Holy Spirit [that] completely dominates Luther's theology."[12] Though a bold pronouncement laid upon the Christocentric Luther, Prenter's assertion is not unwarranted. In the final section of the *Large Catechism* concerning the Creed, Luther *reverses* the order of the Trinity to reflect the Christian's encounter with God. Concerning this re-ordering, Timothy J. Wengert draws three conclusions: first, that "Luther's understanding of the Holy Spirit holds the key to his Trinitarian theology"; second, that Luther's understanding of the Holy Spirit leads to his description of the Trinity; and lastly, that "it is the Holy Spirit who turned Luther's (and turns our) understanding of the Trinity on its head."[13] Pekka Kärkkäinen advances a conceptually similar argument in *Luther's trinitarische Theologie Des Heiligen Geistes,* arguing that Luther exhibits strong pneumatological commitments in doctrines historically grounded in the Trinity.[14] One example he offers to support this claim comes from Luther's commentary on the epistle to the Galatians, wherein Luther posits a strong, unified relationship between the Spirit and faith, with the promise of faith being fulfilled by the Holy Spirit indwelling the believer.[15]

---

8. Paulson, "Luther's Doctrine of God," 187.

9. Luther, *The Practice of Theology,* 130–31.

10. Swain, "The Trinity in the Reformers," 228.

11. Kärkkäinen, *Pneumatology,* 80; cf. Lohse, *Martin Luther,* 232.

12. Prenter, *Spiritus Creator,* ix.

13. Wengert, *Martin Luther's Catechisms,* 43–44.

14. Saarinen, "Justification by Faith: The View of the Mannermaa School," 257.

15. Pekka Kärkkäinen, *Luther's trinitarische Theologie des Heiligen Geistes,* 102–12.

This reading of Luther is corroborated and expanded upon by Veli-Matti Kärkkäinen, who believes that Luther's pneumatological outlook is central to his theology of the law, word, and sacraments. V-M. Kärkkäinen claims that there "is not a single doctrine in all theology in which the activity of the Spirit was not fundamental" for Luther.[16] To be sure, this does not mean that Luther was proto-Pentecostal. He was explicitly Christocentric and intended to ground every doctrinal position in both the person *and* work of Christ.[17] Still, V-M. Kärkkäinen asserts that this healthy Christocentrism provided a prominent role for the Holy Spirit in Luther's theology. For Luther, the Holy Spirit is the primary agent who testifies concerning Christ's person and mediates Christ's work. Stated differently, Luther argued that Christ's personality and activity were both matched by the Spirit's testimony. Lastly, V-M. Kärkkäinen also notes Luther's strong emphasis upon the interrelationship between the outward and inward works of the Spirit—an emphasis that is particularly noteworthy when contrasting him with Melanchthon. These dual-concerns formatively shaped Luther's pneumatology, as he prioritized both the "outer" way that God approaches humankind through the preached Word and sacraments as well as the "inner" way God approaches humankind—through the Holy Spirit and pneumatologically-infused gifts.[18] Because of these dual-commitments, Luther believed that there was an "incarnational" aspect of the Holy Spirit. Indeed, he persuasively argued that the *real presence of God in Christ* is analogous to the *real presence of the Holy Spirit in the Christian*.[19]

We thus see that Luther (1) prioritized a Trinitarian theological framework; (2) linked doctrinal positions to the person *and* work of Christ; (3) committed to the pneumatological mediation of Christ both linguistically and sacramentally; and (4) prioritized pneumatological commitments. Against these positions, one could (perhaps facetiously) delineate Melanchthon's theological commitments by placing a 'not' before each of the above statements. To be sure, this *is* a jocose suggestion—it would be disingenuous to state that Melanchthon was 'not' Trinitarian merely, 'not' Christocentric, 'not' sacramental, or 'not' pneumatological without further context. He did affirm each of Luther's commitments—yet, he promulgated starkly different conceptions of each position, and, as will be shown, did not prioritize any of them within his theological corpus.

16. Kärkkäinen, *Pneumatology*, 80–87; cf. Lohse, *Martin Luther's Theology*, 234–35.

17. The "and" here is key to differentiating Luther from Melanchthon—i.e., Luther's dual-emphases on the Person *and* work of Christ. Kärkkäinen, "The Holy Spirit and Justification," 32.

18. Kärkkäinen, *Pneumatology*, 81, 84–85

19. Kärkkäinen, *Pneumatology*, 85.

For example, one of the greatest scandals of the early Reformation was the 1521 edition of the *Loci Communes Theologici,* a work that Melanchthon purported to be an "outline of the Christian faith"—a work that did not discuss the Trinity. Shockingly, his rationale for its exclusion was that the Trinity did not "belong to the essence of theology."[20] A charitable reading of Melanchthon might suggest that he espoused a doctrine of hyper-perspicuity, whereby he considered only items *clearly* explicated in the Scriptures as "central" to the Christian faith.[21] If taken to be true, his impetus to gloss over the doctrine of the Trinity is perhaps understandable—though, Robert Jenson rightly asserts that the writings of the early Melanchthon (and others) had a "regrettably negative impact on trinitarian reference in liturgy, preaching, and personal piety."[22]

Such a charitable reading of Melanchthon is undermined by later editions of the *Loci* in which he aimed to assuage his critics. By the time the final edition was published in 1559, his *longest* locus was devoted to the Trinity. Its foreword contained the following statement: "the highest concern of man would be to learn the true teaching concerning God, just as also the First Commandment specifically demands this duty."[23] Yet, his theological evolution led to a different, but equally problematic orientation. Though more closely aligned with theological contemporaries in Trinitarian formulation, Melanchthon paradoxically became, in the words of Samuel M. Powell, "most amenable to the speculative method" he previously eschewed.[24] This predilection is apparent in the 1559 locus where he places Plato in dialogue with Irenaeus and Origen—in other words, he provides an equal platform to a pagan philosopher and patristic theologians, something that would have been anathema to him just three decades prior. However, here a charitable reading of Melanchthon may be better-warranted, as the cause for his about-face is likely historical. As contentions with the Socinians and Michael Severtus concomitantly occurred alongside pressure from Roman Catholic theologians, it became necessary for Melanchthon to explicate orthodox Trinitarian claims—as evident in his numerous refutations of Severtus and likeminded theologians in this locus. Notwithstanding, Melanchthon's doctrinal promulgation in the face of opposition did not abrogate his earlier view of the Trinity as an unessential Christian doctrine. Rather, as readily apparent in his corpus at-large, Melanchthon's Trinitarian

20. Swain, "The Trinity in the Reformers," 228.

21. Powell, *The Trinity in German Thought,* 16.

22. Schlitt, *German Idealism's Trinitarian Legacy,* 198.

23. Melanchthon, *The Chief Theological Topics: Loci Praecipui Theologici 1559,* 10.

24. Powell, *The Trinity in German Thought,* 6.

presentation was *not* a central theological commitment. Rather, as Michael Rogness rightly states, Melanchthon's Trinitarian views are "hardly inspiring" and serve only as "a *prolegomena*, a foundation for the doctrine of the redemption through the Logos, the Son."[25]

Though presented more lucidly than Luther, Melanchthon's treatments of the person of Christ and the Holy Spirit are similarly uninspiring. Rogness masterfully summarizes their divergent interests: for Melanchthon, "the Gospel was not so much about Christ himself, but the truth or Gospel *about* Christ, the proclamation of Christ's saving work on the cross. Luther dwelt on the person of Christ, Melanchthon on Christ's work."[26] To be clear, Melanchthon did *affirm* the personhood of both Christ and the Spirit, both in the *Loci Praecipui Theologici*[27] and in the *Augsburg Confession*.[28] Still, his affirmation of Christ's personhood served a secondary role in his theology. Moreover, Melanchthon's prioritization of Christ's work over personhood led to difficulties in articulating a cogent presentation of the Holy Spirit, as he had difficulty defining distinctive *works* of the Spirit.[29] Due to this difficulty, the presence of the Spirit is scant in Melanchthon's theological system and is relegated only to the interiority of the Christian, strikingly absent from any meaningful public actions.[30] Moving to the next section, this focal shift from person *and* work of Christ in Luther to only Christ's *work* in Melanchthon is central to understanding the divergence of their conceptions of the doctrine of justification by faith.

Justification by Faith

V-M. Kärkkäinen notes that there is a "general consensus of most recent Luther scholarship that the commonly held forensic doctrine of justification by faith, as articulated by later confessional writings under the leadership of Philipp Melanchthon, is a one-sided understanding of Luther's theology."[31] To the old-guard Lutheran scholar, this may be an incendiary claim. Notwithstanding such considerations, this new line of inquiry allows for a more thorough consideration of an "other-sided" understanding of Luther's soteriology. In *Christ Present in Faith*, Tuomo Mannermaa articulates this

25. Rogness, *Melanchthon: Reformer without Honor*, 80.
26. Rogness, *Melanchthon: Reformer without Honor*, 62.
27. Melanchthon, *Loci Praecipui Theologici*, 17–39.
28. Melanchthon, *Augsburg Confession*, 100.
29. Rogness, *Melanchthon: Reformer without Honor*, 79–80.
30. Hinlicky, *Paths not Taken*, 149.
31. Kärkkäinen, *Pneumatology*, 85.

other-side by asserting that Luther's central conception of justification is not primarily located in legal terminology, but rather, in the imagery of a "happy exchange."[32] Hinlicky expounds upon this imagery and asserts that it is this exchange of the Christian's sin and Christ's righteousness that "provides the operative model in Luther's mind of how the event of justification transpires in uniting the believer with Christ in His death and resurrection."[33] For Luther, this happy exchange presupposes that Christ serves a dual-role in the economy of salvation, both as God's favor and God's gift.[34] Furthermore, Mannermaa asserts that for Luther, this justifying act was in continuity with sanctification, and that Christ ruling alongside the Holy Spirit is the primary agent making the Christian holy.[35] Concerning this, Hinlicky notes that the conclusion of this event is that the Spirit "bonds the believer to Christ in time by faith, just as eternally He bonds the Son to the Father and the Father to the Son in love."[36]

> This is not the case for Melanchthon. Consider Article IV of the *Augsburg Confession*:And they teach that men cannot be justified before God by their own abilities, merits or works, but are justified freely by Christ through faith, when they believe they have received it by grace, and that their sins are forgiven by Christ who in his death made satisfaction for our sins. God imputes this faith for righteousness in his sight.[37]

It is the final sentence of the above passage, containing the term "imputes," which is particularly striking. Rogness rightly notes that Luther never favored this term, nor was it present in Melanchthon's early writings. Yet, beginning with the *Augsburg Confession* this linguistic formula became the official description of justification in Lutheranism. According to Wilhelm Mauer, this new description meant that Melanchthon believed that justification was "not made at a joyful wedding; it is a legal transaction in which God rewards faith by imputing to it what still remains to fulfill the law—whereby God himself makes full satisfaction to the law."[38] This is a key development, as it is at odds with Luther's strong belief that justification is primarily related to a believer's unity with Christ.[39]

32. Mannermaa, *Christ Present*, 17.
33. Hinlicky, *Paths not Taken*, 146.
34. Mannermaa, *Christ Present*, 19.
35. Mannermaa, *Christ Present*, 53.
36. Hinlicky, *Paths not Taken*, 148.
37. Melanchthon, *Augsburg Confession*, 101.
38. Maurer, *Historical Commentary on the Augsburg Confession*, 343.
39. Rogness, *Melanchthon: Reformer without Honor*, 113.

Melanchthon introduced the word, "forensic," in the *Formula of Concord*, where he defined the phrase "to be justified" as an agent being "pronounced righteous in a forensic way."[40] Hinlicky notes that this statement, alongside many others made by Melanchthon, includes "no personal encounter with Christ (one encounters a report *about* Christ)" nor "any public work of the Holy Spirit to supply justifying faith to the stricken sinner."[41] Here, Melanchthon's doctrine of justification coheres with his deemphasis of the Trinity. For Melanchthon, it is not the *person* of Christ that is primary in justification, but rather the *work* of Christ and its *benefits* for the Christian. This differs from Luther who believes that both Christ *"as a person in us"* and the work of Christ are central to a Christian's justification.[42] This same divergence exists in articulating the role of the Holy Spirit. Prenter explicates that Luther prioritizes both the *person* and the *work* of the Spirit as really present in the justified agent,[43] whereas Melanchthon prioritizes neither—as Hinlicky bluntly states, "this legal transaction is to all appearances also Spirit-less."[44]

THE PHILOSOPHER-THEOLOGIAN: FINDING LUTHER IN GEORG WILHELM FRIEDRICH HEGEL

In *Paths not Taken*, Hinlicky posits that the slow disappearance of the Holy Spirit in Lutheranism (here understood as primarily shaped by Melanchthon's theology) was due to the rise of a "general pneumatology."[45] Ephraim Radner suggests that this tendency toward a general pneumatology is the result of a pneumatological expansionism which occurred during the early-modern period and resulted in disparate, vaguely pneumatized outlooks within disciplines ranging from metaphysics to physical sciences to history.[46] Though Hegel likely falls both within Hinlicky's category of "general pneumatology" and Radner's portrayal of "pneumatological expansionism," he differs from predecessors such as Gottfried W. Leibniz[47] in one key respect—while philosophers such as Leibniz drew from the Lutheran

40. Rogness, *Melanchthon: Reformer without Honor,* 112.
41. Hinlicky, *Paths not Taken,* 149.
42. Rognass, *Melanchthon: Reformer without Honor,* 63.
43. Prenter, *Spiritus Creator,* 31–65.
44. Hinlicky, *Paths not Taken,* 148.
45. Hinlicky, *Paths not Taken,* 177.
46. Radner, "The Holy Spirit and Unity," 1 n.1.
47. Leibniz is mentioned in the conclusion as a philosopher who inherited the theological tendencies of Melanchthon.

tradition at-large, Hegel was directly influenced by Luther's writings alone. Indeed, there is a discernible difference in how pneumatology is incorporated within the grand philosophical system of Hegel, even to the extent that the Spirit undergirds his entire corpus. In this regard, it can be persuasively argued that he was an ardent disciple of Luther.

Karl Barth once proclaimed that though Hegel was known primarily as a philosopher, his foremost desire was theological: to be the Protestant Aquinas.[48] This claim is echoed by Robert C. Solomon who states that Hegel's "Christian ambitions, however unorthodox, [are] the very heart of his philosophy."[49] This is readily evident in the breadth of Hegel's engagement with *Geist,* a concept informing his metaphysics, understanding of history, conception of human progress, and, implicitly, his entire philosophical outlook. It is most comprehensively delineated in *Phänomenologie des Geistes,* and *Vorlesungen über die Philosophie der Religion* (VPR).[50] Though *Geist* is understood differently in these two works, the importance of Hegel vis-à-vis this essay is his explicit affinity for Luther's pneumatology. In this regard, Hegel believed that he was "more Lutheran than Lutherans," insofar as he believed that Lutheranism had "become a pale reflection of its former self, especially with respect to the power of the Spirit undergirding Luther's passionate and imaginative theological assertions."[51] To this end, Alan M. Olson posits that Hegel had an "instinctive appreciation of Luther's dialectical conception of the Holy Spirit,"[52] from which he structured his own pneumatology. Hence, J.M. Fritzman rightly characterizes Hegel's theological-philosophy as "largely a radicalization of Luther's."[53]

At this juncture, one might ask: what pneumatological commonalities with Luther can be observed in Hegel? At least three exist: (1) the priority of the Holy Spirit in elucidating the Trinity; (2) an emphasis placed upon the linguistic mediation of the Spirit; and (3) the "incarnational" aspect of Luther's pneumatology as it relates to personal and communal unity with God. Concerning the first item, it was previously noted that Luther inverted the order of the Trinity in his *Large Catechism* to mirror the experience of the believer. As a reader of Luther, Hegel extended this inversion and speculatively reimagined his Trinitarian framework "from the concept of God as

48. Solomon, *In the Spirit of Hegel,* 62.

49. Solomon, *In the Spirit of Hegel,* 62

50. Hegel, *Phänomenologie Des Geistes,* passim; Hegel, *Vorlesungen Über die Philosophie Der Religion,* passim.

51. Olson, *Hegel and the Spirit,* 155.

52. Olson, *Hegel and the Spirit,* 155.

53. Fritzman, Hegel, 23.

Spirit."[54] This is evident in his 1821 manuscript of VPR, where he states that "God is *spirit*—that which we call the *triune* God."[55] This pneumatological priority is noteworthy, as similar to Luther, the Trinity is central to Hegel's worldview. In fact, Dale Schlitt argues that without the doctrine of the Trinity, Hegel's categories of history of the world, principle of freedom, and true religion all cease to be coherent.[56] Though there is some uncertainty as to how far Hegel removes the notion of personhood from the Trinity,[57] and for that matter, "being" itself from the Trinity,[58] Olson aptly notes that Luther's catechetical instruction was highly formative for Hegel, both for his doctrine of the Trinity and his philosophical corpus as a whole.[59]

Second, Luther's insistence on the Spirit's mediation of Christ through the preached Word is reworked in Hegel's emphasis on the linguistic mediation of *Geist*.[60] This is most readily observed in *First Philosophy of Spirit*, where Hegel asserts that "language is the first and primary manifestation (or *potency*, as he puts it, emulating Schelling) of Spirit separating itself from 'air' as its primal element and positing itself as speech."[61] This emphasis of both Hegel and Luther may be contrasted with Melanchthon's understanding of the spoken word as primarily testifying to salvific work—a linkage which Powell claims "did not loom large in Hegel's thought."[62] As a note, Hegel's (and Luther's) emphasis on the Spirit's linguistic mediation will be revisited when discussing Karl Rahner.

Third, Luther's parallel of God in Christ with the Holy Spirit in the Christian—V-M. Kärkkäinen's posited "incarnational" language in Luther's pneumatology—is incorporated into Hegel's expansive panentheism[63] Unlike Luther, Hegel articulates *Geist* (and God) as not a Creator apart from the creation, but rather, a substance permeating the created order.[64] This extensive presence of *Geist* extends to human individuals in history via the

---

54. Kärkkäinen, *Pneumatology*, 60.

55. Williamson, *An Introduction to Hegel's Philosophy of Religion*, 293.

56. Schlitt, *German Idealism's Trinitarian Legacy*, 23–24.

57. O'Regan asserts that "Hegel's Trinitarianism is not tri-personal" ("Kant, Hegel, Schelling," 260–61).

58. Powell notes that "it is necessary to use quotation marks with 'being' because. . .God is not, according to Hegel, a being" (*The Trinity in German Thought*, 120–134).

59. Olson, *Hegel and the Spirit*, 15–16, 41.

60. Kärkkäinen, *Pneumatology*, 83–85. Olson, *Hegel and the Spirit*, 10.

61. Olson, *Hegel and the Spirit*, 33.

62. Powell, *The Trinity in German thought*, 139.

63. Kärkkäinen, *Pneumatology*, 85.

64. Hodgson, *Hegel and Christian* Theology, 129.

historical event of the Incarnation. For Hegel, the unification of the divine and human in the historical Jesus de-particularized the incarnation (and the Holy Spirit), and thus, universalized both the possibility of unification of these natures and the Incarnation *itself* for all human agents.[65] Although the notion of Hegel's universal incarnation would be anathema to Luther, Hegel's emphasis on unity with the Divine certainly resembles both the mystical language present in Luther's early writings and Mannermaa's Finnish interpretation of Luther. Moreover, other assertions of Hegel regarding the Incarnation event, such as it being the moment of God's self-revelation,[66] are exactly in tandem with Luther's positions. Evidence of Hegel's close-reading of Luther's "unity language" is also apparent in his description of communal unity, where he posits—in agreement with Luther—that the mark of the hurch is the "indwelling of the Holy Spirit in the gathered community."[67] Additionally, Hegel borrowed Luther's understanding of the Spirit's work as the Agent who "calls, gathers, enlightens, and sanctifies" the Body of Christ.[68] For all of the above reasons, in *some* strange way, Hegel was as he claimed to be, "more Lutheran than Lutherans."

Several decades after Hegel (1770–1831), an extraordinary pneumatologically-shaped historical development arose in the work and theology of Roman Catholic theologian Karl Rahner (1904–1984). What was extraordinary was not merely the novel content of Rahner's theology. Instead, the adage of fashion (or history!) repeating itself every so often was transposed to the sphere of theology and manifestly exhibited in modern Catholic theology. Perhaps stranger than Hegel's "Lutheran-ness," the pneumatology of the rabble-rouser Luther—an individual who casually called the Pope the "Antichrist"—heavily influenced Rahner's theology due to his appropriation of Hegelian philosophy. It is to this striking development that we now turn.

LUTHERAN HEGELIANISM IN KARL RAHNER

Rahner's theological career could have ended before it started when he failed to defend his first dissertation (*Geist in Welt*) in 1936.[69] But Rahner, despite that initial difficulty, went on to produce a staggering literary output. He also

---

65. This is a contested point; see Jamros "Hegel on the Incarnation," 167–199. Also, see Kärkkäinen, *Pneumatology*, 60.

66. Fritzman, *Hegel* 134.

67. De Nys, *Hegel and Theology*, 110.

68. Olson, *Hegel and the Spirit*, 127.

69. For further reading see Pearl "Dialectical Panentheism," 119–37, and Bradley, "Rahner's *Spirit in the World: Aquinas or Hegel?*," 167–99.

made immense contributions to Vatican II, and concretized his legacy as the foremost Catholic theologian of the twentieth century.[70] Relevant to this essay, Rahner marked a decisive shift in theological scholarship as he sought to recapture the centrality of Trinitarian concerns in popular discourse. Like Luther, Rahner's Trinitarian framework undergirded his theological program, yet unlike Luther, he spent extensive time explicitly articulating this framework via logic and speculative philosophy. Indeed, outside of Catholic circles, he is best known for a statement known as Rahner's Rule: "The 'economic' Trinity is the 'immanent' Trinity and the 'immanent' Trinity is the 'economic' Trinity."[71] His Trinitarian commitments are most clearly delineated in *The Trinity* and *Foundations of the Christian Faith*. However, most of his corpus engages the Trinity and does so in a manner bearing a striking resemblance to what may be called "Lutheran Hegelianism." This kinship is so evident that Olson argues that Rahner's masterworks are inconceivable apart from Hegel's influence.[72]

Aside from Trinitarian commitments, there are three additional commonalities between Rahner and Lutheran Hegelianism: (1) a healthy Christology that supports a robust pneumatology; (2) an emphasis on the linguistic mediation of the Spirit; and (3) the universalization of the Spirit. Concerning the first item, one must examine Rahner's doctrine of the Trinity. Specifically, Rahner refers to the Trinity as the "self-communicating" God. In this conception of the Trinity, the Father serves as the eternal "mystery of God," while both the Son and the Spirit serve as the *one* communication of God.[73] One important note: though the Trinity is the framework of Rahner's theology, it is the Incarnation that serves as its historical referent. Hence, the notion of *one* Divine communication is interesting, as Rahner insists that it is *only* the Son who participated in the Incarnation event.[74] Yet, Rahner concomitantly argues that the Spirit is inextricably united with this communicative act. This union is due to his presupposition that it is the Spirit Himself who brings about acceptance of the appearance of Christ.[75] Hence, Rahner—alongside Luther and Hegel—believes that it is the Spirit

---

70. Schlitt, *German Idealism's Trinitarian legacy,* 125; Kärkkäinen, *Pneumatology,* 111.

71. Schlitt, *German Idealism's Trinitarian legacy,* 129.

72. These 'masterworks' particularly refer to *Geist in Welt and Hörer de Worts*; see Olson, *Hegel* 201.

73. Holzer, "Karl Rahner, Hans Urs von Balthasar, and Twentieth-Century Catholic Currents on the Trinity," 321.

74. Burke, *Reinterpreting Rahner,* 80–81.

75. Schlitt, *German Idealism's Trinitarian Legacy,* 131.

who guides and communicates with humankind, both about God's being and God's will.[76]

As observed with Luther, Rahner's healthy Christology undergirds a robust pneumatological presentation. For Rahner, this is both possible and necessary due to his equating of the immanent and economical Trinities with one another. Based upon this equivalence, he postulates four Trinitarian acts of communication—Origin/Future, History/Transcendence, Invitation/Acceptance, and Knowledge/Love—that equally elucidate the *single* (and equal) mission of the Son and Spirit in their mission of declaring the unique God.[77] Interestingly, Rahner (like Hegel) understood the Trinity as "a single movement of divine subjectivity" from initial self (in the Father) to recognition and realization of that self through the act of communication (in the Son and Spirit).[78] In other words, both in his Trinitarian and Christological commitments, Rahner is squarely situated within Lutheran Hegelianism.

Secondly, as evident above, communication and language play a central role in Rahner's theology. This is because Rahner—like Luther and Hegel—believed that the mediation of the Spirit occurs linguistically. Of supreme import, this emphasis is explicitly due to Rahner's direct reading of Luther, where he shrewdly notes Luther's pneumatology and concept of faith as linguistic, that is, as *word-act*.[79] That said, Rahner departs from Luther (yet remains well-within Hegel's "radicalization" of Luther) by arguing that the Spirit is not limited to these mediatorial channels. Rather, he claims that the Spirit is universally present and active amongst Christians and non-Christians alike.

Like Hegel, Rahner envisions a universal Spirit that permeates the created order. For Rahner, the *one* communication act of God occurs on two levels: the presence of the Spirit on the "transcendental" level and the presence of Jesus Christ on the "categorical level." Of these two levels, Rahner prioritizes the transcendental.[80] For Rahner, this transcendental aspect of the Spirit is understood by humankind as grace. Like Hegel, he believes that this grace orients all humans toward God. Thus, he asserts that "the world is drawn to its spiritual fulfillment by the Spirit of God, who directs the whole history of the world in all its length and breadth toward its proper

---

76. Burke, *Reinterpreting Rahner*, 81.

77. Burke, *Reinterpreting Rahner*, 81–82.

78. Schlitt, *German Idealism's Trinitarian Legacy*, 145; cf. 139–140.

79. Olson, *Hegel and the Spirit*, 203.

80. Schlitt, *German Idealism's Trinitarian Legacy*, 128.

goal"[81] V-M.Kärkkäinen notes that it is from this expansive pneumatology that Rahner derives another theological commitment: that of the "anonymous Christian." For Rahner, the Spirit is efficacious in all religions, albeit to varying degrees. Thus, persons who are aimed toward the transcendent grace of God may be "justified by God's grace and possess the Holy Spirit[82]" without faith. This understanding of the Spirit as present in world religions throughout history is classically Hegelian,[83] as is the Spirit's "incarnational" action within the Christian and non-Christian alike.

CONCLUSION: AREAS FOR FUTURE RESEARCH AND ITEMS FOR PRESENT REFLECTION

Where does this exploration leave us? As a cursory study, the above proposition likely created more questions than concrete answers or practical solutions. Additionally, it should be noted that many of the claims regarding these interlocutors are contested; thus, this chapter lays *one additional claim upon all of them.* Nevertheless, it should be readily evident that *at least* two divergent pneumatological streams exist in 'Lutheran' thought—one found in Luther's writings and another espoused by Melanchthon and his later followers. In this chapter, a rudimentary outline of the first stream was presented: that is, one extending from Luther's robust pneumatology through Hegel's expansion and radicalization; and another to Rahner's universalization and appropriation of Lutheran Hegelianism in Catholic thought.

Luther, the progenitor of this pneumatological lineage, was a Christocentric, Trinitarian theologian who prioritized the personhood and presence of the Holy Spirit in his theology. It was argued that three major items supported his robust pneumatological framework: (1) he tied the person *and* work of Christ directly to the testimony of the Spirit, (2) he prioritized the linguistic mediation of the Spirit, and (3) he posited that justification was based upon the Spirit's unity with the believer instead of being a mere legal transaction. Though Mannermaa has often been credited with retrieving Luther's pneumatological focus, this chapter traced this 'retrieval' back to the philosophical theology of Hegel, an individual who considered himself "more Lutheran than Lutherans," and, as a result, unearthed this predilection of Luther's decades earlier. Indeed, Hegel retained Luther's linguistic

---

81. Kärkkäinen, *Pneumatology* 116; cf. Rahner, "The One Christ and Universality of Salvation," 203.

82. Rahner, "Jesus Christ in the non-Christian Religions," 43.

83. E.g. *Vorlesungen Über die Philosophie Der Religion* which posits that successive religions increasingly revealed a single truth.

mediation, prioritization of the Spirit, and "unity" language. In this sense, one can say that he "radicalized" and expanded Luther's pneumatology to encompass the structures of the Trinity, human history, and universal metaphysics. Broaching Protestant bounds, this stream expanded into Rahner's transcendental theology. Like Luther, Rahner retained the personhood of the Spirit in tandem with a strong Christology. Like Hegel, Rahner universalized the Spirit as present and active amongst Christians and non-Christians alike. In consonance with both Luther and Hegel, Rahner affirmed both the linguistic aspect of pneumatological mediation and the unity of the Spirit with/within Christians.

This essay also examined several divergences from Luther that were present in the theology of Melanchthon. These included a weak Trinitarian framework, a neglect of the personhoods of both Christ and the Spirit, and a primarily legalistic formulation of the doctrine of justification. Though space limited the possibility of examining persons within this Melanchthonian stream, future research endeavors should pursue this fruitful line of inquiry—it will likely unearth surprising theological consequences in areas ranging from ecclesiology to eschatology. As previously mentioned, it has been argued that Melanchthon's divergence from Luther's robust doctrine of the Holy Spirit was instrumental in the early-modern theological shift toward a "general pneumatology." Hinlicky contends that the most prominent philosopher-theologian to inherit this problematic pneumatological paradigm was Leibniz—a claim that is not without warrant. In *Law and Protestantism*, John Witte Jr. sheds light on a shared Platonic tendency in the theology of Melanchthon and Leibniz (a tendency that places both of them at-odds with Hegelian idealism). One of Witte's starkest examples is a quotation from *Corpus Reformatorum*, wherein Melanchthon asserts that God as the "light of lights" has implanted his divine wisdom in all humans, with this knowledge differing only in quantity.[84] This same thought (and near-identical verbiage) is articulated in Leibniz's *Theodicy*: "This portion of reason which we possess is a gift of God, and consists in the natural light that has remained with us in the midst of corruption; thus, it is in accordance with the whole, and it differs from that which is in God only as a drop of water differs from the ocean."[85] Due both to their shared philosophical underpinnings and other commonalities (such as their weak Trinitarian formulations), Powell proclaims that Leibniz was squarely situated within Melanchthonian Protestantism.[86] Tracing the Melanchthonian

84. Witte Jr., *Law and Protestantism*, 123–124.

85. Leibniz, *Theodicy*, 107.

86. Powell, *The Trinity in German Thought*, 46.

pneumatological stream beyond Leibniz, one may also investigate the pneumatology of prominent twentieth-century theologian Karl Barth, whom Hinlicky argues "appropriated the sequenced scheme of 'imputative justification—effective sanctification', that, following Melanchthon, became normative also for the Reformed tradition."[87] In fact, though Barth's theology is explicitly Trinitarian and anti-Platonic, his retention of a Melanchthonian view of justification led him to de-emphasize the Spirit in a manner wholly consistent with what may be considered "general pneumatology."

Regarding this tendency, Theodora Hawkley underscores Barth's understanding of the Cross as the "decisive end of history," which in turn diminishes the present role of the Spirit.[88] Joseph L. Mangina similarly notes that Barth's pneumatology only allows the Spirit to "appear as a predicate of Christ's reconciling work, a *manifestation* of the latter rather than an *agency* of its [sic] own."[89] For these reasons, Hawkley rightly concludes that for Barth (as well as for Melanchthon and Leibniz), "the Spirit ceases to be a salvific entity in its [sic] own right."[90]

Despite his generalizing tendencies, Barth once called pneumatology "the future of Christian theology." In saying so, he joined many others such as Eastern Orthodox theologian Nikolay Berdayev who proclaimed that pneumatology is "the last unexplored theological frontier."[91] In agreement with such luminaries, the broadest purpose of this chapter was to explore this future, this unexplored frontier; whether this was done successfully or not is another matter. To do so, an inchoate articulation of a posited pneumatological stream—admittedly elementary—was offered to serve as an entry-point for readers to consider what theological commitments and metaphysical outlooks may be necessary to support a robust pneumatology. However, this is not merely an academic exercise. My hope is that a reinvigorated theology of the Holy Spirit may offer a more successful approach to some of the exigent issues of the present era, such as the increasing interest in 'mystical' or 'inward' spirituality against traditional Christendom; the growth of third-world Christianity (bolstered largely by Pentecostalism) in contrast to decreasing numbers in the West; and the desire for ecclesial unity to address the visible brokenness of the Body of Christ. These issues (and many more) provide a practical impetus and rationale for this study.

87. Hinlicky, *Paths not Taken,* 128.
88. Hawksley, "The Freedom of the Spirit," 182.
89. Mangina, "Bearing the Marks of Jesus," 270.
90. Hawksley, "The Freedom of the Spirit," 183. Attention is called to the non-personal pronoun of "its" rather than "his."
91. Kärkkäinen, *Pneumatology* 13.

This chapter does not claim that the 'fruits' of the Luther-Hegel-Rahn-er pneumatological stream are entirely positive or biblically sound; nor does it claim that the above crises may *only* be remedied within a pneumato-logical sphere. I believe that troubling theological developments occurred within this stream, and thus, Iam apprehensive to offer this pneumatologi-cal stream (at least, in its portions that are untethered from Scripture) as a panacea for all ills of the present Christian faith, whether related to praxis or doctrinal concerns.

Additionally, one might argue that the Melanchthonian theological stream, with its resultant "general pneumatology," is not *so* different from the stream originating with Luther that results in the "universalized pneu-matology" of Hegel and Rahner. Yet, I contend that there *is* a key differ-ence. Within the latter pneumatological stream there is an implicit honor, dignity, and priority assigned to the Holy Spirit, with a strong impulse to secure his personhood; indeed, a central focus that saves the Spirit from becoming *theos agraptos*—the God about whom no one writes—or whom V-M. Kärkkäinen playfully terms the "Cinderella of the Trinity; when the two other 'sisters' went to the ball, Cinderella was left at home."[92] If only for this reason, the robustly pneumatological stream of Luther-Hegel-Rahner is worthy of consideration and careful study.

Lastly, this chapter should not be viewed as an attempt to castigate or discredit the theological contributions of Melanchthon, nor should it be used as a vehicle to transform him into the "whipping boy" of all Reformation or Lutheran maladies.[93] Rather, it aims to delineate common theological ele-ments that have undergirded a robust pneumatology across denominational and philosophical frameworks. Moreover, within the context of this collec-tion of essays, this chapter serves to elucidate the expansive effects of the Reformation's legacy—spanning well beyond Protestantism to idealist phi-losophy and modern Catholic thought. Most important, a final description of this chapter is that it aims to function as a hortatory: a desperate call both to scholars and to faithful Christians to reflect upon how their theological commitments can be brought into dialogue with the ecclesial realities of the twenty-first century, a period oft-called the "post-Christian era."

Five centuries have passed since Luther penned and subsequently nailed 95 *Theses* to a church door in Wittenberg. Yet, we remain tethered to our earthly existence. Hence, all Christians must consider the following questions: If the Lord were to delay His return for additional time, what

92. *Theos agraptos* is originally a term coined by Gregory of Nazianzus; Kärkkäinen, *Pneumatology* 16.

93. Hinlicky, *Paths not Taken*, 154–155.

forces will be shaping future generations of Christians? Will the Reformation be a mere footnote in history? Will the Christian faith be assimilated into secular, political, or ideological arenas? Or will a future class of theologians hold Reformation 600, 700, or 1000 conferences, all proclaiming a robust and faithful presentation of the mysteries bequeathed to all Christians once and for all? Though perhaps speculative, it appears to me that the path from our present-day ambiguities to such future certainties (at least, the certainty that the future will soon become our present reality!) is necessarily bound up with the espousal of the Holy Spirit as the gathering, renewing, and sanctifying Divine Person. With this in mind, I humbly ask each reader to allow the Spirit to flow as rivers of living water (John 7:38), both personally and theologically—as that water will continue to do in the New Jerusalem for eternity (Rev 22:1).

BIBLIOGRAPHY

Bradley, Denis J M. "Rahner's 'Spirit in the World': Aquinas or Hegel?' *The Thomist* 41 (1977) 167–99.

Burke, Patrick. *Reinterpreting Rahner: A Critical Study of His Major Themes.* New York: Fordham University Press, 2002.

De Nys, Martin J. *Hegel and Theology.* Philosophy and Theology. London: T. & T. Clark, 2009.

Fritzman, J.M. *Hegel.* PCTS–Polity Classic Thinkers. Cambridge: Polity, 2014.

Hawksley, Theodora. "The Freedom of the Spirit: The Pneumatological Point of Barth's Ecclesiological Minimalism." *Scottish Journal of Theology* 64 (2011) 180–94.

Hegel, Georg Wilhelm Freidrich. *Phänomenologie Des Geistes.* Norderstedt: Verlag Der Wissenschaften, 2015.

Hegel, Georg Wilhelm Freidrich. *Vorlesungen über die Philosophie der Religion.* Edited by Walter Jaeschke. Hamburg: Meiner, 1993.

Hinlicky, Paul R. *Paths not Taken: Fates of Theology from Luther through Leibniz.* Grand Rapids: Eerdmans, 2009.

Hodgson, Peter Crafts. *Hegel and Christian Theology: A Reading of the Lectures on the Philosophy of Religion.* Oxford: Oxford University Press, 2005.

Jamros, Daniel P. 1995. "Hegel on the Incarnation: Unique or Universal?" *Theological Studies* 56 (1995) 276–300.

Kärkkäinen, Pekka. *Luther's trinitarische Theologie des Heiligen Geistes.* Mainz: von Zabern, 2005.

Kärkkäinen, Veli-Matti. *Pneumatology: The Holy Spirit in Ecumenical, International, and Contextual Perspective.* Grand Rapids: Baker Academic, 2008.

——————. "The Holy Spirit and Justification: The Ecumenical Significance of Luther's Doctrine of Salvation." *Pneuma: The Journal of the Society of Pentecostal Studies* 24 (2002) 26–39.

——————. "Karl Barth and the Theology of Religions." In *Karl Barth and Evangelical Theology: Convergences and Divergences,* edited by Sung Wook Chung, 236–57. Grand Rapids: Baker Academic, 2006.

Holzer, Vincent. "Karl Rahner, Hans Urs von Balthasar, and Twentieth-Century Catholic Currents on the Trinity." In *The Oxford Handbook of the Trinity*, edited by Gilles Emery and Matthew Levering, 314–27. Oxford: Oxford University Press, 2011.

Leibniz, Gottfried W. *Theodicy: Essays on the Goodness of God, the Freedom of Man, and the Origin of Evil*. Edited by Austin Farrer. Translated by E. M. Huggard. La Salle, IL: Open Court, 1985.

Lohse, Bernhard. *Martin Luther: An Introduction to His Life and Work*. Translated by Robert C. Schultz. Philadelphia: Fortress, 1986.

Luther, Martin. *Martin Luther's Large Catechism (1530)*. https://www.creeds.net/lutheran/luther_large.htm.

———. "The Three Symbols or Creeds of the Christian Faith" In *The Practice of Theology: A Reader*, edited by Colin E. Gunton, et. al., 130–132. London: SCM Press, 2001.

Mangina, Joseph L. "Bearing the Marks of Jesus: The Church in the Economy of Salvation in Barth and Hauerwas." *Scottish Journal of Theology* 52 (1999) 269–305.

Mannermaa, Tuomo. *Christ Present in Faith: Luther's View of Justification*. Edited by Kirsi Irmeli Stjerna. Minneapolis: Fortress Press, 2010.

Manschreck, Clyde Leonard. *Melanchthon: The Quiet Reformer*. New York: Abingdon Press, 1958.

Maurer, Wilhelm. *Historical Commentary on the Augsburg Confession*. Translated by H. George Anderson. Philadelphia: Fortress Press, 1986.

Melanchthon, Philipp. *A Melanchthon Reader*. Translated by Ralph Keen. New York: P. Lang, 1988.

———. *The Chief Theological Topics: Loci Praecipui Theologici 1559*. Translated by Jacob A. O. Preus. St. Louis: Concordia, 2011.

Olson, Alan M. *Hegel and the Spirit: Philosophy as Pneumatology*. Princeton: Princeton University Press, 2010.

Paulson, Steve. "Luther's Doctrine of God." In *The Oxford Handbook of Martin Luther's Theology*, edited by Robert Kolb et al., 187–200. Oxford Handbooks. Oxford: Oxford University Press, 2014.

Pearl, Thomas. "Dialectical Panentheism: on the Hegelian Character of Karl Rahner's Key Christological Writings." *Irish Theological Quarterly* 42 (1975) 119–37

Peterson, Rodney L. *Preaching in the Last Days: The Theme of Two Witnesses in the 16th and 17th Century*. Oxford: Oxford University Press, 1993.

Powell, Samuel M. *The Trinity in German Thought*. Cambridge: Cambridge University Press, 2008.

Prenter, Regin. *Spiritus Creator*. Translated by John M. Jensen. Philadelphia: Muhlenberg, 1953.

Radner, Ephraim. "The Holy Spirit and Unity: Getting out of the Way of Christ." *International Journal of Systematic Theology* 16 (2014) 207–20.

Regan, Cyril O. "The Trinity in Kant, Hegel, and Schelling." In *The Oxford Handbook of the Trinity*, edited by Gilles Emery and Matthew Levering, 254–66. Oxford Handbooks. Oxford: Oxford University Press, 2011.

Richard, James William. *Philip Melanchthon: The Protestant preceptor of Germany, 1497–1560*. Miami, FL: HardPress Publishing, 2013.

Rogness, Michael. *Philip Melanchthon: Reformer without Honor*. Minneapolis: Augsburg, 1969.

Saarinen, Risto. "Justification by Faith: The View of the Mannermaa School." In *The Oxford Handbook of Martin Luther's Theology*, edited by Robert Kolb et al., 254–63. Oxford Handbooks. Oxford: Oxford University Press, 2014.

Schlitt, Dale M. *German Idealism's Trinitarian Legacy.* Albany: SUNY Press, State University of New York Press, 2016.

Solomon, Robert C. *In the Spirit of Hegel: A Study of G.W.F. Hegel's "Phenomenology of Spirit."* New York: Oxford University Press, 1983.

Swain, Scott R. "The Trinity in the Reformers." In *The Oxford Handbook of the Trinity*, edited by Gilles Emery and Matthew Levering, 228–39. Oxford Handbooks. Oxford: Oxford University Press, 2011.

Wengert, Timothy J. *Martin Luther's Catechisms: Forming the Faith.* Minneapolis: Fortress, 2009.

Williamson, Raymond Keith. *An Introduction to Hegel's Philosophy of Religion.* SUNY Series in Hegelian Studies. Albany, NY: SUNY, 1984.

Witte, John, Jr. *Law and Protestantism: The Legal Teachings of the Lutheran Reformation.* Cambridge: Cambridge University Press, 2002.

2

Hermeneutica Sacra

Echoes of Martin Luther's Reformation Hermeneutics in Canonical Criticism

SAMUEL W. MUINDI

INTRODUCTION

HERMENEUTICS IS AN EPISTEMOLOGICAL paradigm; it is, in the words of Friedrich Schleiermacher, a "theory of understanding."[1] More specifically, hermeneutics is a discipline that deals with the understanding or interpretation of texts.[2] However, a 'text' is a nuanced concept. Paul Ricoeur, the French philosopher renowned for his extensive work on textual interpretation, notes that a text is "not only expressions fixed in writing but also mediation exerted by all the documents and monuments which have a fundamental trait in common with the written word."[3] Hermeneutics is, thus, not simply a method or a set of techniques but an epistemological paradigm and, hence, not synonymous with exegesis. It is both the translation and application of the meaning of a text into a socio-cultural context as well as an

---

1. Schleiermacher, "The Hermeneutics," 85–100; see also McLean *Biblical Interpretation*, 44–50.

2. Fiorenza, "Method in Women's Studies," 207.

3. Ricoeur, "Toward a Hermeneutic Idea," 35.

attempt to understand the context in the light of the meaning. As Kenneth Archer argues, hermeneutics "cannot be reduced to a static, distinctive exegetical methodology, but must include the important element of the social location of the readers and their narrative tradition."[4] This task entails a dialogic interaction of a text with the "inter-texts" or the experiences of life and worldviews, including belief systems, which one brings to the text as presuppositional analogies for understanding the text.[5] In this sense, therefore, hermeneutics can be viewed as a dialogic meaning-making encyclopedic process and exegesis as the application of hermeneutical principles.[6]

The above definition of hermeneutics is germane to our understanding of the various methods that have been employed in the discipline of biblical interpretation. Far from being objective methodological approaches akin to the dated scientific-positivistic approaches which are, supposedly, not colored by the faith commitments or the ideologies of the interpreters, the worldviews and faith persuasions of the interpreters do, indeed, enter the hermeneutic meaning-making process. As Kevin Vanhoozer rightly observes, "our hermeneutical theories themselves are dependent on our theologies (or a-theologies)."[7]

Biblical hermeneutics—the discipline that is concerned with the interpretations of the texts of the Bible—has employed a variety of approaches in the history of biblical interpretation. In the historical horizon of the early church, the initial biblical study methods of the church fathers, so called because they "established the doctrinal framework of Christianity,"[8] were chiefly concerned with distinguishing Christianity from Judaism and Greek philosophies, defining the nature of Christian divinity and Christology, and demonstrating how the Bible should be read and applied to the Christian life.[9] The patristic hermeneutical approaches, though often negatively portrayed as pre-critical and entailing allegorical, typological, or literalist methods, nonetheless presupposed the texts of the Bible to be the inspired and authoritative Word of God and, hence, sought to hear the voice of God therein. In the sixteenth century Protestant Reformation, however, the church witnessed a paradigm shift in biblical hermeneutics. As is generally acknowledged in Protestant Reformation scholarship, the centerpiece of the

---

4. Archer, *A Pentecostal Hermeneutic*, 180.

5. Darr, "Glorified in the Presence of Kings," 63.

6. Phan, "Method in Liberation Theologies," 54; and Gadamer, *Truth and Method*, 146.

7. Vanhoozer, "Language, Literature," 27.

8. Bray, *Biblical Interpretation*, 77.

9. Bray, *Biblical Interpretation*, 95–96.

sixteenth-century Protestant Reformation was a hermeneutical revolution.[10] Whereas the Reformation is famed for its revolt against the papal tyranny of the time and an awakening of the hurch from spiritual slumber, Luther's influence on biblical hermeneutics in the sixteenth century was the bedrock of subsequent Protestant hermeneutical development from that time onward. Martin Luther's hermeneutical revolution rested on four pillars of emphasis.

LUTHER'S HERMENEUTICAL PILLARS

Luther's first hermeneutic pillar was his *sola scriptura* (Scripture alone) principle, which emphasized the Bible as the central authority for understanding Christianfaith. Although emphasis on the authority of Scripture had been upheld by the church fathers before him, especially by Tertullian and Augustine,[11] Luther's radical emphasis asserted that the authority of the Bible did not need supplementation by the magisterium of the Roman Catholic Church and, thus, the Church did not have the ultimate authority on scriptural interpretation. Luther argued that the Bible was "the only reliable and irrefutable source of all Christian doctrine."[12] The *sola scriptura* principle, which became the watchword of the Reformation, not only emancipated the Bible from ecclesiastical-hermeneutical hegemony but also affirmed the Bible as the supreme objective authority for Christian interpretation. As Luther went on to argue, "Scripture is queen and this queen must rule, and everyone must obey and be subject to her. The Pope, Luther, Augustine, Paul, and even an angel from heaven . . . these should not be masters, judges or arbiters but only witnesses, disciples, and confessors of scriptures."[13]

Luther believed that the Bible did not need the interpretive magisterium of the Church because *Scriptura sacra sui ipsius interpres* (sacred Scripture is its own interpreter). Per this principle, the interpretation of each passage and each book of the Bible should be in harmony with the whole tenor of Scripture, or in accordance with "the analogy of faith."[14]

---

10. See, for example, Sasse, "Luther and the Word of God," 50–72. See also Cameron who observes that it was Martin Luther who led biblical hermeneutics in a new direction with his *sola scriptura* principle, *The European Reformation*, 136–37.

11. Wood, *Captive to the Word*, 405).

12. Sasse, "Luther and the Word of God," 58.

13. Luther, *Luther's Works*, vol. 26, *Lectures on Galatians*, 58.

14. Muller and Thompson, "The Significance of Pre-Critical Exegesis," 335–42. This principle presupposes scriptural harmony, although Luther was quick to acknowledge the existence of textual problems in biblical interpretation. Luther, nonetheless, argued that textual problems did not endanger the *sensus plenior* of Scripture which

Implicit in the *scriptura sacra sui ipsius intepres* principle was a presupposition that each passage of Scripture contained a meaning beyond that which was intended by individual historical authors. As Luther went on to argue, "the historical authors received some of their historical matter by research, and under the grace of the superintendence of the Holy Spirit."[15] Taken together, these meanings constituted the overall meaning of Scripture, or, the *sensus plenior* (fuller sense or meaning) of Scripture, that is, the meaning that was "intended by God though not necessarily consciously intended by the original authors of the texts of Scripture."[16] *Sensus plenior*, in effect, infers a two-dimensional approach to scriptural interpretation. This approach is articulated by Bruce Waltke as follows:

> In interpreting Scripture, there are two horizons. First, there is the finite horizon of the inspired author that encompasses all the knowledge of the author and his historical situation. Second, there is the infinite horizon of God who sees all things holistically. The existence of this larger horizon allows modern interpreters to go beyond the specific historical context of the biblical writers and, in retrospect, pursue connections and themes in the metanarrative that embrace the whole range of biblical material.[17]

Thus, per Martin Luther, Scripture is both divine and human; it has self-authenticating divine power in that it is able to convict the hearer of the Word.[18]

---

constituted the article of the Christian faith. See, for example, Kramm, *The Theology of Martin Luther*, 116. On the other hand, Luther's 'analogy of faith' concept appears to utilize Church tradition, in terms of the accumulated content of Christian doctrine, to interpret Scripture. As Shelton rightly observes, Luther appears to embrace Church tradition at times in his hermeneutical approaches, though with a caveat that tradition should be critically evaluated and must not be allowed to supplant Scripture. See his "Martin Luther's Concept of Biblical Interpretation in Historical Perspective," 391–95.

15. See Shelton, "Martin Luther's Concept," 187. With this argument, Martin Luther eschewed the notion of 'dictation theory' with respect to divine inspiration of Scripture.

16. McLean, *Biblical Interpretation*, 36. However, the *scriptura sacra sui ipsius interpres* principle, together with Luther's declaration that there was no distinction between the spiritual capacity of the clergy and the laity in terms of scriptural interpretation, might have opened the door for arbitrary interpretations of Scripture. As Grondin points out, the Roman Catholic Church's Counter Reformation Council of Tent (1546) saw this as the 'Achilles' heel' of the Reformation hermeneutic and, therefore, reaffirmed the Roman Catholic Church's interpretive magisterium as the sure way to prevent arbitrariness. See Grondin, *Introduction to Philosophical Hermeneutics*, 41.

17. Waltke, *An Old Testament Theology*, 46.

18. See also Kramm, *The Theology of Martin Luther*, 116.

Luther's second hermeneutic pillar was his *sensus literalis* (literal or plain sense) of Scripture.[19] Luther argued that "the literal sense of Scripture alone is the whole essence of faith and of Christian theology."[20] The *sensus literalis* inferred a grammatical-historical sense of Scripture. It entailed an inductive process in which the biblical interpreter studied the grammatical-philological structure of a text to tease out the primary authorial intent contained in the text in its socio-historical context.[21] For this task, Luther emphasized knowledge of original biblical languages.[22] The interpreter had also to be conversant with textual literary theories and designs in order to decipher the meaning conveyed in the literary structures of scriptural texts.[23] For Luther, the "exegesis of the 'letter' of the text was the direct means to grasp the substance and content of Scripture" and, hence, his argument that secular methods of textual analysis were, in principle, appropriate for biblical interpretation.[24]

Whereas Luther acknowledged that there were apparently obscure words and figurative language in Scripture which did not readily yield *sensus literalis*, he, nonetheless, argued that "those statements which have been uttered very simply without any figurative language and obscure words interpret those which are uttered with figurative and metaphorical language."[25] He believed that "the literal meaning, rightly understood, of itself contains its own proper spiritual significance; it is from the right understanding of the words themselves that the spirit of Scripture grows."[26] Luther's *sensus literalis* was, in effect, a repudiation of the uncritical piety of the medieval

19. As Wood notes, Martin Luther argued that the literal understanding of the grammatical-historical details of the biblical text was necessary before the exegete could enter the interpretation of the '*sensus plenior*' of Scripture. Wood, *Luther's Principles*, 24–27.

20. Farrar, *History of Interpretation*, 327.

21. The notion of a "primary authorial intent" has, however, become problematic in modern critical study of the Bible. As Waltke observes, "the reality of the situation is that we cannot talk precisely about an original author of biblical narratives, for these books are mostly anonymous and underwent at least some editing over long periods of time" (*An Old Testament Theology*, 85). Perhaps it is more appropriate to talk about "authorial intent" in terms of the meaning of the texts of the Bible in their final canonical shape.

22. See also Plass, *What Luther Says*, Vol 1: 95.

23. See also Wood, *Luther's Principles*, 11–12.

24. See Poland, *Literary Criticism*, 21. Waltke equally argues that "Since the biblical message is communicated through the impersonal semiotic signs that constitute human language, they are subject to a grammatical-historical analysis." (*An Old Testament Theology*, 86).

25. Luther, *Luther's Works*, vol. 20, *Lectures on the Minor Prophets*, 108.

26. Grondin, *Introduction to Philosophical Hermeneutics*, 40.

church with its allegorical and typological or figurative interpretations of Scripture. The allegorical and typological methods had, per Luther, transformed Scripture into myths and symbolisms.[27]

Luther's third hermeneutic pillar was his Christological-hermeneutical focus. Luther argued that, since Christ is the incarnate word of God, the entire content of Scripture is none other than Christ; "all of Scripture, as already said, is pure Christ . . . everything is focused on this Son, so that we might know Him distinctively . . . To him who has the Son, Scripture is an open book; and the stronger his faith in Christ becomes, the more brightly will the light of Scripture shine on him."[28] For Luther, Scripture was simply a testimony which pointed the reader to Christ who is the infallible and inerrant word: "it is Jesus Christ working in and through the Scripture who is the infallible and inerrant word, and the Scriptures faithfully reveal Jesus Christ through the human instrumentality of the inspired writers . . . Christ is the end of the Law . . . as if to say that all Scripture finds its meaning in Christ."[29]

Luther's Christological-hermeneutical focus was *sui generis* in the history of biblical interpretation. The Christological focus appears to hark back to Jesus' words to the Jews thus: "You diligently study the Scriptures because you think that by them you possess eternal life. These are the Scriptures that testify about me, yet you refuse to come to me to have life" (John 5:39–40 NIV). The Scriptures were, thus, not efficacious conveyors of grace in and of themselves but were pointers to the giver of life, Jesus Christ. Nonetheless, according to Luther's explication, the Scriptures are not, in terms of semiotic theory, mere signs. Rather, they are sacramental symbols in the sense that the salvific efficacy of Jesus Christ is encountered in the proclamation and experience of the Gospel.[30]

27. See Shelton, "Martin Luther's Concept," 392. It is, however, noted that, whereas allegory tendentiously belittled the role of history and imposed arbitrary or even philosophical readings of the Bible, typology has been viewed as having a positive role in biblical interpretation. Barr does not, however, see any methodological difference between allegory and typology; he views both as arbitrary approaches to biblical interpretation, Barr, "The Concepts," 65–102. On the other hand, Childs has persuasively argued that, in patristic hermeneutics, typology was "viewed as an extension of the literal sense of historical events in a subsequent adumbration and served to signal the correspondence between redemptive events . . . typology was considered closely akin to prophecy and fulfillment and thought to be a major New Testament category in relating to the Old Testament." Childs, *Theology of the Old and New Testaments*, 13.

28. Luther, *Luther's Works*, Vol 15, *Ecclesiastes, Song of Solomon*, 339. See also Doermann who observes that Christological interpretation forms the basis of Luther's hermeneutic, "Luther's Principles," 24.

29. Shelton, "Martin Luther's Concept," 190–91.

30. For a detailed explication of the semiotic differences between sign and symbol,

On the other hand, the Christological-hermeneutical approach has been viewed in some quarters of biblical scholarship as a deductive imposition on Luther's otherwise inductive hermeneutical method.[31] Moreover, since not all texts of the Bible contain explicit Christological content, Luther is often accused of using the Christological-hermeneutical criterion to create a canon within a canon. For example, such biblical texts as the *Epistle of James* did not receive much attention from Luther because they did not appear to contain an explicit Christological message for the Church in general.[32] In retrospect, it is apparent that Luther did not have a fully developed Christological-hermeneutical theory. Nonetheless, his Christological-hermeneutical approach, which argues that Jesus Christ is the infallible, inerrant Word of God, is an insightful attempt to overcome textual difficulties in the Bible, which appear to be problematic for the doctrine of biblical inerrancy. As Luther argues, "the authority and infallibility of the Scriptures consist in its ability to accomplish salvation in the hearts of men who hear it . . . It is Jesus Christ working in and through the Scripture who is the infallible and inerrant word."[33]

Luther's fourth hermeneutic pillar was his emphasis on the illuminating work of the Holy Spirit in scriptural interpretation.[34] Luther argued that the word of God was not efficacious in conveying its inspired message apart from the illumining work of the Holy Spirit: "the Word of God is not spiritually effective apart from the work of the Holy Spirit, and the Holy Spirit depends upon the Word of God for the content and means of His revelation . . . the Word of God speaks to the reader and the Holy Spirit enables the reader to hear the Word."[35] Luther went on to observe that, apart from the illumining work of the Holy Spirit, human rationality cannot decipher the divine message in Scripture since "the Holy Spirit is not only involved in the inspirational writing of Scripture but also in the illuminating aspect of the reading of Scripture."[36] This observation was underscored by the sixteenth century reformation theologian, John Calvin, who not only observed that

see my analysis in Muindi, *Pentecostal-Charismatic Prophecy*, 186–190.

31. See, for example, Shelton, "Martin Luther's Concept," 255.

32. See also Shelton, "Martin Luther's Concept," 239–55.

33. Luther, *Luther's Works*, vol. 4, *Lectures on Genesis Chapter 21–25*, 68.

34. Martin Luther argued that divine illumination was necessary for the true interpretation of the Bible. Thus, the Holy Spirit was the true interpreter of the word which He had inspired: "for if God does not open and explain Holy Writ, no one can understand it; it will remain a closed book, enveloped in darkness" (*Luther's Works*, vol. 13: *Selected Psalms II*, 17).

35. Shelton, "Martin Luther's Concept," 239, 255.

36. Shelton, "Martin Luther's Concept," 255.

"the authority of Scripture derived not from men, but from the Spirit of God," but also that the Holy Spirit, who "is superior to reason," illumines the minds of believers to understand the Scriptures; "these words will not obtain full credit in the hearts of men, until they are sealed by the inward testimony of the Spirit."[37]

Luther's biblical hermeneutic had both objective and subjective dimensions. Whereas the Bible is the object that is studied using objective critical methods, the biblical interpreter "is the subject who must be influenced by the Holy Spirit for spiritual discernment of the inspired message in the biblical text."[38] Luther's hermeneutical process thus entails two moments: The first moment is a focus on the *verbum externum* (verbal external "word"). This involves a literal understanding of the philological-grammatical and historical aspects of the text. As Luther argued, "this literal understanding is necessary before the exegete enters interpretation of meaning."[39] The second moment is when the exegete, through the illuminating work of the Holy Spirit, is enabled to discern the spiritual significance of the text. Luther was, however, careful neither to embed the Holy Spirit in the "letter" of the Bible nor to separate the Holy Spirit from the Scriptures: "The Spirit is not bound to the Word . . . the Word may exist without the Spirit, but when it does so, it is just a letter . . . Similarly, the Spirit can exist apart from the Word; He is not bound to the Word, but He cannot be God's revealing Spirit without the Word."[40] The deciphering of the spiritual sense of Scripture is, thus, not simply an outcome of the philological exegesis of Scripture. Rather, it entails the illuminating work of the Holy Spirit. Without the illuminating work of the Holy Spirit, Scripture is simply letter or Law. As Luther put it, "All Scripture is Law without the Spirit; with the Spirit, all Scripture is grace."[41]

According to Luther, the spiritual sense of Scripture is appropriated by faith, and faith is created by the Holy Spirit in the believer through the proclamation of the Word; "only God can create faith as the Holy Spirit works faith in man through the preaching of the Word, and the Word provides

37. See Calvin, *Institutes*, 1:52–55. See also Torrance, *The School of Faith*, 23.

38. Shelton, "Martin Luther's Concept," 231.

39. Schultz, "The Problem of Hermeneutics," 44. See also Poland who notes that, for Luther, "the proper understanding of Scripture concerns not only the 'outer clarity' of the theological content gained from exegesis, but also the 'inner clarity' of the reader's heart—the experience of grace and salvation given by the Holy Spirit through the external word of Scripture." (*Literary Criticism*, 19). See also Grondin, who understands Luther to mean that "the literal meaning rightly understood, contains its own proper spiritual significance," (*Introduction to Philosophical Hermeneutics*, 40).

40. Larry Shelton, "Martin Luther's Concept," 239–50.

41. See Wood, *Luther's Principles*, 32.

authority for the basis of faith."[42] Not only does faith resolve the hermeneutical tension between the letter and the Spirit, but faith is, indeed, central in the interpretive process. Thus, the Holy Spirit not only inspires the Word but also creates faith in the hearer of the Word in order to appropriate the Word's spiritual sense.

The above arguments show that Martin Luther's hermeneutic of Scripture is, indeed, pneumatic hermeneutic. The centrality of the Holy Spirit in Luther's hermeneutic represents a *sui generis* integration of the third person of the Trinity, who had largely been neglected by the medieval Church, in the development of Christian theology. Martin Luther's unique contribution to Christian theology in this regard is, arguably, the integration of Christology and pneumatology in biblical hermeneutics. This is a development in biblical theology that should be instructive for contemporary developments in biblical theology. In some quarters of the Church, the Holy Spirit is largely ignored, and hardly ever invoked, in biblical hermeneutics. In other quarters of the Church, particularly in the Pentecostal-Charismatic tradition, an overemphasis on the work of the Holy Spirit has tendentiously undervalued Christology in the task of biblical interpretation.

Luther augments his hermeneutic pillars with a significant rider that the context for biblical interpretation is the Church community. As James Smart aptly notes, "Luther sees the church as the matrix in which interpretation takes place, but is careful to ensure that the Church does not stifle the freedom of critical scholarship and also that critical scholarship does not bring alien concepts to the Church."[43] All in all, Luther's Reformation hermeneutic constituted a paradigm shift in biblical interpretation; his hermeneutical method not only integrated biblical exegesis with Christological-pneumatic theological reflection but was, indeed, a *hermeneutica sacra* (sacred hermeneutics)—a biblical-hermeneutical approach which presupposed the Bible to be the sacred inspired Word of God and which, though utilizing critical or scientific methods of textual exegesis, nonetheless, sought to not only discern the divine message in the biblical text but also to render the biblical message meaningful for the contemporary communities

---

42. Luther, *Luther's Works*, vol. 6, *Genesis Chapters 31–37*, 40.

43. Smart, *The Interpretation of Scripture*, 59. However, in the contemporary church world of denominational sectarianism, the notion of the "the church context" is problematic. Different church traditions are apt to emphasize different hermeneutical principles as their faith distinctive. Perhaps Luther's notion of "church context" is best understood in terms of sacred hermeneutics, that is, the biblical hermeneut should be a believer rather than a secular critic who is a stranger to sacred life. As the Chicago Statement of Faith (1978) aptly states, "The Holy Spirit, the Scripture's divine author, both authenticates it to us by His inward witness and opens our minds to understand its meaning" (Packer, *God Has Spoken*, 143).

of faith.[44] As Lynn Poland remarks, concerning Luther's hermeneutic, "the meaning of Scripture extends . . . *hodie usque ad nos* (even to us day)."[45]

POST-REFORMATION PROTESTANT HERMENEUTICS

Luther's grammatical-historical method of biblical interpretation became the foundational paradigm for the development of Protestant biblical hermeneutics from the sixteenth century onward. However, whereas Luther espoused the grammatical-historical method in order rescue biblical interpretation from the magisterium of the Roman Catholic Church and to provide a secure historical and rational foundation for biblical faith, the subsequent developments, under the influence of the eighteenth century European 'Age of Reason' (the Enlightenment), reduced the historical critical method to historicism. This ideologically -driven hermeneutical approach viewed biblical texts as mere historical phenomena which had value of their own without any relevance for the contemporary communities of faith. Thus, biblical faith was reduced to a preoccupation with historical phenomena.[46] A variant of historicism, the so-called minimalist view of biblical history, held that the narratives contained in the texts of the Bible had little or no historical connection to the events they depicted. They were thus viewed as mere religious legends to be studied as literary artifacts from the past.[47]

Historicism, as it applied to biblical hermeneutics, was enunciated in the hermeneutic thought of the nineteenth-century German theological scholar, Friedrich Schleiermacher, who developed a universal hermeneutic. Schleiermacher's universal hermeneutic posited that "a text is a text,

44. Grondin defines *hermeneutica sacra* as "the art of practical interpretation that applies general hermeneutical rules to Scripture" while still upholding the Scriptures as sacred writings, see his *Introduction to Philosophical Hermeneutics*, 58.

45. Poland, *Literary Criticism*, 12. See also Waltke who remarks that "Ours is a sacred hermeneutic because the Author is spirit and known in the human spirit through the medium of the Holy Spirit." Waltke, *An Old Testament Theology*, 80; and Brueggemann who remarks that "there is no innocent or neutral scholarship, but that all theological and interpretive scholarship is in one way or another fiduciary," that is, based on faith or ideological presuppositions (*Theology of the Old Testament*, 18).

46. For a detailed account of the development of historicism, see McLean, *Biblical Interpretation*, 31–67.

47. For contemporary arguments for the minimalist view of the Bible, particularly with respect to the Old Testament, see Davies, *In Search of Ancient Israel*, 11–18; Lemche, "Is it Still Possible to Write a History of Ancient Israel," 156–90; and Thompson, *The Mythic Past*, 20–25.

whether secular or religious."[48] Schleiermacher's universal hermeneutic thus maintained that the Bible did not require any unique interpretive approach. Schleiermacher, in effect, "collapsed the distinction between *hermeneutica sacra* and *hermeneutica profana* in order to create a universal hermeneutic."[49] Unlike Luther's *hermeneutica sacra* which, though utilizing secular methods of textual exegesis, held that the biblical texts were divinely inspired and that they revealed God's will for humankind in all time, the universal hermeneutic reduced biblical interpretation to a *Religionsgeschichte Schule* (history of religions school) approach which, akin to the minimalist view, argued that "the Bible represents only what certain people thought at a particular time about divine matters, but their thoughts carry no absolute truths for today."[50] Little wonder that Friedrich Nietzsche, the nineteenth-century German philosopher, disparaged historicism, calling it "historical sickness."[51] Nietzsche observed that "we require history for life and action . . . but there is a degree of doing history and an estimation of it which brings with it a withering and degenerating life."[52]

Historicism also postulated that the Bible was plausibly fallible as a historical source and diverse in its origins as a literary entity. The Bible was thus tendentiously atomized into various hypothetical source components.[53] Moreover, historicism presupposed that the Bible, as a religious and theological document, might be less unique than had been supposed.[54] The Bible was, hence, studied anti-supernaturally with "cold objectivity" and as mere religious literature.[55] Moreover, the anti-supernaturalistic bias tended to privilege the hypothetical source components over the extant

---

48. See Schleiermacher, "The Hermeneutics: Outline of the 1819 Lectures," 85–100. See also Ricoeur, for a further development of the universal hermeneutic, *Hermeneutics*, 45–48; and McLean, *Biblical Interpretation*, 37.

49. See Ricoeur, "Philosophical Hermeneutics and Theological Hermeneutics," 30. It is worth noting that the universal hermeneutic had a humanistic orientation; it was a product of the European Enlightenment which was viewed as "the era when human rationality overthrew religious myth and blind superstition and liberated civilization from ignorance, installing humanity as master of its own destiny." See McLean, *Biblical Interpretation*, 83; and Lyotard, *Postmodern Condition*, 7–32.

50. Waltke, *An Old Testament Theology*, 68.

51. Nietzsche, *On the Advantage*, 7.

52. Nietzsche, *On the Advantage*, 7.

53. The Pentateuchal documentary hypothesis associated with Julius Wellhausen, which atomizes the Pentateuch into Yahwist, Elohist, Priestly, and Deuteronomist sources, is a case in point. See Wellhausen, *Prolegomena*.

54. Barr, *The Concept of Biblical Theology*, 19.

55. These ideas are readily embraced in such works as Gunkel, *The Legends of Genesis* and Wellhausen, *Prolegomena*.

texts of the Bible, in their canonical form, in deciphering the meaning conveyed in the Word of God. As Hans Frei laments concerning the modern historical-critical approaches, "Interpretation was a matter of fitting the biblical story into another world with another story rather than incorporating that world into the biblical story."[56]

In the course of its development, historicism also tended to disaggregate the texts of the Bible into what was considered to be authentic and inauthentic sources and, hence, introduced a hermeneutic of suspicion into the task of biblical interpretation.[57] Furthermore, the idea of a canonical context for the study of the texts of the Bible was largely spurned by the tradents of historicism; they held that the texts of the Bible should be studied in their own right as independent texts freed from the "arbitrary constraints" imposed upon them by the Synagogue and the Church in the act of canonization.[58] Failure to read the texts of the Bible in their canonical context negated Luther's dictum that *scriptura sacra sui ipsius intepres* (sacred scripture is its own interpreter). This dictum, as noted above, meant that each text of Scripture should be interpreted in terms of the theology of the Bible as a whole.

The early part of the twentieth century saw the rise of a nuanced form of literary criticism, the new literary criticism, which, as Brevard Childs notes, "shifts biblical study away from historical referentiality."[59] As Gerald Bray observes, the new literary criticism "abandoned history as a model and insisted that works of art be judged primarily on aesthetic grounds."[60] Thus, the new literary approach tendentiously undermined the historical veracity of the biblical accounts. The new literary criticism also sought to break up the Christian canon by incorporating into its repertoire of texts extra-canonical epigraphic materials that were discovered in the course of the twentieth century. In particular, such epigraphic finds as the Dead Sea Scrolls or the *Nagi Hammadi* texts were read as though they were at par

---

56. Frei, *The Eclipse*, 130.

57. A hermeneutic of suspicion, a term coined by Ricoeur to depict the hermeneutic methods of Sigmund Freud, Friedrich Nietzsche and Karl Marx, is the tendency to approach a text with the presupposition that there are authentic and inauthentic elements in the text and an attempt to strip away what is considered to be inauthentic. It is a deconstructionist critique which, in effect, sows doubts in the minds of readers of the text. See Paul Ricoeur's discourse on hermeneutics of suspicion in his *Freud and Philosophy*. See also Stewart, "The Hermeneutic of Suspicion," 296–307.

58. Barton, *Reading the Old Testament*, 79.

59. Childs, *Biblical Theology of the Old and New Testaments*, 16.

60. Bray, *Biblical Interpretation*, 483.

in meaning and theological value as the texts of the Christian canon.[61] In some extreme cases, the new literary criticism went as far as attempting to emend the texts of the Christian canon in the light of the twentieth century epigraphic finds.[62] Hence Peter deVilliers' notion of attempts to "contaminate" the Christian canon.[63] As deVilliers observes, the attempts to emend the texts of the Christian canon in the light of the recently discovered texts is, in effect, an attempt to revise the Christian canon.

Some versions of the new literary criticism, notably the ideologically-driven reader-response critical approaches, argue that meaning is not derived from the texts of the Bible; meaning is "created by the readers in the act of reading."[64] Thus, as historicism privileged a hypothetical extra-biblical world over the texts of the Bible, the new reader-response critical approaches have tended to privilege the extra-biblical world of the reader who searches for the meaning conveyed in the Bible's texts. The implication of this 'privileging' is that the extra-biblical worlds impose their meaning upon biblical texts. The biblical-textual meanings derived therefrom are, hence, idiosyncratic and indeterminate.[65] Stanley Fish, an ardent reader-response proponent, argues that "Since the locus of meaning has proved so elusive, perhaps we should entertain the possibility that there is no determinate meaning in the text to begin with . . . The text yields no meaning. The only option is to play with the text."[66] Little wonder that the contemporary discipline of biblical studies is, in the words of Brevard Childs, "in crisis."[67]

By ignoring the canonical context of the texts of the Bible, both historicism and the new literary-critical approaches have attempted to

61. See de Villiers, "Perspectives on Canon History," 11–26.

62. Childs considers this attempt as very absurd indeed; he argues that "a corpus of religious writings which have been transmitted within a community for over a thousand years cannot be properly compared to inert shreds which have lain in the ground for centuries" (*Introduction to the Old Testament*, 79).

63. de Villiers, "Perspectives on Canon History," 11–26.

64. See Clines and Exum, "The New Literary Criticism," in 18–19.

65. Whereas it is acknowledged that the reader's worldview influences understanding of the text, some extreme versions of the reader-response criticism are decidedly ideological viewpoints. For extreme versions of the reader-response criticism, see, for example, Fish, *Is There a Text?*, 322–26; and Fish, "Interpreting the Variorum," 182–87. A moderate reader-response approach is posited by Iser, who observes that, since the text is external to the reader, it serves as a restraint on the reader's understanding of the text. See Iser, *The Act of Reading*, 19–24.

66. Fish, *Is There a Text?*, 108–9. Another reader-response critic, Clines, privileges the reader by arguing that "Since there is no determinate meaning, we should tailor our interpretation to meet the needs of the group we are addressing." (*Interested Parties*, 113).

67. Childs, *Biblical Theology in Crisis*, 1.

"de-canonize" the texts of the Bible.[68] Also, as already noted above, both historicism and the new literary-critical approaches have misused textual criticism (which is usually the first stage in their methodological processes) by rewriting the texts through unwarranted emendations.[69] The Bible reader who comes to the biblical text to hear the Word of God is therefore ill-served by the extant historical-critical and the new literary-critical methods of biblical interpretation. Hence a continuing search is needed for hermeneutical paradigms that serve the needs of the communities of faith, both in the academy or in the church.

ECHOES OF LUTHER'S HERMENEUTICS
IN CANONICAL CRITICISM

Some recent developments in the canonical-critical approach to biblical interpretation have been billed, in some quarters of biblical scholarship, as constitutive of a hermeneutical paradigm that seeks to interpret the Bible, not as an antiquarian artifact studied for its literary artistry only, but as the Word of God. As explained below, some aspects of the novel canonical criticism, particularly in the works of the Yale University biblical scholar, Brevard Childs, resonate with Martin Luther's Reformation hermeneutics.

The canonical approach to biblical interpretation is often viewed as having had its modern provenance in the early twentieth century Anglo-American biblical theology movement. The movement appears to have been a reaction against the historicism of European theological liberalism, which, as noted above, tended to 'de-canonize' the Bible and atomize it into hypothetical source components. Instead, the biblical theology movement advocated for a study of the received textual corpus of the Bible as a canonical whole as well as a theological unity of the Old and New Testaments. As Brevard Childs notes, the task of the biblical theology movement had been "to engage in the continual activity of theological reflection which studies the canonical text in detailed exegesis, and seeks to do justice to the witness of both Testaments in the light of its subject matter who is Jesus Christ."[70]

The term 'canonical criticism', at least in its modern usage, appears to have been popularized by James Sanders of Claremont School of Theology, California, with reference to the hermeneutical presuppositions of the compilers of the Hebrew *Torah*, and, in a more nuanced fashion, by Brevard

---

68. So argues Childs, *Introduction to the Old Testament*, 79.

69. See also Sanders, "Text and Canon," 8.

70. Childs, *Biblical Theology of the Old and New Testaments*, 78–79.

Childs of Yale University.[71] Sanders argued that the starting point of biblical interpretation is the received canon, that is, the final form of the texts of the Bible in their canonical context.[72] Robert Carroll, in his critical review of Sanders' canonical approach, remarks that:

> This concentration on the final form of the literary units making up the Bible takes seriously the work of the editors and tradents who put together the various traditions and attempts to discern their intentions . . . it was the final product of their work which was canonized rather than the primary or original traditions, so the central issue for the theologian must be the canonical form of the work. Taking the canon seriously means treating the books of the Bible as they stand and relating them to the concerns of the community which gave them their canonical status[73.]

Thus, as Sanders goes on to argue, the texts of the Bible, taken separately, may not appear to present a univocal message. However, taken together, they bear witness to God's manifold revelation of His character and will for His covenant people.[74] This point is also reiterated by John Barton who remarks that biblical critics "were not wrong to identify detailed points of diversity and inconsistency, but they were in danger of not seeing the wood for the trees, ignoring the equal and greater volume of evidence that pointed to unity and singleness of purpose" in the canon of Scripture.[75]

Reading the texts of the Bible in their canonical context implies that the meaning of the text is not only informed by its literary and thematic designs but also by the canonical inter-textual context. The interpretation of any one text of the Bible must thus be cognizant of the overall message of the canon of Scripture. Moshe Halbertal makes a cogent observation that the canonization decision was, *ipso facto*, an interpretive act.[76] The canonical meaning is, therefore, "the meaning the text has when it is read as part of the

---

71. Childs, *Biblical Theology in Crisis*, 84–99; and Childs, *Introduction to the Old Testament*, 56–85.

72. See Sanders, "Biblical Criticism," 157–165, Sanders, "Text and Canon," 5–29, and, Sanders, *Canon and Community*, 2–7.

73. Carroll, "Canonical Criticism," 73.

74. See Sanders, "Biblical Criticism," 157–165, and Sanders, "Text and Canon," 5–29.

75. Barton, *Old Testament*, 61.

76. Halbertal, *People of the Book*, 19.

canon, with full allowance made for the other texts that also form part of the canon, in their overall coherent pattern."[77]

The act of canonization has, however, as noted above, been viewed in some quarters of biblical scholarship as a subjection of the texts of Scripture to some external magisterium of the synagogue and the church, a "subjugation of Scripture to external authority."[78] Nonetheless, as Brevard Childs argues, "although historically the decision of the Church actually shaped the canon, the Church itself envisioned its task as acknowledging what God had given."[79] In other words, the act of canonization was simply the Church's recognition and delineation of God's revelation to the community of faith. The Church was simply the receptor and preserver of the divine revelation.[80] The canon is, therefore, both a collection of divinely inspired authoritative texts as well as an authoritative compendium that is constitutive of the rule of faith for the community of believers. On the other hand, the canonical approach neither ignores apparent textual problems or peculiarities of individual texts of the canon nor does it overlook tensions among the texts of the canon. As John Peckham, commenting on the canonical approach, remarks, "Where apparent tensions arise, they should be properly acknowledged rather than glossed over. However, it should be recognized that apparent tensions do not necessarily rule out undergirding theological consistency, especially if consistency is not improperly conflated with simplistic univocity."[81]

A further question that is often raised in biblical scholarship is: which canon is authoritative? For example, there are variants of the Hebrew canon (Old Testament), namely, the Hebrew Version (notably the Masoretic text) and the Greek Version (the 'Septuagint' or the pre-Christian Greek translation of the Hebrew Bible, often referred to as the 'Alexandrian canon'). The two versions differ markedly in a number of texts; for example, the Septuagint edition of the book of Jeremiah is much shorter than the Hebrew version of the book and has a different ordering of its contents.[82] There are also other collections of texts, the so-called deuterocanonical texts, notably

---

77. Barton, *Reading the Old Testament*, 81.

78. Barton, *Reading the Old Testament*, 97.

79. Childs, *Theology of the Old and New Testaments*, 64.

80. See Childs, *Biblical Theology in Crisis*, 105. Sanders, on the other hand, argues that the canon is community determined but this view is problematic in the sense that this would imply that the church has an ongoing authority to determine the canon. Sanders, *Canon and Community*, 15. See also Peckham, "The Analogy of Scripture," 44.

81. Peckham, "The Analogy of Scripture," 47–48.

82. For a detailed analysis of the two versions of the book of Jeremiah, see, for example, Stulman, *Jeremiah*, 7–8

the apocryphal texts, some of which are included in the canons of some Christian traditions but regarded as extra-canonical in other Christian traditions.[83] Brevard Childs wades into the question of 'which canon' and argues that the Masoretic text (the Hebrew Bible version that was preserved by Jewish rabbinic scholars known as the *Masoretes*) should be the normative canon because it is what the Jews and Christians have in common.[84] On the contrary, Albert Sundberg argues that the Greek canon (the Septuagint) has primacy over other Old Testament versions because it was the canon of the early church.[85] The debate rages on, but as some critics have pointed out, the canonical controversy plausibly boils down to differences between inspired autographs and corrupt transmissions.[86] Nonetheless, the Masoretic text, which was preserved by the Jewish rabbinic scholars, the *Masoretes*, has generally been accepted, both in the academy and the Church, as the canonical norm of the Hebrew Bible.[87]

Whereas Sanders' canonical approach is essentially a holistic literary reading of the Bible in canonical context, Brevard Childs' canonical approach is more nuanced and is, indeed, a canonical theology that harks back to Luther's *hermeneutica sacra*. Childs readily embraces the historical-critical study of the texts of the Bible in a canonical context utilizing scientific exegetical tools. However, Childs' canonical approach is more focused on the presuppositional-hermeneutical paradigm which guides the exegetical methods. His approach is, thus, not simply a technical method of biblical interpretation. Rather, it is a hermeneutical paradigm in which the Bible is read as the divinely inspired and authoritative Word of God. As Earle Ellis aptly points out, "Method is inherently a limited instrumentality, and, indeed, a secondary stage in the art of interpretation. More basic are the perspective and presuppositions with which the interpreter approaches the

---

83. For a detailed discussion on the controversy of variant canons, see Sundberg, "The Protestant," 194–203; and Sundberg, "The Canon," 352–71. See also Barton, *Reading the Old Testament*, 91–92.

84. Childs, *Introduction to the Old Testament*, 72–74, 659–71.

85. Sundberg, "The Protestant," 194–203.

86. See Waltke, *An Old Testament Theology*, 33, and Hays, "Jeremiah, the Septuagint," 133–49.

87. It can also be argued that since, per Scripture, it is to the Jews that "the giving of the law" was committed (Rom 9:4; cf. Rom 3:2), it is the version preserved by the Jews that should be the authoritative canon for the Church. See also Waltke who underscores the need "to take seriously enough the widespread use of the Masoretic text before the Christian era" instead of capitulating to the popular opinion that the Septuagint was the canon of the early church, *An Old Testament Theology*, 33 n.15.

text."[88] Childs' canonical approach is, indeed, *hermeneutica sacra*, or confessional hermeneutics. As he argues:

> Biblical theology has, as its proper context, the canonical scriptures of the Christian Church . . . The Christian Church responded to this literature as the authoritative Word of God, and it remains existentially committed to an inquiry into its inner unity because of its confession of the one Gospel of Jesus Christ which it proclaims to the world. It was therefore a fatal methodological mistake when the nature of the Bible was described solely in categories of the history of religions.[89]

Childs' confessional approach to biblical criticism is also noted by John Barton, who remarks that it "is currently the most influential" attempt to rescue biblical studies from "secular specialism." John Barton goes on to observe that:

> In the work of Brevard Childs (more properly called the canonical method or approach) it aims at a new, post-critical reading of the finished form of biblical texts; but unlike holistic literary readings with their addiction to modern literary theory, a 'canonical' reading is concerned with the religious meaning of the Bible. At the same time, it tries to help the critics themselves to be more theologically and religiously sensitive . . . It wants to bring the critics with their skills back into the fold of the Church; to enable them to share with simpler believers the experience of finding again in the Bible the living word of God.[90]

Childs decries the historical-critical method's tendency to disaggregate the texts of the Bible into hypothetical original or earlier sources, thus confining the Bible into the past. He also laments that the historical-critical methods not only fail to consider any dialectical relation between the biblical texts and their canonical context but also that, in their present form, the historical-critical methods fail to consider whether the canon of Scripture might have a coherent theological truth for the present community of faith, notwithstanding any biblical-textual tensions therein.[91] As John Barton surmises, the apparent biblical-textual inconsistencies pointed out by the historical-critical scholars are plausibly subordinate to a higher unity. Barton grants that the texts of the Bible may not all speak with "a single voice,

88. Ellis, *Prophecy and Hermeneutics*, 163.
89. Childs, *Biblical Theology of the Old and New Testaments*, 8.
90. Barton, *The Old Testament*, 150–51.
91. Childs, "The Canonical Shape," 53–55.

yet taken together, they witness to a unified truth . . . the scriptural texts have a unity of purpose and message which is more important than their mutual tensions and disagreements in detail."[92] It is the "more important" theological message arising from the canon as a whole that Brevard Childs' hermeneutical paradigm seeks to rescue back for the communities of faith, both in the academy and the church.

Brevard Childs' hermeneutical paradigm is, however, not a naïve attempt to harmonize apparently disparate or inconsistent texts of the Bible, as some of his detractors have argued.[93] Rather, akin to Martin Luther's *hermeneutica sacra*, it is a hermeneutical presupposition with which the reader approaches the texts of the Bible as the divinely inspired Word of God and the authoritative rule of faith.[94] For Childs, the unifying factor in the canon is that it is sacred Scripture. Childs, much like Martin Luther, opposes the historical-critical or any other scientific critical methods of textual interpretation. His concern is that the method's atomizing analysis of the texts of the Bible should not be an end in itself; a synthesizing attempt is necessary to discern the coherent message from the canon of Scripture. Dale Brueggemann aptly remarks that Childs' confessional approach to biblical criticism is not a capitulation to literalistic biblicism; "literalists and fundamentalists can only take false comfort in what is happening in this regard; they should not be deceived into thinking that critical scholarship has come to its senses in repentance of its errant ways."[95] Brevard Childs' embrace of scientific methods of textual interpretation is premised on the understanding that "interest in the sources from which the biblical books were composed, or the forms they use, or the skills with which they were assembled by redactors, is a natural consequence of attending to the givenness of the text, and of realizing that if the Bible does mediate knowledge of God, it does it through these means and not otherwise."[96]

It is not just from the historical-critical scholarship's "errant ways" that Childs' *hermeneutica sacra* seeks to recover the Bible for the community of faith. It is also from the secular literary critics who read the Bible as a literary classic devoid of any divine authority. Thus, as John Barton remarks, Brevard Childs' "canonical approach is a proposal about how Christians should

---

92. Barton, *The Old Testament Canon*, 59–60.

93. See, for example, Barr's critique of Childs' Canonical approach in "Childs' Introduction to the Old Testament as Scripture," 12–23.

94. See also Waltke, *An Old Testament Theology*, 79–80.

95. Brueggemann, "Brevard Childs' Canon Criticism," 313.

96. Barton, *The Old Testament*, 155.

read the Bible within the context of faith."[97] Nonetheless, Barton rightly cautions that "whereas biblical critics should be sensitive to the church's call to be more theological, they should also reckon that the church is not best served by an academy that simply capitulates to the uncritical whims of the communities of faith."[98] Consistent with this caution, Brevard Childs adopts a centrist stance which, as Kathleen M. O'Connor notes, "seeks to preserve biblical studies from both the dogmatism of biblicizing conservatives and much more from the historicism of wide-eyed children of the Enlightenment."[99] Childs' fiercest critic, James Barr, who often terms Childs' theologies as "canonical fundamentalism" or "theological fundamentalism," nonetheless, acknowledges that "Childs touches on aspects which for many are religiously very important, and these are likely to produce other expressions in the future."[100]

THE REFORMATION LEGACY IN PNEUMATIC HERMENEUTICS

Martin Luther (1483–1546), the monk of Wittenberg, has been credited with many theological, ecclesiological, and even political achievements. However, as Derek Wilson aptly cautions, "we have to resist the temptation to recreate him in our own image."[101] Nonetheless, Martin Luther is rightly renowned for fanning the sixteenth-century revolt against the papal tyranny of the time and an awakening of the Church from spiritual slumber. The particular thesis of this paper is that a critical aspect of Martin Luther's legacy, often overlooked in Reformation studies, is his influence on biblical hermeneutics. Luther's sixteenth-century biblical hermeneutics became the bedrock of subsequent Protestant theological-hermeneutical development. Luther's Reformation hermeneutic was a *hermeneutica sacra*; it was a hermeneutical paradigm shift which not only rescued biblical interpretation from the magisterium of the church of the day but also utilized scientific tools of textual analysis to interpret the Bible as sacred Scriptures. Luther's Christological-hermeneutical focus, and his embrace of the illumining work of the Holy Spirit in biblical interpretation, were hermeneutical moves that sought to combine biblical interpretation with theological reflection. Thus,

97. Barton, *The Old Testament*, 50.
98. Barton, *The Old Testament*, 156.
99. O'Connor, "How the Text is Heard?" 91.
100. Barr, *The Concept of Theology*, 437–38.
101. Wilson, *Out of the Storm*, 34.

his hermeneutical method integrated biblical exegesis with Christological-pneumatic-theological reflection.

Although Luther's Reformation paradigm was foundational for Protestant hermeneutical development from the sixteenth century onward, this paradigm was derailed in the eighteenth-century European Enlightenment in which biblical hermeneutics were not only secularized but also divorced from theological reflection. Recent developments in canonical criticism not only hark back to Luther's Reformation hermeneutics but also seek to render the biblical message meaningful for the contemporary communities of faith, for the meaning of Scripture extends *hodie ueque ad nos* (even to us today). Luther's integrative *hermeneutica sacra* is particularly instructive for the contemporary Church, which, on the one hand, studies the Bible with cold objectivity as though the Bible has no divine relevance for the Church today; while on the other hand, the Pentecostal-Charismatic wing of the Church, whose pneumatic hermeneutic apparently underrates the value of scientific tools of textual exegesis and tendentiously privileges pneumatology over Christology in its theological reflection, has a lot to learn from Luther's *hermeneutica sacra*.

BIBLIOGRAPHY

Archer, Kenneth J. *A Pentecostal Hermeneutic for the Twenty-First Century: Spirit, Scripture, and Community.* Journal of Pentecostal Theology Supplement Series 28. London: T. & T. Clark, 2004.

Barr, James. 1980. "Childs' *Introduction to the Old Testament as Scripture.*" *Journal for the Study of the Old Testament* 16 (1980) 12–23.

———. *The Concept of Biblical Theology: An Old Testament Perspective.* Minneapolis: Fortress, 1999.

Barton, John. *The Old Testament: Canon, Literature, and Theology: Collected Essays of John Barton.* Aldershot, UK: Ashgate, 2007.

———. "Reading the Bible as Literature: Two Questions for Biblical Critics." *Journal of Theology and Literature* 1 (1987) 135–53.

———. *Reading the Old Testament: Method in Biblical Study.* Louisville: Westminster John Knox, 1996.

Bray, Gerald. *Biblical Interpretation: Past and Present.* Downer's Grove, IL: InterVarsity, 1996.

Brueggemann, Dale A. "Brevard Childs' Canon Criticism: An Example of Post-Critical Naïvete?" *Journal of Evangelical Theological Society* 32 (1989) 311–26.

Calvin, John. *Institutes of the Christian Religion.* Vol. 1. Translated by H. Beveridge, edited by John McNeill. Philadelphia. Westminster. 1970.

Cameron, Euan. *The European Reformation.* Oxford: Oxford University Press, 1991.

Carroll, Robert. "Canonical Criticism: A Recent Trend in Biblical Studies?" *Expository Times* 92 (1980) 73–78.

Childs, Brevard S. *Biblical Theology in Crisis.* Philadelphia: Fortress, 1970.

————. *Biblical Theology of the Old and New Testaments: Theological Reflection on the Christian Bible*. Minneapolis: Fortress, 1992.

————. "The Canonical Shape of the Prophetic Literature." *Interpretation* 32 (1978) 53–55.

————. *Introduction to the Old Testament as Scripture*. Philadelphia: Fortress, 1979.

Clines, David J. A., and J. Cheryl Exum. "The New Literary Criticism." In *The New Literary Criticism and the Hebrew Bible*, edited by J. Cheryl Exum and David J. A. Clines, 19–38. Valley Forge, PA: Trinity, 1994.

Darr, John. "Glorified in the Presence of Kings: A Literary-Critical Study of Herod the Tetrarch in Luke–Acts." PhD diss., Vanderbilt University, 1989.

De Villiers, Peter G. R. "Perspectives on Canon History and Canonical Criticism in the Light of Biblical Spirituality." *Scriptura* 91 (2006) 11–26.

Doermann, Ralph W. "Luther's Principles of Biblical Interpretation." In *Interpreting Luther's Legacy*, edited by F. W. Meuser and S. D. Schneider, 111–23. Minneapolis: Augsburg, 1969.

Ellis, Earle E. *Prophecy and Hermeneutics in Early Christianity*. 1993. Reprint, Eugene, OR: Wipf & Stock, 2003.

Farrar, Frederick W. *History of Interpretation*. New York: Dutton, 1886.

Fiorenza, Elizabeth S. "Method in Women Studies in Religion: A Critical Feminist Hermeneutics." In *Methodology in Religious Studies: The Interface with Women's Studies*, edited by Arvind Sharma, 26–39. McGill Studies in the History of Religion. Albany: State University of New York Press, 2002.

Fish, Stanley E. *Is There a Text in this Class?: The Authority of the Interpretive Communities*. Cambridge: Harvard University Press, 1980.

Fish, Stanley E. "Interpreting the Variorum." In *Reader-Response Criticism: From Formalism to Post-Structuralism*, edited by J. P. Thompson, 38–51. Baltimore: John Hopkins University Press, 1980.

Frei, Hans W. *The Eclipse of Biblical Narrative: A Study in Eighteenth and Nineteenth Century Hermeneutics*. Revised edition. New Haven: Yale University Press, 1974.

Gadamer, Georg. *Truth and Method*. Translated by G. Barden and J. Cumming. New York: Continuum, 1975.

Grondin, Jean. *Introduction to Philosophical Hermeneutics*. New Haven: Yale University Press, 1994.

Gunkel, Hermann. *The Legends of Genesis: The Biblical Saga and History*. Translated by W. H. Carruth. Chicago: Open Court, 1901.

Halbertal, Moshe. *People of the Book: Canon, Meaning, and Authority*. Cambridge: Harvard University Press, 1997.

Hays, Daniel. "Jeremiah, the Septuagint, the Dead Sea Scrolls and Inerrancy: Just What Exactly Do We Mean by 'Original Autographs'?" In *Evangelicals and Scripture, Tradition, Authority, and Hermeneutics*, edited by Vincent Bacote, Laura C. Miguelez, and Dennis L. Ockholm, 116–27. Downer's Grove, IL: InterVarsity, 2004.

Iser, Wolfgang. *The Range of Interpretation*. New York: Columbia University Press, 2000.

Kramm, H. H. W. *The Theology of Martin Luther*. London: James Clarke, 1947.

Lemche, Niels Peter. "Is It Still Possible to Write a History of Ancient Israel?" *Scandinavian Journal of the Old Testament* 8/2 (1994) 165–90.

Luther, Martin. *Luther's Works*. Vol. 4, *Lectures on Genesis Chapter 21–25*, edited by J. Pelican. St Louis: Concordia, 1964.

————. *Luther's Works*. Vol. 6, *Lectures on Genesis Chapter 31–37*, edited by J. Pelican. St Louis: Concordia, 1970.

————. *Luther's Works*. Vol. 13, *Selected Psalms II*, edited by J. Pelican. St Louis: Concordia, 1956.

————. *Luther's Works*. Vol. 15, *Ecclesiastes, Song of Solomon, Last Words of David*, edited by J. Pelican. St Louis: Concordia, 1969.

————. *Luther's Works*. Vol. 20, *Minor Prophets III: Zechariah*, edited by J. Pelican. St Louis: Concordia, 1973.

————. *Luther's Works*. Vol. 26, *Lectures on Galatians Chapters 1–4*, edited by J. Pelican. St Louis: Concordia, 1963.

Lyotard, Jean-Francois. *The Postmodern Condition: A Report on Knowledge*. Translated by Geoff Bennington and Brian Massumi. Theory and History of Literature 10. Minneapolis: University of Minnesota Press, 1984.

McLean, Bradley H. *Biblical Interpretation and Philosophical Hermeneutics*. Cambridge: Cambridge University Press, 2012.

Muindi, Samuel W. *Pentecostal-Charismatic Prophecy: Empirical-Theological Analysis*. Oxford: Lang, 2017.

Muller, Richard, and John Thompson. "The Significance of Pre-Critical Exegesis." In *Biblical Interpretation in the Era of the Reformation*, 39–57, edited by Richard Muller and John Thompson. Grand Rapids: Eerdmans, 1996.

Nietzsche, Friedrich. *On the Advantage and Disadvantage of History for Life*. Translated by Peter Preus. Indianapolis: Hackett, 1980.

O'Connor, Kathleen M. "How the Text Is Heard: The Biblical Theology of Brevard Childs." *Religious Studies Review* 21 (1995) 91–95.

Phan, Peter C. "Method in Liberation Theologies." *Theological Studies* 61 (2000) 40–63.

Peckham, John C. "The Analogy of Scripture Revisited: A Final Form Canonical Approach to Systematic Theology." *Mid-America Journal of Theology* 22 (2011) 41–53.

Plass, Ewald. *What Luther Says*. Vol. 1. St. Louis: Concordia, 1959.

Poland, Lynn M. *Literary Criticism and Biblical Hermeneutics: A Critique of Formalist Approaches*. Chico, CA: Scholars, 1985.

Ricoeur, Paul. *Freud and Philosophy: An Essay on Interpretation*. New Haven: Yale University Press, 1989.

————. *Hermeneutics and the Human Sciences: Essays on Language, Action, and Interpretation*. Edited and translated by John B. Thompson. Cambridge Philosophy Classics. Cambridge: Cambridge University Press, 1981.

————. "Philosophical Hermeneutics and Theological Hermeneutics." *Studies in Religion* 5 (1975) 14–33.

————. "Toward a Hermeneutic Idea of Revelation." *Harvard Theological Review* 70 (1977) 1–37.

Sanders, James A. "Biblical Criticism and the Bible as Canon." *Union Seminary Quarterly Review* 32 (1977) 157–65.

————. "Text and Canon: Concepts and Method." *Journal of Biblical Literature* 98 (1979) 5–29.

————. *Canon and Community: A Guide to Canonical Criticism*. 1984. Reprint, Eugene, OR: Wipf & Stock, 2000.

Sasse, Hermann. "Luther and the Word of God." In *Accents in Luther's Theology*, edited by Heino O. Kadai, 123–39. St. Louis: Concordia, 1967.

Schleiermacher, Friedrich. "The Hermeneutics: Outline of the 1819 Lectures." In *Hermeneutics Tradition from Ast to Ricoeur*, edited by Gayle L. Ormiston and Alan D. Schrift, 119–37. Intersections. Albany: SUNY Press, 1990.

Shelton, Larry. "Martin Luther's Concept of Biblical Interpretation in Historical Perspective." ThD diss., Fuller Theological Seminary, 1974.

Shultz, Werner. "The Problem of Hermeneutics in Current Continental Philosophy and Theology." *Luther's World* 6 (1959) 38–53.

Stulman, Louis. *Jeremiah*. Abingdon Old Testament Commentaries. Nashville: Abingdon, 2005.

Sundberg, Albert C. "The Canon and the Christian Doctrine of Inspiration." *Interpretation* 29 (1966) 352–71.

———. "The Protestant Old Testament Canon: Should it Be Re-examined?" *Catholic Biblical Quarterly* 28 (1966) 194–203.

Vanhoozer, Kevin. "Language, Literature, Hermeneutics, and Biblical Theology: What's Theological about a Theological Dictionary." In *New International Dictionary of Old Testament Theology and Exegesis*, 197–216, edited by Moisés Silva. Grand Rapids: Zondervan, 1999.

Waltke, Bruce K. *An Old Testament Theology: An Exegetical, Canonical, and Thematic Approach*. Grand Rapids: Zondervan, 2007.

Wellhausen, Julius. *Prolegomena to the History of Israel*. New York: Meridian, 1957.

Wilson, Derek. "The Luther Legacy." *History Today* 57 (2007) 34–39.

3

Pentecostal Reception of Luther and Lutheranism

An Analysis of Early Devotional Literature

Donald W. Kammer

INTRODUCTION

EARLY PENTECOSTAL LITERATURE OCCASIONALLY appeals to the authority of Luther and the Reformation as a means of establishing credibility and continuity with the past. Pentecostals, while working out the formational kinks in their theology, sought ideological connectivity to the Protestant Reformation as an analogous renewal movement. They embraced Luther as a "foremost" church father. As Pentecostals imbibed an assortment of experiential and spectacular charismatic demonstrations, Luther's pioneering life became one stabilizing lens through which they interpreted their developing Pentecostal identity and experience. For them, the Reformation and the reformers became emblematic, a prophetic testimony in history of the faithful intervention of God, validating their modern-day experience which they saw pointing them toward even greater reform and renewal of the church and the world. Pentecostals never did see the Protestant Reformation as a static or settled reality. They saw the Reformation as one stage in the continuing reformation of the Church.

With a thorough survey of early Pentecostal periodicals and other texts, it is possible to conclude that Pentecostals held a positive view of Martin Luther and embraced the Reformation as a proof text of their own religious transformation. In view of recent discussions related to Pentecostal identity, understanding the Pentecostal affinity for Luther may offer added value and perspective to ongoing and unresolved discussion and debate.[1] Indeed, observers of Pentecostalism in the modern context need only skim the pages of *Pneuma: The Journal of the Society for Pentecostal Studies* to witness vibrant discussion related to Pentecostal identity.[2]

So how does Luther or Lutheranism fit into this ongoing conversation in connection to Pentecostal identity? For this chapter, the primary method of research has been a thorough survey of online archived texts from the *Consortium of Pentecostal Archives*, the *Flower Pentecostal Heritage Center*, and early published documents from the first few decades of the twentieth century.[3]

HOW DID EARLY PENTECOSTALS VIEW LUTHER AND LUTHERANISM?

On what might have been a cold Sunday morning in Minneapolis, Minnesota during September 1907, an unnamed individual reported in *The Apostolic Faith*, the voice of the Azusa Street community:

> . . .the power of God came upon us in the morning meeting and in the evening the Pentecost began to fall, and by 11:30 the next morning six had received Pentecost, "For they heard them speak with tongues and magnify God." It was like some

1. Dempster, "The Search for Pentecostal Identity," 1–8. Menzies, *Pentecost: This Story is Our Story*, Introduction, loc 117 of 2373,.

2. Recent issues of *Pneuma* have addressed identity matters, such as the loss and recovery of a Wesleyan vision of Pentecostalism, the Pentecostal mystical tradition, the relevance of the #MeToo Movement, and the Future of the Pentecostal Movement, all themes related to introspection on identity or emerging identity. See Coulter, "Recovering the Wesleyan Vision of Pentecostalism: 5 Theses," 457–488; Waddell and Althouse, "Pentecostalism as Mysticism: The Catholicity of the Tradition," 453–455; Ambrose and Alexander, "Pentecostal Studies Face the #MeToo Movement," 1–7; and Oliverio, "The Work of Charles Taylor and the Future of Pentecostalism," 5–16. In 2018, *Pneuma* editors, Waddell and Althouse, in view of this identity seeking, opined, "the study of Pentecostal and charismatic Christianity is likely to see many new changes in the future." Waddell and Althouse, "A Brief History of Pneuma: The First Forty Years," 4.

3. *Consortium of Pentecostal Archives*, https://pentecostalarchives.org/ (accessed 10 July 2019) and *Flower Pentecostal Heritage Center*, https://ifphc.org/ (accessed 10 July 2019).

scenes in Azusa, all around lay the slain, Methodists, Baptists, and Lutherans.[4]

The distant memory of "slain" Methodists and Baptists in worship services in American religious circles certainly had historical precedent in frontier revivals such as Cane Ridge, Kentucky in 1801 and the Second Great Awakening, which were prone to catch Lutherans up in a frenzy of "Arminian-powered revivalism" which Lutheran leaders saw as a threatening "religious enthusiasm."[5] Lutheranism has not typically been associated with such religious expression. One might possibly go back to the Pietists or radical reformers to find documented "religiously" slain Lutherans.[6] A glaring American exception to a less expressive Lutheranism certainly can be discerned on the frontier, where Lutherans often eagerly joined in with the revivalism of Methodists and Baptists. It should be no surprise that the same presence of "religious enthusiasm" would occur when Lutherans encountered Pentecostals in the first few decades of the twentieth century.

This chapter will highlight how early Pentecostals appropriated the heritage of Luther and select aspects of Lutheranism. These Pentecostals desired to preserve a continued connection to and identity with the Reformation and to Luther as a foremost church father. Although Pentecostals became known for their experiential demonstrations, they still were drawn to Luther, although less so to Lutheranism. In the first year of the Azusa Street Mission's existence, *The Apostolic Faith* described God's continuing work by raising up men to "bring back the truth to the church." In 1906 the unnamed author of "The Pentecostal Baptism Restored," in the second issue of *Apostolic Faith,* asserted the following: "All along the ages men have been preaching a partial Gospel." The author then explained that this "darkness" was pierced as God "raised up Luther to bring back to the world the doctrine of justification by faith." The author, possibly Clara Lum,[7] next cites several other reformers and makes the claim that God "is now bringing back the

---

4. "In the Last Days," 1. Quote is found in *The Apostolic Faith*, an early Pentecostal periodical established at the Azusa Street Mission by William Seymour in Los Angeles in 1906. It existed only a few years in Los Angeles. Florence Crawford relocated to Portland, Oregon. She took the entire mailing list, in what some have argued was a takeover. See Warner, "Periodicals," 974–982, and Robeck Jr., *The Azusa Street Mission and Revival,* 99, 104–105, 301–302.

5. Granquist, *A New History: Lutherans in America,* 128–129.

6. Alexander, "Slain in the Spirit," 1075.

7. Robeck Jr., *The Azusa Street Mission and Revival,* 99, 301–302. The Azusa Mission's *The Apostolic Faith* was "more or less a regular newspaper," a cooperative effort "for which Clara Lum took primary editorial responsibility." Robeck asserts that Lum wrote many anonymous articles in the periodical, so it is frequently nearly impossible to identify specific authorship of individual pieces.

Pentecostal baptism to the church.[8] For these Pentecostals, the Reformation and the reformers were emblematic of their own experience of Pentecost. They viewed their own efforts at reformation as related.

Pentecostal periodicals during the early decades of the twentieth century mention the man, Martin Luther, regularly. However, there are fewer references to Lutheranism when one searches the periodicals of the first twenty-five years of the Pentecostal movement. References to Luther and things Lutheran do not delve deeply into theological constructs, but they do represent a steady attempt to associate Pentecostalism with the Protestant Reformation in general, a desire to embrace Luther's ethos and a deliberate choice to identify with commonly held theological positions of Protestantism. This interest, specifically in Luther, gradually shifts over the years to an intentional appropriation of Luther to justify and support distinctive Pentecostal doctrines and experiences, even when such associations are highly debatable and, for most Lutherans, unimaginable. Indeed, Pentecostals identified with Luther's religious experience and components of his theology by molding Luther to fit their own Pentecostal experience and belief.

Pentecostals Identified with Luther and Lists of Reformers

When one surveys early Pentecostal literature, Martin Luther's name is prominent on various lists of reformers. Luther's name on such lists reflects a desire for a return of "real" Christianity, which to Pentecostals had been taken away by Rome during the centuries-long devolution of the Roman Catholic Church.[9] In 1915, the missionary Kate Knight wrote in *Confidence*, "Since the days of Luther, God has been lifting the remnant of the church up again into truth until for the past century there has been steady progress both in regaining a knowledge of the truth once delivered to the saints, and a zealous purpose to come into the power of it."[10] Pentecostals certainly identified with the recovery of Christian truth which occurred because of the Reformation, but they also wanted to encounter the power of that truth. In the life of Martin Luther, truth was manifested in a theology that led to conversion experience.

Pentecostals saw in their own Holy Spirit experiences examples of renewal encounters that were complementary to those of the reformers. For Pentecostals, the turn of the twentieth century witnessed a recovery of truth and a return to the New Testament experience of the Holy Spirit, the real

8. "The Pentecostal Baptism Restored," 1.
9. Piper, "But Also to Suffer for His Sake," 8.
10. Knight, "The Baptism in the Holy Spirit," 133.

old-time religion, which others had forged. This return was not merely an embrace of pneumatology in terms of doctrine. It was both the reception of intimate and demonstrative new experiences of the Holy Spirit as well as an acknowledgment of the contribution of prior reformers.

A typical example of a list of reformers can be found in a 1919 issue of *The Bridegroom's Messenger*. The author included on the list the following prominent reformers: "John Wycliff... John Huss [*sic*]... Jerome of Prague ... Savonarola ... Martin Luther ...Ulric Zwingle [*sic*]... Meno Simon ...William Tyndale... Philip Melancthon [*sic*]... John Calvin."[11] At the beginning of the Pentecostal movement, Pentecostals envisioned themselves as part of a stream of renewal history set in motion during the Reformation. Occasionally the Pentecostal publications would also print articles by non-Pentecostals such the evangelist, Billy Sunday, or Presbyterian S. Edward Young from Brooklyn as a means of identifying with the broader Christian world, "Dearly, dearly would we enjoy this sacrament side by side with Paul and Timothy and Saint Augustine and Luther and Calvin and David Livingston and our own promoted kith and kin, whom the angel, black winged, tore from our embrace."[12] Printed articles from non-Pentecostals listing the names of great reformers suggest that Pentecostals were less sectarian and more ecumenical in orientation then some might expect. Clearly, a resilient sense of belonging and longing to be a part of the larger Christian family existed with these Pentecostal believers from the start.

Pentecostals Embraced Luther as an Exemplar

Occasionally, encouraging quotes from Luther were printed in Pentecostal periodicals. In 1917 *The Weekly Evangel* was one of the most popular Pentecostal periodicals in North America. Its name was later changed to the *Pentecostal Evangel*, a periodical published by the Assemblies of God out of Springfield, Missouri. E. N. Bell, who served as editor from 1917–1919, wrote a regular column, "Questions and Answers," which placed quotes

11. "Prominent Reformers," 1. Other such lists of Luther among a cloud of reformers can easily be located. See "Latter Rain Sermon—Go Forward: Reinforced by the Voice of the Spirit Launching the Latter Rain Evangel," 9. Here "Luther, Wyclif, Savonarola, Knox and Huss" are listed. Billy Sunday's sermon [Sunday was not a Pentecostal] appeared in Boddy's *Confidence*. See Sunday, "Reward," 177–179, 183–185. *Confidence* attributes the source to "The North American" Philadelphia, March 22nd, 1915. The sermon includes "Luther and Wesley and Calvin and Moody" on a list of Reformers.

12. Young, "The Empty Seat at the Master's Table," 20. The editor noted that the article was taken from a periodical named *Homiletic Review*, although no further information was provided in the article.

alongside Bell's response to questions sent to the periodical from readers. One such quote was attributed to Luther, appearing alongside an answer related to Pentecostal participation in war. The column included Luther's advice to a young preacher, "Stand up cheerfully, speak out manfully, leave off speedily."[13] Willis C. Hoover, the founder of Pentecostalism in Chile, also was drawn to Luther for encouragement. For Hoover, Luther provided a mentorship of sorts from history.[14] Facing expulsion from his denomination for his Pentecostalism while the pastor at the Methodist Episcopal Church in Valparaiso, Hoover embraced the words of Luther, "You may expect everything from me. . . except flight and recantation. Fly I cannot, and still less retract." Hoover saw his circumstance in the same light as that of Luther.[15] For Hoover and many other Pentecostals, the knowledge that their experience of rejection, troubles and diverse forms of persecution approached that of the persecuted Luther, was therapeutic amid their dire circumstances.

Other devotional uses of "Luther's words" include P. D. Smith's comment that Martin Luther viewed the interview of Nicodemus in the Gospel of John, the John 3:16 passage, as "the Bible in miniature"[16] *The Latter Rain Evangel,* early in 1909 contained an article appealing for Pentecostal women to have children and not to follow the ways of the world, where women were shifting from interest in childbearing. In this article, Luther is quoted, "God makes children and he will provide for them."[17] The editor of *Confidence,* Anglican vicar, Alexander A. Boddy, a Pentecostal as well, was caught in bad weather in the middle of Nebraska while taking a preaching tour of the United States. In a country church, he had been talking to a group of "earnest Mennonites" in the middle of a thunderstorm. According to Boddy, "not a few Germans" were present. In the middle of Boddy's sermon, lightning and drenching rain struck, killing a German farmer's horse outside. Boddy commented, ". . .some of us felt that it was meant also as an endorsement of the appeal to be ready for the Judgement Throne."[18] Boddy then reminded everyone that Martin Luther also "had turned to the Lord in such a thunderstorm," and suggested that they all should do likewise.[19] Another story spoke of Luther encountering Satan at the foot of his bed. Satan presented

13. Bell, "Luther's Advice to a Young Preacher," 9. Warner, "Bell, Eudorus N. (1866–1923)," 369.

14. Bundy, "Hoover, Willis Collins (1856–1936)," 770.

15. Hoover, "The Wonderful Works of God in Chili, Part Two," 21.

16. Smith and Smith, *Delivered from Bandits,* 30.

17. Bolce, "Blasting at the Rock of Ages," 8.

18. Boddy, "Can Prayer Change the Weather?" 166.

19. Boddy, "Can Prayer Change the Weather?" 166.

a list of Luther's sins and Luther responded to the Devil, saying that Jesus had interceded and cleansed him from all such sin.[20] Many other stories from Luther lore appeared in early Pentecostal literature, quite regularly. Official contact and dialogue between Lutheran denominational leaders and Pentecostal leaders, many of whom had been thrown out of their churches because of their religious experiences, was rare. Yet, Pentecostals seemed to cherish their relationship with a popularized image of Martin Luther, despite sometimes strained relations with his ecclesial successors.

Pentecostals Connected Luther's Reformation to Their View of History

An editorial in *The Bridegroom's Messenger* in 1917 showed the high estimation Pentecostals had for Luther as the leading reformer. Pentecostals generally thought the Church was "going to hell" until reformers, such as Martin Luther, most importantly, appeared as spokesmen of God:

> It was needful that such a leader be very courageous at such a crisis in the history of the apostate church of Rome. He declared that the time of silence was gone, the time to speak had come. He proclaimed justification by faith with holy boldness. He was God's chosen vessel for the hour. His life and work marked a crisis in the history of civilization. The bold utterances of this Reformer shook the foundation of the ecclesiastical bigotry and unholy authority.[21]

This restorationist view of history envisioned an evil apostasy, which was exposed by the doctrinal light shed by the reformer of God, Luther, who heard from God and boldly spoke delivering truth to a blinded sixteenth-century Cchurch.[22] Protestants have a long history of the providential in telling their story, and Pentecostals found that a similar approach fitted their Pentecostal story as well.

One Early Pentecostal historian, Carl Brumback, in *A Sound from Heaven: The Dramatic Beginning of the 20th Century Pentecostal Revival*, paints a similar picture, yet it is one that sees the focal point of renewal set at the beginning of the twentieth century, not the sixteenth:

20. "Illustrations from Gospel Themes: Luther and Satan," 11.

21. "Suffering for Jesus," 2.

22. Blumhofer, *The Assemblies of God*, 17–22. Blumhofer's first chapter, "Origins of Pentecostalism: Restorationism, Premillennialism, Healing" is useful to understand this restorationist element.

Christendom had been profoundly disturbed by Darwinism and Biblical Higher Criticism. One by one the academic and theological institutions which had been established to preserve "the faith. . .once delivered unto the saints" had become cradles of liberalism. Men who held the historic position of the Church vigorously opposed the antisupernaturalists, but victory for the latter became only a matter of time after they gained control of the schools. The overwhelming majority of Protestant denominations gradually shifted their allegiance to the way which their fathers called heresy.[23]

Pentecostals have generally adopted a providential approach to historiography, preferring to embrace a view of their own genesis that portrays God's direct intervention. Brumback's history of the movement, originally titled, *Suddenly from Heaven*, made this claim. Brumback saw the twentieth-century Pentecostal outpouring with similar thinking.[24] "Church historians are prone to interpret revivals solely on the basis of the earthly, rather than the heavenly."[25] Pentecostals such as Brumback saw God's heavenly hand in both Luther's Reformation and their own Holy Spirit Renewal.

Pentecostalism: "It Will Not Fit into the Past"

David McDowell, speaking at the Assemblies of God General Council in 1919 reported, "Whatever Luther had to accomplish has been accomplished. Whatever Wesley has had to do has been accomplished . . . God has called the Pentecostal people together for a specific ministry and it will not fit into anything in the past.[26] Pentecostals were convinced that they were indeed a part of the great trajectory of Christian history, a road that took them to more than what the Reformation had offered. The Reformation awakening under "Wycliff, Luther, Hus, Jerome and others" was a preparation for the future, according to Bert McCafferty.[27] McCafferty argued further that through the Pentecostals, God was pouring out a blessing; "God was preparing the church for the last rain before the harvest, the latter rain, and today we are living in that time."[28] McDowell was also convinced of the limitations

23. Brumback, *A Sound from Heaven*, 2–3.

24. Cerrillo Jr. and Wacker, "Bibliography and Historiography of Pentecostalism in the United States," 382–405.

25. Brumback, *A Sound from Heaven*, 1.

26. McDowell, "Redigging the Old Wells," 19.

27. McCafferty, "The Time of the Latter Rain," 5.

28. McDowell, "Redigging the Old Wells," 22.

of the Reformation in terms of changing the human heart. The Reformation was incomplete and insufficient. Something more powerful was needed to penetrate the closed wells of the heart, argued McDowell. He described a picture of people who were so closed to the Gospel, so "filled with personal attainments, with money-making and so forth, until all our associations, all our doings do not measure much higher than our own head in this life."[29] McDowell suggested that these closed wells must be dug open, "If you dug them open you will find the water flowing freely. Does not God talk to you? Get your well open brother, and you will find out. That is the ministry of Pentecost. It gets away down where Luther and some of these other men never reached."[30] This comment might not be considered a criticism of Luther or the reformers as much as it was McDowell's appeal to something better than what he perceived to be a limited Reformation spiritual template. McDowell was suggesting that Pentecostals go further than Luther was able to go in terms of experiencing God, that Pentecostalism was a better fulfillment of God's plan. For these early Pentecostal leaders, the Protestant Reformation was insufficient without Pentecost.

Pentecostalism: Limits to Luther and the Reformation

McDowell's suggestion that Martin Luther was unable to reach some people in his time because he did not possess the power of Pentecost, hints at other criticisms by Pentecostals. Such sentiment may be present in a 1910 article in *The Later Rain Evangel*, which describes the noble fight waged by the reformers.[31] Yet, according to W. H. Cossum, the fight, "which speaks of the ancient valor of Paul, Luther and Wesley. . .was a losing fight . . ."[32] Cossum connects the followers of the Reformation with unrepentant Judaism of the Old Testament. He saw in Protestantism a tragic struggle, "just as Jerusalem went down in an awful crash by the persistence of the enemies who had no God with them except the God of providence."[33] Cossum may have granted Luther credit in terms of his being faithful in the spiritual fight, but he was not impressed with the accomplishment of the mainstream Protestant churches nor their activities, especially worship events with large numbers

29. McDowell, "Redigging the Old Wells," 22.

30. McDowell, "Redigging the Old Wells," 22.

31. Cossum, "Mountain Peaks of Prophecy and Sacred History," 11.

32. Cossum, "Mountain Peaks of Prophecy and Sacred History," 11.

33. Cossum, "Mountain Peaks of Prophecy and Sacred History," 11. "No God but the God of providence" may be considered a comment on the limitations of a more Reformed or Calvinist theology.

of attendees. Cossum writes, ". . .the fight the churches are putting up today is a noble fight. You like to hear of the big meetings, but to me they are the desperate sorties of a dying apostate church which has brought its weakness upon itself."[34] Another author commented that in a large district in Finland, "there was no other church than the Lutheran State Church, but many of the people were not free in the midst of its formalism.[35] So, for the early Pentecostals the problem was not as much Luther as it was Lutheranism. The formalism of State Churches frustrated the Pentecostals, but they still sought to hold onto Luther and embrace Lutherans, who Pentecostals saw as blinded to the truth of the Holy Spirit, until awakened.

Stanley Frodsham, in *Things Which Must Shortly Come to Pass*, one of the early theological texts of the Assemblies of God, comments upon a falling away that he saw taking place in the churches of America "The apostasy is making itself evident in the disintegration of the Christian Churches.[36]" He quotes Dr. H. Carroll, as Carroll identified significant church membership losses:

> The United Lutheran Church has had a loss of membership in the last seven years of sixty-four thousand four hundred and fifty-nine. The Protestant Episcopal Church estimates the loss in that church from "disappearing Communicants" at about twenty-two thousand a year. . ."The church, the body of Christ, is apparently running down hill. . . If we are losing thousands of valuable members, with the possibility of larger losses in the near future, it is certainly not too late to call upon God in repentance for our negligence and indifference and to "repent and do the first works."[37]

Frodsham explained in a chapter with the title of "The Coming Apostasy," that most of the churches rooted in the Reformation in America were terribly apostate. The rejection of miracles and cardinal doctrines, such as the virgin birth and other beliefs indicated that divine judgment was close. Frodsham then expressed the same pessimism about the church worldwide.[38] For Frodsham, the future of the church, including Protestantism, looked gloomy.

34. Cossum, "Mountain Peaks of Prophecy and Sacred History," 11.

35. "The Finnish Gold Story," 2.

36. Frodsham, *Things Which Must Shortly Come to Pass*, 33–34.

37. Cossum, "Mountain Peaks of Prophecy and Sacred History," 11. Frodsham without offering sourcing specifics identifies the quote as coming from the *Christian Advocate*, 7 July 1927.

38. Cossum, "Mountain Peaks of Prophecy and Sacred History," 31–42.

Pentecostalism: An Ecumenism of the Holy Spirit

The Pentecostal periodicals record frequent responsiveness of Lutheran people to the message of Pentecost but also indicated the spiritual impoverishment of these same communities. Evangelist Hardy W. Mitchell reported in 1915 the results of a several-week revival in Milwaukee, Wisconsin:

> The altar has been filled continually with from fifteen to fifty. Many of these are Lutherans and Roman Catholics and God is saving and baptizing them. . . Sunday night, . . . we had a most wonderful meeting. At least seventy-five came to the altar; eleven were struck down by the power of God and held for hours with visions of heaven and hell, and given warnings for the unsaved.[39]

To Pentecostals, such displays of Lutherans prostrate upon the altars in Pentecostal churches were not necessarily an example of victorious proselytization as much as evidence of the Spirit working among the heirs of the Reformation. The standpoint of Pentecostals related to other Christians at this time reflected a desire for inclusion, with the hope to connect with Christians from the Reformation mainstream and bring them to a new Reformation. The editor of *Confidence* portrays this attitude in a 1909 conference which was attended by individuals who came from many different mainstream denominations:

> Those beloved German brethren! Our hearts went out in extra yearnings of love towards them. No denominatinalism! Anglicans, Lutherans, and every kind of Nonconformist, all assented in a common "Yea and Amen" to the Bible faith which has been once for all delivered unto the saints. Here is the witness to the world, that Pentecost is of God. . . Nothing has ever so united the children of God, scattered abroad, as this blessed experience.[40]

Pentecostals saw the responsiveness of other Christians to the gifts and experience of the Holy Spirit as an evidence of God's approval and sanction.

Pentecostals, in the early years of their movement, often showed remarkable interest in the unity of the Christian church. *The Latter Rain Evangel* suggested such an ecumenical orientation in 1908, quite early in the movement's history.[41] An anonymous article, probably written by the

---

39. "Signs Following in Milwaukee," 14–15.

40. [Boddy?], "Sunderland International Pentecostal Congress: General Impressions," 128.

41. [Piper], "The Prayer of Jesus Must Be Answered," 21–23.

editor, William Hamner Piper, who was also Pastor of the influential Stone Church in Chicago, observed that "The Baptist, the Presbyterian and the Lutheran all agree, after all, on the great fundamental doctrines of Jesus." Then Piper suggests that the prayer of Jesus, that diverse Christians would all become one, must be realized. Such an answered prayer would include bringing together these diverse Christian communities through experience in the Holy Spirit. The author clearly understood the Pentecostal movement as important to this ecumenical enterprise.[42] Piper also argued that there was still a need for such great men as Paul, Luther, and Wesley, "men who will give humbly their lives and take the lowest place and keep humble before God."[43] Piper believed there was more need "now of Spirit-filled leaders than in the early Church," and that God was calling Christians to come together through the Pentecostal movement.[44]

PENTECOSTAL APPROPRIATION OF LUTHER'S TEACHING AND PRACTICE

Pentecostals have not been known for their academic or critical theological reflection, especially in the early years of the movement. They "favored testimonies, choruses and prayers" as an expression of their theological convictions, and still do.[45] Frank Macchia, one of the few systematic theologians of the movement in our time maintains, "large areas of theological concern have to date not yet been consciously or methodically explored by Pentecostals, especially in a fashion that is consistent with their origins and the diverse historical ethos of a unique Christian movement.[46] That said, no one should assume that Pentecostals were not interested in theology. They were interested, but their priority was not "ideological or dogmatic as much as it was dialogical and humble, open to legitimate pluralism."[47] Many Pentecostals today have failed to comprehend the nature of the "humble and dialogical" rootedness of the movement. Instead, they have often adapted to ideological and dogmatic theologies common among communities closely tied to the Reformation, which are sometimes more prone to marginalize

---

42. [Piper], "The Prayer of Jesus Must Be Answered," 21–23. The editor includes a short explanation of the policy of the periodical, that no other name would be represented in the paper as the editor because the Holy Spirit was truly the editor.

43. [Piper], "The Prayer of Jesus Must Be Answered," 23.

44. [Piper], "The Prayer of Jesus Must Be Answered," 23.

45. Macchia, "Theology, Pentecostal," 1120–1141.

46. Macchia, "Theology, Pentecostal," 1140.

47. Macchia, "Theology, Pentecostal," 1140.

charismatic expressions. Early North American Pentecostals were less ideological and more dialogical then they are in this century. Early Pentecostals
also showed an openness to an ecumenical orientation that, in the case of
Luther, became a means by which Pentecostals were able to translate elements of his message and his ethos into a Pentecostal framework.

Pentecostals Valued Luther's Key Ideas

Pentecostals concluded that God placed a focus on certain "great scriptural
truths," such as Luther's justification by faith and Wesley's sanctification.
The reformers were represented as major theological forerunners to the
Latter Rain truths; that is, they made a distinct contribution to the later
Pentecostal theology and experience.[48] These Reformation doctrines were
held to be essential features of the full Gospel. Martin Luther's justification
by faith, and Wesley's sanctification and holiness, were combined with the
power of the "Latter Rain Gospel." These doctrines were harnessed to battle
the "latter day delusions that are threatening to engulf the earth with their
deception; to say nothing of the opposition from the nominal church that
has joined hands with the world, placing billiard tables in their basements,
along with their ice cream socials and oyster suppers. . ."[49]

   Piper observed that the reformers were essential for a balanced church
to exist. One of the reoccurring problems in the Pentecostal movement was
the occurrence of self-appointed prophets and apostles, "Individuals who
think they have been called of God to set the movement right and to keep
it right."[50]

> These fellows go into cities or assemblies and split everything up
> with some great revelation they have just gotten from heaven, so
> they claim; they are far superior to the universally acknowledged
> leaders of the past. Before their greatness, Luther's divinely in-
> spired message on justification and Wesley's on sanctification
> pale into insignificance. May God give His people some sanc-
> tified common sense and save them from these ravenous and
> theological wolves.[51]

---

48. Myland, "The Latter Rain," 11.

49. "Spiritual Slumber and the Awful Awakening," 1.

50. Piper, "The Unity of the Spirit in the Body of Peace," 15.

51. Piper, "The Unity of the Spirit in the Body of Peace," 15. This warning reminds
one of *Didache* 12. See. Holmes, Michael W, ed. and trans. "The Didache," 318–319.

Luther exemplified the true doctrine of Christianity for these Pentecostal leaders, and pointing to Luther was a common way to appeal to reason and sanity during times of theological turmoil in the Pentecostal churches. For Pentecostals, the name of "Luther" was primarily wielded as a symbol of sound theology. Pentecostals were interested in the Reformation idea of justification by faith. Other doctrines of Luther gained much less focus from Pentecostals. Indeed, Pentecostals visiting Germany expressed shock that Germany itself had diverged from sound doctrine. These Pentecostal leaders saw definite signs of apostasy there in wicked doctrine, disrespect of the Bible, skepticism, and the presence of Higher Criticism. They found little evidence of an "alive" church in the homeland of Luther.

> But it is sad and strange to discover that in Germany, the land of Luther where we expect abundance of Bibles, there is almost as much skepticism as in any other part of Europe. However, I am told that in many Protestant families the Bible is never seen and never read. "All the Broad Church clergy have accepted the Higher Criticism. Very many of the High Churchmen endorse it, with some noticeable exception.[52]

Pentecostals Appropriated the name of Luther

Pentecostals did not neglect to make use of Luther's name to support their own theological commitments. Frank Bartleman claimed that "the Lord was bringing a greater revelation," that "in Luther's time God brought to the church a fresh revelation, and just as in Wesley's time God brought forth revelation . . ."[53] Bartleman was convinced that if God brought His revelation through a Luther and other reformers, the Lord would do so through humans in his own generation.

D. M. Panton asked if Luther should have kept silent when challenged by those opposing his teaching on justification by Faith.[54] The answer to that question was a sharp, "No!" In the same way, Panton argued that Pentecostals could not be silent regarding their distinctive message of Spirit baptism. He argued that Pentecostals must understand that they are part of a great movement that is intent upon bringing people out of darkness. As Martin Luther was used by God in the sixteenth century, God could again deliver "the church out of what awful darkness and spiritual poverty" in

52. "Importance of Sound Doctrine," 1.

53. Bartleman, "God's Onward March through the Centuries," 2.

54. Panton, "Earnestly Contend for the Faith," 1.

which it was found.[55] The work of Luther would thus continue, with the Pentecostals assuming the call to see it forward.

Pentecostals Embraced a Luther of Prayer

Pentecostals looked to Luther as a model for their experience. The most common element in this modeling of Luther was the tradition of prayer. Intercession, for Pentecostals, was essential to their religious experience, and prayer was closely connected to Spirit baptism, the life of the Spirit and Christian living. Many periodicals highlighted Luther as a man of prayer. "Luther and his coadjutors were men of such mighty pleadings with God that they broke the spell of ages and laid nations subdued at the cross."[56] Stanley Frodsham observed that Luther "felt he could not afford to have less than three hours a day in prayer."[57] Even Sunday school literature communicated that Luther was a man of prayer to be emulated, by offering a motto that Luther was said to live by, "He that has prayed well has studied well."[58] Andrew D. Urshan pointed out that revivals in history started with prayer, and the reason they died was that prayer ceased. According to Urshan, "Luther, Wesley, Finney, Moody, and others prayed more than they preached and ate, that is why they though dead yet speak loudly."[59] For Pentecostals, the prayer of the Reformation, modeled by Luther, was appealing and emblematic.

Pentecostals Embraced Luther as a Healer

Luther's prayer connected to healing was used to support the healing prayer practices of Pentecostals. One pastor suggested that as Luther prayed for healing, Pentecostals should emulate this practice. He claimed that Luther, at the bedside of a dying Melanchthon, "whose eyes were set and whose jaw dropped, knelt at the bed and told God that if He expected him to continue working for Him He would have to answer prayer.[60] According to Piper, Luther appealed to the Scripture from the Old Testament and New Testament:

55. "Reasons Why Many, Even Christians Fight the Pentecostal Movement," 4.

56. Rist, "Intercession," 17.

57. Frodsham, "Praying Always," 6.

58. "February 27, 1816: The Seven Helpers," 10.

59. Urshan, "A Life of Continual Prayer," 2.

60. Piper, "Jesus the Healer," 16.

God, You say, 'I am the Lord that healeth thee';" and he quoted one promise after another. "Surely He hath born away our sickness and carried away our pains,. . .and by His stripes we are healed;" "Who healeth all thy diseases;" "Unto you that fear My Name shall the Sun of righteousness arise with healing in his wings."[61]

These texts are quotes from the Bible often used by Pentecostals to encourage prayer for the sick. Joining them to Luther made Luther more "Pentecostal" for Pentecostals.

Piper maintained that God healed Melanchthon and said, "Listen, You Lutherans! Get back to Luther, for you have largely lost even justification by faith that Luther gave his life for."[62] Florence L. Burpee maintained that the early church had prayed for healing for hundreds of years after Christ's death and that both Luther and Wesley "as well as other devout men prayed for the sick."[63] Likewise, Lilian B Yeomans in *Healing from Heaven* (1906) claimed that along with the Protestant Reformation came "a revival of faith for healing, and the tide has been gradually rising ever since that time."[64] Yeomans included in her list of healers Martin Luther, George Fox, John Wesley, Charles Finney, and others, to include Aimee Semple McPhearson.[65]

Pentecostals Embraced Luther as a Speaker in Tongues

A central Pentecostal practice has been speaking in tongues, and for many people, this practice has been the movement's distinctive feature. E. N. Bell, who served both as Chairman of the General Council of the Assemblies of God and as editor of the *Pentecostal Evangel*, wrote a regular column, "Questions and Answers," in the *Pentecostal Evangel*. In 1923, Bell published *Questions and Answers*.[66] Bell considered the question, "How did the church lose this supernatural power?" He answered, "The church has never entirely lost it."[67] He discussed the general loss of "full gospel light, through sin and disbelief," and observed that people like the Methodists under John Wesley, the Quakers, Charles Finney and D. L. Moody spoke in tongues. According to Bell, "Luther is also said to have spoken in tongues." In 1926,

61. Piper, "Jesus the Healer," 16.
62. Piper, "Jesus the Healer," 17–18.
63. Burpee, "Divine Healing," *Word and Witness*, 5.
64. Yeomans, *Healing from Heaven*, 105.
65. Yeomans, *Healing from Heaven*, 105–106.
66. Bell, *Questions and Answers*, 22–23.
67. Bell, *Questions and Answers*, 22–23.

Stanley Frodsham, published *"With Signs Following."* Frodsham asserted Luther spoke in tongues by citing a "German church history text, Sour's *History of the Christian Church*, Vol. 3., page 406."[68] Frodsham stated, "the following words are found: 'Dr. Martin Luther was a prophet, evangelist, speaker in tongues, and interpreter, in one person, endowed with all the gifts of the Spirit.'"[69] Clearly, Pentecostals would welcome a tongues talking Martin Luther to their community, even if the claim rested on dubious claims and evidence.

Pentecostals Embraced Luther as One Who Was Also Persecuted

Persecution was a quite common occurrence for Pentecostals in the early years of the movement, with persecution reports coming from many nations. Pentecostals in Latin America, like other Protestants, bore the name, "Cursed sons of Luther" with honor.[70] In 1909 Swedish Pastor Thomas Barratt wrote Alexander Boddy, editor of *Confidence*, reporting multiple occasions of persecution while in Copenhagen, Denmark. Barrett wrote about "the *Socialists* determined to strike a blow against us," "outrageous pictures" being produced in papers, shouting and disruptions and "all kinds of sounds" being made in worship services.[71] Barratt reported that control was gained over one attack when "the greatest part of the congregation arose and sang Luther's grand hymn."[72] For many, such persecution of Pentecostals was a signifier of qualification and approval, one that the reformer Martin Luther had also endured.

CONCLUSION

At the start of the Pentecostal Reform and Renewal Movement at the turn of the twentieth century, Pentecostals sought to retain their identity as children of the Reformation and to cultivate a friendship with the reformer, Martin Luther. It was a tumultuous time in terms of growth, revival, and persecution. Pentecostals also sought to cultivate relationships with fellow believers in a spirit of ecumenism and welcome. Lutherans were a part of these

68. Frodsham, *"With Signs Following,"* 329.

69. Frodsham, *"With Signs Following,"* 329.

70. Bailey, "The Spirit and the Bride," 21.

71. Barratt, "The Revival Campaign in Copenhagen," 3.

72. Barratt, "The Revival Campaign in Copenhagen," 3.

encounters. Pentecostals understood that the connection to the broader Christian Church was essential and that they were part of a continuity of Christianity. They desired to embrace some of the fundamental theological concepts of the Reformation, as well as the ethos of Martin Luther, to whom they appealed as a popular exemplar.

Although Pentecostals became most known in society and the broader Christian world for their experiential demonstrations, they remained drawn to Luther, and were even tempted to convert Luther to Pentecostalism by identifying in him the same experiences and motivations which moved them. Therefore, one can read the literature of these twentieth-century men and women of Christian renewal and discern a Protestant Luther who presents himself in a fashion attractive to Pentecostals. I find little criticism of Luther in early Pentecostal devotional literature; and a reader can easily find many occasions that approvingly cite Luther as a man of prayer and a man of healings. If one looks closely, one can even find a Luther who speaks in tongues. To these early Pentecostals, Luther, like them, was a persecuted prophet of truth. As seen through the unique prism of their literature, they welcomed him as their own church father.

BIBLIOGRAPHY

Ambrose, Linda M., and Kimberly Alexander. "Pentecostal Studies Face the #MeToo Movement." *Pneuma* 41 (2019) 1–7.

Bailey, Gerard A. "The Spirit and the Bride." *The Latter Rain Evangel* 5/4 (1913) 19–22.

Barratt, Thomas B. "The Revival Campaign in Copenhagen." *Confidence* 3/1 (1910) 3–5.

Bartleman, Frank. "God's Onward March through the Centuries: the Pentecostal Experience Opens to Us a New Realm." *The Latter Rain Evangel* 2/10 (1910) 2–8.

Bell, E. N. "Luther's Advice to a Young Preacher." Questions and Answers, *The Weekly Evangel* 185 (April 14, 1917) 9.

Boddy, Alexander A. "Can Prayer Change the Weather? A Recent Experience." *Confidence* 7/9 1914) 165–67.

[Boddy, Alexander]. "Sunderland International Pentecostal Congress: General Impressions." *Confidence* 2/6 (1909) 127–31, 134.

Bolce, Harold. "Blasting at the Rock of Ages: Some Startling Facts about American Universities." *The Latter Rain Evangel* 1/7 (1909) 6–9.

Brumback, Carl. *A Sound from Heaven: The Dramatic Beginning of the 20th Century Pentecostal Revival*. Springfield, MO: Gospel Publishing, 1961.

Burgess, Stanley M., and Eduard M. van der Maas, eds. *New International Dictionary of Pentecostal and Charismatic Movements*. Grand Rapids: Zondervan, 2002.

Burpee, Florence L. "Divine Healing." *Word and Witness* 12/5 (1915) 5.

Cerillo, Augustus, Jr., and Grant Wacker. "Bibliography and Historiography of Pentecostalism in the United States." In *New International Dictionary of Pentecostal and Charismatic Movements*, 382–405. Grand Rapids: Zondervan, 2002.

Cossum, W. H. "Mountain Peaks of Prophecy and Sacred History: Jerusalem the City of History and Destiny." *The Latter Rain Evangel* 2/10 (1910) 8–13.

Coulter, Dale M. "Recovering the Wesleyan Vision of Pentecostalism: 5 Theses." *Pneuma* 40/4 (2018) 457–88.

Dempster, Murray W. "The Search for Pentecostal Identity." *Pneuma* 15 (Spring 1993) 1–8.

"February 27, 1916: The Seven Helpers." Sunday School Lesson. *The Weekly Evangel* 127 (February 19, 1916) 10.

"The Finnish Gold Story." The Works of God. *The Weekly Evangel* 167 (December 2, 1916) 2–3, 9.

Frodsham, Stanley. "Praying Always." *Weekly Evangel* 126 (February 12, 1916) 6–7.

———. *Things Which Must Shortly Come to Pass*. Springfield, MO: Gospel Publishing, 1928.

Holmes, Michael W, ed. and trans. "The Didache," in *The Apostolic Fathers: Greek Texts and English Translations*, 345–69. Grand Rapids: Baker, 2007.

Hoover, Willis C. "The Wonderful Works of God in Chili: Part Two, Continued from April 1911." *The Latter Rain Evangel* 3/10 (1911) 21–24.

"Illustrations from Gospel Themes: Luther and Satan." *The Weekly Evangel* 167 (December 2, 1916) 11.

"Importance of Sound Doctrine." *The Bridegroom's Messenger* 4.94 (September 15, 1911) 1.

"In the Last Days." *The Apostolic Faith* 1.9 (June–September 1907) 1.

"January 13, 1918: Jesus Begins His Work." Sunday School Lessons. *The Weekly Evangel* 221 (January 5, 1918) 12.

Kendrick, Klaude. *The Promise Fulfilled*. Springfield, MO: Gospel Publishing, 1961.

Knight, Kate. "The Baptism in the Holy Spirit." *Confidence* 8/7 (1915) 129, 133–34.

"Latter Rain Sermon—Go Forward: Reinforced by the Voice of the Spirit Launching the Latter Rain Evangel." *Confidence* 1/1 (1908) 7–13.

Macchia, Frank. *Justified in the Spirit: Creation Redemption, and the Triune God*. Grand Rapids: Eerdmans, 2010.

McCafferty, Burt. "The Time of the Latter Rain." *The Weekly Evange* 188 (May 5, 1917) 45.

McDowell, David. "Redigging the Old Wells for the Flowing of Pentecostal Springs." *The Latter Rain Evangel* 12/1 (1919) 18–22.

McGee, Gary. *People of the Spirit: The Assemblies of God*. Springfield, MO: Gospel Publishing, 2004.

Menzies, Robert P. *Pentecost: This Story Is Our Story*. Springfield, MO: Gospel Publishing, 2013. Kindle edition.

Myland, D. Wesley. "The Latter Rain: Its Design and Operation." *The Latter Rain Evangel* 2/8 (1909) 11–18.

Olivero, L. William Jr. "The Work of Charles Taylor and the Future of Pentecostalism." *Pneuma* 40/1–2 (2018) 5–16.

Panton, D. M. "Earnestly Contend for the Faith." *The Pentecostal Evangel* 334 and 335 (April 3, 1920) 1.

Piper, William H. "But Also to Suffer for His Sake." *The Latter Rain Evangel* 1/4 (1909) 7–9.

———. "Jesus the Healer: Divine Healing as Contained in the Three Great Commissions." *The Latter Rain Evangel* 3/5 (1911) 16–18.

[Piper, William H.]. "The Prayer of Jesus Must Be Answered: His Body Must Be United; The Gifts and Offices of the Early Church Must Be Restored." *The Latter Rain Evangel* 1/1 (1908) 21–23.

———. "The Unity of the Spirit in the Bond of Peace." *The Latter Rain Evangel* 3/9 (1911) 14–17.

"The Pentecostal Baptism Restored." *The Apostolic Faith* 1/2 (1906) 1.

"Prominent Reformers." *The Bridegroom's Messenger* 12/215 (1919) 1.

"Reasons Why Many, Even Christians Fight the Pentecostal Movement." *The Bridegroom's Messenger* 3/69 (1910) 4.

Rist, Trena. "Intercession." *The Latter Rain Evangel* 11/3 (1918) 17.

Robeck, Cecil M. Jr. *The Azusa Street Mission and Revival: The Birth of the Global Pentecostal Movement.* Nashville: Nelson, 2006.

———. "Ecumenism." In *Studying Global Pentecostalism: Theories and Methods,* edited by Allan Anderson et al., 286–307. Anthropology of Christianity 10. Berkeley: University of California Press, 2010.

"Signs Following in Milwaukee." *The Latter Rain Evangel* 7/4 (1915) 14–15.

Smith, P. D. and Mrs. Smith, P. D., comp. *Delivered from Bandits, Cannibals and Lions: And Other True Stories.* Springfield, Mo.: Gospel Publishing, 1932.

"Spiritual Slumber and the Awful Awakening." *The Apostolic Faith* 48 (1920) 1.

"Suffering for Jesus." *The Bridegroom's Messenger* 10/202 (September 1917) 2.

Sunday, William. "Reward." *Confidence* 9/11 (November 1916) 177–79, 183–85.

Urshan, Andrew D. "A Life of Continual Prayer is the Life of Victory over the Flesh, World and the Devil." *The Weekly Evangel* 201 (August 4, 1917) 2.

Waddell, Robby and Althouse, Peter. "A Brief History of *Pneuma.*" *Pneuma* 40/1–2 (2018) 1–4.

———. "Pentecostalism as Mysticism: The Catholicity of the Tradition." *Pneuma* 40/4 (2018) 453–55.

Warner, W. E. "Periodicals." In *New International Dictionary of Pentecostal and Charismatic Movements,* 974–82. Grand Rapids: Zondervan, 2002.

———. "Bell, Eudorus N." In *New International Dictionary of Pentecostal and Charismatic Movements,* 369. Grand Rapids: Zondervan, 2002.

Young, S. Edward. "The Empty Seat at the Master's Table." *The Latter Rain Evangel* 1/11 (1909) 18–20.

4

Re-forming Formative Spirituality in the Matrix of the Protestant Reformation

MARA LIEF CRABTREE

INTRODUCTION

DURING THE BIBLICAL ERA and throughout the history of the Church, numerous approaches or models of spiritual formation were developed. However, for an approach or model to be faithful to the biblical example of formative spirituality in the Christian faith, several specific elements are required. Those nine elements are Call/Conversion/Empowerment, Holy Scripture, Sacraments or Ordinances, Community, Disciplines (spiritual practices), Ministry, Mission, Joy/Suffering, and Eternal Life. These major elements each have various sub-categories that define and describe them more fully. During the matrix—that point from which the Reformation developed—and during that movement's continuing impact on the Church, these various elements continued to be discussed, argued, defined, and re-defined, constituting a re-formation of formative spirituality. This process of re-formation continues in the contemporary Church. It is important to emphasize that not a single one of those nine major elements of Christian formative spirituality was absent from the dialogue and the writings arising from the Reformation and its reformers. Three of those elements will be considered here, especially in the light of Martin Luther's beliefs concerning the Word of God, the Sacrament of Holy Communion, and the realities of Christian life in the dialogical experiences of both joy and suffering.

MARTIN LUTHER'S SPIRITUALITY

Luther's "works have shaped the trajectories of Western Christian theology."[1] His ideas and convictions extend to the area of spiritual theology. In examining the elements of formation as they developed in the matrix of the Reformation, it is important to understand that Martin Luther's formative spirituality was that of an Augustinian monk. Luther was "trained in the doctrines and ethics of Scholastic theology . . . and in the strict discipline of the monastic order to which he had dedicated himself . . . ."[2] Luther's desire in life, his pathway of spirituality "was to find peace with God."[3] The Reformer "started his career as a tortured German academic whose spiritual [struggles] were tangled up with biblical exegesis—a state of constant agitation . . . ."[4] The Reformer penned a letter "on October 27, 1527, [to] his colleague Philip Melanchthon with the request: 'pray for me, miserable and despised worm that I am . . . for I seek and thirst only for a gracious God.'"[5] "Luther was disgusted that priests were using their sermons to preach the benefits of indulgences instead of preaching the gospel."[6] His spiritual development resulted in reframing the tradition in which he had been formed; a tradition he considered in disagreement with his interpretation of Scripture. Ultimately, the reformer's convictions also resulted in a re-formation of certain aspects of Roman Catholic spirituality.[7]

> Luther was not primarily a herald of the modern era as much as a medieval thinker seeking truth. His work inexorably changed the future–whether through intended or unintended consequences. But it is deeply embedded within the mystical piety of the monastery, the nominalist approaches to logic he learned

1. Durheim, *Christ's Gift*, 29.

2. Brewer, *Martin Luther*, 1.

3. Brewer, *Martin Luther*, 1.

4. Kay, "It took years for Luther's ideas to spread," Sec. B 1, 4 (n.b. newspaper pages are not numbered in consecutive order; section identification is needed before page number).

5. Brewer, *Martin Luther*, 1.

6. Lascelles. *Pontifex Maximus*, 200.

7. Lascelles. *Pontifex Maximus*, 200.

at the university, humanism's call to return to primary sources, and his deep engagement with the Scriptures through teaching, prayer, and study. He reworked all these and other matters and made them conform to evangelical faith.[8]

In Luther's personal re-formation he abstained from practicing certain forms of spiritual disciplines. His spiritual theology eschewed any belief which credited the disciplines themselves as having the ability to make one holy. Martin was vehement in his condemnation of such practices:

> All manner of religion, where people serve God without his Word and command, is simply idolatry, and the more holy and spiritual such a religion seems, the more hurtful and venomous it is; for it leads people away from the faith of Christ, and makes them rely and depend upon their own strength, works, and righteousness. In like manner, all kinds of orders of monks, fasts, prayers, hairy shirts, the austerities of the Capuchins, who in popedom are held to be the most holy of all, are mere works of the flesh; for the monks hold they are holy, and shall be saved, not through Christ, whom they view as a severe and angry judge, but through the rules of their order.[9]

His *Small Catechism* and *Table Talks* embrace a spiritual life which is centered in Holy Scripture, in participation in the Sacraments and the practice of disciplines related to both. Luther understood that the practice of particular disciplines in and of themselves did not form one's spirituality. Loving God, devoting oneself to God, and living obediently in response to God's commands are those practices that result in spiritual growth and maturity.

The disciplines' value was in the fact that attention to spiritual practices required one to become sensitive to the Holy Spirit in focusing one's attention upon the Lord. In the presence of the Lord, through the power of His love, the Christian is formed, conformed, and transformed, developing in mature faith. Rather than doing away with all disciplines, Luther reframed the spiritual theology concerning these practices. His views appear to align with St. Paul's theology who compares the Christian life to that of a qualified athlete (*athlasis*): one whose focus and dependence are upon the Lord, and who therefore lives in a disciplined way, for the purpose of maturing in Christ.

8. Mattes, *Martin Luther's Theology* of Beauty, 3.
9. Luther, *Table Talk*, 57.

GUTENBERG'S PRINTING PRESS:
INTEGRATING *VISIO DIVINA* AND *LECTIO DIVINA*

Although Martin Luther published his *Ninety-Five Theses* in 1517, it was German Johannes Gutenberg's development of a printing system using metal, movable type, circa 1440, that would prove to be the technology essential to advancement and wide assimilation of written materials. The invention of the press provided the means to an open door of communication for the expansion of Protestantism throughout the continuing history of the Christian faith. The continuing legacy of the Reformation would have been impossible without the invention of an advanced method of printing. "Luther was the first to harness the power of print to create a popular movement. The Reformation was, in its first manifestation, a media event, deploying a powerful new invention to speak over the heads of the clergy."[10] The explosive essence of the movable type printing press was its ability, quickly and relatively inexpensively, to transmit masses of information widely across space and time. For the first time, general laypeople could own and read their own Bibles. The Reformation resulted, much due to this development.[11] These momentous changes in communication were the results of words created for reading by the "flow from oily ink on slugs of alloy . . . ."[12]

Prior to advancements in communication available to the Church through the invention of an advanced printing system, spiritual formation was, for most Christians, a form of *visio divina*; the practice or process called "sacred sight" or "sacred seeing." Although access to individual copies of the Bible or to other types of Christian literature was not common, Holy Scripture was proclaimed in corporate worship through the liturgy. Formation in Christ was also greatly aided by a visual process. The sublime beauty of cathedrals, their flying buttresses soaring upward to the sky, their windows visually portraying biblical realities formed in glass and lead, were places of numinous reality. These holy places, open to the light of heaven shining into worship spaces and resting on the faces of the worshipers, witnessed the reality of God, the Father, the Son, and the Holy Spirit, and symbolized biblical truths in stone, in glass, and in filtering light. Sculptures in marble, granite, and metal representing Jesus, the Apostles, various other saints, and events in the Bible, provided believers with visual depictions of truth. When Bibles are not available, *visio divina*, the process of encountering, seeing, and meditating on solid images created to glorify God, provides

10. Pettegree. "The Talented," Sec. B 6.

11. Von Drehle. "Steve Jobs," Sec. A 21.

12. Von Drehle. "Steve Jobs," Sec. A 21.

the means to enliven and encourage Christians' faith and spiritual growth. It is important to note that these visual symbols were never meant as objects of worship. As icons of the faith, their purpose was to raise one's spiritual sight to a reality beyond oneself; the reality of the living God.

When Luther's *Small Catechism* and additional writings became available, they often included illustrations in the relief printing technique of woodcut art. These illustrated publications represented an integration of the tradition of *visio divina* (sacred seeing) with a generalized version of *lectio divina*, (sacred reading) for those with the ability to read. The action of seeing visual images of words on a page, and woodcut illustrations followed by sacred reading of the biblical text, allowed these two disciplines to become integrated as elements of spiritual formation. To see holy words made visible (*visio divina*) through God's gift of the printing process provided an opportunity for individuals to experience an encounter with truth via reading silently or reciting aloud the ancient words of both the biblical text and contemporary writings. God's gift of the printed page, now widely distributed, enhanced the process of formative spirituality, connecting individuals with their faith in new ways. First seeing, then reading, meditating, and contemplating what one has seen and read (*lectio divina*) resulted in the Holy Spirit's guidance in providing new dimensions of knowledge and understanding for many believers' journeys of faith.

The importance of visual communication to the process of spiritual formation cannot be overestimated. Symbols, in Christian tradition, are often used to represent the realities of Christian spirituality. The architecture of a church or cathedral, the symbol of a cross on the steeple, an altar prepared with paten and chalice awaiting the celebration of Holy Communion: these are symbols experienced by Christians, often daily, throughout much of Church history. When Scripture, inspired by the Holy Spirit, provides context and meaning to the symbols of the Christian Church, the text communicates the truth of Christian faith through seeing, through reading, through hearing, and through understanding: all necessities in one's formation in Christ.

Today, many may take the printed word for granted because of its wide and easily accessed availability. However, it should not be forgotten that the printed word, which integrates *visio divina* with *lectio divina,* is essential to spiritual formation in the Christian tradition. The Church should not forget those believers in past ages who depended upon *visio divina* and hearing the Word of God. They did not have opportunities to experience the integration of symbols on the page with the ability to read and to understand those symbols, the formational process which allowed them to engage in divine reading.

DIVERSE THEOLOGIES
REGARDING HOLY COMMUNION

Luther's drew his sacramental theology from Augustine's view of the sacraments. "Augustine referred to them as 'visible signs' and 'visible words' through which God would sanctify by 'invisible grace through the Holy Spirit'. The Spirit of God was said 'to give fruit to the visible sacraments'. And these sacraments Augustine saw described in the New Testament 'give salvation' to the believer."[13]

One can well argue that Luther's views on the nature of the Mass or the Holy Communion and the views of other reformers emerged as perhaps the most singular differentiation in the ways Christians understand spiritual formation. The Roman Catholic view of transubstantiation had much ancient development but was not named until the twelfth century; and not made formal doctrine the counter-reformational Council of Trent (1552). This doctrine states that the bread and wine are truly transformed into the actual Soul, Divinity, Body, and Blood of Jesus Christ. However, arising from the Reformation was a diversity of other understandings concerning the nature and meaning of the Lord's Supper. Following are summaries of these various understandings:

Consubstantiation: There is no change in the substance of the elements, however, Christ is with those elements.

Memorialism: Posits Holy Communion as a memorial to Jesus Christ. The belief maintains that his Body and Blood are not in any way present in the elements. The celebration of Communion is spiritually supportive to believers' experience and growth in faith. This was the position of the reformer Huldrych Zwingli.[14]

Objective Reality: Views the elements as truly changed to the Body and Blood of Christ The position avoids any precise explanation of how this occurs referring to the reality simply as a mystery of God.

Pneumatic Presence or Real Presence: Maintains that the Body and Blood of Christ are truly received, by those who have faith, through the power of the Holy Spirit. In this view of Holy Communion there is no specific explanation of how this occurs other than an explanation that the process is in the realm of the Mystery of God.

Sacramental union: Purports that the elements, as consecrated, are united with the Body and the Blood of Jesus Christ.

13. Brewer, *Martin Luther*, 8.

14. Bromiley, "General Information." *Zwingli and Bullinger*, 36–37.

Suspension: The view accepted by Quakers, also the Salvation Army, which purports that Holy Communion was not meant as a continuing ritual for the Church to observe.

"'Because Christians in the sixteenth century considered the correct understanding of the sacraments to be essential for ecclesial life and salvation, to be wrong about the sacraments was not merely to hold a mistaken idea, but not to be a Christian at all, observed a Reformation era scholar.'"[15]

> During this time Christians were in disagreements concerning the meaning, as well as the number and the power attributed to sacraments as they related to the church's spiritual life corporately and individually. Protestants did not agree that the elements conveyed grace either in a mechanical sense or is attributed to the guest of ordination in the priest. The Protestant view emphasized a strong Christology: salvation is through Christ alone. However, Protestants did see that faith was a central factor required for not only receiving the sacraments but understanding their meaning. Only by understanding the sacraments rightly, they thought, could one understand God and salvation rightly, too. A right understanding of the sacraments was considered necessary in understanding God and salvation. "The sacraments were seen as inextricably related to God's redeeming work in the world. One cannot appreciate Protestant theology and what Luther and the succeeding Reformers proposed without reference then to these ordinances of the church."[16]

Article X of the Augsburg Confession of 1530 states: "Of the Supper of the Lord they teach that the [true] body and blood of Christ are truly present [under the form of bread and wine] and they are communicated to [and received by] those who eat in the Lord's supper and they disapprove of those that teach otherwise."[17]

> The Lutheran theory teaches a real and substantial presence of the very body and blood of Christ, which was born of the Virgin Mary, and suffered on the cross, in, with, and under (*in, sub, cum*) the elements of bread and wine, and the oral manducation of both substances by all communicants, unworthy and unbelieving, as well as worthy and believing, though with opposite effects. The simultaneous coexistence or conjunction of the two substances is not a local inclusion of one substance in

---

15. Miller, "Sacraments," 141–42.

16. Brewer, *Martin Luther*, 3–4.

17. Schaff, "The Eucharistic Theories," 531–32.

the other (impanation), nor a mixture or fusing together of the two substances into one; nor is it permanent, but ceases with the sacramental action. It is described as a sacramental, supernatural, incomprehensible union. The earthly elements remain unchanged and distinct in their substance and power, but they become the divinely appointed media for communicating that heavenly substance of the body and blood of Christ.[18]

Lutheran doctrine teaches that the efficacy and power of God's Word, not transubstantiation nor the priest's ecclesial consecration, allows the elements to communicate substantively the body and blood of Christ. "The eating of the body is by the mouth, indeed, yet it is not Capernaitic, and differs from the eating of ordinary food. The object and use of the Lord's Supper is chiefly the assurance of the forgiveness of sins, to the comfort of the believer."[19] This doctrinal statement, was specified by *Formula Concordiae* framers and Lutheran scholastics of the seventeenth century.[20]

In addition, Luther writes in his *Large Catechism:*

> Now, what is the Sacrament of the Altar! Answer: It is the true body and blood of our Lord Jesus Christ, in and under the bread and the wine which we Christians by command of the Word of Christ to eat and to drink. And as we have said of Baptism that it is not simple water, so here we say the Sacrament is bread and wine, but not mere bread and wine, such as are ordinarily served at the table, but bread and wine comprehended in, and connected with, the Word of God.
>
> It is the Word (I say) which makes and distinguishes this Sacrament, so that it is not mere bread and wine but is, and it's called, the body and blood of Christ. For it is said, *Accedat verbum ad elementum et At sacramentum.* If the Word is joined to the element, it becomes a Sacrament. This saying of St. Augustine is so properly and so well put that he has scarcely said anything better. The Word must make a Sacrament of the element, else it remains a mirror element. Now, it is not the word or ordinance of a prince or Emperor, but of the sublime Majesty, and whose feet all creatures should fall, and affirm it as He says, and accept it with all reverence, fear, and humility.[21]

---

18. Schaff, "The Eucharistic Theories," 530–31.

19. Schaff, "The Eucharistic Theories," 530–31.

20. Schaff, "The Eucharistic Theories," 531.

21. Luther, *Large Catechism*, 84–85.

The importance of one's knowledge and understanding of the sacrament of Holy Communion—its meaning and value to Christian faith and life—cannot be overestimated in view of the ways in which the sacrament relates to spiritual formation. The frame of mind in which one participates in Holy Communion must also be considered as important to the continuing process of formation, conformation, and transformation in Christians' lives. An argument can be made that no other single belief so differentiates spiritual formation in the Roman Catholic tradition from spiritual formation in various Protestant traditions than each one's theology of Holy Communion. There are those who maintain that sacramental theology is the most difficult bridge to cross in making progress toward unity among Roman Catholics and Protestants.

Why is sacramental theology, particularly theology concerning the Holy Communion, so very important to spiritual formation? First, the various theological points concerning Holy Communion attempt to define the ways in which Christ is truly present in the Christian's life, particularly whether the Lord is or is not present in some way during the celebration of the sacrament. The apostle Paul explained two interacting metaphors to define the Christian's life with and in Jesus Christ: participation in Christ (*participatio Christi*)[22] and imitation of Christ "(*imitatio Christi*)."[23] Also, Christian worship, in particular Holy Communion, is strongly related to one's ethical life.[24]

Sacramental theology endeavors to understand the reality of Holy Communion: How does the Christian's understanding of the sacrament relate to one's understanding of Jesus? What is the sacrament's meaning relative to the Holy Trinity? Is there a spiritual reality to the sacrament that clearly relates to the believer's life and faith in the here and now, and if so how? The question arises for the individual believer: Am I practicing a ritual simply to honor Christ, or are there spiritual realities which I receive as I participate in receiving the sacrament? These are primary questions that Protestant theologians struggled with in the Reformation era; as do contemporary theologians! However, those open-ended questions are worth the struggle and should not be overlooked, given their importance to one's formative spirituality and the whole of one's life in Christ.

One's understanding of spiritual reality regarding the Holy Communion—those beliefs concerning if and how Christ is present at, or with, or in the sacrament—are essential beliefs and understandings which greatly

---

22. Phil 1:21; 1 Cor 1:9; 6:17; Heb 3:14.

23. 1 Cor 11:1; Phil 2:3–8; 2 Cor 3:18; 1 John 2:6.

24. Durheim, *Christ's Gift*, xi.

influence, even transform, the worship life of the Christian. Those beliefs are also significant factors in how one approaches and understands spiritual formation. The Christian's understanding of what is transpiring in one's life relative to participation in the sacrament of Holy Communion powerfully facilitates the forming of Christian character.

Luther believed the power of the sacrament is grounded in God's promise. One cannot render oneself worthy to receive the gift of the sacrament. One comes by faith as one hears "this is my body given for you," and then receives the elements. The promise of salvation in Jesus Christ is received simply by trusting his Word, by faith alone.[25]

> Gordon T. Smith emphasizes the ongoing debate and the church's history concerning the efficacy of the sacraments. Do the sacraments truly confer grace upon the recipients? Is the essential factor of the sacraments the corporate faith of the church, the individual faith of believers, God's bestowal of supernatural power on the elements of wine, water, and bread as consecrated and then administered by an ordained priest? Although all of the above factors have significance, it is the presence and action of the Holy Spirit which are critical in understanding the efficacy of the sacraments.[26] Smith affirms that " . . . the epiclesis—the prayer for the presence and anointing of the Spirit—is pivotal in the celebration of baptism, the Lord's Supper, and any other sacramental rite or practice."[27]

Brian Brewer maintains that "one of the great ironies of contemporary Christianity is that most Christians within Protestantism today do not give much consideration to sacramental theology at all."[28] Although some denominations have endeavored to strengthen their understanding and practice of the sacraments for the purpose of worship, other Protestant denominations and groups "further deemphasized both sacramental theology and even the observance of the sacraments themselves in the pursuit of seeking 'relevance' for people's lives."[29]

25. Stroho, "Luther," 592

26. Smith, "Sacrament," 729.

27. Smith, "Sacrament," 729.

28. Brewer, *Martin Luther and the Seven Sacraments*, 4.

29. Brewer, *Martin Luther and the Seven Sacraments*, 4.

LUTHER'S UNDERSTANDING OF SUFFERING
IN THE CHRISTIAN'S LIFE

Ronald Rittgers explains that "According to Luther, divinely-ordained suffering is to be embraced and patiently endured, not avoided or rejected in favor of sacramental penalties or indulgences.[30]

> In a sermon on *Indulgence and Grace* Luther teaches that Christians should seek to endure the tribulations [allowed] by God, not because they render satisfaction for sin but because they contribute to Christians' spiritual improvement, which he argues is God's purpose in sending them. This was a radical break with late medieval penitential theology and its teaching about suffering; this break had profound implications for how Luther understood the role of tribulation and adversity in the Christian life. Here Luther makes it abundantly clear that he will not allow suffering to be placed on some kind of soteriological scales in order to tip them in the Christian's favor. From the beginning of his career as a Professor of Theology, Luther was silent on the issue of suffering as a work of satisfaction. This silence is no doubt owing to the fact that he was simply not interested in human merit and the role it might play in salvation: he was not interested in soteriological scales because in his mind sinful humanity had nothing to place on them, aside from its sin. This silence also created a rather significant pastoral problem for Luther, for it meant the rejection of one of the primary ways Christians had interpreted and coped with suffering in the Later Middle Ages.[31]

Luther described those he called "theologians of the cross." These individuals spoke of the crucified and hidden God, embracing the truth and teaching the reality that God often revealed himself "under the contrary" (*sub contrario*). Human beings were called to humility in order to follow Christ and become active and instrumental in being used by God. He defines the many struggles, difficulties, and traumas of life as "sacred relics . . . to be embraced, quoting St. James' admonition to 'count it all joy, my brethren when you meet various trials.' (James 1:2)."[32]

Hummel maintains that "Luther's theology of God—of the hidden God and the revealed God who is, ultimately, one God—is complex" as is the life of the Christian who struggles to understand, be consoled, and

30. Rittgers, "Luther's Reformation," 4.

31. Rittgers, "Luther's Reformation," 5.

32. Rittgers, "Luther's Reformation," 6–7.

strengthened during events of suffering.[33] "Luther understood the suffering of this world to be, somehow, under the providence of God—a God whose reasons for and place amidst suffering are unknowable. In that strict sense, one may say that suffering is sent us by God who, in doing so, hides God-self from us.[34] Luther's theology did not ascribe inherent value or benefit to suffering. "Luther did not do so because the primary aim of all his teaching, preaching, and writings was this: to lead people to have faith in God."[35] As Ronald Rittgers explains, Luther's theology of suffering understood that forgiveness was a certainty, as was the peace resulting from forgiveness. The Christian could embrace tribulation with joy because tribulation was not divine punishment for sin due to Christ's suffering in entirety for sin. Instead, trials and tribulations were instances of strengthening and testing the quality and depth of one's love for the Heavenly Father. One's salvation was not at stake; however, the Christian's redemption from the effects of sin as a fruit of salvation was at stake.[36] "The rejection of suffering as penance signaled a crucial break with late medieval penitential theology and much of the Latin Christian tradition."[37]

Luther's Theology of Purgatory

In his break with Roman Catholicism Luther developed, over time, a new understanding concerning the theology of Purgatory:

> Luther's understanding of Purgatory differed from much of the tradition that preceded him. Purgatory could not be a *punitorium* where one suffered the remaining punishment for sin, rather it could only be a *purgatorium* where one was purged of self-love and caused to love the divine will. Luther kept this modified view of Purgatory for some time, and did not finally reject the idea of a post–mortem purification from sin until 1530.[38]

The reformer did subscribe to a pre-mortem Purgatory. He expressed a sense of forsakenness at times, the experience of *Deus absconditus*: God's absence. He believed, along with mystic Johannes Tauler, in a pre-mortem purification. Luther admonished Christians to avoid a flight from suffering,

33. Hummel, "Consolation for Suffering," 94.
34. Hummel, "Consolation for Suffering," 98.
35. Hummel, "Consolation for Suffering," 98.
36. Rittgers, "Luther's Reformation," 6–8.
37. Rittgers, "Luther's Reformation," 8.
38. Rittgers, "Luther's Reformation," 8–9.

embracing life's trials and traumas while trusting in God, and thus experiencing peace in one's conscience. He taught that believers should avoid viewing their life's sufferings in a penitential way. He viewed suffering as no longer salvific but redemptive in the sense that experiences involving suffering may result in one's growth in love for and obedience to God and overall in purification of character and spiritual maturity.[39] Luther was in agreement with St. Paul, who referred to suffering in this world and this life as " . . . momentary light affliction . . . producing for us an eternal weight of glory far beyond all comparison . . . ."[40] Luther's view of purgation, as with many of his other views, had a profound impact on the understanding of spiritual formation in the Christian tradition. If purgation was not penitential, but a purification of character, and a molding of character into Christ-likeness, then how one understood the experience of suffering was irrevocably changed for those who adhered to Martin Luther's theology.

The Reality of Joy

On the other side of Christians' suffering, however, was the gift of joy. Luther understood that:

> . . . faith at its core is markedly aesthetic, awakening the senses, opening receptivity, kindling wonder, and evoking gratitude. Such an aesthetic core to the faith is expressed in worship that is sensitive not only to ecstatic joy but also to complaint or accusation against God when life seems terribly unfair, seen for instance in the laments in the Psalter, and even spiritual attack (*Anfechtung*) when God appears to be against us. The latter is an inevitable result of Luther's threefold spirituality of prayer, meditation, and attack (*oratio, meditation, and tentatio*).[41]

When it came to the dialogical relationship between suffering and joy (for each one informs the other), Luther's spiritual theology of aesthetics was not, as Mattes asserts, based

> . . . on a theology of glory but rather aesthetics shaped by the theology of the cross . . . . The cross offers a strange beauty and that it is defined through Christ as deliverer, one who absorbs our sins bodily on the tree of the cross in opposition to propelling sinners to ascend into heaven through merit. Hence

---

39. Rittgers, "Luther's Reformation," 8–9.

40. 2 Cor 4:17, NASB.

41. Mattes, *Martin Luther's Theology of Beauty*, 3.

genuine participation in God is baptismally configured as dying and rising in Christ and not as greater degrees of mimetically embodying beauty or goodness.[42]

ECCLESIAL STANDARDS FOR PRIESTLY FORMATION: A COUNTER-REFORMATION LEGACY

The Council of Trent, the Nineteenth Ecumenical Council of the Roman Catholic Church, met between the years 1545–1563 and addressed issues relating to the faith and practice of the Church in the face of the Reformation. The Council's members attempted to understand and clarify doctrines of the Protestants with the idea of bringing revitalization to the Church. This Council proposed and inaugurated specific standards for priestly formation in seminaries. In its Tridentine Decree on Seminaries, the Council carefully distinguished and separated intellectual formation from spiritual formation. Among the decree's statements were the following standards:

- Every cathedral and metropolitan church is obliged to have a seminary of its own.

- Smaller and poorer jurisdictions might band together to form what today would be called a regional seminary.

- While every diocese is obliged to have a seminary, not every candidate whom a bishop ordains has to be educated in a seminary.

- Candidates for the seminary should be at least twelve years of age with skills in reading and writing and be of suitable moral character.

- Preference is to be given to the sons of the poor.

- Intellectual formation is to be suited to a candidate's age and abilities.

- However, a curriculum of sorts is specified: they are to study letters, the humanities, chant, and the science of 'ecclesiastical computation,' scripture, dogmatic, moral and pastoral theology, and rubrics.

- Spiritual formation includes wearing the clerical dress, receiving the tonsure, assisting at daily Mass, going to Confession once a month, and to Holy Communion as often as the advice of one's spiritual director permits.

42. Mattes, *Martin Luther's Theology of Beauty*, 14.

- Professors in the seminary are to be qualified academically with master's, licentiate, or doctoral degrees in the particular field of their expertise and are to be competent in discharging their offices.[43]

Continuing through the centuries, various encyclicals have deleted certain of these requirements and added others. It is important to note that the spiritual formation of clergy was considered distinct from their intellectual formation and of vital importance to the revitalization and renewal of the Church. A well-educated and trained priest would be prepared to minister to a parish in such a way as to facilitate and promote the formation of parishioners in the Roman Catholic faith. However, in the Protestant movement's continuing development, the formation of spiritual leaders was not always carefully defined and applied. In the twenty–first century with its diverse and numerous Protestant denominations and groups, there is significant diversity in how each denomination or group understands the biblical, historical, and theological aspects relative to the spiritual formation of church leaders and laity. Certain denominations and groups prioritize the importance of formative spirituality while others may rarely address, or address in a limited way, the process of Christian formation. Without an understanding of spiritual formation from its biblical roots through its historical and theological development, individuals have little or no knowledge concerning the believer's formation, conformation, and transformation in Christ. If communities do not prioritize the need for individuals to understand spiritual formation, there is then little or no awareness of Christian formative spirituality and how this relates to the context of personal life and participation in one's faith community. Luther's legacy, emerging from the re–forming of formative spirituality in the Reformation era, emphasizes the need for contemporary spiritual renewal in order to understand and practically apply the biblical, historical, and theological realities of formative spirituality in the body of Christ.

CONCLUSION: THE REFORMATION LEGACY
OF SPIRITUAL RE-FORMATION CONTINUES

Visio divina begins the process of seeing Holy Scripture, then reading the text's written symbols, followed by understanding and applying their meaning to life situations and needs, integrates divine seeing and divine reading as essential to spiritual formation. The Reformation brought about an integration of spirituality's visual aspects with studying, learning, and applying

---

43. Seminary of Christ the King, "History of Priestly Formation," lines 168–187.

the Scriptures. Increased availability of the biblical texts, beginning with the Reformation, emphasized the reality that Christian faith development requires formation in and by the Holy Spirit as the written word was published and available to God's people.

The Reformation, in effectuating the integration of *visio divina* and *lectio divina,* allowed the community of faith to communicate with God and with one another in a singular and unparalleled way. These elements of both divine seeing and divine reading coalesce in the liturgy of the Eucharist. This holy meal of Christ's body and blood communicates the truth of Jesus Christ which transcends all technological communication, including that of the present age. The Christian is formed in part by understanding both symbol and reality as encountered in the vessels of chalice and paten and their precious contents, and through the written and spoken words of liturgy in the celebration of the Eucharist. The sacrament strengthens, renews, heals, and inspires the experience of joy. Participation in the Eucharist, for both the individual and the faith community together, also emphasizes the relatedness of the sacrament with Christians' experience of suffering. The reality of Christ to the people of God as they celebrate this holy meal prepares believers for those familiar, ongoing human struggles endured in this present life by individuals and communities of faith.

Together, these formational elements and others, re-formed in the matrix of the Protestant Reformation and the Counter-Reformation, comprise the process of formation in Christ, conformation to the will of God, and transformation through renewal of the mind. These elements of formation, which are biblically expressed, embrace both the kataphatic understanding of spirituality, which is God revealed, as well as the apophatic understanding of spirituality, which is God concealed: the mystery of God.

The Word of God--in *visio divina, lectio divina,* Holy Communion, and the experience of suffering--is essential to Christian formative spirituality. What Christians understand and believe about these elements of formation and the ways in which believers participate in them forms, changes, and prepares disciples of Jesus Christ, not only for this life but for the life to come. It is from the matrix of the Reformation, beginning with the struggling, searching faith of an Augustinian monk, that the Protestant community has journeyed forward over 500 years. The Christian community is ever-reminded by the legacy of Luther's life, his writings and his example of faith, that Christian spiritual formation, in all its elements, is wholly a biblically-grounded formation of, in, and by the Father, the Son and the Holy Spirit.

BIBLIOGRAPHY

Bromiley, Geoffrey W., ed. *Zwingli and Bullinger*. Library of Christian Classics 24. Philadelphia: Westminster, 1953.

Brewer, Brian C. *Martin Luther and the Seven Sacraments: A Contemporary Protestant Reappraisal*. Grand Rapids: Baker, 2017.

Durheim, Benjamin. *Christ's Gift. Our Response: Martin Luther and Louis-Marie Chauvet on the Connection between Sacraments and Ethics*. Collegeville, MN: Liturgical, 2015.

Hummel, Leonard M., "Constellation for Suffering in Luther and the Lutheran Confessions: Notes and Comments on the 2016 Luther Colloquy." *Seminary Ridge Review* 19 (2017) 90–100.

Kay, Jonathan. "It Took Years for Luther's Ideas to Spread. That's Why He Succeeded." *The Washington Post* (October 29, 2017) Sec. B 1, 4.

Lascelles, Christopher. *Pontifex Maximus: A Short History of the Popes*. London: Crux, 2017.

Luther, Martin. *The Large Catechism*. Grand Rapids: Christian Classics Ethereal Library, n.d. http://www.ccel.org/ccel/luther/largecatechism.pdf.

———. *Table Talk*. Translated by William Hazlitt. Grand Rapids: Christian Classics Ethereal Library, 2004. http://www.ntslibrary.com/PDF%20Books/Luther%20 Table%20Talk.pdf.

Mattes, Mark C. *Martin Luther's Theology of Beauty: A Reappraisal*. Grand Rapids: Baker, 2017.

Pettegree, Andrew. "The Talented, Heedless Man Who Changed the Direction of History." *The Washington Post* (October 29, 2017) sec. B 1, 6.

Rittgers, Ronald K. "Luther's Reformation of Suffering." *Seminary Ridge Review* 19 (2017) 1–17.

Schaff, Philip. *History of the Christian Church*. Vol. 7, *Modern Christianity. The German Reformation*. "The Eucharistic Theories Compared: Luther, Zwingli, Calvin," 370–71. Grand Rapids: Christian Classics Ethereal Library, 2002. https://www.ccel.org/ ccel/schaff/hcc7.pdf.

Smith, Gordon T. "Sacrament." In *Dictionary of Christian Spirituality*, edited by Glen G. Scorgie, 729. Grand Rapids: Zondervan, 2011.

Stroho, Jane. "Luther, Martin (1483–1546)." In *Dictionary of Christian Spirituality*, edited by Glen G. Scorgie. 591–92. Grand Rapids: Zondervan, 2011.

Seminary of Christ the King. "History of Priestly Formation." http://sck.ca/priestly-formation/history-of-priestly-formation/.

Von Drehle, David. "Steve Jobs Gave Us Our President." *The Washington Post* (September 7, 2017) sec. A 1, 4.

Von Hildebrand, Dietrich. *Liturgy and Personality*. Manchester, NH: Sophia Institute Press, 1943.

Wengert, Timothy J. et al., eds. *Dictionary of Luther and the Lutheran Traditions*. Grand Rapids: Baker, 2017.

5

A Pentecostal Paradigm that Reconciles

*The Theology of the Cross
and Christian Perfection*

LANCE BACON

INTRODUCTION

A gap between expectation and experience that was evident in the early days of Pentecostalism has significantly widened in recent years as pluralism and biblical illiteracy have given rise to materialistic hyper-faith and deficient hyper-grace theologies that seek blessing without growth, or growth without struggle. A reconciliation of Martin Luther's Theology of the Cross and John Wesley's Christian Perfection is necessary to bring reversal and renewal.

Though the doctrines appear to be at odds, they are compatible and arguably symbiotic when informed by a pneumatic hermeneutic. Luther's insights would restore a right understanding of salvation, centered on the loss of brokenness over sin that is missing in many modern theologies (and sometimes superseded by sanctification in Wesleyan thought). They would further restore the understanding that God reveals Himself in suffering rather than prosperity. Wesley's doctrine presents sanctification as the necessary reformation of the believer: beginning with the Spirit-led transformation initiated at the cross (an aspect lacking in Luther's forensic justification), and continuing with empowerment for gospel witness. Such reconciliation would address the error of Luther, who was unwilling or unable to find a satisfactory pneumatological victory beyond struggle, as well as the error of many modern Wesleyan Pentecostals who wrongly desire a life without struggle.

Though the well-established "already/not yet" paradigm is of immeasurable worth, Pentecostal renewal demands a third element be included to develop an "already/becoming/not yet" paradigm in which the saved and positionally sanctified believer (already), living in the process of perfection through cooperating grace and anointing (becoming), does so in the sure hope of fulfillment in the eschaton (not yet). Though the believer can never arrive at "not yet" through becoming,[1] such an approach recognizes and rightly responds to God's explicit will that believers not remain stagnant in what He has already done, but rather endeavor in covenant progression toward Christ-likeness.

THE RISE OF PENTECOSTALISMS

Theological deficiencies and errors have created gaps between expectation and experience since the inception of the modern Pentecostal movement.[2] In the words of Finnish Pentecostal systematician Veli-Matti Kärkkäinen, Pentecostalism was "birthed out of dynamic experience rather than a theological discovery."[3] That is not to discount the critical role that experience plays in Pentecostal formation and progression. However, the advancement of experience from penultimate to ultimate has proven detrimental from the early days of the Azusa Mission. Indeed, William Seymour's "fundamental concern was with the increasing reliance he saw within the Pentecostal movement on outward signs as opposed to inward realities—the substitution of mere experience for the word of God."[4] Initial cracks in the theological structure were soon evident amid firm assertions that speaking

---

1. Wesley and Luther held that salvation involved not only the removal of guilt, but the transformation of life, but that transformation would not be complete until the eschaton. While Wesley felt it the Christian duty to strive for that perfection, Luther felt such effort resided within the Theology of Glory rather than the Theology of the Cross.

2. For this chapter, I present the term "Pentecostalism" in the context of Allan Anderson's definition, which includes Classical Pentecostalism, Charismatics, and Neo-Pentecostalism. See Anderson, "Varieties," 14–15.

3. Kärkkäinen, "Pneumatologies," 224–25.

4. Jacobsen, *Thinking in the Spirit*, 78.

in tongues referred only to xenolalia for missionary witness,[5] and when faith cure theologies rejected all medical means.

Those cracks have only widened as diversity within, and continuing development of, the modern Pentecostal movement have opened the door to a staggering variety of methods and messages. That no serious academic work on Pentecostalism began until the 1950s has contributed significantly to this conundrum. Academic Pentecostal pneumatology has barely begun, yet this relatively young theology has already moved beyond what its initiators experienced and declared it to be.[6] Such development and definition are made difficult by the movement's repeated renewing and re-forming; as noted by Amos Yong, "there are tensions between the historic versus contemporary aspects of Pentecostalism. The former seems to some more exclusive, antiecumenical, and anti-interreligious, whereas the latter seems to others too open-ended and ideologically pluralistic."[7]

Amid these developments, there has emerged a wide variety of Pentecostal faith groups that have adapted to radically different social and global contexts. Indeed, it is more accurate to speak of *Pentecostalisms*, according to Anderson, who uses the family resemblance analogy to acknowledge similarities, yet account for differences, in this diverse and eclectic group.[8] Nevertheless, the family tree of Pentecostalism has emerged with four primary roots: Conversion: A radical personal change of worldview and identity; Confession: A radical submission to the lordship of Christ; Sanctification: A purifying perfection of motives and desires; Empowerment: A move beyond God's presence to an infilling and indwelling that manifests through the operation of spiritual gifts.

These four roots stand in contrast to many Christian doctrines and denominations that, while being firmly anchored at the cross, are unwilling or unable to move beyond it. They either fail or refuse to acknowledge the ongoing work of justification, lifelong sanctification, Spirit baptism, and subsequent charismata that are the defining essence of the Pentecostal tradition.

While Pentecostals lament such omissions outside their ranks, an opposite approach within Pentecostalism is increasingly evident and problematic. Hyper-faith and hyper-grace messages now inundate adherents,

---

5. Xenonalia refers to speaking intelligbiby in a human language that the speaker has not learned, as at Pentecost. There are many documented cases of xenonalia; but the biblical gift of tongues also includes "tongues of . . . angels" (1 Cor 13:1) and speaking "mysteries in the Spirit" (1 Cor 14:2).

6. Kärkkäinen, "Pneumatologies," 230.

7. Yong and Richie, "Missiology," 251.

8. Anderson, "Varieties," 13–15.

promising the blessings of the resurrected life and the power of Pentecost while quickly moving past conversion (often "achieved" through a quick, formulaic prayer) and circumventing, even negating the subsequent works of confession, sanctification, and restoration. While this chapter does not allow a fuller analysis of such doctrines, it progresses with an eye toward hyper-faith movements that promise God's power and blessings through marketable catchphrases, and the emerging hyper-grace movement that teaches that God does not see the sins of His children because believers have allegedly been made righteous by the blood of Jesus and all sins—past, present, and future—have already been forgiven. Such "faith" and "grace" negate any further conviction by the Holy Spirit, as well as further repentance by the believer.[9] Though both approaches offer Scripture to support their theologies, they are tantamount to the third temptation of Christ, which offered a kingdom without a cross (Matt 4:8–10).

These two movements undermine the various Pentecostalisms when their congregants desire the blessing and power of God but take the path, much like electricity, of least resistance (contra the hard path that Luther would call "struggle"). While such devolution is not exclusive to Pentecostalism, hyper-grace and hyper-faith doctrines and dispositions are increasingly embraced by and arguably prevalent within their ranks. As David J. Courey rightly notes, North American Pentecostalism often elevates charismatic experience from penultimate to ultimate, and has made biblical interpretation a servant to experience.[10] The result for Pentecostalism is "a series of expectations that cannot be sustained, and are constantly being called into question by the harsh reality of disappointed existence."[11] Martin Luther's Theology of the Cross provides an unlikely and refreshing solution.

BACK TO THE CROSS

Luther's Theology of the Cross is one of revelation, as opposed to the "Theology of Glory," which presumes to ascend to the divine by human work and ingenuity. Conclusions about the reality of God drawn from human reason or natural theology are misleading, in Luther's view. The Reformer taught that God's revelation is recognized not in works but in suffering—our

9. For example, Ellis contends believers are "just as holy and righteous as [Christ] (1 Cor. 1:30); God dealt with our sins once and for all on the cross (Heb. 10:12); consequently, the Holy Spirit remembers our sins no more (Heb. 10:17)." ("Confronting the Error," para. 2).

10. Courey, *What Has Wittenburg?*, 226.

11. Courey, *What Has Wittenburg?*, 12–15.

personal sufferings bring an end of self and the revelation of the hidden God, who is revealed in His humanity, weakness, and the foolishness of the cross.[12]

Luther's insight is critical for an era in which problematic theologies seek power and possession above all else, with congregants crowding to seek the blessings of a God they have not met, and seeking to be formed into the image of a God they do not know. The cross is not only the place where believers come to know the hidden God but is also the place of reordering of such erroneous desires; a place Jürgen Moltmann describes as "repugnance and devastation before it is anything else. It may become the place from which I derive joy and hope, but from the moment I first see the light, from the moment I received my sight, it must be the place of desolation and godforsakenness."[13]

This "theology of suffering" is increasingly foreign in most Pentecostal circles, yet remains the centerpiece of Paul's theology of power through weakness. Within 2 Cor 10–13, Paul declares weakness to be the source of godly power and the mark of true ministry. Just as holiness is the proof of justification, weakness is the proof of power. The evidence of this truth is the spiritual fruit among believers—Christ is not weak in dealing with you; Christ is powerful in you (2 Cor 13:3).

The term *astheneia* (weakness) and its cognates occur fifteen times in 1 Corinthians, fourteen times in 2 Corinthians, and eight times in Romans, but only seven times in all of Paul's other letters. Paul develops his concept of weakness in four ways:

- Anthropologically: Weakness presupposes that a person's whole being is dependent on God. Limitations include the inability of human beings to obtain God's favor by themselves (1 Cor 9:22).

- Christologically: Weakness is the platform from which the power of God is exhibited in the world. Weakness is the place where God's power is perfected (2 Cor 12:9).

- Ethically: Weakness is the catalyst of servanthood. Due to the priority of love over knowledge and gift, believers must hold their Christian freedom in check, in deference to the sensibilities of weak Christians (1 Cor 8–10). A failure to help the weak (1 Thess 5:14) is a failure to recognize the mutual dependence of every member of the unity that is characterized in Christ's body (1 Cor 12:12–13).

12. Courey, *What Has Wittenburg?*, 154–156.
13. Courey, *What Has Wittenburg?*, 152.

- Theocentrically: God depends neither on human strength nor human achievement, but instead seeks out the weak, the ungodly, and the hostile to redeem them and fit them as vessels of his strength.[14]

Paul identifies himself as a testimony to the power of weakness. He stated that if he had achieved anything, it was only because of God's power working through a weak but consecrated vessel (cf. 2 Tim 2:20–21). Therefore, Paul did not deny, justify, or excuse his weakness, but instead embraced it as the conduit through which the power of God worked. In three pericopes in which Paul reflected on power (2 Cor 4:7—5:10; 6:3–10; 11:16—12:10) he also addressed the hardships that beset his ministry. Such hardships and his weakness enabled the power of Christ to be revealed in miracles (2 Cor 12:12, Rom 15:19; Gal 3:5), in Paul's preaching (1 Cor 2:4), and in the conversion of sinners who were washed, sanctified, and justified (1 Cor 6:11).[15]

The significant problem of Luther's theology is that it keeps Christianity at Calvary. Many Pentecostals and Charismatics see this doctrine as insufficient because it goes no further —the reformer's forensic justification overcomes the *penalty* of sin, but not the *power* of sin in the life of a believer. Luther can only cast himself on faith in the revealed God, and find relief from the pressure of *Anfechtung* by clinging to the Word and looking to the cross. Such an approach is insufficient for Pentecostalism, which is not a theology of relief, but one of progressive covenant reformation leading to ultimate victory and perfection in the eschaton. This progression necessitates the understanding that Luther's God, once hidden at the cross, can and will continue to reveal himself through the cross—and beyond it.[16]

Despite the power provided in Paul's theology, three dominant views soon crippled the role of the cross within the development of Pentecostal doctrine. While Paul presents the cross as providing power amid our weakness, to embrace one's weakness is seen by many as a denial of Pentecostal power. This is certainly the case for the William Durham's "Finished Work" theology that split Pentecostalism soon after its inception. This predominate Pentecostal doctrine does not deny human inability but moved beyond Luther's shortfall by claiming victory over sin's penalty and power through Christ's finished work on the cross. However, this approach neglected any

14. Black, "Weakness," 966.

15. Gräbe, *The Power of God*, 154.

16. This is captured in the Greek word *hilasterion*, which appears only twice in Scripture. In Rom 3:25, it is used to describe the expiation of sin and propitiation of God's wrath. When used in Hebrews 9:5, the word is translated "mercy seat," where the presence of God would manifest. Therefore, when the blood of Christ is applied (at the cross), expiation leads to propitiation, and God is revealed anew to the believer.

need to return to the cross for continued growth in holiness, even when the lives of adherents proved deficient in this regard.

The earlier theologies of John Wesley have a stronger exegetical basis and provide a far better solution. The nineteenth-century Holiness Movement embraced those theologies that then proved foundational to the modern Pentecostal movement. Wesley's theology of sanctification sees the work of the cross as continuing beyond rather than being finished at the cross. That work is completed through lifelong maturation and perfection in love. However, Wesley's theological emphasis on the cross was later diminished by others through the encroachment of Enlightenment thinking that "democratized" entire sanctification within the Holiness Movement.[17] The subsequent development of Wesleyan Christocentric theology in Holiness and Pentecostal streams did not emphasize the cyclical return to the cross demanded by Wesley but stressed the transformative aspects of maturation and perfection instead.

From this developed the idea that faith was a voluntary act that brought the immediate guarantee of holiness to the believer who would merely accept what had already been provided, a belief best captured in Phoebe Palmer's "shorter way to holiness." Such thought replaced the cyclical return to the cross and the tarrying for empowerment common to Wesley's theology and gave little heed to Luther's correct contention that brokenness over emergent sin is necessary for true and continual repentance. The Holiness approach to transformative growth was bolstered by Wesley's writings, though these were arguably being applied in error. For example, Wesley used the word "repent" only twice in his classic work, *On Christian Perfection*, while expressing the Arminian view that one can forfeit one's salvation. However, many Wesleyan adherents hold that one who is proceeding toward perfection will not be in jeopardy of such loss—a view that is not consistent with Scripture.[18] Sin must be forgiven at the cross before human tendencies and temptations can be overcome through sanctification. This is true not only at the moment of salvation but as sins are uncovered through growth and maturation. While the various Wesleyan streams would certainly demand repentance, the Pentecostal failure to demand brokenness over sin enabled a tendency to minimize, or even abate the need for continued repentance in practice. Such an approach is self-serving and arguably heretical. As Dieter

17. Bebbington, *Holiness*, 65–66.

18. Despite their spiritual growth, believers still struggle with sin (1 John 2:1) and are susceptible to deception (1 John 3:7–8; 5:21).

rightly asserts, "[t]he same love for and of God that draws us toward perfection should drive us to the cross."[19]

Though Christ's blood has provided absolute positional sanctification, continuous cleansing by that same blood is needed (1 John 1:7–9). Such an understanding remains a hallmark of the Keswick view of consecration, which holds that "individuals must clearly see their own bankruptcy and God's abundant provision before they can adequately respond to the challenge of unconditional surrender."[20] This truth was not lost on the founders of the modern Pentecostal movement. William Seymour, the "Apostle of Pentecost," was critical of the way many holiness-oriented preachers tended to "[depreciate] justification, in order to exalt the state of Holy sanctification," and urged the need to "repent and do the first works, and consecrate to receive sanctification."[21]

The *theologia crucis* presented in The Heidelberg Disputation (1518) can be of immeasurable worth in this endeavor. It boldly declares that human pretension is powerlessness, our will is limited, and the hidden God reveals Himself in suffering and the cross. Luther's contrary Theology of Glory is defined as one that seeks to manipulate the divine and searches for God in wisdom, glory, and power, largely to obtain these for one's self—a scenario that is increasingly common and immeasurably dangerous. Still, it is necessary that Pentecostals donot fall into the tendency of Luther and remain at Calvary.

While Courey provides a strong argument for a return to Luther's Theology of the Cross and then goes to great efforts to show that Luther shares more similarities with Pentecostals than some may realize, it is his search to find an all-encompassing application of *theologia crucis* that falls short. Specifically, Courey asserts that the failure of Pentecostalism resides in triumphalism, which he sees as an inherent weakness in North American Pentecostalism (and that may well be). However, his analysis blames this weakness on restorationism and perfectionism, which the author also considers a Theology of Glory. I argue that the Theology of the Cross is a pillar of Pentecostalism that predates John Wesley or the Holiness Movement, emerging from within Luther's camp. These concepts are evident in Johann Arndt's *Pious Desires*, and further developed in Philip Jakob Spener's Pietism (a reform movement that sought "heart religion" and personal spirituality within confessional Lutheranism), as well as Moravian theology, all of which profoundly influenced Wesley and subsequent Pentecostal pioneers.

19. Dieter, "The Wesleyan Perspective," 20.
20. McQuilkin, "The Keswick Perspective," 155.
21. Jacobsen, *Thinking in the Spirit*, 71–73.

Furthermore, it is a significant step to ascribe triumphalism, which Courey defines as an attitude that leaves "little if any room for debate or difference of opinion" to a movement that, by his own admission, has progressed through many paradigms. Indeed, its constant state of renewal has made it near-impossible to categorize and systemize the Pentecostal movement.

Courey also sets the locus of the baptism in the Holy Spirit primarily as an eschatological event. To anticipate the fullness of eschatological fulfillment in the here-and-now is tantamount to triumphalism, he argues, constituting a Theology of Glory. In this, the "finished work" heritage of his own Pentecostal Assemblies of Canada is unmistakable. His solution is to construct instead an *eschatologia crucis* that apprehends "the powers of the age to come" through the appropriate lens of the cross and the resurrection. Such a view is hard to reconcile with numerous scriptures that advocate perfection.[22] Furthermore, to render Wesley's Christian Perfection as triumphant is simply in error. When rightly approached, perfection is steeped in humility—its very title is a pronounced admission that the believer is not perfect.

BEYOND THE CROSS

While Durham rejected, and Wesleyan Pentecostalism does not emphasize, a return to the cross, the forgiveness of subsequent sins and need for a deeper revelation of God demands the pursuit of Pentecostal power be centered on a cyclical return to the cross and subsequent submission to greater reformative work through Christ's resurrection.[23] Paul's declaration of strength in 2 Cor 13:1–4 stands as testimony to this truth: Christ lives and rules not only by God's resurrection power but also as the crucified Lord. The prepositional phrases in 13:4 indicate that Paul's weaknesses are manifestations of his participation in Christ; evidence that he has been crucified with Christ (cf. Rom 6:6; Gal 2:20; 6:14) and carries around the "death of Jesus" in his own body that the life of Jesus and power of God may also be revealed in him and others (2 Cor 4:10–12). Power and weakness/submission belong equally and inseparably to the Christ event. Thus, divine power is experienced amid sufferings.[24]

22. Lev 11:44–45; 19:2; Matt 5:48; Eph 4:13; Phil 3:12; Heb 10:14.

23. 1 Co 11:27–32; 2 Cor 7:1; Jas 5:14–15; Rev 2–3.

24. Gräbe, *The Power of God*, 155–157. Notably, the apostle's weakness is portrayed in the Greek present tense, which signifies a continuous kind of action, while his life with Christ through the power of God is presented in the future tense. Thus it can be said that weakness dominates in the present, but has a temporary nature, while power

The Pentecostal believer, having emerged from a return to the cross, can then advance further in Wesley's "Christian Perfection," a doctrine centered on his conviction that the Christian should not be "content with any religion which does not imply the destruction of all the works of the devil, that is of all sin"[25]—and full recovery of the *imago dei*. Christian Perfection, or entire sanctification, is the Spirit's cleansing of the heart. This cleansing purifies one's dedications and desires, heals the crippling wounds caused by original sin, and frees the soul to love.

Wesley saw sanctification by faith to be the logical step from justification by faith. Justification is not merely a matter of what God *did for us*, but what God is *doing in us*. Sanctification is the moment-by-moment obedience to God's will through which God's grace eradicates the sinful tendencies that reside even after justification. It stands as a symbiotic unity between our freedom to respond and the grace on which we depend.[26] With every submissive and obedient decision, the believer dies to self and allows more of God to reside within (cf. Gal 2:20).

The central purpose of the cross, in Wesley's view, was to positionally sanctify a people that God desires for intimate fellowship (Eph 5:25-27; 1 Thess 5:23; Heb13:12). The result is a responsibility and power to express from a perfected and undivided heart the pure love of God in relationship with God and with others. Thus, sanctification is a faith that works by divine love, and love becomes the true test of holiness. Such holiness stands as a position and a proposition:a verb as well as an adjective.

It is worth noting the symmetry between Wesley's understanding of "faith that works by divine love" and Luther's conviction that "works without faith is dead." While James the biblical author declared that faith without works is dead (Jas 2:18-20), Luther emphasized a converse conviction.[27] Without faith, one is not in right standing with God, and works are pointless. But one who acts in faith will exhibit love flowing forth and will experience evangelical freedom—not in the sense that the individual has freedom from works, but that he does not rely on works for justification. Drawing on Luther's work *On the Freedom of a Christian*, Bayer rightly echoes that "a Christian is a free Lord over all things and is subject to no one. A Christian is a ready servant of all things and is subject to everyone."[28] Thus, the Christian is freed from having to seek his identity in anything but God. To emphasize

reveals an eschatological promise.

25. Wesley, "The End of Christ's Coming," 376.

26. Rom 6:12; 2 Cor 7:1; 10:5; Eph 4:22, 24; Phil 2:5; Heb 12:1.

27. Luther's struggles with the book of James are well known.

28. Bayer, *Martin Luther's Theology*, 289.

this, Luther cites 1 Cor 9:19, in which the apostle declares "because I am free with respect to all, I have made myself a slave to all," Luther notes that Paul did not say, "though I am free," but "because I am free."

Bayer thus argues for a continued return to Luther's Theology of the Cross. As Stanley Horton asserts, "through the Holy Spirit we are able not to sin, even though we never come to the place where we are not able to sin."[29] Holiness cannot progress beyond the sinful tendencies that find a residence, or even dominance, in the life of the believer. These tendencies must be taken to the cross, where deeper measures of divine grace and revelation await.

This approach is not contrary to Wesley's theology but instead serves to enhance subsequent sanctification and maturation. In his view, Christian Perfection is initiated at the cross, not in the eschaton (Luke 1:69–75; Titus 2:11–14; 1 John 4:17). Also, Wesley allowed no stopping point or conclusion in the holiness quest, even beyond this life; progress ever-propels the Christian forward. In this progressive process, the believer recovers the *imago dei*, which Wesley would call the "glorious privilege of every Christian." Such growth in holiness, which occurs by cooperating with the Spirit-led transformation, renders one free from evil thoughts and evil tempers, and allows the love of God to guide all actions and attitudes. Such a believer is "purified from pride, for Christ was lowly of heart. He is pure from self-will or desire, for Christ desired only to do the will of his Father and to finish his work. And he is pure from anger, and the common sense of the word, for Christ was meek and gentle, patient and long-suffering."[30]

Wesley would call a believer's unwillingness or inability to achieve this perfection a "failure to thrive." Still, it should be understood that is is not a doctrine of works. While Luther would hold the pointedly paradoxical formula *simul iustus et peccator* (righteous and at the same time a sinner), Wesley argued there is much more to the Christian life: a victory through and growth in holiness. He developed such understanding through sanctification, theological broadening, and experience.

Macchia develops this understanding further in his demand that justification be pushed beyond the cross, where it has comfortably resided throughout Christian history, and instead be seen in the resurrection and Pentecost. There, he pointedly redefines justification as an active and continuous event that is not complete until glorification, and one that must be

---

29. Horton, "The Pentecostal Perspective," 125.

30. Wesley, "Christian Perfection," 411.

viewed in the context of a pneumatological soteriology within a Trinitarian theology.[31]

In Macchia's view, justification, as defined through the imparted grace of Catholicism and the imputed grace of Protestant theology, is woefully inadequate. The idea that justification was accomplished at the cross causes "an unfortunate fracture" between the objective Christological and subjective pneumatological understanding. He further couches Luther's imputed righteousness as a "questionably biblical notion," a passive justice that removed all human transformation and cooperation. While Luther drove the doctrine of justification from anthropology into Christology, Macchia holds that the journey is not complete until it arrives at pneumatology, where it can facilitate synergistic participation of transformation with the Spirit. This is necessary because the right definition of justification sees it as not only addressing the penalty of sin but also the power of sin.

Justification cannot be confined to cooperation or imputation, but instead finds a fuller and truer definition in participation within an intimate *koinonia* of divine love shared with Father, Son, and Spirit. Such an understanding sees God not as merely accepting sinners, but embracing sinners; God takes them into the divine life and puts that divine life in them, that the individual can be reformed and returned to the created image in the likeness of God.[32] Justification, in this view, was initiated by the divine self-giving in the incarnation, and the incarnation enabled the divine self-giving at Pentecost. In this divine self-giving, humanity is given its very being as God's living presence dethrones sin and death as reigning powers in order to reign in their place (1 Cor 15:44–46; 2 Cor 5:4).[33]

Our cooperation, which Macchia defines as "graced synergy," brings the life of the Spirit (Rom 5:18; 1 Cor 15:45) and participation in the Triune life. This process is cyclical (Rom 3:21–26), which again necessitates the believer's repeated return to the cross. It is worth noting that contrary to Wesley's Christian Perfection, Macchia (who more closely aligns with the Finished Work theology) does not see God as giving the believer who emerges from the cross a power or assistance to help him mature. Instead, God gives Himself. This divine indwelling enables conveyed grace, such as charismatic and spiritual fruit. These, in turn, enable further sanctification

---

31. Macchia, *Justified in the Spirit*, loc. 325.

32. Macchia, *Justified in the Spirit*, loc. 2576.

33. Macchia, *Justified in the Spirit*, loc. 2794. This aligns with Martin Hengel in the understanding that the New Testament defines atonement not as a human abatement of God's wrath, but God's reconciliation to himself unfaithful creatures who had become his enemies.

and deification and enable a deepening of the love-based restorative relationship.

PNEUMATOLOGICAL DEVELOPMENT
OF A CHRISTIAN ETHIC

A Renewal theology that affirms sanctification, and also finds its fulfillment at the cross and beyond, demands an embracing of Lutheran and Wesleyan theologies. It is equally necessary that the discussion of holiness move beyond debates over positional and conditional sanctification to establish a Christian ethic that more adequately addresses social responsibility and transformation.

Left unto themselves, the respective theologies of Luther and Wesley can result in over-reliance on external and experiential observances; the danger is a preference for religious ritual that soon becomes a substitute for moral development and integrity (Amos 5:21–24).[34] Jesus encountered such tendencies in the rabbinic tradition of his day and responded with an emphasis on internal character and the root causes of behavior (Mark 7:1–23).

While it may appear that Jesus was deconstructing the Law, he was actually attacking the rabbinical system that taught that believers could achieve righteousness through obedience and purity. It is critical to note that Jesus (and Paul) interpreted spiritual formation in the context of "the Law and the prophets," rather than the rabbinical tradition. The Torah is thus viewed as a divine covenant of grace rather than a legal list of dos and don'ts. As Cartledge rightly notes, the "Ten Commandments set the basic parameters within which covenant loyalty is to be demonstrated (Exod 20:1–17; Deut 5:6–21) and life is to be lived in a holy way. The book of Leviticus stipulates in terms of sacrifices that which can be offered to God in order to rectify the breach. The Aaronic priesthood is provided in order to mediate between the people and it is the mechanism used to deal with sin through the sacrificial system."[35]

The prophetic view of the Law (one of mercy and grace) places greater emphasis on its moral rather than cultic aspects—a necessary approach in the development of a Renewal soteriology. Such a model—one that is instantaneous, yet continuous—stands contrary to numerous Evangelical doctrines that have long argued to keep salvation and sanctification either synonymous or subsequent. It also reassesses the divine *oikonomia* within the justification matrix. Justification has long held a heavy forensic

---

34. Stassen and Gushee, *Kingdom Ethics*, 91.

35. Cartledge, *Encountering the Spirit*, 87.

perspective in Evangelical (especially Reformed) thought, with the Spirit's role centered in His work as counselor, advocate, intercessor, and the Spirit of adoption (all legal metaphors). Wesley interpreted justification through the perspective of regeneration rather than judgment, but his efforts were beleaguered by the inherent degrees of regeneration, leading to his doctrines on sanctification and Christian Perfection.

Renewal theology more closely aligns with the Pietist emphasis on moving from imputation to transformative indwelling; from a christological imputed righteousness to a pneumatological imparted righteousness. Notably, Hollenweger's classic work *The Pentecostals* does not even mention the traditional Lutheran doctrine of forensic justification; it focuses instead on regeneration and healing. In keeping with this trajectory, Macchia approaches justification as the active gift of righteousness (or "just relation") that is granted to the sinner, what the author calls a "rightwising" or "righteousing" of flesh.[36] Such justification is an active and continuous event that is not complete until glorification.

Macchia offers exegetical analysis to develop and support this definition further. For example, he points out that "righteousness" is rarely used in the Old Testament in a legal or forensic context, but instead speaks of covenant faithfulness—meaning that righteousness has mainly to do with "loyalty rather than legality."[37] The challenge to obey is never softened in the Old Testament, making the person ultimately depend on the mercy of God for the gift of righteousness, because the law cannot create singleness of heart in devotion to God, give new life, or fulfill righteousness. The Messiah is responsible for applying this mercy, then to make his victorious life available to believers through the indwelling Spirit (Isa 11; 42:1; 61:1–3; Ezek 36:27–29; cf. Heb 2:10).

Humanity is thus given its very being in this divine self-giving. While the Reformation-based Evangelical soteriology sees God as providing a justified believer the power or assistance to mature, this paradigm considers the individual justified because God gives himself. This divine indwelling conveys grace, such as charismatic and spiritual fruit. This fruit, in turn, enables further sanctification and deification, enabling also a deepening of the love-based restorative relationship.

The need for this Spirit-driven transformation is perhaps most evident in the emptiness of the Christian ethic meant to guide moral and social development. As Hollinger rightly asserts, the ethics discipline, for much of the twentieth century, has "carried on much of its discourse as if Jesus had

36. Macchia, *Justified in the Spirit*, loc. 52.
37. Macchia, *Justified in the Spirit*, loc. 1277.

never existed."[38] Much of what passes as a Christian ethic is little more than Scripture sprinkled atop a secular ethic. Christianity is laden with ethical egoism (choose what will give the best result for the individual) and utilitarianism (the greatest good for the greatest number of people). Those who oppose subjective analysis tend to center their ethic on principles such as the Socratic method, which views knowledge as the key to the moral life, or Immanuel Kant's view that reason is the final arbiter of ethics. The inherent deficiencies of these and similar approaches carry serious implications to include malformed Christian practices, moral beliefs, and moral witness; a crisis of Christian identity; and outright idolatry as believers substitute other "moral authorities" for Jesus and his way of discipleship.[39]

Character, or virtue ethics (rather than principles) are the foundation of the Christian ethic. These judge not what a person does, but who he or she is. The key is not what we ought to do, but what we ought to be, and the way that we become is through cooperation in the sanctifying work of the Holy Spirit. Neither holiness nor the subsequent ethic it enables is based on rigid legalism, which was prevalent in the early days of Pentecostalism (and flatly denounced by Jesus in his repeated assessment of the rabbinic tradition). The legalistic approach has resulted in a decrease in the standards of holiness.[40] Neither should we swing from legalism to libertinism, as this diminishes the resistance to sin and temptation.[41] Instead, we should recapture the purity of God's essence and character, with the understanding that purification enables the Spirit to use graced socio-critical charisms for the kingdom of God (2 Cor 8:1). As Cartledge rightly notes, "the social and charismatic experience of God in worship should flow out into social and political commitment. To be inspired by the Spirit will mean action on behalf of others (James 2:15–17)."[42]

Only by losing our lives will we receive God's life. In doing so, we will not withdraw from society in the name of holiness but employ our holiness to transform society.[43] Holiness does not abandon or condemn society; it redeems society. Such redemption can flow only from one who has been redeemed. This holiness requires a rejection of religion's legalistic tendencies to ensure that we not neglect the weightier matters of the law: justice,

---

38. Hollinger, *Choosing the Good*, 67.

39. Stassen and Gushee, *Kingdom Ethics*, 11–15.

40. Warrington, *Pentecostal Theology*, 21

41. Warrington, *Pentecostal Theology*, 213.

42. Cartledge, *Encountering the Spirit*, 94–95.

43. Green, *Sanctifying Interpretation*, 91.

mercy, and faith (Matt 23:23). Such goals reflect the heart of God and the call of God and are only fulfilled by God.

CONCLUSION

The need for renewal is amplified by the diluted doctrines, cheap grace, and biblical illiteracy that consume modern Pentecostalisms. The prevalence of such dynamics demands a return to (and repeated returns to) the cross of Calvary. As Berkouwer rightly asserts, "[g]enuine sanctification—let it be repeated—stands or falls with this continued orientation towards justification and the remission of sins."[44]

A renewal of the church must begin with a renewal of the mind. To have the mind of Christ, one must first be crucified with Christ (Phil 2:5–9). But it is necessary that, like Christ, we move beyond the cross. Paul mentions that Christians are "in Christ," "in him," or "in the Lord" in all but one of his letters, one hundred and sixty-four times in all. Christ is also in the Christian (John 14:20, 17:23; Gal 2:20; Eph 3:17; Col 1:26–27). If we are in Christ, and Christ in us, we must progress from the cross to resurrection to Pentecost.

Luther's Theology of the Cross is powerful, yet deficient in that it goes no further. It brings the believer to the place of forgiveness, but not to the freedom; it overcomes the penalty of sin, but not the power of sin. Pentecostal renewal must move beyond the cross and embrace the Spirit's function. Macchia's approach is refreshing as it rightly asserts that the theology of justification must move beyond the cross to include the Spirit's function, which must be seen to carry communal, cosmic, and eschatological dimensions. The desired renewal could also be strengthened by the cooperative sanctification common to Wesley's approach. Unlike a fideistic atonement through the written and preached Word, supplemented by God's spiritual and vocational gifting, a Pentecostal transformative atonement must hold to the "fivefold gospel" in which the believer is provided salvation, transformation through sanctification, healing and deliverance, empowerment for witness, and eschatological redemption. Justification is not a matter of grace alone, faith alone, or mystical union alone—it demands a personal transformation through lifelong sanctification.

While Luther would be suspicious of any approach that moved beyond his Theology of the Cross, Christian Perfection does not mark a transition to Luther's Theology of Glory as long as experience remains penultimate to Scripture. It can well be argued that such re-formation would enable a

44. Berkouwer, *Faith and Sanctification*, 78.

stronger understanding of the mediated Word, thus protecting against the theology of glory that has threatened Pentecostalism.

Such renewal would address the error of many modern Pentecostals who wrongly desire a life without struggle. Such renewal would address the error of Luther, who was unwilling or unable to find a satisfactory pneumatological victory beyond struggle. The victory comes through a Christian life initiated on the cross (and arguably returning there with frequency), progressing to a place of resurrection (new life in the Spirit) and ultimately into a Pentecostal experience (power for witness through the Spirit) with an eye toward the ultimate fulfillment in the eschaton. As such, Luther's Theology of the Cross provides an invaluable and necessary element of renewal in Pentecostalisms that tend to diminish their dealings with sin. Similarly, Wesley's Christian Perfection embraces experience and the necessity for transformative discipleship through growth in the Spirit, both of which are deficient in Luther's theology.

Renewal theology must be founded on the understanding that Kingdom is not a place, nor a period, but a performative act by God in which we participate. Similarly, holiness is not merely a matter of the individual living a life that is pleasing to God but allowing God to live His life through the individual. In this, we see that biblical holiness is neither objective legality, nor is it measured by one's ability to follow the letter of the Law. Rather, it is the work of the Holy Spirit to help and empower the believer.

BIBLIOGRAPHY

Anderson, Allan. "Varieties, Taxonomies, and Definitions." In *Studying Global Pentecostalism: Theories and Methods,* edited by Allan Anderson et al., 13–29. Anthropology of Christianity 10. Berkeley: University of California Press, 2010.

Bayer, Oswald. *Martin Luther's Theology: A Contemporary Interpretation.* Grand Rapids: Eerdmans, 2003.

Bebbington, David. *Holiness in Nineteenth-Century England.* Carlisle, UK: Paternoster, 2000.

Berkouwer, G.C. *Faith and Sanctification.* Grand Rapids: Eerdmans, 1952.

Black, D. A. "Weakness." In *Dictionary of Paul and His Letters,* edited by Gerald F. Hawthorne et al., 966–67. Downers Grove, IL: Intervarsity, 1993.

Cartledge, Mark J. *Encountering the Spirit: The Charismatic Tradition.* Maryknoll, NY: Orbis, 2006.

Courey, David J. *What Has Wittenburg to Do with Azusa?* New York: Bloomsbury T. & T. Clark, 2015.

Dieter, Melvin E. "The Wesleyan Perspective." In *Five Views on Sanctification,* edited by Stanley N. Gundry, 11–46. Grand Rapids: Zondervan, 1987.

Ellis, Paul. "Confronting the Error of Hyper-Grace—A Response to Michael Brown." *Escape to Reality* (Feb. 12, 2013). https://escapetoreality.org/2013/02/22/error-of-hyper-grace-michael-brown/.

Gräbe, Petrus J. *The Power of God in Paul's Letters.* Wissenschaftliche Untersuchungen zum Neuen Testament 2/123. Tübingen: Mohr/Siebeck, 2008.

Green, Chris. *Sanctifying Interpretation.* Cleveland. TN: CPT Press, 2015.

Hollinger, Dennis P. *Choosing the Good: Christian Ethics in a Complex World.* Grand Rapids: Baker Academic, 2002.

Horton, Stanley M. "The Pentecostal Perspective." In *Five Views on Sanctification,* edited by Stanley N. Gundry, 105–35. Grand Rapids: Zondervan, 1987.

Jacobsen, Douglas. *Thinking in the Spirit: Theologies of the Early Pentecostal Movement.* Bloomington: Indiana University Press, 2003.

Kärkkäinen, Veli-Matti. "Pneumatologies in Systematic Theology." In *Studying Global Pentecostalism: Theories and Methods,* edited by Allan Anderson et al., 223–44. Anthropology of Christianity 10. Berkeley: University of California Press, 2010.

Macchia, Frank D. *Justified in the Spirit: Creation, Redemption, and the Triune God.* Grand Rapids: Eerdmans, 2010. Kindle edition.

McQuilkin, J. Robertson. "The Keswick Perspective." In *Five Views on Sanctification,* edited by Stanley N. Gundry, 149–83. Grand Rapids: Zondervan, 1987.

Stassen, Glen H., and David P. Gushee. *Kingdom Ethics: Following Jesus in Contemporary Context.* Downers Grove, IL: InterVarsity Academic, 2003.

Warrington, Keith. *Pentecostal Theology: A Theology of Encounter.* London: T. & T. Clark, 2008.

Wesley, John. "Sermon: Christian Perfection." In *The Essential Works of John Wesley: Selected Books, Sermons, and Other Writings,* edited by Alice Russie, 397–414. Uhrichsville, OH: Barbour, 2011. (Original date of the sermon: Nov. 11, 1739.)

———. "Sermon: The End of Christ's Coming." In *The Essential Works of John Wesley: Selected Books, Sermons, and Other Writings,* edited by Alice Russie, 367–376. Uhrichsville, OH: Barbour, 2011. (Original date of the sermon: Dec. 9, 1758.)

Yong, Amos, and Tony Richie. "Missiology and the Interreligious Encounter." In *Studying Global Pentecostalism: Theories and Methods,* edited by Allan Anderson et al., 245–68. Anthropology of Christianity 10. Berkeley: University of California Press, 2010.

6

Katharina Luther and the Changing Role of Women in Christianity

BARBARA ELKJER

INTRODUCTION

THE REFORMATION WAS THE beginning of profound changes for women in Western Christianity. While women were not yet permitted to serve as ordained clergy or contribute to the scholarly, written body of Reformed theology, they were not passive recipients of the Reformation. They actively supported and spread the ideals of Luther and Calvin through a whole host of activities, some of which were permitted because of Martin Luther's teaching on marriage, especially marriage for the clergy, and his valuation of women within godly marriages. We have Katharina von Bora to thank for Luther's good opinion. Their trailblazing marriage was seen at the time as one of the most scandalous and intriguing of the Reformation. Yet, against all the odds, this unlikely union worked, and in time, flowered into the most tender of love stories.

Luther and Katharina's obvious affection and respect for each other, lived out before the hundreds of theologians, students and visitors who passed through their home, set an example that planted seeds of freedom and dignity for both men and women. Their relationship was documented by many observers during mealtimes around their table and can be seen in

Luther's personal letters to his beloved wife. Luther was a prolific writer, and much of his correspondence was preserved. In these letters, he addressed his Katie playfully as an empress, a gift of God, loyal and trustworthy, one who comforted him with the Word of God, a theologian, his rib, and a woman worthy to be loved.[1]

Unfortunately, as was the case throughout much of history with the writings of women, Katharina's writings—her correspondence or any journals she may have written—were not preserved. Only eight letters written by her—none of them addressed to Luther—are extant today. However, through the letters that Luther wrote to her, it is possible to get a glimpse inside their marriage.

Their marriage is a story of freedom unfolding for women in Protestant Christianity. It would be difficult to understand how the role of women in Christianity began to change gradually, beginning with the Reformation, without examining the history of the theology of women in the Western church. Therefore, this chapter will first briefly survey the theological history of women in Western Christianity and reflect on possible sources and the effects of that theology. Then we will consider the state of marriage just before the Reformation and how Luther and Katharina lived out Luther's teachings before the watching world. Finally, we will analyze the effects of the Reformation, both immediate and long term, on the roles of women in Christianity.

Martin Luther, the Man Katharina Admired

When people think of Luther, two iconic events usually come to mind. The first is his nailing the Ninety-Five Theses on the wooden doors of the Wittenberg Castle Church naming practices of the Roman Catholic Church that needed examination and reform, especially indulgences. The second is when, at the Imperial Diet in Worms, he made it clear as he stood before some of Christendom's most powerful men—men who could burn him at the stake—that he feared God's judgment more than he feared their power. The audacity of this mere monk to elevate the Word of God above the traditions of the Roman Church! The brazen suggestion that the Holy Roman Emperor Charles V, along with an impressive array of German nobles—and perhaps most importantly, the Pope's representative Thomas Cajetan—did not speak for God, but instead, the Scriptures spoke for God, was a watershed moment in world history. Luther humbly but boldly defied these men, thus changing the meaning of freedom, religion, politics, economics, and

---

1. Markwald and Markwald, *Katharina von Bora*, 142.

Christian marriage forever. As Eric Metaxas observes, "Those of us in the West have lived on the far side of it ever since."[2]

Until that time, the Roman Catholic Church brooked no dissent. The significant earlier attempts at reform by Jan Hus, Peter Waldo, and John Wycliffe were met with violent force and ruthlessly suppressed. Perhaps the most poignant tale of the early Reformation is that of William Tyndale. In 1536 Tyndale was betrayed and martyred for daring to translate the Bible into English.

The Most Dangerous Thing Luther Did

New Testament scholar Ben Witherington III says that the most dangerous thing Luther did was to translate the Bible directly from the Hebrew and Greek into common German so that it could be made widely available.[3] Church historian Philip Schaff observed, "The richest fruit of Luther's leisure in Wartburg [Castle], and the most important and useful work of his whole life, is the translation of the New Testament, by which he brought the teaching and example of Christ and the Apostles to the mind and hearts of the Germans in life-like reproduction. . . . He made the Bible the people's book in church, school, and house."[4]

As Luther stood on the truth of God's Word, he had no idea of the door that he was opening through its translation. The idea that all believers, even women, had the right to read the Bible for themselves, thus allowing the opportunity for the Holy Spirit to speak to them and bring personal revelation of God's truth, was truly revolutionary. Calvin called this an illumination of the heart. He taught that "The Word of God is made alive to the individual by the "secret testimony of the Spirit" (*testimonium Spiritus Sancti internum*). This testimony is superior to that of the Church, the enthusiasts, or even reason itself, but it adds no new revelation to the word of the gospel."[5]

As Catholic scholar José Comblin has pointed out, by the time of the Reformation the Holy Spirit had been effectively set aside in favor of the Church—not in formal doctrine but in practice.[6] The human actions of the church were assumed to be the actions of the Spirit. In doctrinal creeds, the Holy Spirit was dutifully acknowledged, but in policy and practice, for the

---

2. Metaxas, *Martin Luther*, 2."

3. Witherington, "The Most Dangerous Thing Luther Did," n.p. Web.

4. Witherington, "The Most Dangerous Thing Luther Did," n.p. Web.

5. Burgess, "The Doctrine of the Holy Spirit in the Reformation Traditions," loc31743.

6. Comblin, *The Holy Spirit and Liberation*, 78.

most part, the Spirit was relegated to an invisible, secret, mysterious role. An examination of Luther's writings shows that he limited the Spirit's operations to divine acts in the inner being of humankind. According to Lutheran scholar Regin Prenter, Luther conceived the Spirit's purpose as "to bring to humans the great treasure of Christ for the purpose of conforming them to his image, especially to his death and resurrection."[7]

However, he did add a critical new element that set the Scriptures free from the bondage of church tradition. He taught that the Spirit not only "searches all things, even the deep things of God,"[8] but then reveals these transcendent secrets to us through the Scriptures, that "We may understand what God has freely given us."[9] This understanding reflected what Jesus told his disciples, "[The Spirit] will bring glory to me by taking from what is mine and making it known to you . . . That is why I said the Spirit will take from what is mine and make it known to you."[10]

Luther joked to colleagues, "I simply taught, preached, and wrote God's Word; otherwise I did nothing. And then, while I slept, or drank Wittenberg beer with my Philip [Melanchthon] and my [Nicolaus von] Amsdorf, the Word so greatly weakened the papacy that never a prince or emperor did such damage to it. I did nothing. The Word did it all."[11] The idea that the Spirit would reveal truth, not only to popes and cardinals but to ordinary priests and monks—even to nuns and housewives—exploded on the landscape of late medieval Europe. "Suddenly the individual had not only the freedom and possibility of thinking for himself [or herself] but the weighty responsibility before God of doing so."[12]

This humble truth from the Word of God, that the Holy Spirit would illuminate God's Word to anyone, so dramatically changed the circumstances of Western culture that it was hardly recognizable from what it was before. While some of Luther's ideas took hundreds of years to develop fully as they were expanded and built upon by others,[13] the forces that he unleashed

---

7. Prenter, *Spiritus Creator,* 148.

8. 1 Cor 2:10b

9. 1 Cor 2:12b

10. John 16:15–16

11. Tucker, *Katie Luther,* 34–35.

12. Metaxas, *Martin Luther,* 2."

13. In November of 1520 Luther wrote, *On the Freedom of the Christian,* one of the most enduring treatments on Christian freedom ever in Christendom. The tract begins with two seemingly contradictory propositions: "A Christian is a perfectly free lord of all, subject to none. A Christian is a perfectly dutiful servant of all, subject to all." (See Luther, *Three Treatises,* 277.) Even though this revolutionary truth sparked the "Peasant's War," the biblical idea of freedom was taken up by many other theologians,

led eventually to this momentous statement, "We hold these truths to be self-evident, that all men are created equal, that they are endowed by their Creator with certain unalienable rights, that among these are life, liberty and the pursuit of happiness."[14] While it took an additional two hundred years for that statement to apply fully to women in Western culture, it was Martin and Katharina Luther who cracked open the door to such freedom and equality.

THE EVOLUTION OF WESTERN THEOLOGY TOWARD WOMEN

However, to understand the profound change for women brought about by the Reformation we must first understand how Western Christianity viewed the status and role of women in the centuries leading up to it. As Barbara MacHaffie outlines in her history of the roles and status of women in the theology of the Church,[15] the pendulum swung from depicting women as inferior, evil seductresses luring holy men away from their devotion to God, to the Victorian-era "Cult of True Womanhood," where women were idealized as paragons of virtue and piety while men were cast in the role of sensual beasts.[16] It has taken until the twenty-first century to realize that women are neither of these extremes of the theological pendulum, but it was Katie Luther and her fellow wives of pastors who began to move the opinion of the Church in a positive direction.

The Violent Suppression of Women

By the time six-year-old Katharina von Bora was taken by her newly re-married father to live in a Benedictine convent in Brehna, misogyny was firmly entrenched in the Church. By the late Middle Ages, witch hunts were well underway. The general consensus among historians is that between 1400 and 1750 AD, a conservative estimate of women who were hanged or burned as witches is 40,000 to 50,000, with some estimates as high as

---

preachers and philosophers and finally resulted in the United States. Preaching on freedom was so prolific in the years leading up to the American Revolution that the British Parliament named the courageous American clergy "The Black Robed Regiment" referring to the black robes that ministers wore.

14. Spalding, "The Declaration of Independence," 2.

15. MacHaffie, *Her Story*, passim.

16. MacHaffie, *Her Story* 160.

100,000.[17] Several years before Katharina was born, Dominican Inquisitors Jacob Sprenger and Heinrich Kramer published the notorious *Malleus Maleficarum* (*Hammer Against the Evildoers*). Because of the newly invented printing presses, this purported guidebook and source of information about witches and witchcraft enjoyed a wide readership. It carried great authority because it was prefaced by a bull from Pope Innocent VIII ordering the annihilation of witchcraft. "The book was banned by the Church in 1490, and Kramer was censured, but it was nevertheless reprinted in 14 editions by 1520 and became unduly influential in the secular courts."[18]

In their attempts to explain why witchcraft was predominantly practiced by women, the authors stated:

> A woman was a "liar by nature"; vain in gait, posture, and habit; and insatiable in carnal lust, as well as wicked: "a foe to friendship, an unescapable punishment, a necessary evil, a natural temptation, a desirable calamity, a domestic danger, a delectable detriment, an evil of nature, painted with fair colors! A woman either loves or hates; there is no third option," wrote the authors, quoting Seneca, "When a woman thinks for herself, she thinks only evil."[19]

These words reflect a genuine hatred for women. This ancient prejudice, misogyny, had been institutionalized in Roman Catholic theology for centuries. However, some scholars suggest that some Protestant leaders used accusations of witchcraft to rid communities of "rebellious" women who refused to conform to the ideal of the submissive, obedient wife.[20] Indeed, the cry of "Witch!" was a real danger to the women of the Reformation like Katharina Luther, Katherine Zell, and Elizabeth Bucer, who were intelligent, educated and capable. This atrocious, violent suppression of women lasted until 1721 when the last accused witch, Jenny Horne, was burned in Europe.

Being burned as a witch was not the only danger to educated, outspoken women. Anyone could be tried in court by either the church or state, to be pilloried, drowned, publicly flogged, tortured, and/or imprisoned. Such was the case of Margery Kemp, a fourteenth/fifteenth-century mystic, who was repeatedly tried for witchcraft because she claimed to have an intimate, conversational friendship with Jesus.[21] During her frequent prayer, she

17. MacCulloch, *The Reformation*, 544.

18. Jolly et al., *Witchcraft and Magic*, 241.

19. Kors and Peters, *Witchcraft in Europe*, 121.

20. MacHaffie, *Her Story*, 67. This thesis is found, for example, in Brauner, *Fearless Wives*, 87–88.

21. MacHaffie, 73.

heard the promise of Jesus that he would "give her victory over her enemies, give her the ability to answer all clerks, and that [He] will be with her and never forsake her, and to help her and never be parted from her."[22] She did indeed avoid the gamut of common punishments. Not all women were so fortunate. Prior to the mid-1800s, most legal systems viewed wife-beating as a valid exercise of a husband's authority over his wife.[23] A husband or father could also imprison or starve his wife or daughters for disobedience.

THE DEVELOPMENT OF THE THEOLOGY OF WOMEN IN THE WEST

How do we explain this oppression and brutalization of half the world's population by the other half, throughout history? It is most evident that the basis of the institutionalized degradation of women in Christianity can be laid at the feet of Greek philosophy and its philosophers, especially Plato and Aristotle. The Greek culture gave the world many good things—the language of the New Testament, architecture, art, poetry and the first version of democracy—"but in the history of misogyny, the Greeks also occupy a unique place as the intellectual pioneers of a pernicious view of women that has persisted down to modern times."[24]

Women in First Century Christianity and Judaism

To understand the profound changes for women begun during the Reformation it is necessary to get a brief overview of the evolving worldview of Western Christianity and how women were thought of theologically in the context of that worldview. Barbara MacHaffie maintains that very early Christianity was attractive to women. Inscriptions from synagogues in various parts of the Roman Empire give women leadership titles such as "mother" and "elder."[25] Bernadette J. Brooten concludes that these titles were more than honorific; they revealed that women had liturgical, teaching, judicial, and financial responsibilities. Both Jewish and Greco-Roman culture reinforced the silencing and subordination of women; but Paul's specific greetings in his writings to at least fifteen women are evidence that

22. Beal, "Margery Kempe," n.p.
23. Felter, "A History of the State's Response to Domestic Violence," 5–7.
24. Holland, *Misogyny*, loc. 305.
25. MacHaffie, *Her Story*, 3.

Christianity accepted active women members and powerful female leaders such as Phoebe and Priscilla.[26]

There is biblical evidence that women were included as full members of early Christian communities. Luke tells us in Acts at the birth of the Church that the "the women and Mary the mother of Jesus" all received the exact same sign of membership in God's people, the baptism in the Spirit, and publicly prophesied in tongues to the Pentecost crowd.[27] Saul, before his conversion, rode out to arrest both men and women who were propagating the faith.[28] Another passage in Acts claims that the Bereans, both men and women, "received the word with all eagerness, examining the Scriptures daily to see if these things were so."[29] Of the thirty-nine co-laborers Paul specifically mentioned by name, more than one fourth were women,[30] such as the church deacon, Phoebe, whom he trusted to deliver his letter to the Romans.[31]

Although there were diverse opinions in first-century Judaism, many rabbis regarded women as socially and religiously inferior to men, and some even expressed contempt for them. However, this Hellenization of Jewish thought had originated much earlier—after the conquest of Judea by Alexander the Great and his generals. Many of the Jews welcomed the customs and philosophy of the Greeks. They found them refreshing. In 1 Maccabees 1:11–15, the author described a Hellenizing process that led many Jews to adopt not only Greek philosophy but the attitudes about women that came with it. Still, not all Jewish scholars agreed with the Aristotelian view of womanhood nor welcomed the Greek attitude toward females. One notable exception was Gamaliel, the teacher of Saint Paul. Just as Luther wrote in his treatises on marriage,[32] Gamaliel subscribed to the proverb, "He who finds a wife finds what is good and receives favor from the LORD."[33] Centuries later, church leaders who themselves were a product of a resurgence in the study of the Greek philosophers interpreted Paul's writings, not from the Hebrew perspective of Gamaliel, but the Greek perspective of Aristotelian and Stoic philosophy.

26. Brooten, "Early Christian Women," 65–91.

27. Acts 1:14; 2:4; 10:44–47.

28. Acts 8:3; 9:2

29. Acts17:11–12

30. Cunningham and Hamilton, *Why Not Women?* loc 858–859.

31. Rom 16:1–2.

32. Luther, "The Estate of Marriage," 38.

33. Prov 18:22.

The Influence of Greek Philosophy

During the first three centuries of the early church a new worldview began to infiltrate Christianity that was heavily influenced by Greek philosophy, especially Platonic dualism. This view radically challenged the Judeo-Christian belief that God's creation is good. In this dualistic view, the spiritual is ideal and good, and the physical is flawed and evil.[34] Creation was thought to be the result of a fall from a perfect spirit realm into the prison of bodily existence. Thus, having become trapped in physical bodies, human spirits became subject to the evil powers that ruled the material realm. Consequently, the body and its appetites such as sex and hunger were considered evil snares to be mortified. The widespread and influential heresy of Arianism promoted this view in the early centuries after Christ.

In the Hebrew account of the creation of humankind, the first woman, Eve, is a delightful gift from God so that Adam would not be alone.[35] She was exactly the same species, bone of his bone, flesh of his flesh, and created in God's image.[36] In the Greek version, woman is also a gift but a most spiteful, malicious one given as a punishment by the gods. In Greek mythology, males were created by the gods and lived in blissful bachelorhood as companions to the gods, "apart from sorrow and from painful work—free from disease."[37] Women were characterized as sly, manipulating deceivers whose morals were described by Plato as a female dog in heat. Since women were inflicted upon men, "mankind has been doomed to labor, grow old, get sick, and die in suffering."[38]

Speaking in the science of his day, Aristotle taught that women were subhuman—somewhere between an animal and a human—and the result of a birth defect. He wrote, "A woman is an infertile male; [she] is female [because she] lacks the power to concoct semen."[39] He said that the reason for this was the "coldness of her nature."[40] The belief that males were the singular begetters of life, providing the life-giving "seed," with females providing only the place or the "soil," in which the seed could grow, underscored women's inferior status. Aristotle maintained that this was only a reflection of the created order, the way things were meant to be. According

---

34. MacHaffie, *Her Story*, 22.

35. Gen. 2:18–25.

36. Gen 1:26–28; 2:18, 23.

37. Hesiod, *Theogony*, 61–62.

38. Holland, *Misogyny*, 325–26.

39. Aristotle, *Generation of Animals*, 1.20 (728a 18–21).

40. Aristotle, *Generation of Animals*, 1.20 (728a 18–21).

to Aristotle, male insemination normally produced another male in the image of his father. However, if there was too much fluid in the womb, the male body was "subverted" and a defective specimen—a female—was produced. The female was thus accounted inferior in every way: weaker in body, less capable of reason, and morally less capable of will and self-control. Arisotle's teachings were revived and venerated by Philo, who was then followed by Augustine, Thomas Aquinas and among numerous other theologians as these unbiblical ideas flourished and were reintroduced into Christian theology again and again.

Greco-Roman culture was dominated by an honor/shame ideology in which men were rewarded for public effort and achievement while women were to hide their "shame" [their inherent inferiority] . . . by remaining obedient and secluded.[41] Demosthenes, the great Greek orator, repeated an often-quoted Athenian saying, "We have courtesans for our pleasures, young female slaves for daily physical use, and wives to bring up legitimate children."[42] The Greek historian Xenophon described the ideal marriage partner this way: "She was not yet fifteen when I introduced her to my house, and she had been brought up always under the strictest supervision; as far as could be managed, she had not been allowed to see anything, hear anything or ask any questions."[43]

In the generation after Aristotle, another Athenian philosopher named Zeno founded a school of thought, Stoicism, that greatly influenced Greek and Roman society. He taught that all passions and pleasures are to be disdained by those who would truly pursue wisdom. Zeno's followers championed the value of asceticism and celibacy for the sake of higher goals, the search for truth. The asceticism of Stoicism profoundly influenced the early church.

Thinkers in the early church, supping these societal influences, quickly turned away from the high value of women shown in the New Testament. Women were characterized as evil seducers whose delight was to lure godly men away from their devotion to God. The blame for the fall of humankind was placed squarely on Eve's shoulders. Tertullian wrote, "You [women] are the Devil's gateway. You are the unsealer of that forbidden tree. You are the first deserter of the Divine law. You are she who persuaded him whom the Devil was not valiant enough to attack. You destroyed so easily God's image

---

41. Stegemann, "Paul and the Sexual Mentality," 161.

42. Demosthenes, "Apollodorus: Against Neaera," 121.

43. Xenophon, "Within the Home," 625.

man. On account of your desertion, that is death, even the Son of God had to die."[44]

This attitude persisted into the Middle Ages and beyond. Aristotle and his ideas were admired by influential men of the church and were used to support their views that women were intrinsically weaker, more easily deceived, and a trap for men. Bonaventure, a medieval Franciscan, contemporary of Aquinas, and scholastic theologian emulated Aristotle when he preached, "What is woman but an enemy to love, an inescapable punishment, an unavoidable evil, a temptation built into nature, a disaster made of desire and a danger to every household."[45] This wording so resembles the later wording in the *Malleus Maleficarum* that it is likely that Kramer and Sprenger copied them directly from Bonaventure or, that this misogyny was so entrenched as to be "common knowledge."

In this Greek spiritual/material dualism the male was more aligned with the ideal of the spirit realm, and the female was identified with the corruption of the fallen material, earthly realm.[46] Interpreting a verse such as Paul wrote to the Colossians, "Set your minds on things above, not on earthly things,"[47] through the Aristotelian and Stoic lens would mean that devout men seeking the transcendent God should shun women as earthly and evil. This Greek interpretation goes directly against God's first command to his newly created humans to "be fruitful and increase."[48] Both Luther and Calvin pointed out, "Man and woman were made for the purpose of sexual union according to God's design."[49] And, as Luther pointed out in his writings on marriage, assuming that taking a vow of chastity could somehow thwart God's good design of reproductive biology was not only arrogant but foolish.

This dualistic thinking that the body and its God-given appetites were evil invaded the Church and dominated its theology for centuries. Both males and females in religious orders, as they suppressed, redirected, or erased their sexuality, assumed that they were already participating to some extent in the new order of the kingdom of God. This kind of thinking was clearly influenced by Platonic dualism and Stoic philosophy, which deemed all bodily appetites disruptions in the pursuit of the spiritual. Therefore, the religious task was to dominate the flesh so that one's spirit could rule

44. Tertullian, "On the Apparel of Women," loc 1117.

45. Mills and Grafton, *Conversion*, 9.

46. MacHaffie, *Her Story*, 14.

47. Col 3:2.

48. Gen 1:28.

49. MacHaffie, *Her Story*, 90.

and thus regain the spiritual realm. Such views of the flesh are evidenced in the veneration of virginity, excessive forms of asceticism, equating poverty with holiness, renunciation of the material world, and other denigrations of earthly human existence. Monastic communities especially prized celibacy as the highest spiritual estate.

The Virtue of Virginity

In the writings of the church fathers, virginity became the one means in the Christian community through which women could acquire some measure of practical equality with men and some sort of official standing within the church. "The price a woman paid was dear; she had to obliterate her 'female-ness'. She did this by denying her childbearing ability, by fasting to eliminate her menstrual cycle, and by making herself as unattractive as possible."[50] The equality in Christ that Paul advocated in Galatians was only allowed, in part, in the virgin life within the convent.[51]

While these cloistered women were not allowed to leave the premises or speak with anyone outside, women were allowed to use their gifts of leadership and scholarship within the monastic walls. In addition to performing the Daily Office, which is the official set of prayers marking the hours of each day, the nun Katharina von Bora would likely have had specific tasks assigned to her by the Abbess of the community. "Nuns during the Middle Ages often translated religious texts, illuminated manuscripts with elaborate artwork, or did embroidery or other handiwork."[52] Even if Katharina did not participate in this kind of work, it is evident from the competence she displayed immediately after her marriage in organizing and directing the tremendous amount of work needed to feed and house the many residents of the Black Cloister that she was knowledgeable and trained. "Convent life provided women with the opportunity to hold many different positions of responsibility," says German Reformation historian Charlotte Woodford. After the Abbess, one of the most important offices for a professed nun was that of Cellaress, the convent business manager, responsible for the economy. She presided over the convent's income from its farms and estates, both in-kind—grain, livestock, and wine—and money, be it from trade, taxes, or elsewhere.[53]

50. MacHaffie, *Her Story*, 25.

51. Gal 3:26–28.

52. DeRusha and Prior, *Katharina and Martin Luther*, 53.

53. Woodford, *Nuns as Historians*, 6–7.

That is precisely the role that Luther's wife Katharine, as the First Lady of the Reformation, undertook for her husband, freeing him to teach, preach, write, debate, and discuss with the students, distinguished theologians and noblemen who stayed in their home. Luther brought his brilliant mind, his teachable spirit, some smelly clothes, foul bed sheets, and old books to the marriage. After only a short time, Luther came to trust his wife and her decisions and turned over the finances and the administration of the enormous household to her completely.

Both Luther and Calvin, and a host of other reformers, argued that marriage was preferable to celibacy on biblical grounds.[54] The very first commandment that God gave to humanity was to procreate. Men and women were created for the purpose of sexual union, according to God's good design. Since this was part of God's strategy for his creation, Luther argued they should feel joy and not guilt in their natural inclinations.[55] God's design was one of Luther's main points in advocating for marriage, especially marriage of the clergy, as an honorable estate preferable to celibacy.

The Scandalous State of Marriage

When the Reformers arrived in the late Middle Ages, the institution of marriage was a mess. Marriage during Luther's time was considered part of the Church's jurisdiction and thus was not managed by the state. At the Council of Verona in 1184 the Roman Catholic Church officially claimed it as one of the seven sacraments. Nevertheless, marriage was not managed within the framework of the Church's liturgy. In other words, it was not required that the marriage ceremony take place in a church or be officiated by a priest.[56] The Church viewed marriage as a gift from God and an act of consent between a man and a woman; therefore, canon law failed to regulate the act of marriage in any substantive way.[57] A couple who promised to love one another and live together until death was considered officially married, especially if the couple had consummated their vows.

By the late Middle Ages, it became increasingly common for boys as young as fourteen and girls as young as twelve to betroth themselves to one another without any parental involvement. Then there was the problem of clandestine marriages either by amoral reprobates who seduced multiple women with lies, or unscrupulous fortune hunters who kidnapped

54. MacHaffie, *Her Story*, 90.
55. MacHaffie, *Her Story*, 90.
56. DeRusha and Prior, *Katharina and Martin Luther*, 137.
57. MacCulloch, *The Reformation*, 612.

rich heiresses and raped them into compliance. A couple who exchanged vows were considered by the Church to be married, regardless of whether they had announced their engagement publicly, exchanged their vows in a church, obtained the consent of their parents, or the bride was tricked or forced into consummation.

The ecclesiastical courts were flooded with thousands of hotly contested lawsuits. Cases involved "girls seduced on alleged promises of marriage, parents challenging the secret unions of their children, bigamous 'Casanovas' accused of secretly promising marriage to two or more women, and possibly, most embarrassing of all, men and women sincerely attempting to make public their private vows, only to be challenged by someone claiming to have been secretly promised marriage by one of the partners."[58]

Luther had already written and preached on marriage several times when he returned to Wittenberg from the Wartburg Castlein March 1522. The scandalous state of marriage much concerned him, but even more frustrating to Luther was the fact that the Church charged fees to dissolve marriages or grant dispensations to marry relatives—as in the case of Henry VIII of England. Because the Church made a lot of money from the marriage mess that it had created, it was not motivated to improve it. Luther railed in *The Babylonian Captivity of the Church*, "The Romanists of our day have become merchants. What is it that they sell? Vulvas and genitals—merchandise indeed most worthy of such merchants, grown altogether filthy and obscene through greed and godlessness. For there is no impediment nowadays that may not be legalized through the intercession of mammon."[59]

With the writings of the Reformers the European understanding of marriage underwent a radical shift until it did not resemble the distorted institution of marriage that had developed over centuries. Because women had almost no political rights and little social standing, they were very vulnerable to abuse until the reforms began to take root. Even though a father could still force a daughter into an unwanted marriage, the new regulations that were put in place, such as parental consent, meeting with a priest, the public posting of bans, the avoidance of premarital sex, and a requirement of a public ceremony in the presence of witnesses, were real protections that benefited women.

58. Ozment, *When Fathers Ruled*, 25.
59. Luther, in *Luther's Works*, Vol 45, "The Estate of Marriage," 96.

LUTHER'S RELUCTANCE TO MARRY

Three of Luther's works on marriage, *Sermon on the Estate of Marriage* (1519), *The Babylonian Captivity* (1520), and *On Monastic Vows* (1521), were written before he married and are much more theoretical and idealistic than his more practical treatise, *On Marriage Matters* (1530), written after he married Katharina. For years Luther was not inclined to marry partly because, as a declared heretic, he could be hunted down and burned at the stake and, most probably, because at forty-two, he was comfortable living as a bachelor. His close colleagues Philipp Melanchthon and Justus Jonas thought that marriage would distract Luther from his work and tried to discourage him. But finally, Luther wrote to friends that he had decided to marry for two reasons. First, to please his father and provide him with a grandchild and second, perhaps in reaction to the Peasant's War, to spite the devil. Later, Luther claimed his marriage would "please his father, rile the pope, cause the angels to laugh and the devils to weep."[60]

Luther and Katharina's Courtship

Katharina was not Luther's first choice. "If I had wanted to get married thirteen years ago, I would have chosen Eva Schonfeld," he said. "I didn't love my Kathie at the time, for I regarded her with mistrust as someone proud and arrogant. But it pleased God, who wanted me to take pity on her."[61]

Katharina von Bora was a feisty, aristocratic, runaway nun who escaped her cloistered convent and her vows with the help of a renegade monk who had been shocking Western Christendom with his treatises criticizing the state of Christian marriage. Because her personal papers were not preserved, we can only speculate on how Luther's writings were smuggled into her locked and guarded convent and how she came to admire him and his reforms. We do know that Luther, in response to a smuggled letter, learned that twelve nuns wanted to escape to freedom and asked for his help. He arranged for a merchant, Leonhard Koppe of Torgau, who delivered herring and other goods to the convent, to smuggle them out in his wagon. The law considered this to be the kidnapping of nuns and named it a capital offense. The Religious faced dangers, too. If recaptured, they were treated as vow breakers subject to severe punishments, flogging, starvation, and imprisonment in the convent dungeon.

---

60. Markwald and Markwald, *Katharina von Bora*, 70.
61. Karant-Nunn and Wiesner, eds., *Luther on Women*, "Marriage and Family," 132.

Luther learned the hard way that advocating on paper for the closing of monasteries and cloisters was one thing; however, the reality of dealing with it personally was a much different story. When Koppe and the twelve nuns arrived on his doorstep, Luther graciously welcomed them, praised them for their courage, and set about finding temporary quarters for the refugees. He pleaded with his friend George Spalatin to beg for money from the wealthy noblemen, "so I can get food for the refugees for at least eight or fourteen days and also some dresses, since they have no shoes or clothing."[62]

Luther found husbands or employment for all the nuns except for Katharina. She was taken in by Lucas Cranach, the Elder, the famous court painter, and his wife, Barbara. They were very kind to Katharina—providing clothing, food, and housing for her—but she could not impose on their hospitality indefinitely. Luther at first attempted to marry her off to two other men. The first proposal, from Hieronymus Baumgartner, was annulled when he went home to Nuremberg for his parents' approval. They emphatically objected to a runaway nun with no dowry as an unacceptable bride for their son. Luther next offered Katherine the choice of Kasper Glatz, an elderly theologian and pastor, but she refused because she heard he was stubborn, opinionated, argumentative, and miserly. Luther became increasingly frustrated with her and accused her of aristocratic snobbery. Desperate and running out of options, Katharine made a daring move and asked Luther to marry her—to which he agreed!

So, they married. Because of the marriage reforms, Luther and Katie had to endure a new regulation that might seem repulsive to modern couples. The consummation of their marriage had to be witnessed by a trustworthy observer. The guest they picked for this uncomfortable wedding ritual, Justus Jonas, wrote, "Yesterday I was present and saw the bridegroom on the bridal bed—I could not suppress my tears at the sight. Now that it has happened, and God has desired it, I implore God to grant the excellent, honest man all the happiness."[63]

The Marriage that Changed the World

Luther had met his match. Even though he wrote to his friend, Nikolaus von Amsdorf, that he was neither romantically nor physically attracted to Katharina, he cared about her.[64] Yet, it wasn't long before he greatly admired Katharina and then fell deeply in love with his wife. His many letters

62. Markwald and Markwald, *Katharina von Bora*, 52.

63. Oberman, *Luther*, 282.

64. Luther, *Luther's Letters II*, vol. 49, 117.

to her express his tender regard, respect, and the absolute confidence he had in her. Roland Bainton, in his biography of Martin Luther, *Here I Stand*, relates that after one year of marriage, Luther wrote to a friend, "My Katie is in all things so obliging and pleasing to me that I would not exchange my poverty for the riches of Croesus."[65]

He not only discussed the practical problems of feeding and housing so many guests, but he also discussed with her his meetings with other Reformers. In one letter, Luther asked for advice on who should fill a vacant pastorate because he had confidence that she would make a good suggestion.[66] In another letter, in 1535, Luther gave a glimpse into her activities: "My lord Katie greets you. She plants our fields, pastures and sells cows, et cetera [Bainton asks, how much does that et cetera cover?]. In between she has started to read the Bible. I have promised her 50 gulden [Where did he expect to get them?] if she finishes by Easter. She is hard at it and is at the end of the fifth book of Moses."[67] In yet another, he asked Katie to relate his explanation of a Gospel passage to his friend Philip Melanchthon.[68]

Katie listened to her husband's progress on the translation of Scripture and to his theological musings.[69] She was his secretary and publishing agent, printing and distributing his works.[70] Katie was also his counselor and comforter. She was his devoted nurse when he suffered from gout, insomnia, catarrh, hemorrhoids, constipation, kidney stones, dizziness, and ringing in the ears.[71]

Luther liked to joke, and his humor was often earthy and coarse. As a man of his times, Luther would remind Kathie in their lighthearted banter that women were subservient to men, especially because of the fall. Guests around the table observed and recorded that, while Katie was always respectful, calling her husband *Herr Doktor*, she often returned his witty quips with her own.

As "Luther's wife, Katherine von Bora, presided over barnyard, fields, fishpond, orchard, a host of servants, [six natural] children [and three adopted ones], sick visitors, student boarders, church leaders and theologians in their huge Augustinian cloister, which had forty rooms on the first floor

---

65. Bainton, *Here I Stand*, loc 3985.
66. Markwald and Markwald, *Katharina von Bora*, 110.
67. Bainton, *Here I Stand*, Kindle loc 3979.
68. Markwald and Markwald, *Katharina von Bora*, 118.
69. VanDoodewaard, *Reformation Women*, 3.
70. Markwald and Markwald, *Katharina von Bora*, 124.
71. Bainton, *Here I Stand*, loc 3985.

alone."[72] It was like running a hotel. She most likely served an average of 30 people at each meal with provisions she raised or grew herself. Along with her few servants, she did their laundry and cleaned their rooms. She cultivated and prepared herbal medicines to use when nursing was required. In later life, Luther called marriage the school for character.[73] Visiting leaders of the Reformation closely observed how the Luthers' marital relationship, and their family life with their children, set the example and tone for clergy marriage and Protestant family life. Because of their example of love and mutual respect, loving companionship and collaboration became the watchwords of Christian marriage.

TWO IMPORTANT CHANGES FOR WOMEN

The marriage of clergymen affected the status of women in two important ways. First, theologically, because of the Reformers' commitment to the Scriptures, women progressed from being evil seductresses of Satan intent on luring good men away from God, to becoming godly wives undergirding and strengthening good men. This profound change in how the Church viewed women was especially evident in Luther's marriage. Luther found great comfort and companionship in his relationship and quickly came to recognize and greatly appreciate his Katie's contribution and support of his work.

Make no mistake, Luther and Calvin were still men of their age who had been steeped in a theology of women influenced by Greek misogyny. Women were still thought of as weak-natured, second-class citizens, and blamed for the fall of humankind. However, their sexuality was no longer a tool of the devil. Instead, sexual attraction within godly marriages had been shown to be the good design of God. Luther's sola Scriptura opened the way for the Word of God, instead of Greek philosophy, to define God's creation of men and women and his design for their relationship.

Second, MacHaffie observed more practically, "Married clergy in both Lutheran and Calvinist circles also meant a new sphere of activity and power for some women as 'ministers' wives."[74] The Protestant home became an important center for teaching the gospel and passing on the tenets of the reformed Christian faith. Within this community of families, the minister's home acquired a preeminent status. Luther's doctrine of the priesthood of all believers applied, theoretically, to both men and women. It was at home

---

72. MacHaffie, *Her Story*, 92.

73. Barrett, "Martin Luther on Marriage as a School for Character," n.p.

74. MacHaffie, *Her Story*, 91.

that children were taught the Bible, the catechism, and basic Christian doctrines. Mothers, as well as fathers, were accountable for imparting the faith. Luther wrote, "Most certainly father and mother are apostles, bishops, and priests to their children, for it is they who make them acquainted with the gospel."[75] Because of this, he advocated the education of both girls and boys so that they could teach the Bible in the home.

Although many modern Christians have difficulty equating the position of the minister's wife with liberation, the sixteenth century offers examples of just such circumstances. "Women who married Lutheran or Calvinist ministers often found themselves presiding over households that were the centers of cultural and intellectual activities. They offered hospitality to theologians, advice to other clergy, and bed and board to young students."[76] Toward the end of her life Katherine Zell, wife of Strasbourg pastor Matthew Zell reviewed some of her accomplishments: "I honored, cherished and sheltered many great, learned men, with care, work and expense . . . I listened to their conversation and preaching, I read their books and their letters, and they were glad to receive mine."[77] At the same time, however, clergy wives were expected to set the example for obedience and charity for the rest of the community.

Unfortunately, the depopulation of convents had regretful, negative consequences for female scholarship as the departed nuns, now wives, had little time for composition amid their household duties. Yet the larger theological shifts in attitude toward women laid the foundation for subsequent changes that are still happening today. While obedient, submissive women were no longer considered evil, the roles of women were still limited to those of motherhood and homemaking. The Reformers, though, raised these roles to the level of a vocation ordained by God. The understanding of vocation in the Roman Catholic Church was narrowly restricted to those who entered religious orders or the priesthood. In contrast, the Reformers taught that all honest works performed by all baptized Christians were vocations "as working for the Lord, not for men."[78] Thus, "a faithful wife and mother serves God in her family, and God blesses that effort and uses it to change cultures."[79]

75. Luther, *Luther on Women*, 108.

76. MacHaffie, *Her Story*, 92.

77. Chrisman, "Women and the Reformation," 157.

78. Col 3:23.

79. Crapuchettes, *Popes and Feminists*, loc 4065.

CONCLUSION

If we ask the question, "Did the Reformation of Luther and Calvin enhance or diminish the status of women in the Christian community?" we would have to answer that the immediate effects of the Reformation were mixed, but the long-term effects were world-changing. There is very little evidence that the Reformers made any conscious efforts to alter the social or political status of women, who atthat time they were still considered second-class, weaker, and inferior to men. Women were not allowed to contribute to the written body of the new reformed scholarship, nor were they allowed to teach, preach or govern in the new churches; and they lost the convent, which was the only place women could exercise such leadership and scholarly gifts.

The most significant theological impact of the Reformation for women came from recognizing godly marriage as an honorable estate designed by God for both men and women, which terminated the association of women with evil because of their reproductive functions. The transformation from, ". . .an unescapable punishment, a necessary evil, a natural temptation, a desirable calamity, a domestic danger, a delectable detriment, an evil of nature,"[80] to a godly helpmeet created in the image of God as a gift to humankind to be nourished and cherished was, in actuality, a deep and profound change both in theology and in the status of women.

This change from evil necessity to godly asset removed the stranglehold on women's voices. While the immediate effect was that a wife could advise her husband, one hundred years later, Quaker women were preaching and prophesying in congregations' meetings.[81] Two hundred years later, Methodist women were leading Bible studies, giving public testimonies, and writing religious pamphlets.[82] Three hundred years later, Presbyterians like Harriet Beecher Stowe were leading abolitionist campaigns,[83] being ordained as deacons,[84] and writing influential books on women's equality in the Spirit, such as Phoebe Palmer's, *The Promise of the Father*.[85] Four hundred years later, newspapers were reporting on Maria Woodward-Etter's nation-wide healing ministry, and Amy Semple McPherson was the

---

80. Kors and Peters, *Witchcraft in Europe*, 121.

81. MacHaffie, *Her Story*, 141.

82. MacHaffie, *Her Story*, 136.

83. Stowe, *Uncle Tom's Cabin*. Stowe's novel revealed the evils of slavery to the average citizen of the United States by personalizing the plight of the characters.

84. MacHaffie, *Her Story*, 206.

85. Palmer, *The Promise of the Father*. Palmer was one of the first to explain why, in a pneumatological context, there is gender equality

founder of the Pentecostal Foursquare denomination. Five hundred years later, women are regularly admitted to seminaries, earn Ph.D.s in theology, write for professional journals, and are ordained in many denominations. Without the scriptural basis for the godly creation of women proclaimed by the Reformers and lived out before the watching world by their wives, these hard-won victories would not have happened.

Nevertheless, two ground-breaking factors of the Reformation cracked opened the door for freedom and equality for all people—for both men and women. The first was the direct translation of the Bible from Hebrew and Greek into the common languages, making it more widely available. The second was the accompanying necessary call for education so that everyone could read and understand the Bible for themselves, thus allowing the opportunity for the Holy Spirit to speak to them and bring personal revelation of God's truth. This call was borne out in the early years of America. During the first 150 years as English colonies, children were homeschooled. Parents took seriously their role to not only teach their children how to read, write, and cipher, but to cultivate virtuous character and Christian conscience for future citizenry. The Bible was their primer and children were catechized.[86] With the expectation of being the primary teacher of the Bible in the home, this granted dignity and opened educational opportunities for all women, not just those committed to the virgin life of the convent.

The second was the idea of the priesthood of all believers. Reflecting on the women of the Reformation, Roland Bainton wrote, "The weaker vessel when filled with the Holy Spirit is powerful to pull down strongholds."[87] The idea that all Christians had the right and responsibility to tell others about the Gospel eventually paved the way for female proclamation, scholarship and teaching. While these ideas set in motion by the Reformers may have taken several centuries to bear fruit, these two factors alone—the God-given right to read the Bible for oneself, guided by the Holy Spirit, and the personal responsibility to evangelize—eventually brought about spiritual, political, and social freedom for both men and women.

BIBLIOGRAPHY

Aristotle. *Generation of Animals.* Translated by A. L Peck. Loeb Classical Library. Cambridge: Harvard University Press, 2012.

Bainton, Roland H. *Here I Stand: A Life of Martin Luther.* Nashville: Abingdon, 2013. Kindle edition.

86. Youman, "The Remarkable Role of the Bible in Early American Education," n.p.

87. Bainton, *Women of the Reformation,* 211.

Bainton, Roland H. *Women of the Reformation in France and England*. Minneapolis: Fortress, 2007.

Barrett, Matthew. "Martin Luther on Marriage as a School for Character." The Gospel Coalition, August 13, 2011. https://www.thegospelcoalition.org/article/martin-luther-on-marriage-as-a-school-of-character.

Beal, Jane. "Margery Kempe." In *British Writers Supplement*, edited by Jay Parini. Scribner Writers Series 12. New York: Scribner, 2007N.P. .

Brooten, Bernadette J. "Early Christian Women and Their Cultural Context: Issues of Method in Historical Reconstruction." In *Feminist Perspectives on Biblical Scholarship*, edited by Adela Collins, 65–91. Chico, CA: Scholars, 1985.

Burgess, Stanley M. "The Doctrine of the Holy Spirit in the Reformation Traditions." In *Dictionary of Pentecostal and Charismatic Movements*, edited by Stanley M. Burgess, Gary B. McGee, and Patrick H. Alexander. Grand Rapids: Regency Reference Library, 1988. Kindle edition.

Chrisman, Miriam U. "Women and the Reformation in Strasbourg, 1490–1530." *Archive for Reformation History* 63 (1972) 143–67.

Comblin, José. *The Holy Spirit and Liberation*. Maryknoll, NY: Orbis, 1989.

Crapuchettes, Elise. *Popes and Feminists: How the Reformation Frees Women from Feminism*. Moscow, ID: Canon, 2017. Kindle edition.

Cunningham, Loren, and David J Hamilton. *Why not Women?: A Biblical Study of Women in Missions, Ministry, and Leadership*. Seattle: YWAM, 2000. Kindle edition.

Demosthenes. "Apollodorus: Against Neaera." In *Selected Speeches of Demosthenes*, edited by Christopher Carey, translated by Robin Waterfield and Mervin R Dilts. Oxford World's Classics. Oxford: Oxford University Press, 2014.

DeRusha, Michelle, and Karen Prior. *Katharina and Martin Luther: The Radical Marriage of a Runaway Nun and a Renegade Monk*. Grand Rapids: Baker, 2017.

Felter, Elizabeth. "A History of the State's Response to Domestic Violence." In *Feminists Negotiate the State: The Politics of Domestic Violence*, edited by Cynthia Daniels, 5–20. Lanham, MD: University Press of America, 1997.

Hesiod. *Theogony and Works and Days*. Translated by Dorothea Wender. London: Penguin, 2016.

Holland, Jack. *Misogyny: The World's Oldest Prejudice*. New York: Carroll & Graf, 2006. Kindle edition.

Jolly, Karen Louise et al. *Witchcraft and Magic in Europe: The Middle Ages*. Philadelphia: University of Pennsylvania Press, 2002.

Kors, Alan Charles, and Edward Peters. *Witchcraft in Europe, 400–1700: A Documentary History*. Philadelphia: University of Pennsylvania Press, 2001.

Luther, Martin. *Luther on Women: A Sourcebook*. Edited by Susan C Karant-Nunn and Merry E. Wiesner. Cambridge: Cambridge University Press, 2003.

———. *Luther's Letters II*. Edited by Jaroslav Pelikan et al. Vol. 49. St. Louis: Concordia, 1972.

———. *Luther's Works*. Edited by Jaroslav Pelikan et al. Vol. 49. St. Louis: Concordia, 1986.

———. "The Estate of Marriage." In *Luther's Works*, edited and translated by Walter I. Brandt, 45:38–46. Philadelphia, PA: Fortress, 1962.

MacCulloch, Diarmaid. *The Reformation*, 2005. http://www.myilibrary.com?id=713497.

MacHaffie, Barbara J. *Her Story: Women in Christian Tradition*. Philadelphia: Fortress, 1986.

Markwald, Rudolf, and Marilynn Markwald. *Katharina von Bora: A Reformation Life*. St. Louis: Concordia, 2004.

Metaxas, Eric. *Martin Luther: The Man Who Rediscovered God and Changed the World*. New York: Viking, 2017.

Mills, Kenneth, and Anthony Grafton. *Conversion: Old Worlds and New*. Rochester, NY: University Rochester Press, 2003.

Oberman, Heiko A. *Luther: Man between God and the Devil*. Translated by Eileen Walliser-Schwarzbart. New Haven: Yale University Press, 2006.

Ozment, Steven. *When Fathers Ruled: Family Life in Reformation Europe*. Cambridge: Harvard University Press, 1983.

Palmer, Phoebe. *The Promise of the Father Or, A Neglected Specialty of the Last Days, Addressed to the Clergy and Laity of All Christian Communities*. 1859. Reprint, Eugene, OR: Wipf & Stock, 2015.

Prenter, Regin. *Spiritus Creator*. Translated by John M. Jensen. 1953. Reprint, Eugene, OR: Wipf & Stock, 2001.

Spalding, Matthew, ed. "The Declaration of Independence and the Constitution of the United States." The Heritage Foundation, 2010.

Stegemann, Wolfgang. "Paul and the Sexual Mentality of His World." *Biblical Theology Bulletin* 23 (1993) 161–68.

Stowe, Harriet Beecher. *Uncle Tom's Cabin*. New York: McCann, 1851.

Tertullian. "On the Apparel of Women." In *Ante-Nicene Fathers: The Writings of the Fathers Down to A.D. 325*, edited by Alexander Roberts et al. Translated by S. Thelwall. Edinburgh: T. & T. Clark, 1995. Kindle edition.

Tucker, Ruth A. *Katie Luther, First Lady of the Reformation: The Unconventional Life of Katharina von Bora*. Grand Rapids: Zondervan, 2017.

VanDoodewaard, Rebecca. *Reformation Women: Sixteenth-Century Figures Who Shaped Christianity's Rebirth*. Grand Rapids: Reformation Heritage Books, 2017.

Wenham, Gordon John. *Genesis 1–15*. Word Biblical Commentary 1. Grand Rapids: Zondervan, 2014.

Witherington, Ben, III. "The Most Dangerous Thing Luther Did." Christian History | Learn the History of Christianity & the Church, October 2017. /history/2017/October/most-dangerous-thing-luther-did.html.

Woodford, Charlotte. *Nuns as Historians in Early Modern Germany*. Oxford: Clarendon, 2005.

Xenophon. "Within the Home." In *The Greek Reader*. Translated by Arthur L Whall. New York: Duell, Sloan & Pearce, 1950.

Youman, Elizabeth. "The Remarkable Role of the Bible in Early American Education." Christian Education. Disciple Nations Alliance. https://www.disciplenations.org/. . ./The-Remarkable-Role-of-the-Bible-in-Early-American-Education.

PART TWO

The Legacy of John Calvin

7

John Calvin and the Holy Spirit
Pneumatological Union with Christ

ANDREW SNYDER

INTRODUCTION

ALTHOUGH THE PROTESTANT REFORMATION was by no means a homogenous movement, its central *dynamis* entailed a rejection of Semipelagian tendencies in favor of an essentially theocentric faith based upon the written Word of God. With a repudiation of supposed anthropic righteousness, leading figures such as Luther and Calvin emphasized that it is God who saves and sinful man who is saved, for it is God alone who plays the active role in salvation. As Christ did not die to potentially to save sinners, but to actually save sinners, the Holy Spirit is said definitively to unite the elect unto Christ, thereby guaranteeing that the gospel benefits of Christ are rightly administered in accordance with gracious providence. This doctrine is clearly taught by the primary leaders of the Reformation, but it is demonstrably treated with the greatest scrutiny by John Calvin, who has often been aptly dubbed the theologian of the Reformation. Although Calvin maintains a doctrine of *sola scriptura*, his core theological framework is distinctly and intentionally Augustinian, as even a cursory reading of the *Institutes of Christian Religion* will demonstrate. With Augustine, Calvin maintains a fundamentally Trinitarian soteriology, with the Holy Spirit operating as the bond of love between the Father and Son in intra-Trinitarian fellowship as well as between the Christian and Christ the Mediator, thereby bringing the Christian into this eternal fellowship. Despite recent interest in doctrines of *theōsis*, however, this Creator-creature fellowship ought not to entail fellowship in essence, but rather fellowship in society, volition, and felicity through union with Christ the Mediator. As this is said to be the *telos* of genuine humanity, as created in the divine image, the means by which sinners might join the Trinitarian fellowship play a central role in Calvin's theology. Thus, the person and work of the Holy Spirit, as the bond of love uniting sinners to God through Christ, is paramount for Calvin. As the Holy Spirit is considered such a bond, Calvin's pneumatology cannot be separated from his Christology or soteriology. This chapter will demonstrate that Calvin's theology was not, at its core, an innovation, but rather a return to late Augustinianism. It will present Augustine's theology of a pneumatologically-driven soteriology as the foundation for Calvin's theology, which thereby served as a renewal of a profoundly theocentric, pneumatologically-driven faith.

This chapter will demonstrate that Calvin does not teach a union between the elect and Christ's divine nature, but rather a union between the elect and Christ as the second Adam—a union which is established and maintained by the Holy Spirit. Some recent scholars, such as Carl Mosser, have suggested that Calvin taught a doctrine of *theōsis*, as though Christ's divinity was communicated to his human nature and, consequently, to the elect as well. Although language closely resembling this can certainly be found in patristic writings, Calvin is careful to ensure that he is in harmony with the Chalcedonian teaching that Christ's divine and human natures remain distinct while being united in his one person. Furthermore, he insists on maintaining that the gospel benefits of Christ's obedience are only apprehended through a faith that is impossible for depraved humans to produce. Therefore, the same God who created and ordered the cosmos must create and order new life in the Christian, which then manifests itself as faith. Closely following Augustine, Calvin teaches that the Holy Spirit is the bond of love in the Trinitarian fellowship that also binds the elect to Christ. This bond is established by the Father through the Spirit in Christ by grace alone, and not according to human merits. Because of Calvin's great debt to Augustine, this chapter will begin by exploring Augustine's moral ontology and Trinitarianism with a particular focus on his pneumatological soteriology. This section will demonstrate that Augustine did not teach a substantial union between the elect and Christ's divinity, but instead references a reformed humanity through pneumatological union with Christ in his earned righteousness as a man. It will next demonstrate that Calvin relies heavily on these Augustinian themes to form his soteriology and sacramentology, which centrally entails a union between the elect and Christ the Mediator, a role which necessitates his divinity but is earned through his humanity.

THE INFLUENCE OF AUGUSTINE

Foundational to Augustine's doctrine of divine election is his moral ontology and related understanding of grace. He maintains that God, as the only ontologically independent being and source of all that is, is the only pure reality. As all existence is from God, whatever exists is good, as he writes in the *City of God*, "No nature is contrary to God; but a perversion, being evil, is contrary to good."[1] Thus evil, while not being dismissed as an illusion, is not a substantial entity, but rather a pulling away from goodness. Inasmuch as Man is oriented unto God, therefore, he shines with the light of being; and inasmuch as he pulls away from God and is directed unto lesser goods, he is darkened by the void that is identified as evil. Augustine thusly describes the Fall, writing, "This then is the original evil: man regards himself as his own light, and turns away from that light which would make man himself a light if he would set his heart on it."[2] Man's evil, therefore, is in volitional posturing away from God, the only Good. Being deprived of all goodness, the soul is thereby incapable of attaining goodness apart from an act of recreation. He writes, "For the evil of the soul, its own will takes the initiative; but for its good, the will of its Creator makes the first move, whether to make the soul which did not yet exist, or to recreate it when it had perished through its fall."[3] Therefore, Augustine maintains that the sinfulness of Man, by which he means the lack of spiritual being, requires that God bring into being that which is not, i.e., a soul in fellowship with God through theocentric orientation.

Augustine's solution to the apparent problem of theodicy, i.e., the question as to how an omnipotent and omnibenevolent God and evil could exist simultaneously, is that evil does not, in fact, exist but is instead an ontological negation that brings serious consequences. This "privation theory" of evil provides it with a conceptual framework relative to a substantial standard. Goodness is tied to ontological reality and, therefore, the concept of goodness can have meaning apart from evil; however, evil is a privation and therefore, can only have meaning in a negative relation to goodness. This deviation from reality and goodness does not indicate that evil is a chimera,

---

1. Augustine, *City of God*, Book XII, 474.
2. Augustine, *City of God*, Book XIV, 573.
3. Augustine, *City of God*, Book XIII, 523.

i.e., a concept that lacks existential substantiation, for a chimera was never an integral component of reality. Evil, however, refers to the negation of ontologically significant goodness, which is ultimately sourced in God, who is the only pure and independent substance. Evil therefore has serious repercussions, even as the negation of sustenance results in starvation. Augustine explains this as follows: "Since we have already learned that sin is not a substance, let us consider whether abstinence from food is also not a substance. . . . But to abstain from food is not a substance—yet nevertheless if we abstain entirely from food, the substance of our body languishes."[4] Just as the lack of sustenance leads to bodily languishing, so too does the lack of spiritual sustenance lead to spiritual languishing.

As God is the only independent substance and, as is particularly significant for the current discussion, and the sole basis for a living human soul, the negating effect of sin results in a negation of the soul, or at the very least a negation of the soul's proper faculties which are necessary to look unto God. Augustine writes, "For, as I have already said, what can those who have been deprived of the light of justice and thereby plunged into darkness produce except all those works of darkness which I have noted, until it is said to them, and they obey the command, 'Rise, you that sleep, and arise from the dead, and Christ shall enlighten you?"[5] Apart from a resubstantiation of spiritual life from the supreme substance and source of all substance, the ontologically deficient soul is only capable of being ontologically deficient and thereby unable to fulfill the purpose for which it was created. To comprehend Augustine's ontological soteriology, one must begin with the nature of God as the foundation for both being and goodness.

For Augustine, the *telos* of genuine humanity, bearing the image of God, is to reflect upon the source of that image, even as God eternally reflects upon himself in the Trinitarian relationship. In keeping with Nicene orthodoxy, Augustine presents the Trinity as Father, Spirit, Son, "not three gods but one God; although indeed the Father has begotten the Son, and therefore he who is the Father is not the Son; and the Son is begotten by the Father, and therefore he who is the Son is not the Father; and the Holy Spirit is neither the Father nor the Son . . .[6] Thus, Augustine maintains plurality and unity in the Godhead, i.e., that there is relational differentiation amongst the divine persons, yet they are indeed *homousious*. The Son is eternally begotten of the Father and, due to this "eternal" qualification, is indeed a participant in the ontological independence of the Father. The Son,

4. Augustine, *Four Anti-Pelagian Writings*, "On Nature and Grace," 37.
5. Augustine, *Four Anti-Pelagian Writings*, "On Nature and Grace," 40.
6. Augustine, *De Trinitate*, Book I, 70.

who is the very form of God, took the form of man so that he might serve as Man's mediator and, therefore, Augustine writes, "The Son of God is God the Father's equal by nature, by condition his inferior."[7] In that he took the form of a servant through the incarnation, the Son is inferior to the Father, but, as maintaining the form of God, the Son is equal to the Father and, therefore, Augustine continues, "who can fail to see that in the form of God he too is greater than himself and in the form of a servant he is less than himself? And so it is not without reason that scripture says both; that the Son is equal to the Father and the Father is greater than the Son."[8] Augustine continues his Trinitarian doctrine in the Latin tradition by stating, "Nor is the Spirit of each separable from this unity, the Father's Spirit, that is, and the Son's, the Holy Spirit which is given the proper name of the Spirit of truth, which this world cannot receive."[9]

The Spirit, therefore, while maintained as a distinct person, is viewed as a type of binding relationship between the Father and Son. Augustine explains this concept as follows: "And if the charity by which the Father loves the Son and the Son loves the Father inexpressibly shows forth the communion of them both, what is more suitable than that he who is the common Spirit of them both should be distinctively called charity?"[10] This identification of the Holy Spirit with love is of great significance for the Augustinian economy of salvation.

Augustine teaches that God does not merely love the saint in a manner that would be implied through a lover-beloved analog in human relationships, but that God *is himself love* and, therefore, to give love is to give himself. He writes, "As then holy scripture proclaims that charity is God, and as it is from God and causes us to abide in God and him in us, and as we know this because he has given us of his Spirit, this Spirit of his is God's charity."[11] In his *Historical Theology,* Alister McGrath describes the implications of this doctrine, writing, "God already exists in the kind of relation to which he wishes to bring us. And just as the Spirit is the bond of union between God and the believer, so the Spirit exercises a comparable role within the Trinity, binding the persons together."[12] Just as it is the Spirit that binds together the Father and the Son, so too is the Spirit said to bind the elect to Christ and thereby grant access to the divine fellowship. Augustine teaches that this is

---

7. Augustine, *De Trinitate*, Book I, 77.

8. Augustine, *De Trinitate*, Book I, 77.

9. Augustine, *De Trinitate*, Book XV, 429.

10. Augustine, *De Trinitate,* Book XV, 429.

11. Augustine, *De Trinitate,* Book XV, 429.

12. McGrath, *Historical Theology,* 67.

indeed the *telos* of redeemed humanity: "to enjoy God the three in whose image we were made."[13]

There have been many attempts to utilize Augustine's participatory soteriological language to demonstrate a thoroughgoing theology of *theōsis*, i.e., a substantial divinization of the elect. In his article, "You Made Us for Yourself": Creation in St. Augustine's Confessions," Jared Ortiz writes, "For Augustine—to make the point as stark as possible—creation reveals the truth about who God is, who human beings are, and also reveals God's intention to deify humanity through the incarnation by participation in the sacraments of the church."[14] Such a position, however, is in stark contrast to Augustine's Christology. Although operating shortly before Chalcedon, Augustine exhibits sound Chalcedonian theology concerning the one Christ who fully and distinctly remained God while fully and distinctly taking the form of man. So he evidences in a number of his teachings, such as in *De Trinitate,* where he writes. "I say that the very Word of God was made flesh, that is, was made man, without however being turned or changed into that which he was made; that he was of course so made that you would have there not only the Word of God and the flesh of man but also the rational soul of man as well.[15] Thus Augustine teaches a separation between the two natures of Christ, thereby indicating that the divinity he possesses as the Word of God is not transmitted to the human nature he assumed. If even Christ's human nature is distinct from his divine nature, though united in his one person, there is no reason to maintain that he taught a divinization of the elect's human nature.

Augustine makes it clear that it is to Christ's human nature that the elect are united, as he writes, "But being clothed with mortal flesh, in that alone he died and in that alone he rose again; and so in that alone he harmonized with each part of us by becoming in that flesh the sacrament for the inner man and the model for the outer one."[16] As the elect are united to Christ by virtue of his human nature and his human nature is not divinized by virtue of his divine nature, the elect are not deified in essence, although they are blessed to *partake* of the divine nature, i.e., they enjoy specific blessings of divinity, such as immortality, that they receive on behalf of the vindicated man, Christ. That this fellowship is primarily one of society, volition, and felicity, rather than substance, is evident in Augustine's discussion of John 17, in which he writes of the disciples, "split as they are

13. Augustine, *De Trinitate,* Book I, 81.

14. Ortiz, *You Made Us for Yourself,* 229–34.

15. Augustine, *De Trinitate,* Book IV, 156.

16. Augustine, *De Trinitate,* Book IV, 157.

from each other by clashing wills and desires, and the uncleanness of their sins; so they are cleansed by the Mediator that they may be one in him . . . by virtue of one and the same wholly harmonious will reaching out in concert to the same ultimate happiness, and fused somehow into one spirit in the furnace of charity.[17] For Augustine, this "furnace of charity" is synonymous with "the furnace of the Holy Spirit," as he writes, "So the love which is from God and is God is distinctively the Holy Spirit; through him the charity of God is poured in our hearts, and through it the whole triad dwells in us."[18] As the Father is in the Son and the Son is in the Father and the Holy Spirit is said to proceed from the Father and the Son, the indwelling of the Holy Spirit in the elect, by which the elect are united with Christ, entails entry into full Trinitarian fellowship without conversion of ontological essence, even as the Trinitarian indwelling of Christ's human nature did not convert his ontological essence as man into a divinized essence. Thus, for Augustine and Calvin after him, the Holy Spirit is the binding personal tie of love that ushers and maintains the Christian in the bliss of Trinitarian fellowship through Christ, but never in divinized essence.

PNEUMATOLOGY, SOTERIOLOGY, AND CALVIN

As thoroughgoing Augustinianism gave way in the Church over time to an economy of salvation driven by a synergy of merit and so-called grace, mainstream medieval Christianity became increasingly Pelagian and anthropocentric, thereby giving rise to the necessity of religious renewal. In his *Justified in the Spirit*, Frank Macchia aptly comments, "In my view, the great insight behind the elevation of justification in Protestant theology was thus the attempt to return to a theocentric, or God-centered, understanding of the divine-human relationship that held at least the potential of viewing salvation principally as a possession of and participation in the divine life."[19] However, Macchia concludes that this potential was often unactualized by the reformers, as he laments that doctrines of imputed righteousness neglected what "was at the very heart and soul of justification: the gift of the Spirit in embracing the sinners and taking them into the life and *koinonia* enjoyed by the Spirit with the Father and the Son. . . . As such, the justified relationship lacked pneumatological substance and an adequately Trinitarian structure.[20] However applicable this claim may be to certain theologies,

17. Augustine, *De Trinitate*, Book IV, 165.
18. Augustine, *De Trinitate*, Book V, 425.
19. Macchia, *Justified in the Spirit*, 38.
20. Macchia, *Justified in the Spirit*, 39.

it fails to do justice to Calvin's treatment of imputed righteousness, which, at its core, entails a pneumatological bond between the Christian and Christ whereby the Christian participates in Trinitarian fellowship. Thus Calvin's pneumatologically-driven Trinitarian soteriology is at least as robust as that of Augustine, who certainly could not sustain the criticism that Macchia levies against Protestant theology.

Although Calvin does not borrow as heavily from Neoplatonic imagery as Augustine, he describes the depravity of Man in Augustinian fashion, writing in the prefatory address of his *Institutes*, "For what accords better and more aptly with faith than to acknowledge ourselves divested of all virtue that we may be clothed by God, devoid of all goodness that we may be filled by Him . . ."[21] With Augustine, Calvin thusly describes sin as an ontological deficit—that which is devoid of goodness, freedom, light, health, and strength. "In short," he continues, "the object on which all men are bent, is to keep their kingdom safe or their belly filled; not one gives even the smallest sign of sincere zeal."[22] This hamartiological analysis is nearly synonymous with that of Augustine, who writes, "This then is the original evil: man regards himself as his own light, and turns away from that light which would make man himself a light if he would set his heart on it."[23] Being severed from the goodness of God, who alone is the source of goodness, sinful humanity is incapable of utilizing true freedom, as Calvin writes, "Those who, while they profess to be the disciples of Christ, still seek for free-will in man, notwithstanding of his being lost and drowned in spiritual destruction, labour under manifold delusion, making a heterogeneous mixture of inspired doctrine and philosophical opinions, and so erring as to both."[24] The sinner, lost in darkness, must experience a renewal of the soul in order to set his gaze upon God in pneumatologically vivifying faith. Calvin explains this further, writing, "Hence it follows, that he is now an exile from the kingdom of God, so that all things which pertain to the blessed life of the soul are extinguished in him until he recover them by the grace of regeneration.[25] Salvation, therefore, is not to be found in a mere legal *declaration* of imputed righteousness, but through God's personal indwelling in the sinner, which restores the freedom of life unto fellowship with God. According to Calvin, righteousness is not an abstract label that the Christian is given, but is the merit of Christ himself, which is imputed to

21. Calvin, *Institutes*, Prefatory Address, 6.
22. Calvin, *Institutes*, Prefatory Address, 7–8.
23. Augustine, *City of God*, Book XIV, 573.
24. Calvin, *Institutes*, Book I, 169.
25. Calvin, *Institutes*, Book II, 233.

the Christian only because Christ himself is imputed to the Christian in a mysterious union through the Holy Spirit.

Calvin's soteriology certainly grants a foundational role to the doctrine of imputed righteousness through faith in Christ; however, critics such as Macchia would do well to recognize the nature and means of this imputation as something far more significant than a mere legal declaration—though such a declaration is indeed vital. Calvin explains his most fundamental doctrine of justification as "the acceptance with which God receives us into his favour as if we were righteous; and we say that this justification consists in the forgiveness of sins and the imputation of the righteousness of Christ."[26] Although this explanation certainly does imply a legally credited righteousness, closer investigation reveals that Calvin considered the grounds for this imputation of righteousness to be the participation of the Christian in Christ. Describing the bond between the Christian and Christ as a "mystical union," he writes, "Hence we do not view him as at a distance and without us, but as we have put him on, and been ingrafted into his body, he deigns to make us one with himself and, therefore, we glory in having a fellowship of righteousness with him.[27] Therefore, for Calvin, imputed righteousness is not a mere extrinsic label, but the very union of the Christian with Christ. Because it is the Holy Spirit, the bond of love, who establishes this union, an understanding of Calvin's Christological soteriology necessitates an understanding of his pneumatology.

The incarnation, obedience, death, and resurrection of Christ do not benefit any sinner unless he is rendered a beneficiary of the promises of the gospel. Calvin thus writes, in keeping with Augustinian Trinitarianism, "So long as Christ is separated from us we have no benefit from him. We must be engrafted in him like branches in the vine. Hence the Creed, after treating of Christ, proceeds in its third article, *I believe in the Holy Spirit*—the Holy Spirit being the bond of union between us and Christ."[28] As the love of God, both as originating in God and as directed toward God, the Holy Spirit is the gift that binds the elect to Christ. Again, he writes, "The whole comes to this, that Christ, when he produces faith in us by the agency of his Spirit, at the same time ingrafts us into his body, that we may become partakers of all blessings."[29] Of course, by "all blessings," Calvin does not mean all blessings that are befitting of the divine Word, but rather those that are befitting of Christ the Mediator. The Augustinian insistence that this union is with

26. Calvin, *Institutes*, Book III, 38.
27. Calvin, *Institutes*, Book III, 38.
28. Calvin, *Institutes*, Method & Arrangement. 28–29.
29. Calvin, *Institutes*, Book III, 501.

Christ's human nature alone has already been demonstrated, and Calvin not only inherits this doctrine but is very careful to emphasize its significance for the Christian gospel.

As Calvin's doctrine of the Holy Spirit provides an entryway into his Trinitarian soteriology via the person and life of Christ, his pneumatology must be understood in connection to his Christology, lest unmerited arguments for Calvinist *theōsis* arise, as has been the tendency in recent years. In his article, "The Greatest Possible Blessing: Calvin and Deification," Carl Mosser attributes the lack of Calvinist connections to *theōsis* to simple neglect from Western Christianity that was perhaps amplified by Harnack's criticisms of supposed Hellenization. Mosser argues for an interpretation of Calvin in which "Christ unites believers to God because in his person God and humanity are already united. Significantly, this distinction is the very heart of patristic and Orthodox notions of deification. In patristic terms, individual believers can be deified because the incarnation of Christ deified human nature."[30] Thus, Mosser suggests, Christ's human nature participated in the divinity of his divine nature, and, consequently, Christians may be deified through this connection. However, such an argument fails to grasp Calvin's insistence upon strict Chalcedonian and Augustinian Christology, which maintains that Christ's divine and human natures remained distinct. Responding to Mosser, Todd Billings writes in his article, "United to God through Christ: Assessing Calvin on the Question of Deification," that "Calvin teaches deification of a particular sort. Drawing upon the language of participation, ingrafting, and adoption in select Pauline and Johannine passages, Calvin teaches the participation of humanity in the Triune God, affirming the differentiated union of humanity with God in creation and redemption."[31] Although Billings rejects Mosser's interpretation of Calvin as teaching a union of the elect with Christ's divinity unto an undifferentiated humanity, he does insist that Calvin teaches that a kind of participation with Christ is an essential component of spiritual formation. He indicates this belief as he comments on Calvin's concepts of justification and sanctification, writing, "While justification always and necessarily leads to real sanctification, the former is forensic and the latter involves a moral transformation of the believer by the Spirit. In contrast to Osiander, forensic notions of pardon are not opposed to the themes of indwelling and participation in Calvin."[32] With this dichotomy, Billings teaches that justification is a legal declaration, as opposed to sanctification, which is a spiritual transformation.

30. Mosser, "The Greatest Possible Blessing," 46.
31. Billings, "United to God through Christ," 316–317.
32. Billings, "United to God through Christ," 321.

Although Billings argues for a participatory Calvinist doctrine of sanctification, his forensic/transformation dichotomy underemphasizes Calvin's participatory doctrine of justification. As has already been demonstrated, the basis for Calvin's forensic justification is participation in Christ the Mediator as established through the binding role of the Holy Spirit. Sanctification, therefore, is the outworking of the already present reality of spiritual transformation. Michael Horton indicates this simultaneous distinction and fundamental union between Calvin's doctrines of justification and sanctification, writing, "All of those who are justified are united to Christ and become fruit-bearing branches. One never gains the sense that Calvin struggles with a choice between the forensic and mystical, legal and organic, declarative and transformative aspects of God's evangelical word spoken in Christ. One never receives Christ's gifts apart from receiving Christ himself."[33] In "The Question of Deification in the theology of John Calvin," Sung Park further argues that it is participation with Christ's humanity that provides the means of justification, writing, "This imputed righteousness of Christ in the believers' justification is not the divine essential righteousness as Osiander teaches. Instead, it is a righteousness he acquired by his obedience in his humanity to the Father through his whole life from his birth to death."[34] Park further demonstrates Calvin's rejection of a *theōsis* soteriology, writing, "And it follows from Calvin's doctrine of justification that for him, the blessing conferred on the believers in their union with Christ is that which Christ acquired through his salvific work in his humanity, not that which peculiarly belongs to Christ's divinity."[35] Thus Park affirms that Calvin does understand the epitome of salvation to entail fellowship in the Trinity; however, he also recognizes that this is not an ontological union between humanity and divinity, but rather a union between redeemed humanity and Christ as the second Adam, by which humanity is granted access to the Trinitarian fellowship.

Park's understanding of Calvin's thought is readily demonstrated by observing his polemics against Osiander, who maintained that the redeemed acquire the righteousness that is Christ's by virtue of his inherent divinity. While attempting to avoid both Eutychian and Nestorian heresies, Calvin explains his Christological soteriology, writing, "For although Christ could neither purify our souls by his own blood, nor . . . in short, perform the office of priest, unless he had been very God . . . it is however certain that he performed all these things in his human nature. If it is asked, in what way

33. Horton, "Union and Communion," 400.
34. Park, "The Question of Deification," 3.
35. Park, "The Question of Deification," 4.

are we justified? Paul answers, 'by the obedience of Christ.'[36] Thus, while not dividing Christ into two persons, Calvin maintains that it is Christ the man to whom the elect are ingrafted and, as such, it is Christ the man who provides the righteousness of obedience. Therefore, Park concludes, "It can be reasonably concluded that as far as *theōsis* is construed as the believers' participation in the intrinsic divine life, mediated by Christ's humanity in their union with Christ, it is hard to hold that Calvin teaches *theōsis*.[37]

Calvin's pneumatology and Christology are on clear display in his treatment of the sacraments, and most clearly so in his treatment of the Eucharist. Calvin taught that "the sacraments are truly termed evidences of divine grace, and, as it were, seals of the goodwill which he entertains toward us. They, by sealing it to us, sustain, nourish, confirm, and increase our faith."[38] Grace is mediated to the believer through Spirit-driven faith in Christ and his gospel, but the sacraments are said to act as pillars which aid in the sustaining of faith. As symbols, they demonstrate the blessings received by this faith, but they also have a genuine reality behind them as the believer on pilgrimage in this world receives a foretaste of his destination, which is perfect Trinitarian fellowship through union with Christ. As the sacrament is considered to be inseparable from the promises of the gospel, and the promises of the gospel are only actualized through faith which is produced by pneumatological union with Christ, Calvin maintains that sacraments are only truly received by this faith. The Eucharist, therefore, is a means by which the Holy Spirit existentially confirms the partially realized eschatology of the elect's union with Christ in his death and resurrection.

As Richard Topping indicates in his article, "Help My Unbelief: John Calvin on the sacraments", Calvin "decries the mumbling formulas that accompanied the sacramental practice he encountered during his time," which is because Calvin insists that the sacraments are inextricably connected with faith and, consequently, are only received if the partaker is doing so in response to the declared Gospel. Therefore, Topping continues, "For Calvin, when and where the sacrament is celebrated, it should always be accompanied by preaching and the declaration of the sacramental promise attached to the sign made by the minister in a clear voice."[39] Acquiring support for this position, Calvin writes, "Augustine, when intending to intimate this, said that the efficacy of the word is produced in the sacrament, not because

---

36. Calvin, *Institutes,* Book III, 44.
37. Park, "The Question of Deification," 4.
38. Calvin, *Institutes*, Book IV, 332.
39. Topping, "Help My Unbelief," 38.

it is spoken, but because it is believed."[40] Thus, as the sacrament is connected to the gospel, the elements are not made sacramental through ceremony, but by the Spirit working through faith. However, the same sacrament that requires faith to be beneficial is also the instituted means by which the Christian's fragile faith is strengthened. "It's as though God offers help for faith in the sacraments that we are not able to receive because of our lack of it."[41] Topping explains this paradox, writing, "Faith is conceived, nourished, and sustained by the inward illumination of the Holy Spirit. The seed of the Word is made to flourish by the Spirit so that the sacraments allure us toward Christ and his benefits truly offered are received."[42] Thus the apparent problem of the sacraments requiring what they provide is solved in the same manner as the problem of the unregenerate sinner needing faith in order to be regenerated: the Holy Spirit first provides the union with Christ that is required for the redeemed to act unto union with Christ.

Sue Rozeboom argues that Calvin's understanding of the sacraments, and the Eucharist in particular, results from his assimilation of orthodox Trinitarianism and patristic writings on the sacraments, most notably those of Augustine. Rozeboom writes, "Calvin's emphasis on the role of the Holy Spirit with regard to believers' participation in the Lord's Supper is a sacramental-theological result of his assimilation of his expressed understanding of the doctrine of the Trinity, and his assimilation of the thought of his contemporaries and his predecessors." She notes that two explicit expressions of Calvin's Eucharistic pneumatology are prominent in the 1536 and 1539 editions of the *Institutes*. She writes, "The first—concerning the Spirit as 'the bond' who unites believers to Christ and thus affords for them the true, spiritual communication of Christ's true body and true blood—appears already in 1536 in Calvin's second treatment of the sacrament."[43] This language of the Spirit acting as the bond between the elect and Christ clearly demonstrates a harkening to the participatory pneumatological language of Augustine. The second prominent feature of Calvin's Eucharistic pneumatology that Rozeboom notes is the believer's participation in the body and blood of Christ of Christ, i.e., in Christ's humanity as the means of salvation. She continues, "The second concerns "the *virtus* of the Spirit," a phrase Calvin first employs in the 1539 *Institutio* concerning the *communicatio* and even the *exhibitio* of Christ's body and blood in the Sacrament. . . . He declares that Christ truly feeds his people with his own body, and that Christ

---

40. Calvin, *Institutes,* Book IV, 495.
41. Topping, "Help My Unbelief," 38.
42. Topping, "Help My Unbelief," 38.
43. Rozeboom, "The Provenance," 3.

bestows this communion upon them by the power of his Spirit.[44] These two prominent emphases of Calvin's Eucharistic theology both confirm the notion that he emphasizes true union with Christ the Mediator through the Holy Spirit, but not ontological participation in the eternal Word. As has been indicated, it is the acquired righteousness of Christ that provides the remedy for sinner's lost righteousness in Adam and, consequently, it is confirmation of this righteousness that sustains the elect.

The necessity of the Holy Spirit's binding role in the Eucharist is indicated as Calvin rejects that the elements themselves could in any sense be substantially transformed into Christ on Christological grounds, arguing, "As we cannot at all doubt that it (Christ's flesh) is bounded according to the invariable rule in the human body, and is contained in heaven, where it was once received, and will remain till it return to judgment, so we deem it altogether unlawful to bring it back under these corruptible elements, or to imagine it ever present."[45] If the heart of Christian salvation were to be found in essential unity with the divine and omnipresent Word, spatial concerns would be absurd. However, as the Eucharist entails communion with that which provides justification, i.e., the human righteousness of Christ, and humanity is spatially confined, the man Christ Jesus may not both be in heaven and the elements. For this reason, Horton demonstrates the necessary pneumatological emphasis in Calvin's Eucharistic understanding, as he writes, "The Spirit's mediation of Christ's person and work, not an immediate participation in the divine essence, is a critical aspect of his account. We are one with the Son of God; not because he conveys his substance to us, but because, by the power of the Spirit, he imparts to us his life and all the blessings which he has received from the Father."[46] It is Christ's received blessings, received as an award for his obedience, that are therefore imparted to the Christian by the Spirit. Thus Christ is not substantially united to the elements, but the Holy Spirit, the bond of love, unites the faithful to Christ the second Adam, who is in heaven. Through this spiritual eating, Calvin explains that the following occurs: "The Spirit truly unites things separated by space. That sacred communion of flesh and blood by which Christ transfuses his life into us . . . he testifies and seals in the Supper, and that not by presenting a vain or empty sign, but by their exerting an efficacy of the Spirit by which he fulfills what he promises."[47] Therefore, union with Christ through faith, which the sacraments demonstrate and confirm, is

---

44. Rozeboom, "The Provenance," 4.

45. Calvin, *Institutes*, Book IV, 565.

46. Horton, "Union and Communion," 400.

47. Calvin, *Institutes*, Book IV, 563.

obtained through the bonding role of the Holy Spirit that enables the believer to participate in the acquired righteousness of Christ as he sits at the right hand of the Father.

CONCLUSION

Following Augustine's moral ontology and Trinitarian soteriology, Calvin maintains that human sinfulness consists of a volitional turning away from God and that salvation consists of God bringing humanity into the inter-Trinitarian fellowship of society, volition, and felicity that God enjoys. As humanity turned away from the light of God, its members became lost in darkness until the Holy Spirit ontologically renewed them unto faith in Christ, who is the Word of God by eternal nature and who as man became the Mediator for humans. As the elect are ingrafted not into the essential righteousness of Christ, but rather into the acquired righteousness of Christ through the Holy Spirit, they are justified before God and thereby enter into the Trinitarian fellowship in their teleological fulfillment as God's image-bearers. Thus Calvin's use of an essentially Augustinian framework advances a legacy of pneumatological-driven soteriology in keeping with Christ's explicit pneumatological teaching of John 14:6: "He will glorify me, for he will take what is mine and declare it to you" (ESV).

BIBLIOGRAPHY

Augustine. *Concerning the City of God. Against the Pagans.* Translated by Henry Bettenson. 1972. Reprint, London: Penguin, 1984.

———. "On Nature and Grace." In *Four Anti-Pelagian Writings.* Translated by John A. Mourant and William J. Collinge. Washington, DC: Catholic University of America Press, 1992.

———. *De Trinitate.* Edited by John Rotelle. Translated by Edmund Hill. Brooklyn: New City Press, 2012.

Billings, J. Todd. "United to God through Christ: Assessing Calvin on the Question of Deification." *Harvard Theological Review* 98 (2005) 315–34.

Calvin, John. *Institutes of the Christian Religion.* Translated by Henry Beveridge. Grand Rapids: Eerdmans, 1959.

———. "Method and Arrangement." In *Institutes of the Christian Religion.* Translated by Henry Beveridge. Grand Rapids: Eerdmans, 1959.

———. "Prefatory Address." In *Institutes of the Christian Religion.* Translated by Henry Beveridge. Grand Rapids: Eerdmans, 1959.

Horton, Michael. "Union and Communion: Calvin's Theology of Word and Sacrament." *International Journal of Systematic Theology* 11 (2009) 398–414.

Macchia, Frank D. *Justified in the Spirit: Creation, Redemption, and the Triune God.* Pentecostal Manifestos. Grand Rapids: Eerdmans, 2010.

McGrath, Alister E. "The Patristic Period." In *Historical Theology: An Introduction to the History of Christian Thought*. Oxford: Blackwell, 1998.

Mosser, Carl. "The Greatest Possible Blessing: Calvin and Deification." *Scottish Journal of Theology* 55 (2002) 36–57.

Ortiz, Jared. "Conclusion: Creation in the Confessions." In *You Made Us for Yourself: Creation in St. Augustine's Confessions*. Minneapolis: Fortress, 2016.

Park, Sung W. "The Question of Deification in the Theology of John Calvin." *Verbum et Ecclesia* 38 (2017) 1–5.

Persons, Claude O'Shedrick, Jr. "The Deified Citizens of 'The City of God': How Augustine Applies the Patristic Doctrine of *Theōsis* to the Citizens of 'The City of God.'" PhD diss., Southeastern Baptist Theological Seminary, 2010.

Rozeboom, Sue A. "The Provenance of John Calvin's Emphasis on the Role of the Holy Spirit Regarding the Sacrament of the Lord's Supper." PhD diss., University of Notre Dame, 2011.

Topping, Richard. "Help My Unbelief." *The Presbyterian Record* 133 (2009) 37–38.

8

The Influence of John Calvin's Pneumatology on Karl Barth

David M. Barbee

INTRODUCTION

B. B. WARFIELD ONCE described John Calvin as "the theologian of the Holy Spirit."[1] Modern scholars have generally affirmed this assessment. Similarly, Karl Barth has been credited as one of the progenitors of a modern resurgence of Trinitarian theology. In thinking about the Holy Spirit and the legacy of the Protestant Reformation, it seems to make some sense to set these two luminary figures, one from the sixteenth century and one from the twentieth, into dialogue on a doctrinal topic of obvious importance. Barth's reverence for and research into Calvin's theology makes such a dialogue particularly germane. According to Fred Klempa, there "are 297 references to Calvin in the thirteen volumes of the *Church Dogmatics*, exceeded only by 320 references to Luther."[2] Strangely, though several studies seek to evaluate the relationship between Calvin and Barth on an array of topics, pneumatology is a topic that has not brought much attention. There are definite points of contact where Barth actively draws upon Calvin's ideas or offers views similar to those of Calvin, as well as points of contrast where

1. Warfield, "Calvin as Theologian," 484.
2. Klempa, "Barth as Scholar and Interpreter of Calvin," 32.

Barth develops his unique pneumatological interpretation. Their respective historical contexts demanded that both Calvin and Barth had to differentiate the work of the Holy Spirit from human nature. Barth, attempting to construct a pneumatologically oriented theological system, finds resources for this task in Calvin—yet develops a pneumatology that often places him at a distance from Calvin. A closer reading of select pneumatological themes in Calvin and Barth will show that while there appear to be similarities in many instances, there are also substantial differences. Such an evaluation will serve to map out the continued expression of Reformation theology to the present day, as well as shed some light on an area in need of scholarly attention.

Calvin's context itself was shaped somewhat by the dogmatic controversies of the early modern era. The doctrine of the Holy Spirit was not a topic of direct polemical exchange between Roman Catholics and Protestants during the era of the Reformation. However, that does not mean that there were no differences between late medieval scholastics and the early generations of Protestant reformers. Thomas Aquinas, for instance, early in the *Summa Theologiae*, handles the person of the Holy Spirit initially in the context of the *filioque* controversy, presenting a defense of the Latin position.[3] In question 37 of the prima pars, Aquinas affirms the traditional Augustinian understanding of the Holy Spirit as the loving bond between the Father and Son.[4] The final question on the Holy Spirit in the prima pars identifies the Holy Spirit as a gift, again borrowing from Augustine. This is important because Aquinas observes that once the Spirit has been given, "he then becomes the Spirit of someone or the One Given to someone."[5] When Aquinas turns to clarify what precisely is given by the Holy Spirit, he distinguishes the gifts of the Spirit from virtue, which is conceived of as a power which moves an object toward perfection, but still viewed them as "*habitus* by which man is perfected so as to obey the Holy Spirit readily" which are also necessary for salvation.[6] To be clear, Aquinas maintains that the Holy Spirit is given gratuitously, as is fitting with the nature of love.[7] This hinders the charge of Pelagianism, if one were to accuse Aquinas, but, with Gabriel Biel, there is a notable change in the order of salvation. For Biel, the doctrine of *facere quod in se est* ("do what is in oneself") presupposes a created habit of grace in a person that allows one to merit further grace in

---

3. Aquinas, *Summa Theologiae*, I q. 36. a. 2, vol. 7, 59–65.

4. Aquinas, *Summa Theologiae*, I. q. 37 a. 2, vol. 7, 73–77.

5. Aquinas, *Summa Theologiae*, I. q. 38 a. 2, vol. 7, 97.

6. Aquinas, *Summa Theologiae*, I-II. q. 68 a. 3, vol. 24, 19.

7. Aquinas, *Summa Theologiae*, I. q. 38 a. 2, vol. 7, 95.

the form of the reception of uncreated grace. "Uncreated grace as such is the Holy Spirit," Heiko Oberman observes, "which is never given without simultaneous infusion of the *gratia gratum faciens*, after the sinner has succeeded in *facere quod in se est*."[8]

It is the seeming Pelagianism that triggers the Protestant Reformation along with the subsequent reformulation of doctrine. Much scholarly effort has been invested in trying to capture the organizing structure of Calvin's theology as articulated in the *Institutes*. Charles Partee surveys four different expository models. The first sees the *Institutes* as closely modeled after the Apostles' Creed. Partee finds this interpretation unconvincing, amongst other reasons, precisely because Calvin did not identify the Holy Spirit as the content of book three.[9] Edward Dowey represents the second model. Dowey finds Calvin's epistemological statement regarding the *duplex cognitio dei* as programmatic for all of the *Institutes*. He contends that this twofold knowledge of God as creator and redeemer "is the foundation of Calvin's theological writing," and, consequently the *Institutes* ought to be divided according to these forms of knowledge.[10] The next model is found in the work of Philip Walker Butin on Calvin's Trinitarian theology. Butin builds upon a line of interpretation that sees the relationship of God and human beings as the seam that binds together Calvin's theology. Within that, it is the "economic-trinitarian pattern of redemption" that ultimately gives shape to Calvin's reflections.[11] Partee himself advocates for the motif of union with Christ as critical. In this model, the *Institutes* are split in half with the first two books "concerned with what Christ does *for* us and the subsequent discussion will treat what Christ does *within* us."[12] While there is likely some validity to each of these trajectories, the common denominator of the last three is the work of the Holy Spirit in Calvin's thought. For Calvin, it is the Holy Spirit who facilitates knowledge of God, applies the redemptive work of the Trinity, and unites the believer with Christ. Thus to comprehend Calvin's theology, one must come to an understanding of his pneumatology.

---

8. Oberman, *The Harvest of Medieval Theology*, 136. *Gratia gratum faciens* is sanctifying grace in Biel that builds upon *gratia gratis data*, a kind of preparatory grace that often collapses into nature for Biel.

9. Partee, *The Theology of John Calvin*, 35–6.

10. Dowey, Jr., *The Knowledge of God*, 41.

11. Butin, *Revelation*, 24.

12. Partee, *The Theology of John Calvin*, 40.

CALVIN'S PNEUMATOLOGY AND ITS RECEPTION
BY BARTH VIA SCHLEIERMACHER

One of Calvin's central pneumatological concerns is to correlate the work of the Spirit with that of Christ. At points, he detects correspondences between their respective tasks. For instance, in his commentary on John, he notes that the "word Comforter is here applied to both Christ and the Spirit; and justly, for it is an office common to both comfort and exhort and guard us by their patronage. Christ was the Patron of His own so long as He lived in the world. Afterwards He committed them to the protection and guardianship of the Spirit."[13] Calvin more typically drew distinctions between the responsibilities of the members of the Trinity in the economic plan of redemption. Early in the *Institutes*, Calvin states that "to the Father is attributed the beginning of activity, and the foundation and wellspring of all things; to the Son, wisdom, counsel, and the ordered disposition of all things; but to the Spirit is assigned the power and efficacy of that activity."[14] These distinctions of Trinitarian responsibility are a point of consistency across Calvin's literary career. In his 1538 catechism, when he exegetes the phrase "I believe in the Holy Spirit," Calvin directly connects the work of Christ and the work of the Spirit, "For Christ accomplishes whatever good there is through the power of his Spirit. Through that power he empowers and sustains all things, causes them to grow and quickens them; through it he justifies, sanctifies, and cleanses us, calls and draws us to himself, that we may attain salvation."[15] John McIntyre detects a Christological pattern in Calvin's pneumatology by which the will of the Father for salvation is effected through the Son and fulfilled by the Spirit.[16]

The understanding of Trinitarian distinctions will become more concrete through a brief analysis of Calvin's doctrine of election. In his initial discussion of that doctrine in the 1559 *Institutes*, Calvin attributes the act of predestination simply to God.[17] Later, though, Calvin identifies Christ as "the mirror wherein we must, and without self-deception" contemplate our election since it is into Christ that "the Father has destined those to be engrafted whom he has willed from eternity to be his own."[18] Calvin articulates the role of the Holy Spirit more succinctly in an earlier draft of

---

13. Calvin, *The Gospel According to St. John*, 82 (John 14:16).

14. Calvin, *Institutes*, 1.13.18, 142–143.

15. Hesselink, ed., *Calvin's First Catechism*, 25.

16. McIntyre, *The Shape of Pneumatology*, 118–19.

17. Calvin, *Institutes*, 3.21.5.

18. Calvin, *Institutes*, 3.24.5.

the *Institutes* when he contends "that there is no other guide and leader to the Father than the Holy Spirit, just as there is no other way than Christ; and that there is no grace from God, save through the Holy Spirit. Grace is itself the power and action of the Spirit."[19] While it could be said that the process of election is the decree of God, each member of the Trinity has a part in carrying out the decree. Calvin's pneumatology must be placed within the context of the larger Trinitarian pattern of his theology and in the more proximate doctrine of Christ. Doing so effectively thwarts the perceived Pelagianism in scholastics such as Biel while also positively constructing a different approach to soteriology.

In the intervening centuries between Calvin and Barth, theologians transformed and reinterpreted the doctrine of pneumatology.[20] Though it is beyond the scope of this chapter to survey all of that territory, it will be useful to examine one figure, Friedrich Schleiermacher, to see the genesis of Barth's pneumatology. This might seem like a rather odd place to begin with Barth, given his repudiation of much of nineteenth-century theology, but according to Barth's account, Schleiermacher inspired his pneumatological inquiries. In attempting to assess his relationship to Schleiermacher, Barth famously stated, "What I now and again have mentioned occasionally as an explanation of my relationship to Schleiermacher and what I here and there have indicated among friends, is that there might be the possibility of a theology of the third article—predominantly and decidedly, therefore, of the Holy Spirit."[21] Philip Rosato, in his study of Barth's pneumatology, contends that the pneumatology of Liberal Protestant theology is the "one thread which could at least save and justify the whole attempt to start theology with the believing Christian as the focus."[22]

Schleiermacher does not turn to address the doctrine of the Holy Spirit until deep into *The Christian Faith,* and he does so primarily within the context of ecclesiology. He suggests that the Holy Spirit ought to be understood as "the union of the Divine Essence with human nature in the form of the common Spirit animating the life in common of believers."[23] Proceeding to clarify this view, Schleiermacher places the Spirit squarely within the context of the church as something that does not arise from human nature, but

19. Butin, *Revelation,* 28.

20. Thiselton, *The Holy Spirit,* 270–315, for a broad and brief overview of the doctrinal developments.

21. Barth, "Nachwort," 311.

22. Rosato, *The Spirit as Lord,* 5.

23. Schleiermacher, *The Christian Faith,* §123, 569.

also as something divine, yet joined with human nature.[24] If the Holy Spirit is not bound up with human nature, he argues that the unity of a person's being would be sacrificed.[25] There is a kind of ambiguity in which the Holy Spirit is bound to the individual, yet transcends the individual, in much the same way that Schleiermacher understood reason to be in everyone, but a universal principle as well.[26] For Schleiermacher, the Spirit mediates Christ, thereby redeeming those who participate in Christ through the Spirit.[27] By "participation," Schleiermacher means simply that a person spontaneously acts in imitation of Christ as informed by the Spirit within the church.[28] "Schleiermacher makes sense of the Spirit's work by talking about Christ's normative judgments becoming our own as we learn them from those whose judgments have been recognized as going in the same way as his," Kevin Hector summarizes, "and as we in turn are recognized as going on in the same way."[29]

Barth criticizes Schleiermacher's pneumatology as fundamentally lopsided. In his *Dogmatics in Outline*, he observes that all of modern theology, epitomized by Schleiermacher, "became a one-sided theology of the third article, which believed that it might venture with the Holy Spirit alone, without reflecting that the third article is only the explication of the second."[30] It is not merely that the malformed shape of Schleiermacher's theology was due to his overemphasis on the Spirit at the expense of Christ. Rather, Barth sees in Schleiermacher an overemphasis on the subjective element in salvation. While acknowledging that there would be no comfort if all remained objective, Barth understands the accentuation of the subjective element as a result of attempting to bring pneumatology to relevance.[31] The subjective aspect suggests parallels between modern Protestantism and medieval Christianity for Barth. "Christianity appears as a great pedagogy, a pathway along which the human partly walks, is partly led, and is partly carried along by supernatural power," he asserts.[32] However, he adamantly insists on the centrality of the Spirit in theology. "It is clear that evangelical theology

---

24. Schleiermacher, *The Christian Faith*, §123.2, 570–572. Note the non-personal reference to the Spirit.

25. Schleiermacher, *The Christian Faith*, §123.3, 572.

26. Schleiermacher, *The Christian Faith*, §123.3, 573–574.

27. Schleiermacher, *The Christian Faith*, §116.3, 535–536.

28. Schleiermacher, *The Christian Faith*, §122.3, 567–569.

29. Hector, "The Mediation of Christ's Normative Spirit," 9.

30. Barth, *Dogmatics in Outline*, 66.

31. Barth, *Dogmatics in Outline*, 137–8.

32. Barth, *The Theology of the Reformed Confessions*, 207.

itself," Barth contends, "can only be pneumatic, spiritual theology."[33] Barth's challenge, then, is to reconfigure theology that gives pneumatology its proper due. Given the parallels between Schleiermacher and late medieval thought, it is not surprising that Barth would draw upon Calvin.

Barth scholars have often been critiqued for failing to construct an adequate pneumatology. While there are a host of critiques of Barth's pneumatology, the one that is most of interest is the charge that Barth's Christocentrism so eclipses his pneumatology as to make the Holy Spirit absent.[34] Such readings of Barth ignore the principle of *opera trinitatis ad extra sunt indivisa* at work in his theology, meaning, as he states it, "there should be brought to our awareness. . .the truth of the triunity which is in fact undivided in its work and which still exists in three persons." He is simply following a long-standing tradition beginning as early as Augustine and moving through Calvin, as Barth observes.[35] This is the backdrop for Barth's infamous discussion of God as one who exists in three modes, but whose differentiation is also necessarily and absolutely essential. For legitimacy, Barth appeals to Calvin's definition of the divine person as "subsistences in the essence of God."[36] Paul Chung writes that Barth affirms the Trinitarian maxim "in such a way that God *in self* is known from what God has done in historical revelation."[37]

Chung's comment alludes to the cohesion between the economic and immanent Trinity, which then requires some differentiation insofar as the members of the Trinity have been revealed according to different modes. To this, Barth states simply that the "Holy Spirit is not identical with Jesus Christ, with the Son or Word of God," following his quote of question ninety-one of Calvin's 1545 Geneva catechism that enumerates some basic distinctions between Christ and the Holy Spirit, mostly in terms of the economic activities of each member of the Trinity.[38] Barth defines the Holy Spirit as "the awakening power in which Jesus Christ summons a sinful man to his community and therefore as a Christian to believe in him; to acknowledge and know and confess him as the Lord who for him became a servant."[39] In the final volume of the *Church Dogmatics*, Barth writes that, "We cannot say more of the Holy Spirit and His work than that He is

33. Barth, *Evangelical Theology*, 55.
34. See Kim, *The Spirit of God*, 3–5 for an overview of the charges laid at Barth's feet.
35. Barth, *Church Dogmatics*, I/I, 373.
36. Barth, *Church Dogmatics*, I/I, 360. Barth cites Calvin, *Institutes*, 1.13.6, 128.
37. Chung, *The Spirit of God*, 59.
38. Barth, *Church Dogmatics*, I/I, 451.
39. Barth, *Church Dogmatics*, IV/I, 740.

the power in which Jesus Christ attests himself, attests Himself effectively, creating in man response and obedience."[40] The language surrounding a believer's attitude toward the Son and the Holy Spirit have some nuance, as Barth draws distinctions based upon the language of scripture when he observes that those who "believe in (Christ) and confess Him believe in Him and confess Him as the exalted Lord. Thus the Spirit in whom they believe and confess and He who is the object of this faith and confession stand as it were on two different levels."[41] Although the Son and Holy Spirit indeed appear very similar in Barth's thinking, to charge him with accentuating one at the expense of the other would require him to have forgotten not only the Holy Spirit in his theology but also his criticisms of Protestant Liberalism.

Barth's doctrine of election provides a contrast with that of Calvin, one that demonstrates his independence from Calvin and opens up space for conversation regarding other points of pneumatological contact. Suzanne McDonald has identified two different doctrines of election in Barth's theology, "one in the *GD* and the other in *CD* II/2, with each taking a significantly different approach to the Spirit's role."[42] Barth's earlier writings are, ironically, perceived as being more Trinitarian. In the *Göttingen Dogmatics*, Barth argues that everything "that the Father does and the Son does, the Spirit does with them. The Spirit, God's express turning to us, is already Creator, Ruler, and Upholder of all things. He is already Redeemer and Mediator."[43] Insofar as all three members of the Trinity have a shared being, the external works of the Trinity are not divided. Barth, therefore, without qualms, associates all the above titles with the Holy Spirit. When he eventually presents his doctrine of election in the *Göttingen Dogmatics*, it takes a fairly traditionally Reformed shape. Barth even states that he intends to present it in its Reformed form, as opposed to Roman Catholic or Lutheran iterations.[44] By this, he means that God sovereignly elects some to salvation while others are subject to reprobation. The Holy Spirit has a decisive role within the process of election. "The Holy Spirit," Barth comments, "through whose power our weak faith and obedience become the subjective possibility of revelation, is the special thing in the election of grace."[45] This line of thought informs the first volume of the *Church Dogmatics* in language that is oft-repeated almost verbatim. Barth identifies the Holy Spirit as the agent

---

40. Barth, *Church Dogmatics*, IV/I, 648.

41. Barth, *Church Dogmatics*, I/I, 451–52.

42. McDonald, *Re-imaging Election*, 32.

43. Barth, *Göttingen Dogmatics*, 128.

44. Barth, *Göttingen Dogmatics*, 443.

45. Barth, *Göttingen Dogmatics*, 466.

of "divine revelation or reconciliation" by which God makes "His claim on us effective to be our one Lord, our one Teacher, our one Leader."[46] Barth equates the Holy Spirit with that "special element in revelation" that is "the subjective side in the event of revelation."[47] Bruce McCormack is inevitably correct when he connects Barth's conception of the task of the Holy Spirit with his understanding of revelation as the agent of revelation that makes belief possible.[48]

By the time Barth composed the second volume of the *Church Dogmatics*, scholars detect a considerable shift in his views. In McCormack's words, Barth learns to "understand every doctrine from a centre in God's Self-revelation in Jesus Christ. . .this methodological commitment marks an advance over the dogmatic method outlined in each of Barth's prolegomena."[49] That commitment is born out when Barth handles the doctrine of election in the second volume of the *Church Dogmatics*, where he laments that he "would have preferred to follow Calvin's doctrine of predestination much more closely, instead of departing from it so radically."[50] Barth infamously transforms the doctrine of election, making Christ the object of election and reprobation.[51] The decision of election is quite often parsed out in more binitarian terms, rather than Trinitarian. For instance, Barth states that the decision regarding election was "made between the Father and Son from all eternity."[52] This essential point is developed later in the *Church Dogmatics* when Barth comments that, "All God's willing is primarily a determination of the love of the Father and Son in the fellowship of the Holy Ghost."[53] At other places, Barth assigns a specific task to the Holy Spirit within the covenant of election, but the Holy Spirit is more subdued in the doctrine of election.[54]

Barth initially frames his dissent from Calvin in exegetical terms.[55] In reality, there are different understandings of the nature of God and his works, centered upon the revelation of God found in Christ. Barth ponders,

---

46. Barth, *Church Dogmatics*, I/2, 198.

47. Barth, *Church Dogmatics*, I/I, 449.

48. McCormack, *Karl Barth's Dialectical Theology*, 371–72.

49. McCormack, *Karl Barth's Dialectical Theology*, 454. This is covered in great detail by Gockel, *Barth & Schleiermacher*, 158–197.

50. Barth, *Church Dogmatics*, II/2, x.

51. Barth, *Church Dogmatics*, II/2, 94–145.

52. Barth, *Church Dogmatics*, II/2, 90.

53. Barth, *Church Dogmatics*, II/2, 169.

54. Barth, *Church Dogmatics*, II/2, 101–102.

55. Barth, *Church Dogmatics*, II/2, x.

> How can we have assurance in respect of our own election ex-
> cept by the Word of God? And how can even the Word of God
> give us assurance on this point if this Word, if Jesus Christ, is not
> really the electing God, not the election itself, not our election,
> but only an elected means where by the electing God—electing
> elsewhere and in some other way—executes that which He has
> decreed concerning those whom He has—elsewhere in and in
> some other way—elected? The fact that Calvin in particular not
> only did not answer but did not even perceive this question is
> the decisive objection which we have to bring against his whole
> doctrine of predestination. The electing God of Calvin is a *Deus
> nudus absconditus*. It is not the *Deus revelatus* who is as such
> that *Deus absconditus*, the eternal God. All the dubious features
> of Calvin's doctrine result from the basic failing that in the last
> analysis he separates God and Jesus Christ.[56]

As Cornelis van der Kooi explains the differences between Calvin and Barth
on this point, Calvin's formulation allows for the possibility that there might
be another God hidden still behind the decree of election if Christ is not the
decree, as Barth asserts.[57] Paul Chung more directly states that "Barth does
not recognize a connection between the Holy Spirit and predestination in
Calvin's framework."[58]

There is a degree of irony in Chung's point, given that it is precisely
at this juncture, where Barth dissents from Calvin, that Barth is most hotly
criticized for a deficient pneumatology. Paul Nimmo observes that there "is
little directly pneumatological here (in the chapter on election in the *Church
Dogmatics*), either in the material on the election of Jesus Christ or in the
material on the election of the community and the individual in him. Certainly, Barth mentions the Spirit at pivotal moments. . .but there is really no
sustained engagement with the pneumatological dimension of election."[59]
McDonald offers a much more damning critique when she remarks that "it
rapidly becomes apparent that difficulties and inconsistencies surrounding
the Spirit's role are at the heart of many of those aspects of the doctrine that
are usually identified as particularly problematic [in Barth's theology]."[60]

McDonald finds that Barth's system ultimately collapses back into
a form of individual double predestination akin to that in the classical

56. Barth, *Church Dogmatics*, II/2, 111.

57. Van der Kooi, *As in a Mirror*, 381.

58. Chung, *The Spirit of God*, 93.

59. Nimmo, "Barth and the Election-Trinity Debate," 166–7.

60. McDonald, *Re-imaging Election*, 59.

Reformed tradition.[61] The alternative is a kind of universalism in which all are elected to salvation in Christ—a charge sometimes levied against Barth. The work of the Holy Spirit is decisive for Barth. "To be without the Spirit," Barth maintains, "and therefore to live uncalled and godlessly, signifies an evil, perilous, but futile attempt to live the life of one rejected by God."[62] Though Calvin places election within the doctrine of the Holy Spirit and Barth locates it in the larger doctrine of God, as Colin Gunton observes, Barth ultimately implicitly accepts the outworking of Calvin's view.[63] This will become more clear when one compares Calvin and Barth upon doctrinal *loci* related to the work of the Holy Spirit.

To start, one might begin by pointing toward a common foundation. Both theologians naturally presume that one of the primary tasks of the Holy Spirit is the revelation of God to the unbeliever. In their commentaries on Rom 5:5, both point toward this essential revelatory function of the Spirit. Calvin comments simply that "the good things which God has prepared for those who worship Him are hidden from the ears, eyes and minds of men, and the Spirit alone can reveal them."[64] Though Barth pontificates in a bit more forceful language, the result is the same, as he concludes that "the love of God hath been shed abroad in our hearts through the Holy Spirit which was given unto us."[65]

Just under the surface of each of these statements is a further belief about the content and the effect of that revelation. Calvin addresses these concerns most directly at the beginning of the third book of the *Institutes*. He begins by noting the disconnection between Christ as the head of the church and the church as the body of Christ. It is the Holy Spirit that then intercedes to build a bridge. "If the shedding of [Christ's] sacred blood is not to be in vain, our souls must be washed in it by the secret cleansing of the Holy Spirit," Calvin says before concluding that "The whole comes to this that the Holy Spirit is the bond by which Christ effectually binds us to himself."[66] In Calvin's estimation, it is the task of the Holy Spirit to make effective the death of Christ.

The nature of faith further facilitates the Spirit's nature and role. It should be no surprise at all that Calvin's classic definition of faith comes just after he begins to explore the meaning of the work of the Holy Spirit

---

61. McDonald, *Re-imaging Election*, 72.

62. Barth, *Church Dogmatics*, II/2, 346.

63. See Gunton, *The Barth Lectures*, 114.

64. Calvin, *The Epistles to the Romans and Thessalonians*, 107 (Rom 5:5).

65. Barth, *The Epistle to the Romans*, 157.

66. Calvin, *Institutes*, 3.1.1.

in the *Institutes*. Calvin offers a concise definition of faith, "Now we shall possess a right definition of faith if we call it a firm and certain knowledge of God's benevolence toward us, founded upon the truth of the freely given promise in Christ, both revealed to our minds and sealed upon our hearts through the Holy Spirit."[67] Calvin further qualifies the nature of faith, stating that "the Word of God is not received by faith if it flits about in the top of the brain, but when it takes root in the depth of the heart."[68] As Calvin describes it in his commentary on Romans, the Spirit of God simultaneously renews sinners and justifies them graciously.[69] Faith, another gift of the Spirit, verifies the reality of God's disposition toward the sinner.

Calvin can then proceed to speak about the relationship between the believer who possesses faith and Christ, the object of that faith. In his commentary on Gal 2:20, he explicitly connects Christ and the work of the Holy Spirit in the life of the believer. This text, Calvin comments, explains how believers have been "(e)ngrafted into the death of Christ" and derive from it a secret energy, as the shoot does from the root. A few lines later, the idea is explored in more detail when he states that "Christ lives in us in two ways. The one consists in His governing us by His Spirit and directing all our actions. The other is what He grants us by participation in His righteousness, that, since we can do nothing of ourselves, we are accepted in Him by God."[70] Thus comes the concept of participation. Dennis Tamburello helpfully summarizes Calvin's teaching when he notes that the "Holy Spirit brings the elect, through the hearing of the gospel, to faith; in so doing, the Spirit engrafts them into Christ."[71] The primary tasks of the Holy Spirit for Calvin are to point toward Christ and unite him with the believer.

BARTH AND REVELATION

Barth, working in the shadow of Kant, analyzes revelation under the categories of objective and subjective possibilities.[72] Aaron Smith characterizes the "objective possibility of God's revelation [as] the unique freedom and authority of God to place himself before us."[73] The subjective possibility ap-

---

67. Calvin, *Institutes*, 3.2.7.

68. Calvin, *Institutes*, 3.2.36.

69. Calvin, *The Epistles to the Romans and Thessalonians*, 156–7 (Rom 8:2).

70. Calvin, *The Epistles to the Galatians*, 42–43 (Gal 2:20).

71. Tamburello, *Union with Christ*, 86.

72. On the influence of Kant upon Barth's pneumatological reflection as it bears on revelation, see Kim, *The Spirit of God*, 129–38.

73. Smith, *A Theology of the Third Article*, 87.

pears to be almost a function of existence. In *Göttingen Dogmatics*, one of his earlier writings, Barth states that, "If, then, there is a being in God in the very activation of our humanity, or, in other words, if there is an activation of our humanity which is from God and in God, then obviously. . .we will stand before and over and against God. . .There will then be revelation, that is, the establishment of fellowship between God and us by God's communication to us."[74] Left there, this sounds like Barth is disturbingly anthropocentric, a suggestion he thoroughly demolishes in his landmark *Nein!* pamphlet against natural theology, in which he queries Emil Brunner, "And if we really do know the true God from his creation without Christ and without the Holy Spirit—if this is so, how can it be said that. . .man can do nothing towards his salvation?"[75] A large portion of *Nein!* is devoted to the exegesis of Calvin's theology upon this question of revelation in which Barth concedes that Calvin adhered to a theoretical possibility of natural theology, but not a possibility that can be realized by humans independently.[76] Barth clarifies his position in the *Göttingen Dogmatics*, "They stand before God because God's revelation is a here as well as a there, something subjective as well as something objective, because God not only reveals himself in the *Son* but reveals himself in the Son by the *Spirit*."[77] This statement from Barth has very clear resonances with Calvin, as noted above. John Thompson nicely captures Barth's view stating that faith "is thus a human activity (in one sense) though orientated to and coming from Christ by the Holy Spirit, but it is never a human possibility."[78] That is, not without the work of the Holy Spirit.

The quotations here from *Nein!* and the *Göttingen Dogmatics* point toward the important work of the Holy Spirit in Barth's thought. In *Church Dogmatics*, he forges connections between the revelation of God in the incarnation and the revelation given by the Holy Spirit when he observes that the "Lord of our hearing, the Lord who gives faith, the Lord by whose act the openness and readiness of man for the Word are true and actual. . .is the Holy Spirit."[79] In his reflections recorded in *Evangelical Theology*, Barth speaks of the liberating and defining power of faith, over and against deficient forms of faith, observing that what "happens in the event of faith is that the Word of God frees one man among many for faith itself. . .By God's

74. Barth, *Göttingen Dogmatics*, 175–6.
75. Karl Barth, *No!*, 82.
76. Karl Barth, *No!*, 106.
77. Barth, *Göttingen Dogmatics*, 176. Italics in original.
78. Thompson, *The Holy Spirit*, 135.
79. Barth, *Church Dogmatics*, 1/1, 182.

Word, together with the life-giving power and the unique sovereignty of
the Spirit, one man among many is permitted to exist continually as a free
man."[80] George Hunsinger correctly draws our attention to the relationship
between revelation and reconciliation in Barth's thought, "Just as revelation
without reconciliation could only have been empty, so reconciliation without revelation could only have been mute. Revelation in fact imparted the
reality of reconciliation, even as reconciliation formed the vital truth that
revelation made known."[81] Here, too, Calvin is one of the key authorities
that Barth cites to connect revelation with receiving the power of Christ
through the agency of the Holy Spirit.[82]

What then does reconciliation look like for Barth? Buried deep in
the *Church Dogmatics*, Barth states that the "justification of man is the establishment of his right, the introduction of the life of a new man who is
righteous before God."[83] But this is too straightforward and easy for Barth.
He offers a metaphor intended to explain what a righteous person is like
when he comments that the "righteous man is the prisoner become watch-
man. He is the guard at the threshold of divine reality. There is no other
righteousness save that of the man who sets himself under judgement, of the
man who is terrified and hopes."[84] Something of Barth's dialectical method
is suggested here, but it is made more evident in other places. "I was and
still am the former man: man as wrongdoer . . . But I am already and will
be the latter man," Barth observes, "the man whom God has elected and
created for himself . . . the man who is not unrighteous but righteous before
God."[85] Hunsinger contends that few "theologians have ever aligned themselves more meticulously with Luther than did Barth in adopting the great
doctrine of *simul justus et peccator*. Indeed, this is another place where it can
be argued, remarkably, that Barth stands with Luther against Calvin, or at
least against Calvin's ambiguities."[86]

Barth does discuss Calvin's views on sanctification, under the heading
of sanctification, just after affirming Luther's *simul*. Barth affirms Calvin's
distinction in sanctification between mortification and vivification—seen
by Barth as an advancement over medieval theology. "Calvin was quite right
when, renouncing all attempts at plastic representation," Barth states, "he

---

80. Barth, *Evangelical Theology*, 100.

81. Hunsinger, "The Mediator of Communion," 178.

82. Barth, *Church Dogmatics*, I/1, 451.

83. Barth, *Church Dogmatics*, IV/1, 554.

84. Barth, *The Epistle to the Romans*, 41.

85. Barth, *Church Dogmatics*, IV/1, 596.

86. Hunsinger, *Disruptive Grace*, 295.

spoke so inexorably of *interitus, abnegation,* and *reductio ad nihilum,* of the slaying sword of the Spirit, and then of the Spirit as the only principle of what may be seriously called a new life."[87] The problem is that Barth does not match the radical presentation of dying to one's self with an equally profound statement on the corresponding vivification of the new person.[88] To do so might imply a rupture between the work of Christ and that of the Spirit for Barth. As Jeff McSwain explains Barth's position, "to be 'full of the Spirit' for Barth, then, functions as biblical idiom for our operating in the truth of the Spirit's fullness given to humanity. . .To be 'full of the Spirit' is a biblical phrase essentially wedded to Christology and for us purely deriva-tive and relative in nature."[89]

Barth's differences from Calvin did not stop him from returning to Calvin as a source when he reflects upon the believer's experience of union with Christ. Insofar as it speaks to the matters of justification and sanctifi-cation, Hunsinger's comment above gestures toward the doctrine of union with Christ in Barth's theology. McDonald observes that this doctrine is absent in his earlier *Göttingen Dogmatics.*[90] Just a few years later, in his *Eth-ics,* Barth addresses this doctrine in the context of the command of law. Although Luther serves as his entry point, Barth moves quickly to integrate Calvin's theology. In a short paragraph, he cites Calvin no less than five times on the theme of union with Christ, particularly with an eye toward describing how this happens. He ultimately concludes that the doctrine is the "most profound and difficult truth that God's Word of forgiveness is not just spoken, but through the Holy Spirit is spoken to *us* and received by *us.*"[91] However, there is an eschatological tension here in acknowledging that this process is not yet complete, as Barth refers to it as "the goal of rec-onciliation that lies beyond all time."[92] Here, too, Barth draws heavily upon Calvin to correlate the relationship between justification and sanctification, with the understanding that it is the work of the Holy Spirit that actualizes each in the life of the believer.

---

87. Barth, *Church Dogmatics,* IV/1, 575.

88. Barth, *Church Dogmatics,* IV/1, 576.

89. McSwain, Simul *Sanctification,* 71.

90. McDonald, *Re-imaging Election,* 36.

91. Barth, *Ethics,* 290.

92. Barth, *Ethics,* 278.

SIMILARITIES AND DIFFERENCES
BETWEEN CALVIN AND BARTH

At this point, some fairly generic and broad structures have been sketched that, for the most part, suggest some similarities between Calvin and Barth. These similarities should not be altogether surprising given the impact of Calvin upon Barth's theology, or, at least, Barth's interpretation of Calvin's influence upon him. Barth famously referred to Calvin as

> a cataract, a primeval forest, a demonic power, something directly down from Himalaya, absolutely Chinese, strange, mythological; I lack completely the means, the suction cups, even to assimilate this phenomenon, not to speak of presenting it adequately. What I receive is only a thin little stream and what I can then give out again is only a yet thinner extract of this little stream. I could gladly and profitably set myself down and spend all the rest of my life just with Calvin.[93]

Collectively, the Reformed—Calvin and Zwingli, ostensibly—are instructive to Barth because the work of God in Christ is the origin and goal of the Christian life."[94] JinHyok Kim correctly contends that "Barth saw that Calvin's pneumatology plays a key role in doing justice both to the centrality of the Word and to the importance of Christ's moral action. For Barth, Calvin always linked the Spirit with the Word, illustrating that the Spirit not only interprets the Word for human beings, but also enlightens them, and convinces them to live according to it."[95]

Kim's comment, as well as the earlier discussion of the dialectical understanding of anthropology in Barth, suggests some space for differentiation between the two Reformed thinkers. To start, the nature and intent of revelation are subtly divergent. If we again turn to their respective commentaries on Romans, disagreements are evident. On Rom 1:20, Calvin maintains that "God is invisible in Himself, but since His majesty shines forth in all His works and in all His creatures, men ought to have acknowledged Him in these, for they clearly demonstrate their Creator. For this reason the apostle, in his Epistle to the Hebrews, calls the world a mirror or representation (*specula seu spectacula*) of invisible things (Heb. 11.3). He does not recount in detail all the attributes which may be held to belong to God, but he tells us how to come to the knowledge of His eternal power

---

93. Barth, *Revolutionary Theology*, 101.

94. Barth, *The Theology of Calvin*, 77.

95. Kim, *The Spirit of God*, 29.

and divinity."[96] Calvin also refers to a *sensus divinitatis* by which all humans are aware of divinity, though in other places in his corpus, not all are saved.[97]

Barth, of course, rejects any possibility of natural theology. In his reflections upon Rom 1:20, he initially states that if we could simply see clearly, we would reach a moment of crisis when we perceive the divine "No" spoken to us in nature. Since we cannot, Barth queries, "what does this mean but that we can know nothing of God?"[98] Barth appeals to both Calvin's view that the beginning of the knowledge of God is self-knowledge as a means to thwart any solely human attempt to know God, and Calvin's belief that the work of the Holy Spirit creates the possibility for knowledge of God.[99] Calvin has a more generous understanding of revelation that does not necessarily entail salvation, while Barth's stricter construction of revelation through the Holy Spirit as akin to salvation, places him at odds with his source.

This conflict dovetails into contrasting notions of Scripture and its relationship to the Holy Spirit. Barth himself acknowledges that Calvin "handles the Bible like a legal book whose wording must always have the final decision. Calvin forged the dogma of inspiration. Yet we cannot be content to merely say that. He never spoke about the inspiration of the Bible without also advancing the principle of its opposing highly subjective character."[100] Barth tends to see the development of the doctrine of biblical inspiration as a deviation, insofar as it tends to domesticate God into a concrete form.[101] He draws upon Calvin's doctrine of the internal testimony of the Holy Spirit to argue that the authority of Scripture is not intrinsic to Scripture, but is a function of "a conversation with the truth itself."[102] Barth is not entirely wrong here; Calvin does speak of the Holy Spirit testifying to the authority of Scripture.[103] Calvin, though, has a different set of questions in mind.

On the one hand, he has to repudiate Roman Catholics who held that the church had authority over scripture and, on the other, radicals who felt that possession of the Spirit made scripture irrelevant. The former is

96. Calvin, *The Epistles to the Romans and the Thessalonians*, 31 (1:20).

97. See, for instance, Calvin, *Institutes*, 1.3.1, 43–44. Schreiner's *The Theater of His Glory* is important in this regard, as is Dowey, *The Knowledge of God*.

98. Barth, *The Epistle to the Romans*, 46–47.

99. Chung, *Admiration & Challenge*, 149–50.

100. Barth, *The Theology of Calvin*, 167.

101. See the historical excursus of the doctrine in Barth, *Church Dogmatics*, I/2, 514–26, but also Barth's more succinct statement of how Scripture is authoritative in *Church Dogmatics*, I/1, 112–14.

102. Barth, *The Theology of Calvin*, 167.

103. Calvin, *Institutes*, 1.7.4.

not germane to our topic, but the latter is crucial. Over and against these adversaries, Calvin upholds scripture as having "the divine image visibly impressed on it."[104] In his treatise against the libertines, Calvin argues that the "Spirit and Scripture are one and the same . . . we choke out the light of God's Spirit if we cut ourselves off from His Word. . .For preaching and Scripture are the true instruments of God's Spirit."[105] Barth has misread Calvin on this point.

Another point of convergence and contrast is evident when one looks at sanctification. Calvin envisions the process of sanctification as embracing the totality of the Christian life after conversion. In his commentary on Malachi, Calvin remarks that "our salvation, we know, consists of two things—that God rules us by his Spirit, and forms us anew in his own image through the whole course of our life."[106] It is the process by which God adopts those who have been justified through the work of the Holy Spirit, who then works to restore the image of God damaged through sin.[107] More succinctly, Calvin divides the topic under the headings of mortification and vivification.[108] Each of those actions carries with it certain obligations, though Calvin, for the most part, describes the Christian life as a consistent act of self-denial, particularly in the form of bearing the cross through obedience.[109]

When Barth begins to speak of sanctification, particularly in relationship to Calvin's view, he shows dependence upon Calvin even while he reconstructs Calvin's views.[110] In *Göttingen Dogmatics*, Barth sets his opinion in contrast with that of Luther, who believed that all that was required of a Christian was faith. He turns to Calvin, noting that in Calvin's 1545 Catechism for Geneva, "Calvin could even distinguish four categories for what must take place on our part (naturally as the work of the Holy Spirit): faith, obedience, prayer and thanksgiving. Yet only two persist: faith and obedience. This pair is so universal and distinctive that Reformed dogmatics cannot possibly fail to assert them."[111] This emphasis on faith and obedience is likely best understood as a refashioning of the structure, rather than the

---

104. Calvin, *Institutes*, 1.7.4.

105. Calvin, *Treatises Against the Anabaptists*, 224–5. See also Balke, *Calvin and the Anabaptist Radicals*, 320–27.

106. Calvin, *Commentaries on the Twelve Minor Prophets*, vol. 5, 608 (Malachi 3:17).

107. Calvin, *Institutes*, 3.11.6, 731–33.

108. Calvin, *Institutes*, 3.3.5, 597–98.

109. Calvin, *Institutes*, 3.3.7–8, 599–600.

110. See Worthington, *The Claim of God*, 36–60.

111. Barth, *The Göttingen Dogmatics*, 172.

content, of Calvin's thought. Barth's reduction of Calvin's more robust list suits his dialectical method.

When Barth speaks of the content of the doctrine of sanctification, he tends to do so using the language of liberation, but it is freedom to be adopted as God's child through revelation. Barth maintains that one who has experienced divine revelation "is the child of God. As such he is free, he can believe. And he is God's child as he receives the Holy Ghost."[112] Barth sees the theme of sanctification as liberation in Calvin, as is clear in Barth's comments upon the chapter on Christian liberty in the 1537 edition of the *Institutes*.[113] Barth's point in this regard underscores a valuable point of Calvin's influence upon Barth. Sung Wook Chung notes that "Barth viewed the central theme of Calvin's *magnum opus* as the Christian ethical life. . .Barth interpreted Calvin's theology to be a fundamentally ethical one."[114] This is so because of the close connections in Calvin's thought between Word, Spirit, and the Christian life.[115] Given this, it is not at all surprising that Calvin was one of Barth's primary interlocutors when he delivered a series of lectures on theological ethics.[116] Barth invokes Calvin's epigram that "we are not our own masters, but belong to the Lord" as a way to draw attention to the ethical demands of God upon the believer in sanctification.[117] Thanks to the connection between faith and obedience, theology and ethics, Barth follows Calvin in viewing "the Christian life as one of action, if only the action of pointing back to the cross of Christ."[118]

CONCLUSION

In the end, in his lectures on Calvin's theology, Barth tells his reader that "we do not have teaching by repeating Calvin's words as our own or making his view ours. . .Being taught by Calvin means entering into dialogue with him, with Calvin as the teacher and ourselves as the students, he speaking, we doing our best to follow him and the—this is the crux of the matter—making our own response to what he says."[119] Here we see an incredibly apt

---

112. Barth, *Church Dogmatics*, I/1, 457.

113. Barth, *The Theology of John Calvin*, 194–226.

114. Chung, *Admiration & Challenge*, 58.

115. See Kim, *The Spirit of God*, 26–30.

116. See Barth, *The Holy Spirit*.

117. Barth, *Unterricht in der Christlichen Religion*, 314–5. The citation is to the title of Calvin, *Institutes*, 3.7.1, 689.

118. Worthington, *The Claim of God*, 49.

119. Barth, *The Theology of John Calvin*, 4.

self-description for Barth's own method of appropriating Calvin's thoughts on pneumatology. Calvin's and Barth's reflections upon the doctrine of the Holy Spirit look comparable, and their teachings run parallel on several points. Indeed, Calvin's pneumatology runs like rivulet throughout Barth's thought. Barth, however, felt no need to be a slavish interpreter of Calvin's theology. While Calvin's views clearly inspired him, he felt the freedom to revise or refashion the Genevan reformer's beliefs. Much of what differentiates the two theologians likely has to do with the different historical contexts in which each man worked—the milieu each faced demanded responses that diverged, as each addressed diverse criticisms of the doctrine of the Holy Spirit. The degree to which Calvin influenced Barth's pneumatology is the degree to which Calvin indirectly informs modern reflection upon the person and work of the Holy Spirit.

We have now identified a few points of contact and some contrasts between Calvin's and Barth's respective pneumatologies. A more extensive engagement might find still more similarities and differentiation between their teachings on the Holy Spirit.

BIBLIOGRAPHY

Aquinas, Thomas. *Summa Theologiae*. Vol. 7, *Father, Son and Holy Ghost*. Edited by T. C. O'Brien. London: Blackfriars, 1976.

———. *Summa Theologiae*. Vol. 24, *The Gifts of the Spirit*. Edited by Edward D. O'Connor. London: Blackfriars, 1974.

Balke, Willem. *Calvin and the Anabaptist Radicals*. Translated by William Heynen. Grand Rapids: Eerdmans, 1981.

Barth, Karl. *Church Dogmatics*. Edited by G. W. Bromiley and T. F. Torrance. Translated by G. T. Thomson, 5 vols. in 14 parts. Edinburgh: T. & T. Clark, 1936–77.

———. *Dogmatics in Outline*. Translated by G. T. Thomson. New York: Harper& Row, 1959.

———. *The Epistle to the Romans*. Translated by Edwyn Hoskyns. Oxford: Oxford University Press, 1968.

———. *Ethics*. Translated by Geoffrey Bromiley. New York: Seabury, 1981.

———. *Evangelical Theology: An Introduction*. Grand Rapids: Eerdmans, 1992.

———. *Göttingen Dogmatics: Instruction in the Christian Religion*. Edited by Hannelotte Reiffen. Translated by Geoffrey Bromiley. Grand Rapids: Eerdmans, 1991.

———. *The Holy Spirit and the Christian Life: The Theological Basis of Ethics*. Translated by R. Birch Hoyle. Louisville: Westminster John Knox, 1993.

———. "Nachwort." In F. D. E. Schleiermacher, *Schleiermacher-Auswahl mit einem Nachwort von Karl Barth*, edited by Heinz Bolli, 290–312. Munich: Siebenstern Taschenbuch, 1968.

———. *Revolutionary Theology in the Making: Barth–Thurneysen Correspondence 1914–1925*. Translated by James D. Smart. Richmond, VA: John Knox, 1964.

————. *The Theology of Calvin*. Translated by Geoffrey Bromiley. Grand Rapids: Eerdmans, 1995.

————. *The Theology of the Reformed Confessions*. Translated by Darrell L. Guder and Judith J. Guder. Louisville: Westminster John Knox, 2002.

————. *Unterricht in der Christlichen Religion III: Die Lehre von der Versöhnung/Die Lehre von der Erlösung 1925/1926*. Edited by H. Stoevesandt. Zurich: Theologischer Verlag, 2003.

Barth, Karl, and Emil Brunner. *Natural Theology, Comprising "Nature and Grace" by Prof. Dr. Emil Brunner and the Reply "No!" by Karl Barth*. 2nd ed. Translated by Peter Fraenkel. 1946. Reprint, Eugene: Wipf & Stock, 2002.

Butin, Philip Walker. *Revelation, Redemption, and Response: Calvin's Trinitarian Understanding of the Divine-Human Relationship*. Oxford: Oxford University Press, 1995.

Calvin, John. *Commentaries on the Twelve Minor Prophets*. Translated by John Owen. Calvin Translation Society, 5 vols. 1846. Reprint, Grand Rapids: Eerdmans, 1950.

————. *The Epistles of Paul the Apostle to the Galatians, Ephesians, Philippians, and Colossians*. Edited by David W. Torrance and Thomas F. Torrance. Translated by T. H. L. Parker. Calvin's New Testament Commentaries. Grand Rapids: Eerdmans, 1965.

————. *The Epistles of Paul the Apostle to the Romans and to the Thessalonians*. Edited by David W. Torrance and Thomas F. Torrance. Translated by Ross MacKenzie. Calvin's New Testament Commentaries. Grand Rapids: Eerdmans, 1960.

————. *The Gospel according to St. John 11–21 and 1 John*. Edited by David W. Torrance and Thomas F. Torrance. Translated by T. H. L. Parker. Calvin's New Testament Commentaries. Grand Rapids: Eerdmans, 1975.

————. *Institutes of the Christian Religion*. Edited by John McNeill. Translated by Ford Lewis Battles. Library of Christian Classics 20–21. Louisville: Westminster John Knox, 1975.

————. *Treatises against the Anabaptists and against the Libertines*. Translated and edited by Benjamin Wirt Farley. Grand Rapids: Baker, 1982.

Chung, Paul S. *The Spirit of God Transforming Life: The Reformation and Theology of the Holy Spirit*. New York: Palgrave Macmillan, 2009.

Chung, Sung Wook. *Admiration & Challenge: Karl Barth's Theological Relationship with John Calvin*. Berlin: Peter Lang, 2002.

Dowey, Jr., Edward A. *The Knowledge of God in Calvin's Theology*. Grand Rapids: Eerdmans, 1994.

Gockel, Matthias. *Barth & Schleiermacher on the Doctrine of Election: A Systematic-Theological Comparison*. Oxford: Oxford University Press, 2006.

Gunton, Colin. *The Barth Lectures*. Edited by P. H. Brazier. London: T. & T. Clark, 2007.

Hector, Kevin W. "The Mediation of Christ's Normative Spirit: A Constructive Reading of Schleiermacher's Pneumatology." *Modern Theology* 24 (2008) 1–22.

Hesselink, I. John, ed. *Calvin's First Catechism: A Commentary*. Louisville: Westminster John Knox, 1997.

Hunsinger, George. *Disruptive Grace: Studies in the Theology of Karl Barth*. Grand Rapids: Eerdmans, 2000.

————. "The Mediator of Communion: Karl Barth's Doctrine of the Holy Spirit." In *The Cambridge Companion to Karl Barth*, edited by John Webster, 177–94. Cambridge Companions to Religion. Cambridge: Cambridge University Press, 2000.

Kim, JinHyok. *The Spirit of God and the Christian Life: Reconstructing Karl Barth's Pneumatology*. Minneapolis: Fortress, 2014.

Klempa, Fred. "Barth as Scholar and Interpreter of Calvin." In *Calvin Studies VII*, edited by John. H. Leith, 31–49. Davidson: Calvin Studies Society, 1994.

Kooi, Cornelis van der. *As in a Mirror: John Calvin and Karl Barth on Knowing God: A Diptych*. Translated by Donald Mader. Studies in the History of Christian Traditions 120. Leiden: Brill, 2005.

McCormack, Bruce. *Karl Barth's Critically Realistic Dialectical Theology: Its Genesis and Development, 1909–1936*. Oxford: Clarendon, 1995.

McDonald, Suzanne. *Re-imaging Election: Divine Election as Representing God to Others and Others to God*. Grand Rapids: Eerdmans, 2010.

McIntyre, John. *The Shape of Pneumatology: Studies in the Doctrine of the Holy Spirit*. London: T. & T. Clark, 1997.

McSwain, Jeff. *Simul Sanctification: Barth's Hidden Vision for Human Transformation*. Princeton Theological Monograph Series 232. Eugene, OR: Pickwick Publications, 2018.

Nimmo, Paul T. "Barth and the Election-Trinity Debate: A Pneumatological View." In *Trinity and Election in Contemporary Theology*, edited by Michael T. Dempsey, 162–81. Grand Rapids: Eerdmans, 2011.

Oberman, Heiko A. *The Harvest of Medieval Theology: Gabriel Biel and Late Medieval Nominalism*. Grand Rapids: Baker Academic, 2000.

Partee, Charles. *The Theology of John Calvin*. Louisville: Westminster John Knox, 2008.

Rosato, Philip. *The Spirit as Lord: The Pneumatology of Karl Barth*. Edinburgh: T. & T. Clark, 1981.

Schleiermacher, Friedrich. *The Christian Faith*. Edited by H. R. Mackintosh and J. S. Stewart. Edinburgh: T. & T. Clark, 1976.

Schreiner, Susan. *The Theater of His Glory: Nature and the Natural Order in the Thought of John Calvin*. Grand Rapids: Baker Academic, 2001.

Smith, Aaron. *A Theology of the Third Article: Karl Barth and the Spirit of the Word*. Minneapolis: Fortress, 2014.

Tamburello, Dennis. *Union with Christ: John Calvin and the Mysticism of St. Bernard*. Louisville: Westminster John Knox, 1994.

Thiselton, Anthony C. *The Holy Spirit—in Biblical Teaching, through the Centuries, and Today*. Grand Rapids: Eerdmans, 2013.

Thompson, John. *The Holy Spirit in the Theology of Karl Barth*. Princeton Theological Monograph Series 23. Eugene, OR: Pickwick Publications, 1991.

Warfield, Benjamin Breckenridge. "Calvin as Theologian." In *Calvin and Augustine*, edited by Samuel G. Craig, 481–87. Philadelphia: Presbyterian & Reformed, 1956.

Worthington, Ethan A. *The Claim of God: Karl Barth's Doctrine of Sanctification in His Earlier Theology*. Eugene: Pickwick Publications, 2015.

9

John Calvin's Criteria for the Functioning of the Charismata

The Impact on Contemporary Worship

Fitzroy John Willis

INTRODUCTION

Five hundred years after the Reformation inspired by Martin Luther (1483–1546) and systematized by John Calvin (1509–1564), its legacy continues today. Perhaps this effect is nowhere more evident than in the worship service, relative to how Calvin interpreted Paul's exhortation concerning the functioning of the *charismata* (1 Cor 12:8–10, 28; Rom 12:6–8). And if the *charismata* are "a diversity of experienced concretions (sum) of the grace of God, sovereignly bestowed by the Spirit upon members of the community of believers and functioning interdependently for the purpose of the upbuilding of the church in love,"[1] then they are gifts of the Spirit and demonstrations of the grace of God to edify the church. This chapter will focus on the impact of Calvin's criteria for the functioning of the *charismata* on the contemporary worship service.

Undoubtedly, this emphasis includes appropriate communication among worshipers. Indeed, Calvin himself comments that Paul was

1. Schatzmann, *A Pauline Theology*, 51–52.

addressing a communication problem,[2] and contemporary scholars tend to agree. For example, David Aune concludes that Paul is addressing appropriate communication—relative to utterances of prophecy, tongues, and interpretation of tongues—in the worship service.[3] David Ackerman says, "there is a communication problem at Corinth," and as Paul is seeking to position the *charismata* of prophecy and tongues into the context of edifying the church,[4] he is condemning their wrong interpretation of what it means to be spiritual.

Paul also addresses the cessation of the *charismata* in a future of the perfect. In 1 Cor 13:8, Paul says, "Love never fails, but as for prophecies, they will be discontinued, as for tongues, they will cease, as for knowledge, it will be discontinued." He also addresses gender criteria in 1 Cor 14:34–35 when he charges, "let the women be silent in the churches. For it is not permitted for them to speak, but (to) be subject, just as even the law says. And if they wish to learn something, let them ask their own husbands at home, for it is shameful for a woman to speak in church." These verses—commonly referred to as the *mulier taceat* (let the women be silent) —as interpreted by Calvin, continue to have a tremendous impact on the contemporary worship service.[5]

However, it is not just because of *charismata* concerning prophecy, revelation, and tongues that the Apostle Paul's and Calvin's impacts are evident in the contemporary worship service. Indeed, views concerning *charismata* such as faith, gifts of healing, miracles, forms of leadership, exhorting, giving, and mercy are still impacting today's worship service. So, what follows is a focus on how Calvin interpreted such *charismata*, as well as the legacy of his views.

CALVIN'S CRITERIA FOR THE FUNCTIONING OF PROPHECY IN THE WORSHIP SERVICE

For Calvin, prophecy is a "peculiar gift" for interpreting and applying Scripture wisely in the present.[6] Thus, the prophet is an interpreter and administrator of received revelation (canonical Scripture),[7] not interpreting

---

2. Calvin, *Commentary on the Epistle to the Corinthians*, 435.

3. Aune, *Prophecy*, 220.

4. Ackerman, "Fighting Fire with Fire," 350–51.

5. Notwithstanding the context of Paul's recognition that a woman may publicly pray or prophesy, though with her head covered (1 Cor 11:5).

6. Calvin, *Commentary on the Epistle to the Corinthians*, 415.

7. Calvin, *Commentary on the Epistle to the Corinthians*, 438.

the direct will of God, for such interpretation could become purely anthro-pocentric. Moreover, prophecy does not concern foretelling or communi-cation relevant to future events.[8] Such prognostications would be entirely supernatural—attributable only to God. Instead, for Calvin, prophecy is forth-telling, concerning the present, and is based on scriptural revelation.[9] From this perspective, prophecy is a highly regarded interpretation of Scrip-ture, addressing the present needs of the church. Since prophecy is not the directly revealed will of God, the source of "prophetic" communication can be either natural or supernatural.

But even if prophetic revelation is restricted to the content of Scrip-ture, it does not follow that it should preclude foretelling. Though the canon of Scripture has closed, scriptural revelation often speaks into the future, foretelling the will of God. For example, both John the revelator and Paul foretell a future reign of God (see Rev 21:2–22:5 and 1 Thess 4:13–18).

Contemporary Interpretations of Calvin's Criteria

Contemporary interpretations of Calvin's criteria for the functioning of prophecy in the worship service can be categorized based on whether a prophecy is interpreted as being a direct revelation of God's will or an inter-pretation of scriptural content. On the one hand, J. I. Packer, says,

> Prophecy is a God prompted application of truth that in gen-eral terms had been revealed already rather than a disclosure of divine thoughts and intentions not previously known and not otherwise knowable . . . Any verbal enforcement of biblical teaching as it applies to one's present hearers may properly be called prophecy today.[10]

On the other hand, the Lutheran Church of Australia maintains that "to prophesy is to speak God's word to his people on the basis of a special rev-elation by the inspiration of the Holy Spirit."[11]

For George Mallone, prophecy must be under the control of the person (14:32); only two or three are to be given at any one meeting (14:29); and the prophet is reluctant and humble, instead of being presumptuous.[12] Mark

---

8. Calvin, *Commentary on the Epistle to the Corinthians*, 436.

9. Calvin, *The Epistles to the Romans and Thessalonians*, 269; cf., Calvin, *Institutes*, 1057.

10. Packer, *Keep in Step*, 215.

11. Lutheran Church of Australia, "1 Corinthians and 1 Timothy," 62.

12. Mallone, *Those Controversial Gifts*, 33.

J. Cartledge states that both New Testament and contemporary prophecy are based on revelation; the appropriate and expected context for their functioning is the worship service; anyone can prophesy; prophecy should be edifying, encouraging, and comforting (1 Cor 14:3); and prophecy has authority of general content, and therefore requires discernment and judgment (14:29)—in light of Scriptures—from its hearers.[13]

CALVIN'S VIEW ON THE RELATIONSHIP BETWEEN PROPHECY AND PREACHING

Notwithstanding, how have Calvin's and his interpreters' criteria for the functioning of prophecy impacted the contemporary worship service? This speaks to Calvin's view of the relationship between prophecy and preaching—especially relevant to the *charismata* concerning offices of the church. For Calvin, the New Testament office of prophet corresponds to that of the contemporary teacher, and the office of the New Testament apostles corresponds to the contemporary pastor.[14] Teachers and prophets are interpreters of Scripture, but pastors and apostles preach the Gospel, discipline the church,[15] and administer the sacraments.[16] The communication of teachers and prophets, then, is limited to proclamation relative to the present. It is not supernatural and not a direct revelation of God's will. Instead, the teacher and prophet are interpreters of what has already been revealed in Scripture, "to keep doctrine whole and pure among believers."[17] However, their interpretation and exhortation can be attributable to either a human or supernatural source.

Likewise, preaching pertains to the communication of scriptural revelation of the Gospel of Jesus Christ, "for the salvation of the world."[18] Thus, preaching is forth-telling and not foretelling. It is not a direct revelation of God's will—which cannot be limited to the present time. Preaching is a human exhortation or interpretation of scriptural revelation that can be attributable to either a human or supernatural source. So, both prophecy and preaching require listeners in the worship service to discern if the utterance is divine revelation. For Calvin, the relationship between prophecy and preaching is that they are the same.

13. Cartledge, "Charismatic Prophecy," 17–19.

14. Calvin, *Institutes*, 1057–58.

15. Calvin, *Institutes*, 1056–57.

16. Calvin, *Institutes*, 1057.

17. Calvin, *Institutes*, 1057.

18. Calvin, *Institutes*, 1056–57.

Contemporary Interpretations of Calvin's View
of the Relationship between Prophecy and Preaching

In terms of the relationship between prophecy and preaching, contemporary scholars interpret Calvin as either equating prophecy and preaching or distinguishing between the two. Regarding the former, Eduard Schweizer says, "preaching means prophecy," for both forms of communicating translate the Christian faith, making it relevant for the hearer.[19] Such "prophetic preaching," however, should not limit the freedom of the Spirit by allowing only ordained preachers to speak. Moreover, overestimated enthusiasm in which a preacher's "utterance of the Spirit" is contradictory to scriptural revelation should be considered inauthentic.[20] "There needs to be a combination of prophetic utterances of members, by the Spirit of God, with a bold sticking to the unchangeable apostolic truth."[21]

Additionally, Kenneth Gangel says, "the gift of prophecy is congregational preaching which explains and applies God's revelation [in scripture]."[22] Gangel does not allow for the continuous functioning of the *charismata* of prophecy outside of Scripture, and, therefore, not in the contemporary context. Calvin, on the other hand, was open to this notion, for he acknowledged "traces or shadows of them [prophecy in his time]."[23]

However, other contemporary scholars distinguish between prophecy and preaching. One such scholar is Thomas Gillespie. For him, the NT prophets, instead of preaching, were interpreting the *kerygma*—which concerns the Gospel—and should be considered the first theologians of the church.[24] Their interpretation of the *kerygma* is done under the inspiration of the Holy Spirit, and therefore should be considered divine revelation.[25] To Max Turner, preaching is revelation mediated through Scripture, and it may be inspired, but it is not the same as prophecy, which is direct revelation mediated to the person.[26]

Arguably, views on the relationship between prophecy and preaching need to be more balanced and representative of a biblical perspective. Prophecy is revelation from God (1 Cor 14:6), and as such, can either

19. Schweizer, "The Service of Worship," 406.

20. Schweizer, "The Service of Worship," 407.

21. Schweizer, "The Service of Worship," 408.

22. Gangel, *You and Your Spiritual Gifts*, 38.

23. Calvin, *Commentary on the Epistle to the Corinthians*, 416.

24. Gillespie, *The First Theologians*, 32

25. Gillespie, *The First Theologians*, 199, 262.

26. Turner, "Spiritual Gifts," 14.

be foretelling or forth-telling. In terms of preaching, it can be equated to prophecy, if it is based on revelation and is not limited to Scripture, or to an anthropocentric hermeneutic. Preaching, however, should not contradict Scripture. Preaching should be led by the Holy Spirit—who "not only once inspired those who wrote it [scripture], but continually inspires, supernaturally assists, those that read it [scripture] with earnest prayer."[27]

Prophecy receives its content through revelation—whether direct or indirect[28]—but the content of preaching may not be from revelation (1 Cor 2:4). If the objective of all communication is to be authentically revelatory of God, today's preacher—and the church—should, therefore, be eager to prophesy (14:1, 39) and to allow the Holy Spirit to illuminate their mind concerning the Gospel of Jesus Christ and its eschatological implications for all people.

According to John Wimber, preaching should be done charismatically, for it should accompany a demonstration of the Gospel.[29] Preaching should also focus on Christ's redemptive act on the cross that transforms people as they glorify God by the power of the Holy Spirit.[30] It is therefore essential that preachers work at the delivery and reception of their sermon so that it will be appealing to as many people as possible.[31] This issue of communicating in a broadly appealing way is also at the center of discussions regarding tongues in the worship service.

CALVIN'S CRITERIA FOR THE FUNCTIONING OF THE GIFT OF TONGUES AND INTERPRETATION

For Calvin, the gift of tongues refers to "knowledge of languages—specifically the diversity of human foreign languages—and the gift of interpretation."[32] A tongue, for Calvin, is a sign for unbelievers,[33] given by the Holy Spirit "merely for the publication of the Gospel among all nations."[34] But, tongues

---

27. Wesley, *Explanatory Notes*, 794; also see Pinnock, "The Work of the Holy Spirit," 7.

28. Reisling, "Prophecy, the Spirit and the Church," 70.

29. Wimber with Springer, *Power Evangelism*, 79.

30. Harink, *Paul Among the Postliberals*, 244, 256.

31. Fry-Brown, *Delivering the Sermon*, 86.

32. Calvin, *Commentary on the Epistle to the Corinthians*, 417, 419, 435.

33. Calvin, *Commentary on the Epistle to the Corinthians*, 454.

34. Calvin, *Commentary on the Epistle to the Corinthians*, 437.

are a "gift of inferior importance,"[35] for people do not hear and understand the particular language(s), except if there is an interpretation.

Moreover, there is a need for the gift of interpretation of tongues, "for the church can, without any inconvenience, dispense with tongues, except in so far as they are helps to prophesy."[36] Indeed, with the gift of interpretation of tongues, tongues can be exercised in the worship service, and like prophecy, will intelligibly communicate to others. Uninterpreted tongues, however, are for private prayers.[37]

Contemporary Interpretations of Calvin's Criteria for the Functioning of the Gift of Tongues and Interpretation

Calvin's interpretation of Paul, in terms of tongues and the interpretation of tongues, has fueled contemporary debates concerning their functioning in the worship service. Many agree that "interpretation of tongues is an attendant gift to tongues,"[38] for the interpretation of tongues makes possible and meaningful the use of tongues in the meeting for worship."[39] That interpretation of tongues is complementary with the gift of tongues, suggests that interpretation of tongues should not be claimed unless there is a public exercise of tongues—then, it would be equivalent to a prophetic word which is revelatory of the will of God.

Nevertheless, there is disagreement as to whether to consider the interpretation of tongues as prophecy. David Ackerman says, "tongues speaking can become useful to the community only if it is interpreted, which then makes it equivalent to prophecy."[40] David Hill, however, asserts that interpretation of tongues—or one's perception of the will of God from Scripture or some other indirect "revelation" from God—does not correspond to prophecy, as it is more analogous to the role of a teacher.[41]

For Paul, tongues are given by the Spirit (1 Cor 12:4, 11) to benefit the one practicing it (14:4) as well as those hearing it (12:7). They have mystical value (14:2). They can be used in prayer (14:14–15), worship (14:15), and evangelism (14:22). Also, tongues should not be forbidden (14:39). Ernest Best is therefore carefully balanced in saying that:

35. Calvin, *Commentary on the Epistle to the Corinthians*, 459.

36. Calvin, *Commentary on the Epistle to the Corinthians*, 459.

37. Calvin, *Commentary on the Epistle to the Corinthians*, 460.

38. MacGorman, "Glossolalic Error," 389.

39. Bittlinger, *Gifts and Graces*, 51.

40. Ackerman, "Fighting Fire with Fire," 351.

41. Hill, *New Testament Prophecy*, 205–06.

[O]n the basis of scripture, the practice of glossolalia should be neither despised nor forbidden; on the other hand, it should not be emphasized nor made normative for the Christian experience. Generally, the experience should be private, and those who have experienced a genuine renewal of their faith in this way should be on their guard against divisiveness within the congregation. At the same time those who have received no unusual experiences of the Holy Spirit should be alert to the possibility of a deeper understanding of the Gospel and a fuller participation in the gifts of the Spirit.[42]

THE CESSATION OF THE CHARISMATA

The issue concerning whether the functioning of the *charismata* in the contemporary worship service is relevant, or if they ceased in the NT period stems largely from interpretations of Calvin. In his *On the Cessation of the Charismata: The Protestant Polemic on Postbiblical Miracles*, Jon Ruthven explains that cessationism is the idea that the *charismata*—especially "miraculous" ones like tongues and prophecy—were only for the foundation of the church and have since ceased functioning.[43] This notion first appeared in the writings of Augustine (354–430 C.E.) who declared,

in the earliest times, 'the Holy Ghost fell upon them that believed: and they spoke with tongues,' which they had not learned, 'as the Spirit gave them utterance.' These were signs adapted to the time. For there behooved to be that betokening of the Holy Spirit in all tongues, to shew that the Gospel of God was to run through all tongues over the whole earth. That thing was done for a betokening, and it passed away. In the laying of hands, now, that persons may receive the Holy Ghost, do we look, that they should speak with tongues? . . . If then the witness of the presence of the Holy Ghost be not now given through these miracles, by what is it given, by what does one get to know that he has received the Holy Ghost? Let him question his own heart. If he love his brother, the Spirit of God dwelleth in him.[44]

Augustine later retracted this seemingly cessationist view saying,

---

42. Best, "Interpretation of Tongues," 48.

43. Ruthven, *On the Cessation*, 30.

44. Augustine, *The Epistle of St. John*, 497–498.

what I said is not to be so interpreted that no miracles are believed to be performed in the name of Christ in the present time.
For when I wrote that book, I myself had recently learned that a
blind man had been restored to sight . . . and I knew about some
others, so numerous even in these times, that we cannot know
about all of them nor enumerate those we know.[45]

Still, it is variously interpreted that Calvin adopted and popularized the
earlier "cessationism" of Augustine without acknowledging his later retractions.[46] Vinson Synan asserts that Calvin made cessationist statements in
reaction to the Catholics' charge that the Reformers did not have authenticating miracles in their movement like those which the founders of the
Catholic Church had in the New Testament. Calvin said the miraculous
gifts were only intended for the beginning of Christianity and had long
since ceased to operate in the Church.[47] This response not only discounted
the miracles claimed by the clerics of the Catholic mystical tradition of his
day, but seemingly implied that the functioning of the *charismata* ended
with the early church and would not be needed anymore.

To understand Calvin's views regarding cessation of the *charismata*,
however, it is essential to consider all his writings. He states that the gift
of healing is the power to heal all manner of sicknesses and diseases, but
[it] pertains to the offices of the New Testament church, for example, when
a deacon cares for the poor.[48] And, "like the rest of the miracles [such as
tongues and prophecy], which the Lord willed to be brought forth for a
time, [it] has vanished away to make the new preaching of the Gospel marvelous forever . . . it now has nothing to do with us."[49] Stated differently,
having been established, the church no longer needs *charismata* like the
gifts of healing to witness about God, or to hear from God. Nevertheless,
the church should continuously preach about the *charismata* of NT time.[50]

Calvin's writings about the gifts of healing seem to suggest that they
have ceased. His writings concerning the *charismata* of forms of leadership,
however, suggest otherwise. For Calvin, "the offices of pastor and teacher
have not ceased in the church of this day, but relative to the offices of apostles, prophets, and evangelists, the Lord "now and again revives them as the
need of the times demands," but such an action is extraordinary for "in duly

---

45. Augustine, *The Retractions*, 55; cf. Elbert, *Calvin and the Spiritual Gifts*, 253.

46. Engammare, "Calvin," 648; Colver, "The Baptism in the Holy Spirit," 22.

47. Synan, "Speaking in Tongues," 324.

48. Calvin, *Commentary on the Epistle to the Corinthians*, 416.

49. Calvin, *Institutes*, 1467.

50. Calvin, *Institutes*, 1061.

constituted churches it has no place."[51] Such a revival has even happened through Martin Luther, whom he considers an apostle.[52] Additionally, in regards to prophets, Calvin notes, "this class either does not exist today or is less commonly seen."[53]

These statements suggest that Calvin is not a cessationist, for he only considers charismatic activity to be extraordinary, or less commonly seen in the offices of the church. This "soft cessationism" is further evidenced when he says, "if anyone is of a different opinion, I have no objection to his being so, and will not raise any quarrel on that account. For it is difficult to form a judgement as to gifts and offices."[54]

Contemporary Interpretations of Calvin and Cessationism

Calvin's work has influenced contemporary scholars to argue for and against cessationism. Among the latter, Pentecostal scholar Gordon Fee makes clear that Paul and the church expected that God would heal physical bodies.[55] Max Turner asserts that contemporary healing may be weaker than that of the NT, but the gift is nevertheless real,[56] and indicative of a variety of ways and individuals that the Spirit uses to address ailments.

If this is true, the healing of ailments does not come by a particular method. The base of authentic gifts of healing can also be either "spiritual" or "natural" means. Both the use of medicine and the laying on of hands, for example, could be considered part of the gift of healing. Moreover, since the Spirit distributes *charismata* as he wills (1 Cor 12:11), none should claim to be able to heal whenever they want to. Gifts of healing can occur "through whatever instrument or human agent, and whatever time God may choose, as one of many specific gifts."[57]

Those who argue for cessationism do so in at least five different ways. First, there is an exegetical claim that 1 Cor 13:8–10 teaches cessationism, based on an interpretation of "the end goal" in those verses to be Scripture.[58] The text reads, "love never fails, but as for prophecies, they will be discontinued, as for tongues, they will cease, as for knowledge, it will be discontinued.

51. Calvin, *Institutes*, 1057.

52. Calvin, *Institutes*, 1057.

53. Calvin, *Institutes*, 1057.

54. Calvin, *Commentary on the Epistle to the Corinthians*, 416.

55. Fee, *The First Epistle*, 590.

56. Turner, *The Holy Spirit*, 348.

57. Thiselton, *The First Epistle*, 950.

58. Unger, *New Testament Teaching*, 96.

For we know in part, and we prophesy in part, but whenever the end goal comes, that which is in part will be discontinued." That interpretation, however, is not without its detractors,[59] who see Paul referring instead to the *Parousia* of Jesus Christ.

Second, theological dispensationalists assert that *charismata* were for biblical times and not the present age, despite the suggestion in Eph 4:12–13 that the church—regardless of the dispensation—needs to be edified through the *charismata*.

The third view claims that historically, the miraculous gifts ceased after the apostolic period. However, there are at least two reasons to explain why the *charismata* may have appeared to cease in the post-Apostolic era. One of these explanations is that as the post-Apostolic church became more structured, power and the *charismata* were seen as prerogatives of the Bishop or resided in "exceptional Christians," such as those to be martyred. Thus, the laity increasingly did not participate in the *charismata*.[60]

Paul Tillich finds a second reason for the third cessationist claim, observing that after the Second Ecumenical Council at Constantinople (381 CE), when the divinity of the Spirit became "established," the Spirit was no longer "experienced" by most people as immanent, or applicable to their daily lives. Instead, the Spirit became the transcendent God, replaced in piety by the Virgin Mary. The German theologian and existentialist philosopher explains, "in the moment in which he was deified in the same sense that Christ was considered divine, the Spirit was replaced in actual piety by the Holy Virgin. The Virgin who gave birth to God acquired divinity herself to a certain extent."[61]

Fourth, some cessationists want correct theology without the power of which the Bible speaks. For them, after the apostolic era, there is no need for the miraculous since the Gospel has been adequately dispersed. Cessationists have chosen to focus on the doctrine that has been established by the apostles to control those that they consider heretics because of their belief in and continuous practicing of the *charismata*.[62]

However, scholars such as Stanley Burgess have documented the continuance of the *charismata* throughout church history.[63] Whenever the *charismata* appear to cease, it is often due to the institutionalized church forcing those gifts into groups that are considered marginal, fringe, or

---

59. Mallone, *Those Controversial Gifts*, 17–19; Talbert, "Paul's Understanding," 103.
60. McDonnell and Montague, *Christian Initiation*, 41.
61. McDonnell and Montague, *Christian Initiation*, 78.
62. Tillich, *A History*, 41.
63. Burgess, *The Holy Spirit*, passim.

heretical. Montanism is an example of this in the ancient church, and Classical Pentecostalism is an example in the contemporary church.

The final way in which contemporary scholars argue for cessationism is an assertion that those who claim to be functioning in the *charismata* today are practitioners of a "satanic counterfeit," because they do not evidence love, and are emotionally unstable.[64] But even though some may abuse the functioning of the *charismata*, such inauthentic spirituality is no reason to suggest that the *charismata* should cease functioning in the church—any more than inauthentic cessationism by some invalidates its advocates as a whole.

GENDER CRITERIA AND CHARISMATA

We next address another question: Are there gender criteria for the functioning of the *charismata*? This issue is raised in the contemporary context concerning the *mulier taceat* (let the women be silent) of 1 Cor 14:34–36, where the Apostle Paul says,

> Let the women be silent in the churches. For it is not permitted for them to speak, but (to) be subject, just as even the law says. And if they wish to learn something, let them ask their own husbands at home, for it is shameful for a woman to speak in church. Or did the word of God come out from you, or come upon you only?

Is Paul saying that women should not communicate in the worship service? If Paul allows for women to communicate in the worship service, to what extent does he do so? Are some *charismata* gender specific? Can women exercise the charismata of leadership in the worship service, and have authority over males?

Calvin's View on the Mulier Taceat

For Calvin, Paul is merely seeking to advance what is proper and edifying in a duly regulated assembly.[65] In such a gathering, because "it is the dictate of common sense, that female government is improper and unseemly . . . authority to teach (and to preach/prophesy) is not suitable to the station that a woman occupies, because, if she teaches, she presides over all the men while

64. MacArthur, *The Charismatics*, 174–80.
65. Calvin, *Commentary on the Epistles to the Corinthians*, 468–69.

it becomes her to be under subjection."[66] This, however, does not mean that women were not allowed to speak in the worship service, "for a necessity may occur of such a nature as to require that a woman should speak in public."[67] Such exercise of the *charismata* by a woman should not occur "where there is a church in a regularly constituted state," where prophets and other men who can teach are available.[68] Thus, Calvin does not interpret the *mulier taceat* as a command that women cannot speak in the worship service. To Calvin, Paul is saying that the Corinthian women should not be the regular authoritative communicator in the worship service.

Contemporary Views on the Mulier Taceat

Surprisingly, contemporary scholarship agrees in their interpretation of Calvin—at least in terms of the issue of propriety and edification as criteria for exercising the *charismata* in the worship service. However, that is where the consensus ends, for there are various interpretations of what kind of "order" Paul intended.

In line with Calvin's thinking, the Lutheran Church of Australia (LCA) Commission on Theology and Inter-Church Relations concludes that since Paul allowed women to prophesy and pray in public worship (1 Cor 11:5), the *mulier taceat* was "designed to serve Paul's fundamental pastoral and evangelical concern that worship be conducted with order and decorum."[69] The charge to silence, therefore, applies only to authoritative teaching, preaching, and evaluation of prophecies in that setting.

Thus, the women who prophesied as allowed in 1 Cor 11:5 were functioning in the acceptable role of merely being channels announcing what the Lord revealed. Paul is talking about women being silent in terms of functioning charismatically in the higher offices of male teachers and preachers who evaluate prophecies. A woman may prophesy, but not in a public ministry role: "a woman may teach other women, she may teach children, she may take part in the private instruction of a man like Apollos, but when a congregation assembles for public worship, women have no authority to serve as the preachers and teachers."[70]

The LCA also makes clear that the *mulier taceat* is a command that is valid until the *parousia* (1 Cor 14:37). Furthermore, Paul is not affirming an

66. Calvin, *Commentary on the Epistles to the Corinthians*, 468.
67. Calvin, *Commentary on the Epistles to the Corinthians*, 468.
68. Calvin, *Commentary on the Epistles to the Corinthians*, 468–69.
69. Lutheran Church of Australia, "1 Corinthians and 1 Timothy," 66.
70. Lutheran Church of Australia, "1 Corinthians and 1 Timothy," 65.

abusively patriarchal male dominance. Instead, as the Corinthian context (1 Cor 11:2–16) makes clear, he discusses responsible authority and its proper use of serving others.[71] In 11:3, Paul says, "but I want you to understand that Christ is the head of every man, and the husband is the head of his wife, and God is the head of Christ." Women are to be "subject" to their own husbands, as men are to be subordinate to Christ—a relationship that does not negate male and female equality and unity in Christ (Gal 3:28).

The LCA emphasizes that husbands should exercise authority in a self-sacrificial manner. Paul appeals for voluntary submission to God's order for church and its worship service. This relationship of wives to their husbands is analogous to when the members of the church are subject to their pastors, promoting "the peace and harmony that result when every part of Christ's body function properly, and the body grows and build itself up in love (cf. 1 Cor 13; 14:33, 40)."[72]

In his article entitled, "Learning in the Assemblies: 1 Corinthians 14:34–35," Craig Keener offers a second interpretation of the *mulier taceat*: Paul was emphasizing a need to avoid conduct that was offensive to the Graeco-Roman community, for whom, social space was divided along lines of public (males) and private (females); engaging in casual conversation with men would subject a woman to charges of immorality, and it was unacceptable for women to speak when men were present. One exception to this ethos, however, is for inspired utterances like prophecy or tongues.[73]

In light of this context, it is understandable how Paul can allow women to pray or prophesy in the public worship service, but also charge them to be silent—when they were not prophesying. Paul's charge to silence, then, apparently involved conduct that was offensive in his context. What is at stake in the *mulier taceat* is not gender, but propriety, orderliness, and the fitting place in society for learning.[74]

Third, some commentators argue that the *mulier taceat* concerns a need for orderliness in the worship service, to avoid questioning by those who are insufficiently learned. While the asking of questions was common in first-century Graeco-Roman public discourse, Keener notes that such was not the case if the questioner was insufficiently learned, as was the case for most women of the day.[75]

---

71. Lutheran Church of Australia, "1 Corinthians and 1 Timothy," 53–54.

72. Lutheran Church of Australia, "1 Corinthians and 1 Timothy," 57.

73. Keener, "Learning in the Assemblies," 166.

74. Keener, "Learning in the Assemblies," 171.

75. Keener, "Learning in the Assemblies," 168.

But the idea that the *mulier taceat* concerns unlearned women who were interrupting worship with their questioning seems to imply that if the women were learned, they too would have the authority to communicate in the worship service. If this is true, perhaps the outspoken women in 1 Cor 11:5 were speaking with authority and were not just "channels" of divine revelation. Additionally, would it also not be the same scenario for men who were unlearned? That is, since it is frowned upon for the unlearned to ask questions, unlearned men would also have to be silent. If only learned individuals could communicate authoritatively in the worship service, one should then infer that only the gifted and equipped could exercise *charismata* in public worship.

Finally, for some the *mulier taceat* concerns a need for order in the worship service due to an abuse of tongues. Based on the context of 1 Cor 12–14, it is likely that the *mulier taceat* refers to tongues speakers—who are mentioned throughout the entire pericope. They were even commanded by Paul to be silent if their speech would remain unintelligible and disrupt the order of the public gathering (1 Cor 14:30). Contextually, Corinthians were boastful and competitive. They esteemed tongues as a sign of being spiritually mature—a status symbol. Thus, they spoke simultaneously and unintelligibly with little concern about being understood by others. So, it seems reasonable that Paul issued the *mulier taceat* because the women were creating the same type of disorder in the community gatherings that was caused by uninterpreted tongues.

To summarize contemporary interpretations of the *mulier taceat*, it appears that because 1 Cor 14 explains why Christians should pursue spiritual gifts and love, and even more seek to prophesy (14:1); and because Paul notably contrasts the gift of tongues with prophecy that edifies all, the second interpretation of the *mulier taceat* is most reasonable: that Paul emphasized the need to avoid conduct that was offensive to the Graeco-Roman community. Such offensive conduct includes uninterpreted tongues and unlearned questions, but must also include specific prophetic speech. If Paul is encouraging the appropriate exercise of the *charismata* that edifies the church, then the other three interpretations of the *mulier taceat* do not thoroughly address the principles of orderliness and edification in the worship service. Such views do not consider that while 1 Cor 11:5 allows women to both pray and prophesy, this praying, based on the context of discussing prophecy and tongues, is a reference to the private exercise of uninterpreted tongues, unto God—which Paul does not condemn—as well as prophecy exercised in an orderly manner. However, disorderly communication, such as public tongues that is either uninterpreted or not done in turn, must be avoided in the worship service (1 Cor 14:27–28), just as disorderly prophetic speech must not occur (1 Cor 14:29–32).

There are various implications of this. First, it appears that Paul does not imply that the *charismata* of teaching, preaching, and judging in the worship service are off limits to all women, but only to those who communicate in a disorderly manner—whether through uninterpreted tongues, disorderly prophecy, or inappropriate questioning. Second, utterances such as prophecy, tongues, and "learned" questioning were acceptable in the worship service, but they must be exercised in an orderly way, or be silenced. Finally, while in the *mulier taceat* Paul addresses explicitly a situation involving women, it is not just women who are often unlearned. We may deduce, therefore, that all the unlearned should refrain from disrupting the service with their questions.

CONCLUSION

Having considered the contributions of the Apostle Paul, Calvin, and contemporary interpreters relative to prophecy, tongues, the interpretation of tongues, the notion of the cessation of the *charismata*, and gender criteria relative to the functioning of the *charismata* in the worship service, we can make the following conclusions:

First, like prophecy, a tongue has an edifying role in the church, for uninterpreted tongues are edifying to individual members as they mysteriously speak to God. Such speech can serve to give thanks, fellowship with, and develop a relationship with God, and therefore has doxological purposes. For example, tongues can be a form of inspired prayer, or a psalm in which one presents personal supplications to God or sings his praises.

In the context of the gathering of members of the church, however, tongues should not be practiced unless there is an interpreter, for unintelligible tongues cannot edify others. They should therefore only be spoken to God in private. When interpreted, though, like prophecy, tongues can edify those who hear and understand. Such *charismata* require listeners to discern if they are divine revelation. Thus, speaking in tongues should not be forbidden in the church, but the practice must occur decently and in order that the church, and the rest of the world, can be edified for God's glory.

Second, Calvin was not a cessationist, and church history, thoroughly examined, does not support cessationism. That history instead documents the continuance of the *charismata*—including most saliently the contemporary Pentecostal and Charismatic Movements. Most important, the Bible does not teach cessationism, but a charismatic manifestation of the Spirit exercised in loving and edifying ways. It is, therefore, appropriate to declare that the *charismata* have not ceased with the New Testament church, and to encourage the contemporary church to exercise them in the worship service.

Finally, with respect to whether Paul prescribed a gender criterion relative to the exercise of the *charismata* in the worship service, we find that the Triune God gifts both males and females, and that both males and females may gain the learning that enables them to exercise their gifts in the worship service in loving, orderly, and edifying ways. These criteria of gift-edness and education remove barriers of race, gender, and socio-economic status (1 Cor 12:13), allowing all to participate in the worship service. This inclusion allows the optimal communication of God's message to all, such that all can praise God together and all can be edified. We therefore infer not only the value of the *charismata* brought by the people of God but also the need to hold those same people accountable to the discernment of the community—a basis for further growth of community members as they also allow *charismata* to edify them.

Giftedness also suggests that only those exercising the *charismata* in an edifying and orderly manner should be allowed to do so in the worship service. It implies that all are in control of their spirit, such that they can allow and invite the Spirit of God to work through them. Such work should manifest love, which is characteristic of Christ, in the lives of God's people. When such love is shown by those humbly serving to properly exercise the *charismata* in the worship service, not exalting themselves, we see the work of Christ.

Lastly, what is at stake in the *mulier taceat* is not gender, but propriety, orderliness, and learning in society. As it was for Paul, exercising the *charismata* in the contemporary worship service should manage the tension of being in human culture, but not being of that culture. Social roles involving gender should not determine the exercise of *charismata* in the worship service—under the authority of the Triune God—to benefit his people. We have seen that there are no gender criteria relative to the functioning of the *charismata* in the worship service. We have also seen that it is not, in essence, shameful for a woman to speak or exercise any *charismata* in church. Indeed, "the safety of the church is preserved when members impart their gift for the common good and not prevent others from doing the same."[76] May these conclusions be among the enduring legacies of the Reformation, to the glory of God!

---

76. Calvin, *The Epistles to the Romans and Thessalonians*, 268.

BIBLIOGRAPHY

Ackerman, David. "Fighting Fire with Fire: Community Formation in 1 Cor 12–14." *Evangelical Review of Theology* 29 (2005) 350–51.

Augustine. *The Epistle of St. John.* "Homily vi.10." The Nicene and Post-Nicene Fathers, ser. 1, vol. 7. 14 vols. Edited by Philip Schaff. 1886–1889. Reprint, Peabody, MA: Hendrickson, 1994.

————. *The Retractions.* Translated by Mary Inez Bogan. Washington, DC: Catholic University of America Press, 1999.

Aune, David. *Prophecy in Early Christianity and the Ancient Mediterranean.* 1983. Reprint, Eugene, OR: Wipf & Stock, 2003.

Best, Ernest. "Interpretation of Tongues," *Scottish Journal of Theology* 28 (1975) 45–62.

Bittlinger, Arnold. *Gifts and Graces.* Grand Rapids: Eerdmans, 1967.

Burgess, Stanley. *The Holy Spirit: Ancient Christian Traditions.* Peabody, MA: Hendrickson, 1984.

Calvin, John. *Commentary on the Epistles of Paul the Apostle to the Corinthians.* Translated by John Pringle. Grand Rapids: Eerdmans, 1948.

————. *The Epistles of Paul the Apostle to the Romans and to the Thessalonians.* Translated by Ross Mackenzie. Edinburgh: Oliver & Boyd, 1961.

————. *The Institutes of Christian Religion.* Edited by John McNeill. Translated by Ford Lewis Battles. Philadelphia: Westminster, 2011.

Cartledge, Mark J. "Charismatic Prophecy and New Testament Prophecy." *Themelios* 17 (1991) 17–19.

Colver, Randy. "The Baptism in the Holy Spirit, the Charismata, and Cessationism." (2006) 1–26. http://www.netministry.com/clientfiles/62181/mw_colver baptismintheholyspirit.pdf.

Elbert, Paul. "Calvin and the Spiritual Gifts." *Journal of the Evangelical Theological Society* 22 (1979) 235–56.

Engammare, Max. "Calvin: A Prophet without a Prophecy." *Church History* 67 (1998) 643–61.

Fee, Gordon. *The First Epistle to the Corinthians.* New International Commentary on the New Testament. Grand Rapids: Eerdmans, 1987.

Fry-Brown, Teresa. *Delivering the Sermon: Voice, Body, and Animation in Proclamation.* Minneapolis: Fortress, 2008.

Gangel, Kenneth. *Unwrap Your Spiritual Gifts.* Wheaton, IL: Victor, 1983.

————. *You and Your Spiritual Gifts.* Chicago: Moody, 1975.

Gillespie, Thomas. *The First Theologians: A Study in Early Christian Prophecy.* Grand Rapids: Eerdmans, 1994.

Harink, Douglas. *Paul among the Postliberals: Pauline Theology beyond Christendom and Modernity.* Grand Rapids: Brazos, 2003.

Hill, David. *New Testament Prophecy.* Atlanta: John Knox, 1979.

Keener, Craig. "Learning in the Assemblies: 1 Corinthians 14:34–35." In *Discovering Biblical Equality: Complementarity without Hierarchy*, edited by Ronald W. Pierce et al., 161–71. Downers Grove: InterVarsity, 2004.

Lutheran Church of Australia Commission on Theology and Inter-Church Relations. "1 Corinthians 14:33b–38 and 1 Timothy 2:11–14: Permit the Ordination of Women." *Lutheran Theological Journal* 39 (2005) 66–83.

MacArthur, John. *The Charismatics.* Grand Rapids: Zondervan, 1978.

MacGorman, J. W. "Glossolalic Error and Its Correction: 1 Corinthians 12–14." *Review & Expositor* 80 (1983) 389–400.

Mallone, George. *Those Controversial Gifts: Prophecy, Dreams, Visions, Tongues, Interpretation, Healing.* Downers Grove, IL: InterVarsity, 1983.

McDonnell, Killian, and George Montague. *Christian Initiation and Baptism in the Holy Spirit: Evidence from the First Eight Centuries.* Collegeville, MN: Liturgical, 1991.

Packer, J.I. *Keep in Step with the Spirit.* Old Tappan, NJ: InterVarsity, 1984.

Pinnock, Clark. "The Work of the Holy Spirit in Hermeneutics." *Journal of Pentecostal Theology* 2 (1993) 3–23.

Reisling, Jannes. "Prophecy, the Spirit and the Church." In *Prophetic Vocation in the New Testament and Today,* edited by Johannes Panagopoulos, 46–57. Novum Testamentum Supplements 45. Leiden: Brill, 1977.

Ruthven, Jon Mark. *On the Cessation of the Charismata: The Protestant Polemic on Postbiblical Miracles.* Journal of Pentecostal Theology Supplement Series 3. Sheffield: Sheffield Academic, 1993.

Schweizer, Eduard. "The Service of Worship: An Exposition of 1 Corinthians 14." *Interpretation* 13 (1959) 400–408.

Siegfried Schatzmann, Siegfried. *A Pauline Theology of the Charismata.* Peabody, MA: Hendrickson, 1987.

Synan, Vinson. "Speaking in Tongues." *One in Christ* 19 (1983) 323–31.

Talbert, Charles. "Paul's Understanding of the Holy Spirit: The Evidence of 1 Corinthians 12–14." *Perspectives in Religious Studies* 11 (1984) 95–108.

Thiselton, Anthony. *The First Epistle to the Corinthians.* New International Greek Testament Commentary. Grand Rapids: Eerdmans, 2000.

Tillich, Paul. *A History of Christian Thought.* New York: Simon & Schuster, 1967.

Turner, Max. "Spiritual Gifts Then and Now." *Vox Evangelica* 15 (1985) 7–64.

———. *The Holy Spirit and Spiritual Gifts: Then and Now.* Carlisle, UK: Paternoster, 1996.

Unger, Merril. *New Testament Teaching on Tongues.* Grand Rapids: Kregel, 1971.

Wesley, John. *Explanatory Notes upon the New Testament.* Edited by Alec Allenson. Naperville, IL: Epworth, 1958.

Wimber John, and Kevin Springer, *Power Evangelism.* San Francisco: HarperSanFrancisco, 1992.

10

John Calvin, the Gifts, and Prophecy

DANIEL B. GILBERT

INTRODUCTION

CALVIN'S PNEUMATOLOGY FORMS THE foundation for his understanding of the spiritual gifts, causing him to struggle in his understanding of the *charismata*, yet, at the same time, he can interpret the pneumatic *charismata* in a balanced way. The study of Calvin's pneumatology[1] reveals his acknowledgment of the Holy Spirit's work in every element of life—especially in the believer's life. Calvin teaches that without the Holy Spirit, the grace of God and all the benefits of Christ cannot be imparted to believers.

However, there has not been much research done on Calvin's understanding of the *charismata*, and especially his views on the teachings and practices of the pneumatic *charismata*. As we begin to examine Calvin's general concept of the gifts of the Spirit, this section will show how he demonstrated a distinction within and between the natural gifts of God and the spiritual gifts of God. We also will discover that the issue of the pneumatic *charismata* was a concern for Calvin. After giving an overview of Calvin's understanding of the gifts of the Spirit, we will focus on one of the most important gifts, both to Calvin and to the Church: the gift of prophecy.

---

1. See Gilbert, "The Pneumatic Charismata" for a fuller discussion of the material contained in this chapter.

CALVIN'S GENERAL CONCEPTS
OF THE GIFTS OF THE SPIRIT

To the Reformers, the concept of the gifts of the Spirit was vast. They made little distinction between the *pneumatic charismata* and the other gifts of God. This commonality came because all abilities, knowledge, talents, vocations, and special abilities, along with spiritual gifts, both ordinary and extraordinary, were identified both as gifts of God the Father and gifts of the Spirit. This unity is accurate; however, all gifts are given from God the Father and made effectual by the Holy Spirit—some in the unbeliever and others in the believer.

Spiritual Gifts of God

Although Calvin interchanged the phrases "gifts of God," "God's gifts," "gifts of the Spirit," and "spiritual gifts," he made a clear distinction between those gifts that were natural endowments and spiritual gifts which came with or through the gift of salvation.

In his commentary on Exodus, Calvin expounded on the peculiar gift of the Spirit that was bestowed on Bezaleel to perform extraordinary craftsmanship on the Tabernacle and added a significant statement, "For although 'there are diversities of gifts', still it is the same Spirit from whom they all flow, (1 Cor. xii.4;) . . . *Nor is this only the case with respect to the spiritual gifts which follow regeneration . . .*"[2]

Calvin not only distinguished spiritual gifts from natural gifts, but also clarified that spiritual gifts followed regeneration. In other words, he communicated to the reader that there were two main categories of gifts or distinctions between gifts of God—certain gifts that were common in life (the natural gifts), and certain gifts that were granted through and from salvation (spiritual gifts). Calvin also used 1 Cor 12:4 in this passage to emphasize two elements of the gifts. First, he emphasized that the Spirit of God gave a diversity of gifts that were not limited solely to spiritual gifts. Second, Calvin had in mind from 1 Corinthians 12 those extraordinary spiritual gifts imparted to believers through the Holy Spirit.

Calvin continued to clarify the difference between natural and spiritual gifts in his commentary on 2 Pet 1:3, noting, "His divine power has given us everything we need for life and godliness." He clarifies that Peter was not writing here about natural gifts, but only "special gifts of the new spiritual life which take their origin from the kingdom of Christ. . . to be

---

2. Calvin, *Commentary on Exodus*, vol. 3, 291.

included among the supernatural gifts of God"[3] that God gives to the elect. Calvin sees here a clear distinction between the natural and spiritual gifts, a distinction which he emphasizes throughout his works on the gifts of the Spirit.

In his commentary on Eph 1:17, Calvin made the distinction again, stating, "But let us observe that the gifts of the Spirit are not the endowments of nature."[4] He emphasized this same theme in his comments on Isa 11:2, where he identified the gifts of the Spirit as those spiritual gifts of wisdom, knowledge, understanding, counsel, might, and the fear of the Lord that were endowed upon Christ in order to impart them only to believers.[5]

Gifts of Salvation

There is a general difference between the gifts of salvation and the ordinary gifts of God. Calvin mentions in the *Institutes* that all Christians are blessed with the gifts of the Spirit due to Christ's kingly office, and these gifts are different from the ordinary gifts of God. He writes, "hence we are furnished, as far as God knows to be expedient for us, with the gifts of the Spirit, which we lack by nature."[6] By nature, humanity lacks all spiritual gifts. When Adam and Eve sinned:

> the natural gifts were corrupted in man through sin, but. . .his supernatural gifts were stripped from him. . .Therefore, withdrawing from the Kingdom of God, he [Man] is at the same time deprived of spiritual gifts, with which he had been furnished for the hope of eternal salvation. . .Among these [gifts] are faith, love of God, charity toward neighbour, zeal for holiness and for righteousness. All these, since Christ restores them in us, are considered adventitious, and beyond nature.[7]

According to Calvin, certain spiritual gifts were lost when Adam sinned, which could only be restored to those who were regenerated. He classified these gifts of salvation as spiritual gifts of God. He also provided a similar list and understanding in his commentary on Genesis, stating, "In

---

3. Calvin, *Commentary on 2 Peter*, 329 (emphasis mine).

4. Calvin, *Commentary on Ephesians*, 134.

5. Calvin, *Commentary on Isaiah*, Vol 1., 373–77.

6. Calvin, *Institutes*, II.xv.4, 499. Hereafter cited as *Institutes*.

7. *Institutes*, II.ii.12, 270.

short, that we are despoiled of the excellent gifts of the Spirit, of the light of reason, justice, and of rectitude, and are prone to every evil."[8]

Calvin did not simply regard the gifts of the Spirit expressed in 1 Cor 12 as the only gifts of the Spirit. He states, "everything which is concerned with the true knowledge of God is a gift of the Holy Spirit."[9] According to Calvin, the gifts of the Holy Spirit were a part of the gifts or among the gifts of salvation—of which the knowledge of God was one.

Since Calvin understood the salvific gifts as the core of the gifts of the Spirit, he emphasized these salvific gifts more than any other. In the *Institutes* III.i.4, he stated that saving faith was a supernatural gift that was given by the Holy Spirit.[10] Calvin mentioned that redemption was the "first gift of Christ to be begun in us, and the last to be brought to completion."[11] He saw the gifts of salvation, such as repentance,[12] sanctification,[13] justification,[14] special illumination in the knowledge of God,[15] and others as gifts of the Holy Spirit or spiritual gifts of God. No doubt, these gifts were central in Calvin's thought when he discussed the spiritual gifts. However, he did distinguish between the gifts of salvation and the extraordinary gifts.

Pneumatic Charismata

As Calvin continued to develop his view of the gifts of the Spirit, he made a clear differentiation between certain aspects of the spiritual gifts. Although he interchanged the phrase "spiritual gifts" with "gifts of God" or "God's gifts," he made a distinction that several gifts listed in 1 Cor 12 were different in nature from the other gifts of God. In his exposition of 1 Cor 12:28, he distinguished the gifts in 1 Cor 12:8–10 as gifts of powers, over against the gifts listed in verse 28, which were offices of ministry appointed by the Holy Spirit, stating, "At the beginning of the chapter Paul had spoken about 'powers' (*facultatibus*); now he takes up the discussion of offices."[16] Calvin's description of the *charismata* as gifts of powers revealed a variance between other spiritual gifts and those listed in 1 Cor 12:8–10. He also identified the

8. Calvin, *Commentary on Genesis*, vol. 1, 155–56.

9. Calvin, *Commentary on 1 Corinthians*, 259.

10. *Institutes* III.i.4, 541–42.

11. Calvin, *Commentary on 1 Corinthians*, 46.

12. *Institutes*, III.iii.21, 615.

13. *Institutes*, II.i.7, 250; and III.ii.8, 552–53.

14. *Institutes*, III.xi.18, 747–48.

15. *Institutes*, II.ii.20, 278.

16. Calvin, *Commentary on 1 Corinthians*, 270.

charismata, in his *Commentary on Acts*, as visible gifts and visible graces[17] and wonderful gifts or graces[18] to signify a distinction from the other spiritual gifts of God.

Calvin made another distinction by not identifying the other *charismata* listed in Rom 12:6–8 as gifts of powers because he recognized a difference between them, although they too were spiritual gifts.[19] Calvin rightly saw the gifts in Rom 12 as practical and relevant for the Church, whereas he viewed the gifts in 1 Cor 12–14 as extraordinary. This distinction is seen in his comments on Rom 12:6, "It is not clear that he [Paul] intended here to consider only those *wonderful graces* [gifts of powers] by which Christ adorned His Gospel at the beginning. We see rather that he is referring simply to *ordinary gifts* which remain perpetually in the Church."[20] Calvin viewed the spiritual gifts mentioned in 1 Cor 12 as wonderful graces, gifts that were distinctively different from the ordinary spiritual gifts listed in Rom 12. The ordinary gifts were not inferior in any form of understanding. They were still spiritual gifts that followed the gifts of salvation and were only for the Church and its believers. Here, Calvin rightly saw a distinction between the gifts of the Spirit in 1 Cor 12 and Rom 12, even though the same Greek term *charismata* is used in both passages.

Calvin provided more clarity between the gifts of the Spirit than one would imagine. His distinctions between the gifts reveal that he had not merely combined all the gifts into one category, but had considered each of the gifts and identified distinctions and classifications among them. He distinguished in detail the differences among spiritual gifts, suggesting his thoroughness on the subject.

Calvin corrected believers who diminished the use of the gifts of God in the life of the Church, demonstrating his seriousness concerning the practice of God's gifts. When we hold all the gifts of the Spirit, both ordinary and spiritual gifts, "in slight esteem," he declares, "we condemn and

---

17. Calvin, *Commentary on Acts*, vol. 1, 59. Visible gifts or visible graces are the gifts of the Spirit such as gifts of faith, gifts of healings, gifts of workings of miracles, revelations, dreams, visions, gift of tongues and interpretation of tongues.

18. *Institutes*, IV.xix.6, 1454.

19. Bucer held to this point of view to some degree. He acknowledged the differences in the charismata in Rom 12 and 1 Cor 12, but concentrated most of his efforts on the Rom 12 passage when he discussed the gifts of the Spirit needed for the offices of ministry. See Stephens, *Holy Spirit in the Theology of Bucer*, 185–190; van 't Spijker, "Ecclesiastical Offices," 370–83. Luther, Bullinger and Vermigli all acknowledged that there were extraordinary gifts of the Spirit, of which some were listed in 1 Cor 12, but they did not seem to clarify them as much as Calvin did.

20. Calvin, *Commentary on Romans*, 269. (Emphasis mine).

reproach the Spirit himself."[21] He emphasised the need for all the gifts to be used properly and in order. He showed a distinction between the natural gifts given by the Spirit to all people and the spiritual gifts given by the Spirit for the believer. However, as we have seen, he indicated that all gifts were for the common good of the Church.

THE PROPHETIC OFFICE AND THE GIFT OF PROPHECY

The Gift of Prophecy

Aside from love, Calvin considered the gift of prophecy to be the most important gift of the Spirit. The church must have the gift of prophecy in order to function properly, and those called by God to the ministry of teaching elder must be endowed with this gift.[22]

It is important to consider how Calvin relates his understanding of prophecy in the Rom 12:6 passage to his understanding of that gift's function in the 1 Cor 12 passage. Before Calvin defined the gift of prophecy in Rom 12, he first considered how others interpreted this same passage. He noted that some believed this gift dealt strictly with foretelling or the ability to predict. Though Calvin did not deny this element of the gift, he found it to be an extremely rare occurrence. At times he held to the understanding that prophecy was dynamic, inspired preaching.[23] He therefore defined the gift of prophecy in Rom 12:6 as "the peculiar gift of revelation by which a man performs the office of interpreter with skill and dexterity in expounding the will of God . . . Prophecy at the present day is simply the right understanding of Scripture and the particular gift of expounding it."[24] This definition seemed to be the general understanding of the gift by other Reformers.

Calvin's definition of the gift of prophecy in Rom 12:6 was narrower in scope than his definition in 1 Cor 12, which we observe shortly. There were two main reasons for this degree of difference. First, Calvin wrote his *Commentary on Romans* in 1539 and 1540, six years before he wrote his *Commentary on 1 Corinthians* in 1546. There was a progression in his understanding of prophecy, albeit a small expansion in his view. The second reason for a slight difference was that Calvin was interpreting two different passages with different functions, so he approached the passages with

21. *Institutes*, II.ii.15, 274.
22. *Institutes*, IV.iii.11, 1063.
23. Elbert, "Calvin and the Spiritual Gifts," 127.
24. Calvin, *Commentary on Romans*, 269.

different lenses. Romans 12, according to Calvin, was about the proper use of the offices of ministry and being content with the place of ministry God had given each person. He saw Corinthians 12 as addressing the proper use of the extraordinary gifts because the Corinthians were abusing those gifts and using them for selfish gain. Although there were some differences in Calvin's interpretation of the gift of prophecy in the two passages, Calvin did not contradict himself. He just expanded his understanding of the gift.

Calvin further explored prophecy in Rom 12 as he interpreted the phrase that follows Paul's instruction on the gift of prophecy, "if prophecy, according to the proportion of his faith." According to Calvin, "the proportion of his faith" means conforming the prophecies "to the rule of faith . . . the first principles of religion, and any doctrine."[25] He suggested that when an individual was prophesying, that is, preaching and interpreting the Word, that person was preaching on the doctrines of the faith, teaching the Christian faith to the people. He did not consider that the "proportion of faith" related to one's faith in God, or to being given special faith to speak the Word of the Lord to build up the body of Christ. However, his understanding of the gift of prophecy broadened over the years as he came to view it as more than just teaching or interpreting Scripture and the faith.[26]

The gift of prophecy, the sixth spiritual gift listed in 1 Cor 12:10, is the only spiritual gift listed in common among 1 Cor 12:8–10; Rom 12:6–8; Eph 4:11; and 1 Cor 12:28. Due to this abundant scriptural witness, the office of prophet was one of the most discussed offices in Calvin's works. When Calvin discussed the gift of prophecy, he always equated this gift with the prophetic office—but approached its reference in 1 Corinthians a little differently.[27]

When Calvin discusses the gift of prophecy, he embraces the general understanding that the gift is forth-telling and not necessarily foretelling.[28] However, the main interpretation of this gift among Reformers is that the gift of prophecy is strictly forth-telling of the Word of God or, in other words, the interpreting and preaching of the Scripture.

25. Calvin, *Commentary on Romans*, 269.

26. This will be observed later in the chapter.

27. His approach to the gift of prophecy in 1 Corinthians is different from his approach to the gift in his commentary on Rom 12. It is different for two reasons: First, he is writing his commentary on 1 Corinthians six years after he wrote his commentary on Romans. This shows how Calvin has broadened his understanding of this gift in that period. Second, Calvin is addressing different gifts and is writing his commentary for a different purpose.

28. Calvin, *Commentary on 1 Corinthians*, 286. Calvin sometimes described foretelling as flourishing in the Church in the first century only, to solidify the Gospel as he stated in his *Commentary on Romans*, 269.

Calvin sees in 1 Corinthians that the gift of prophecy is more than just preaching. He defines prophecy as "that unique and outstanding gift of revealing what is the secret will of God, so that the prophet is, so to speak, God's messenger to men."[29] It is evident in his definition that prophecy is more than just inspired preaching or teaching. As Calvin states about 1 Cor 14:6, "prophesying does not consist in the simple or bare interpretation of Scripture." He believes it to be, here, an actual reception of revelation from God regarding the Scripture and speaking the right word to build up the community of believers during a time of immediate need.[30] In this case, Calvin sees God's revelation and human prophesying as two sides of the same coin. One cannot prophesy without having a revelation from the Holy Spirit. He states:

> I bracket revelation and prophesying together, and I think that prophesying is the servant of revelation . . . Therefore whatever anyone has obtained by revelation he gives out in prophesying . . . This supports, rather than conflicts with, the definition of prophecy which I gave earlier. For I said that prophesying does not consist in the simple or bare interpretation of Scripture, but also includes the knowledge for making it apply to the needs of the hour, and that can be obtained by revelation and the special influence of God.[31]

For Calvin, prophecy is real and necessary for the church to be strengthened and enhanced. It is a gift given to help the church, particularly times of need such as the time of the Reformation.

Calvin next expresses several functions of the gift of prophecy that he intertwines with the function of the prophet. He sees one function of this gift in 1 Cor 14, where prophesying enriches everybody. This enrichment is due to the gift since the gift is to be an edifying word to encourage and build up the body of believers.[32]

As he writes on the function of the prophet in 1 Cor 12:28, Calvin gives his understanding of the gift of prophecy, stating:

> I am certain, in my own mind that he means by prophets, not those endowed with the gift of foretelling but those who were blessed with the unique gift of dealing with Scripture, not only by interpreting it, but also by the wisdom they showed in making it meet the needs of the hour. My reason for thinking so

29. Calvin, *Commentary on 1 Corinthians*, 263.
30. Calvin, *Commentary on 1 Corinthians*, 271 and 288.
31. Calvin, *Commentary on 1 Corinthians*, 288.
32. Calvin, *Commentary on 1 Corinthians*, 286.

is that Paul prefers prophecy to all the other gifts, because it is a greater source of edification, a statement that can hardly be made to apply to the prediction of future events . . . Prophets are: 1) outstanding interpreters of Scripture; and 2) men endowed with extraordinary wisdom and aptitude for grasping what the immediate need of the Church is, and speaking the right word to meet it . . . I have a reason for not sharing in the opinion of those who confine the task of the prophet to the interpretation of the Scriptures . . . My view is that the prophets referred to here are those who are skilful and experienced in making known the will of God, by applying prophecies, threats, promises, and all the teaching of Scripture to the current needs of the Church.[33]

Calvin goes further as he defines the gift of prophecy as more than preaching or interpreting the Scripture. It is a supernatural gift used to reveal the will of God and to help meet the current needs of the Church.

Another function or purpose of the gift of prophecy, according to Calvin, is its value for unbelievers. He states in considering 1 Cor 14:24, "[Paul] points out the effect that prophecy has, viz., it summons the consciences of unbelievers to the judgement seat of God, and imbues them with such a lively realisation of the judgement of God, that somebody who, in his indifference, used to despise sound teaching, is forced to glorify God."[34]

Calvin, describing in the *Institutes* the office of prophet as found in Eph 4:11, implies that prophecy continues, stating, "Paul applies the name 'prophets' not to all those who were interpreters of God's will, but to those who excelled in a particular revelation [Eph. 4:11]. This class either does not exist today or is less commonly seen."[35] If the prophet is "less commonly seen," then there is the understanding that prophecy, although less common, may be more than preaching and interpreting God's will. It is also a gift given for particular revelation, which may include the gift of foretelling, "so far as it was connected with teaching."[36] Calvin, however, acknowledges the need for this gift within the Church when it is used appropriately through the prophet-preacher-teacher.

33. Calvin, *Commentary on 1 Corinthians*, 271.
34. Calvin, *Commentary on 1 Corinthians*, 298.
35. *Institutes*, IV.iii.4, 1057.
36. Calvin, *Commentary on Ephesians*, 179.

The Temporary-Permanent Distinction

Calvin, as he developed his understanding of the gift of prophecy, remained unclear as to whether that gift is temporary or permanent. He understands the gift of prophecy from three standpoints. First, the gift of prophecy and the office of prophet are virtually synonymous. Second, the specific office of the prophet is temporary for the most part and, therefore, the gift of prophecy as foretelling is temporary. Third, the gift of prophecy, as defined in his *Commentary on 1 Corinthians,* is still available for the church.

To Calvin, that only one who is a prophet can prophesy is a reasonable assumption. Nevertheless, to say that Calvin has a strict, narrow understanding of the gift of prophecy being used only by prophets is debatable. Addressing 1 Cor 14:31–32 where Paul writes, "for you can all prophesy in turn. . ." Calvin emphasizes that the term "all" does not mean the Holy Spirit may use any believer with this gift, but only those who are endowed with the gift of prophecy, whom he defines as prophets.[37]

However, for us to understand how Calvin sees the gift of prophecy as temporary, it is necessary to clarify how Calvin views prophets and the office of prophets. There are four classifications of prophets in Calvin's thoughts: 1) the Old Testament prophet; 2) the New Testament prophet who foretells the future; 3) the New Testament prophet who brings special words of instruction and edification for the Body of Christ, and 4) the false prophet.

Although the role of the Old Testament prophets is very similar to both types of New Testament prophets in Calvin's view, he still makes a distinction between the Old and New Testament prophets. The Old Testament prophets are described by Calvin as:

> the organs of the Holy Spirit for all necessary predictions. . .Besides, they were endowed with the power of adapting their prophecies to a just object and use. Thus, after the Law was promulgated, they were its interpreters. In prosperity they bore witness to the grace of God; in adversity, to His judgments. In fine, their business was to ratify God's covenant, whereby He reconciles men to Himself through Christ.[38]

Calvin reiterates the role or function of the Old Testament prophet in his Preface to his *Commentary on Isaiah.* He states that the role of the

37. Calvin, *Commentary on 1 Corinthians,* 303.

38. Calvin defined prophecy in his comments on Numbers 11:24–27 as, "a special faculty of discoursing magnificently of secret things or mysteries." (*Commentary on Numbers,* vol. 4, 185). Therefore, a prophet would reveal secret things or mysteries, especially related to God or the work of God.

prophet is threefold. First, to be the interpreters of the Law by declaring to the people the doctrine of life and to "explain more fully what is briefly stated in the Two Tables, and lay down what the Lord chiefly requires from us."[39] The second role is to clarify and expand the Laws regarding the promises and threats of God, which Moses declares in general, and which applies to their situation. This second role usually includes visions that foretell in detail, which Calvin describes as prophecies. The third role of the Old Testament prophet, according to Calvin, is to "express more clearly what Moses says more obscurely about Christ and his grace, and bring forward more copious and more abundant proofs of the free covenant."[40] Describing the role or function of the prophet in the Old Testament, he views them as teachers and interpreters of the Mosaic Law, seers[41] who reveal to the people the blessed or adverse events that are to come, and who also foretell the coming of the Messiah and the end of the age.

For Calvin, the Old Testament prophets and their particular role ended once Christ completed His earthly ministry.[42] There was no more need for "special revelation" in which the Israelites needed to know God and His covenant before Christ. Once Christ ascended, and the Holy Spirit came, then the role of the New Testament prophets developed.

There are two kinds of New Testament prophets, according to Calvin, although a prophet may function in both roles. The first type of prophet is one who prophesies future events, foretelling things to come. He writes about Agabus in Acts 11, "since the word prophet is taken in different ways in the New Testament . . . The men called prophets in this verse are those who were endowed with the gift of foretelling, just as the four daughters of Philip will afterwards be distinguished by the same title (Acts 21:9)."[43] These types of prophets were special and few in number and their prophecies were very limited.[44] In his *Commentary on Ephesians*, Calvin defines the two roles or types of prophets in the New Testament, stating:

> some understand those who possessed the gift of predicting future events, like Agabus. But, for my own part, as doctrine is the present subject, I would rather explain it, as in 1 Cor. 14, to

39. Calvin, 'Preface,' *Commentary on Isaiah*, vol. 1, xxvi.

40. Calvin, 'Preface,' *Commentary on Isaiah*, vol. 1, xxvi.

41. Calvin, *Commentary on Isaiah*, vol. 1, 358. See Calvin's thoughts on Isaiah 30:10 for further clarification.

42. Calvin, *Commentary on Isaiah*, vol. 2, 322. See also Calvin, *Sermons on 2 Samuel*, 217–18.

43. Calvin, *Commentary on Acts*, vol. 1, 333.

44. Calvin, *Commentary on Joel*, vol. 2, 94.

mean outstanding interpreters of prophecies, who, by a unique
gift of revelation, applied them to the subjects on hand; but I do
not exclude the gift of foretelling, as far as it was connected with
teaching.[45]

Calvin does not deny that a prophet in the New Testament could function in both giftings, but his definitions of a prophet distinguish both giftings with clear and definite roles. According to Calvin, the gift of prophecy
used in foretelling has ceased. It is a temporary gift and that type of prophet
is no longer needed in the Church. However, Calvin is not as emphatic about
the cessation of the second type of New Testament prophet, as "outstanding
interpreters of prophecies."[46]

The fourth type of prophet is the false prophet who is used by Satan
to deceive people and lead them away from Christ and the truth of Christ.
Calvin believes that false prophets still abound and must be opposed. For
example, he often attacked the teachings and actions of both the Roman
Catholics and the Radical Reformers. In his *Commentary on Jeremiah*, Calvin underscores his regard of the Papacy and monks as being false prophets
in the church, stating:

> It is indeed a detestable thing under the Papacy, when monks
> and similar unprincipled men ascend the pulpit, and there most
> shamefully pretend that they are the true prophets of God, and
> faithful teachers; but still it would be doubly monstrous, were
> any among us to corrupt pure doctrine with their errors and
> infect the people with their superstitions.[47]

Calvin continues in his comments on Jeremiah to give further detail
about false prophets and their ways during his time. In his lecture on Jeremiah 27:15–18, he makes two points, a) how false prophets work, and b)
how to distinguish between true and false prophets. He develops his points
by equating the bishops and monks of the Roman Catholic Church with
false prophets and teachers, attacking their ignorance and false teachings
that draw people away from the true gospel, thus showing his belief that
false prophets abounded in his time, mainly through the Papacy.[48] Calvin
also suggests that false prophets still flourish when writing about Matt
24:11, "[Jesus] says that not only will false prophets come, but they will
be endowed with the art of deception to draw away sects after them. This

45. Calvin, *Commentary on Ephesians*, 179.

46. Calvin, *Commentary on Ephesians*, 179.

47. Calvin, *Commentary on Jeremiah*, vol. 1, 309.

48. Calvin, *Commentary on Jeremiah*, vol. 3, 372–381.

demands no ordinary caution. The great numbers of those that go astray is like a wild whirlwind driving us off our course, unless we are thoroughly tied to God."[49] Calvin implies that many false prophets are leading great numbers away from the truth. No doubt, Calvin is referring to the Roman Catholics and the Radicals such as the Anabaptists and the Libertines. He held that the Anabaptists and especially the Libertines were led by false prophets and teachers, a view which he addresses in much of his writings, especially in his *Institutes*, his treatises, and many of his letters. Calvin wanted not only to warn the people of such false prophets and teachers but to stand boldly against them and their deceptive ways.

Calvin, in his understanding of both the Old Testament and New Testament Prophets as foretellers, believed that the office of the prophet has ended and therefore, that the gift of prophecy has ended for the most part. However, even here, he begins to reveal his ambivalence on the cessation of the office of the prophet and the gift of prophecy.

When Calvin addresses the issue of the office of prophet in his exposition of Eph 4:11, he states that the office of the prophet was needed only for the establishment of the early church before the Scripture was complete, writing:

> It should be observed, also, that, of the offices which Paul enumerates, only the last two [teachers and pastors] are perpetual. For God adorned His Church with apostles, evangelists and prophets, *only for a time*, except that, where religion has broken down, he raises up evangelists apart from Church order, to restore the pure doctrine to its lost position.[50]

Calvin promulgated that view again in his *Institutes*, where he states concerning the five ministry offices mentioned in Eph 4:11 that three of the five offices—the apostolic, the evangelistic, and the prophetic—are no longer needed in the church; but with some exceptions! Regarding the office of the prophet, he states:

> Paul applies the name "prophets" not to all those who were interpreters of God's will, but to those who excelled in a particular revelation [Eph. 4:11]. This class either does not exist today or is less commonly seen . . . According to this interpretation . . . these three functions [apostles, prophets, and evangelists] were not established in the church as permanent ones, but only for that time during which churches were to be erected where none

49. Calvin, *Commentary on Matthew*, vol. 3, 82.
50. Calvin, *Commentary on Ephesians*, 179–180.

existed before, or where they were to be carried over from Moses to Christ.[51]

It is apparent to Calvin that the prophetic office has ceased; therefore, the gift of prophecy has ceased. However, it is here that he introduces a moderate cessationist view of the office of the prophet and the gift of prophecy. To Calvin, the gift of prophecy as foretelling the future has definitely ended, and therefore, the function of a prophet as a predictor of future events has ended.

Even though Calvin states in his commentaries on Acts and in the *Institutes* IV.iii.5 that the gift of prophetic foretelling has ceased, he retreats from his comments on the total cessation of this gift in the *Institutes* IV.iii.4, when he discusses the prophetic office. His description of this office in Eph 4:11 mentions the ability to foretell, which he does not emphatically state has totally ceased. In fact he states, "This class [of prophet] either does not exist today or is less commonly seen."[52] This last phrase, "less commonly seen," reveals, at least theoretically, Calvin's openness or at least his willingness to acknowledge the possibility that God could still use this gift and office if He so willed it. In one sense, Calvin is stating that the gift of prophecy, and the office of the prophet, have ended in due course, yet he also presents the possibility that the gift and office are still available, albeit rare.

The third standpoint Calvin expresses regarding the gift of prophecy as he defines it is that such prophecy is still available. As demonstrated earlier, Calvin emphasized that it was only the prophet who could prophesy. Calvin continues to clarify his understanding of the office of the prophet and the gift of prophecy in his commentary on 1 Cor 12:28. He expands his first thoughts from verse 10 by stating that prophets in this passage were not those who are "endowed with the gift of foretelling, but those who were blessed with the unique gift of dealing with Scripture, not only by interpreting it, but also by the wisdom they showed in making it meet the needs of the hour."[53] Calvin continues his description of the prophet and his function in the New Testament by clarifying that "the prophets referred to here are those who are skillful and experienced in making known the will of God, by applying prophecies, threats, promises, and all the teaching of Scripture to the current needs of the Church."[54] In Calvin's description of the New Testament prophet, he left room for the continuation of the gift of prophecy as he defines it.

---

51. *Institutes*, IV.iii.4, 1057.

52. *Institutes*, IV.iii.4, 1057.

53. Calvin, *Commentary on 1 Corinthians*, 271.

54. Calvin, *Commentary on 1 Corinthians*, 271.

Therefore, if the gift of prophecy is still available, then some form of the office of the prophet is available. How Calvin arrives at this is simple. The office of the teacher is now functioning in the office of the prophet. The modern use of the gift of prophecy is more than interpretation of the Scripture and biblical preaching; it is, in his view, a prophetic teaching gift. As we have discovered, one of Calvin's understandings of the Old Testament prophet's role was interpreting the Law or teaching the Word of God. With this function of the prophet in mind, Calvin transfers this same function over to that of the office of teacher and preacher. Calvin does not limit the gift of prophecy as he understands it (i.e., as prophetic teaching and not prophetic foretelling) strictly to the teacher, but also applies it to the preaching of the Word. Even though he tends to believe that the office of prophet has ceased, he cannot state with conviction that it has, since he believes that some form of the gift of prophecy is crucial for the church of the Reformation.

CONCLUSION

In this chapter, we have given an overview of John Calvin's general understanding of the *pnuematika charismata*, the gifts of the Spirit, and then concentrated on the gift of prophecy. Calvin indeed saw how the Holy Spirit, the Third Person of the Holy Trinity, was active in creation and sustains creation; and that His primary function is for the life of the believer.

We discussed Calvin's general understanding of the gifts of the Holy Spirit and specifically the charismatic gifts of the Spirit, as found in 1 Cor 12. From this overview of the spiritual gifts, we looked more specifically at Calvin's definitions, practice, and understandings of prophecy, the most important gift of the Spirit. We discovered that although he tended to hold to the overall view that this gift primarily consists of anointed preaching and teaching of the Scriptures and the doctrines of the faith, he went further in his understanding. He believed that the gift of prophecy was vital for the church to not only stay true to the Scripture and sound doctrine, but that it addressed the current needs in the church and people's lives. So too, today, we need this gift to function within the church to bring anointed preaching and teaching of the Word of God, but also to give a particular word in the current hour of the church.

BIBLIOGRAPHY

Calvin, John. *Commentary on 1 Corinthians*. Translated by John W. Fraser. Calvin's New Testament Commentaries. 1960. Reprint, Grand Rapids: Eerdmans, 1989.

———. *Commentary on 2 Peter*. Translated by William B. Johnston. Calvin's New Testament Commentaries. 1963. Reprint, Grand Rapids: Eerdmans, 1989.

———. *Commentary on Acts*. Vol. 1. Translated by John W. Fraser and W. J. G. McDonald. Calvin's New Testament Commentaries. 1965. Reprint, Grand Rapids: Eerdmans, 1989.

———. *Commentary on Acts*. Vol. 2. Translated by John W. Fraser. Calvin's New Testament Commentaries. 1966. Reprint, Grand Rapids: Eerdmans, 1991.

———. *Commentary on Ephesians*. Translated by T. H. L. Parker. Calvin's New Testament Commentaries. 1965. Reprint, Grand Rapids: Eerdmans, 1993.

———. *Commentary on Exodus*. Vol. 3. Translated by Charles W. Bingham. Calvin's Commentaries. Edinburgh: Calvin Translation Society, 1843–1855. Reprint, Grand Rapids: Baker, 1984.

———. *Commentary on Genesis*. Vol. 1. Translated by John King. Calvin's Commentaries. Edinburgh: Calvin Translation Society, 1843–1855. Reprint, Grand Rapids: Baker, 1984.

———. *Commentary on Isaiah*. Vol. 1. Translated by William Pringle. Calvin's Commentaries. Edinburgh: Calvin Translation Society, 1843–1855. Reprint, Grand Rapids: Baker, 1984.

———. *Commentary on Jeremiah*. Vol. 1. Translated by John Owen. Calvin's Commentaries. Edinburgh: Calvin Translation Society, 1843–1855. Reprint, Grand Rapids: Baker, 1984.

———. *Commentary on Jeremiah*. Vol. 3. Translated by John Owen. Calvin's Commentaries. Edinburgh: Calvin Translation Society, 1843—1855. Reprint, Grand Rapids: Baker, 1984.

———. *Commentary on Joel*. Vol. 2. Translated by John Owen. Calvin's Commentaries. Edinburgh: Calvin Translation Society, 1843–1855. Reprint, Grand Rapids: Baker, 1984.

———. *Commentary on Matthew*. Translated by A. W. Morrison. 1972. Calvin's New Testament Commentaries. Reprint, Grand Rapids: Eerdmans, 1989.

———. *Commentary on Numbers* Vol. 4. Translated by Charles W. Bingham. Calvin's Commentaries. Edinburgh: Calvin Translation Society, 1843—1855. Reprint, Grand Rapids: Baker, 1984.

———. *Commentary on Romans*. Translated by Ross MacKenzie. Calvin's New Testament Commentaries. 1960. Reprint, Grand Rapids: Eerdmans, 1991.

———. *Institutes of the Christian Religion*. 2 vols. Edited by John T. McNeill. Translated by Ford Lewis Battles. Library of Christian Classics 20–21. Philadelphia: Westminster, 1960–1961.

———. *Sermons on II Samuel*. Translated by Douglas Kelly. Reprint, Edinburgh: Banner of Truth, 1992.

Elbert, Paul. "Calvin and the Spiritual Gifts." In *Essays on Apostolic Themes: Studies in Honor of Howard M. Ervin*, edited by Paul Elbert. Peabody, MA: Hendrickson, 1985.

Gilbert, Daniel B. "The Pneumatic Charismata in the Theology of John Calvin: A Study of Calvin's Pneumatology, Focusing on His Concepts and Interpretation of the

Pneumatic Charismata in His Life and Works." PhD diss., University of Aberdeen, 2005.

Stephens, W. P. *The Holy Spirit in the Theology of Martin Bucer.* Cambridge: Cambridge University Press, 1970.

Spijker, Willem van 't. *The Ecclesiastical Offices in the Thought of Martin Bucer.* Translated by John Vriend and Lyle D. Bierma. Studies in Medieval and Reformation Thought 57. Leiden: Brill, 1996.

PART THREE

Reformation Themes

11

Reformation, Cessationism, and Renewal

CHRISTOPHER J. WILSON

INTRODUCTION

THERE WERE MANY SIDE effects and unintended consequences to the Reformation. The adoption of cessationism by many post-Calvin denominations is just one example. While Reformers such as Luther and Calvin held to concentric cessationism (i.e., miracles still occurring in unevangelized areas), their successors adopted full-blown cessationism. They attributed the ongoing miracles within Catholicism and the Radical Reformation to either fraud or demonic activity. This chapter will show that the adoption of cessationism occurred for several reasons including: an extreme emphasis on *sola scriptura*, a fundamental misunderstanding of the purpose of miracles, and the rejection of ecclesiastical authority.

First, the historical background will be given by surveying Francis MacNutt's text: *The Nearly Perfect Crime: How the Church Nearly Killed the Ministry of Healing* (2005). MacNutt shows how miracles became rarer with each passing era due to numerous causes, including: the prevalence of Platonism, a misunderstanding of the sacraments, and a subsequent lack of expectation.

Next, the Reformation era will be analyzed. This survey will begin with Jon Ruthven's analysis of Reformation-era cessationism as a Protestant polemic against Catholic miracles. Ruthven's central thesis is that the development of cessationism was not based upon theological or hermeneutical grounds; but rather, was used as a means to attack and undermine claims of ecclesiastical authority. Scott Hahn's analysis of the development and influence of the historical-critical method will also be examined. This section will conclude by showing how various other factors such as the enlightenment worldview transformed the soft/ concentric cessationism of the Reformers into full cessationism and even anti-supernaturalism in later generations.

The final section will examine how contemporaneous miracles in the Renewal movement have caused the doctrine of cessationism to become an untenable position, one which is largely in retreat today. Thus, the Renewal movement has helped to reform the Reformation.[1]

Gradual Cessationism (Pre-Reformation) AD 100–1500

> At least in the Western church what Confirmation is supposed to do is precisely release the power of the Holy Spirit in the Catholic's life. So we should all become charismatics when we're confirmed!"[2] —Peter Kreeft

> According to Gibbon, miracles such as healings, exorcism, speaking in tongues, and resurrections of the dead have occurred throughout church history. Many of the early church fathers such as St. Clement of Rome (2nd Pope), St. Ignatius of Antioch (50–98 AD), and St. Justin Martyr (100–165 AD) write extensively of the miracles they have witnessed in the post-Apostolic Era.[3] —John Driscoll

Proponents of cessationism argue that signs and wonders ceased after the apostolic age, as their sole purpose was to authenticate the gospel message preached by the first-century apostles. However, this view does not withstand historical scrutiny. Even a cursory examination of the writings of the early church fathers will show that not only did signs and wonders continue to occur, but they remained a significant part of how the gospel was spread.[4] What is true, however, is that at various times, different fac-

1. This paper is excerpted from my dissertation, Wilson, "Modern Miracles as the Foundation for a Renewal Apologetic," 123–39.

2. Kreeft and Nevins, *Charisms*, 149–54.

3. Driscoll, "Miracle," loc. 437439–437443 of 700382.

4. Ruthven, *On the Cessation of the Charismata*, 15.

tions within the church have embraced the theology of cessationism. This phenomenon occurred in its fullest form within Protestantism (post-Calvin) and caused a dearth of signs and wonders. This drought occurred as proponents of cessationism no longer believed that signs and wonders occurred; thus, they no longer prayed for them or attempted to perform them.

By the time of Saint Augustine of Hippo (354–430 AD), the prominence of signs and wonders within Christendom had lessened. This rarity of signs and wonders is not because they were no longer occurring but instead was due to the isolation of many towns and the lack of an authentication structure. As Stafford notes, signs and wonders were no longer publicized even when they continued to occur. Often signs and wonders would occur, but even people within the same town could be unawareof them.[5]

In this climate, the early Augustine felt that the signs and wonders which were still occurring did not rise to the level of the biblical signs and wonders; this is why they were not written about as much as the former. However, over time, Augustine came to witness numerous signs and wonders. In chapter twenty-two of *The City of God*, Augustine alludes to over seventy miracles which he knows to have occurred within his vicinity.[6] Augustine bemoans the lack of knowledge of these miracles:

> Even now, therefore, many miracles are wrought, the same God who wrought those we read of still performing them, by whom He will and as He will; but they are not as well known, nor are they beaten into the memory, like gravel, by frequent reading, so that they cannot fall out of mind. For even where, as is now done among ourselves, care is taken that the pamphlets of those who receive benefit be read publicly, yet those who are present hear the narrative but once, and many are absent; and so it comes to pass that even those who are present forget in a few days what they heard, and scarcely one of them can be found who will tell what he heard to one who he knows was not present.[7]

Francis MacNutt (Gradual Cessationism)

Francis MacNutt, in his text *The Healing Awakening: Reclaiming Our Lost Inheritance* (2006), argues that signs and wonders were prevalent amongst the church fathers and amid the Roman persecution. He states: "Spirit baptism,

---

5. Stafford, *Miracles*, 120.

6. Augustine, *The City of God*, 749–99.

7. Augustine, *The City of God*, 765–766.

together with healing and exorcism, flourished in those early years follow-ing Pentecost. From those ancient times, long before the printing press, we have only a few records of how the poor, uneducated, ordinary Christians lived, but we have enough to know that they expected to be filled with and led by the Spirit."[8]

However, after Christianity became acceptable, and the Christians left the catacombs, a gradual dissipation in signs and wonders occurred. This dissipation occurred gradually over several centuries, but even so, it was not complete, so it went mostly unnoticed. MacNutt states:

> To destroy a belief as central to Christianity as healing ... the change had to take place so gradually that Christians didn't even realize that they had lost anything. In Part 2 we saw how, for the first three centuries of Christianity, healing prayer was an ordinary practice; any and every Christian had the confidence to pray for the sick. How ironic then that just when Christianity emerged from the catacombs victorious, following the vicious persecutions, healing and deliverance prayer started sliding down the slope into insignificance.[9]

This lack of signs and wonders occurred for numerous reasons and cannot be traced to one single cause. MacNutt gives several different rea-sons, including: a lack of a charismatic view of the sacraments[10] the adoption of Platonism (causing an embrace of suffering), the view that only "heroic Christians" were capable of performing miracles, and the lack of an expecta-tion of miracles.

Sacraments

According to MacNutt, the sacraments of baptism and confirmation were viewed as a means of Spirit baptism by the early church. As MacNutt notes: "In the early Church, adults who were baptized expected, at the same time,

---

8. MacNutt, *Healing Reawakening*, 79.

9. MacNutt, *Healing Reawakening*, 103.

10. MacNutt, *Healing Reawakening*, 91–92: MacNutt recalls a woman he baptized trembling as if deeply touched by the Holy Spirit. She was subsequently able to pray in tongues for the first time. MacNutt believes that this is how sacraments such as bap-tism are supposed to occur; MacNutt states: "Now, I personally believe that something does happen at baptism and confirmation. I met one Roman Catholic bishop who re-members seeing tongues of fire descend on all the other young people who were being confirmed with him. And yet, when he started to share this experience, he found, to his disappointment, that no one else had seen the fire. So he learned not to talk about this marvelous event, for fear of being seen as a fanatic." (*Healing Reawakening*, 93).

to be baptized in the Spirit; they regarded the two experiences as the same event."[11] However, over time, infant baptism became the norm, and by the eighth century, baptism was no longer viewed as a "Pentecost experience." This view has unfortunately persisted until today.[12]

Platonism: Embracing Suffering

Originally the Church viewed disease and suffering as things to be overcome. The witness of Christ was that they were caused by the kingdom of darkness and could be overcome by the Kingdom of God. However, over time, Christian theology was influenced by Platonism and began to embrace suffering instead. According to MacNutt: "Plato saw the body as a prison from which the soul needed to escape. This devaluing of the body was absorbed into Christianity."[13] As this view began to hold sway, the kingdom of God began to be primarily identified with the next world. Suffering was embraced as a means of purification: "A cross in this life—a crown in the next." The body was to be "mortified"—which means, at root, to be "put to death"—for the soul's sake.[14]

Heroic Christians

Over time, the *charismata* were viewed as the sole providence of the saints and holy men. Augustine himself did not initially believe he was capable of performing a healing miracle.[15] "In the early apostolic Church, manifestations of the presence of the Holy Spirit—tongues, joyfulness, prophetic words, visions—were regarded as normal."[16] Over time the connection between healing and sainthood became so strong that even the desert fathers such as Saint Anthony refused to pray for the sick, as "They did not want to appear proud, as if they felt themselves worthy of sainthood."[17]

11. MacNutt, *Healing Reawakening*, 62.

12. MacNutt, *Healing Reawakening*, 92.

13. MacNutt, *Healing Reawakening*, 107.

14. MacNutt, *Healing Reawakening*, 107.

15. MacNutt, *Healing Reawakening*: MacNutt further cites an example wherein Augustine himself had healed a person by laying hands on them and praying for them. Thus 3 years before his death Augustine wrote a book called *Revisions* where he corrected some of his earlier theology including his initial belief in cessationism. Augustine, *Revisions*, 116.

16. MacNutt, *Healing Reawakening*, 91–92.

17. MacNutt, *Healing Reawakening*, 91–92.

Lack of Expectation

In the early church, the examples of Jesus and Paul were followed as the primary method of evangelism. Signs and wonders not only occurred, but they were also expected. Instead of arguing with words and reason alone, they demonstrated their power to heal and cast out demons as the means of demonstrating the power of God. As MacNutt notes:

> In the early Church—as in the Third World today—people not only believed in evil spirits but actively experienced demonic power firsthand. To proclaim the Kingdom of God was not just to get into a persuasive argument about the truth of Christianity; it meant casting out evil spirits and demonstrating God's power. As Paul claimed: "I came among you in weakness, in fear and great trembling and what I spoke and proclaimed was not meant to convince by philosophical argument, but to demonstrate the convincing power of the Spirit, so that your faith should depend not on human wisdom but on the power of God (1 Cor 2: 3–4).[18]

However, MacNutt agrees that a belief in signs and wonders persisted despite these obstacles, even if somewhat diminished. He states: "As late as the thirteenth century Thomas Aquinas explained this passage [1 Cor 2:3–4] as meaning that Paul confirmed the truth of his teaching by the power of the Holy Spirit—namely, by demonstrations of healing and transformed lives rather than by logic and philosophy."[19]

Despite this general trend away from the *charismata* and toward cessationism, miracles continued throughout the Middle Ages. For example, in the case of Bernard of Clairvaux (1090–1153), Stafford states: "Miracles gave tremendous prestige to the Catholic Church in the Middle Ages. Many, many miracles were recorded, sometimes in a form that seems almost modern in its historical detail. Bernard of Clairvaux, for example, healed hundreds of people as he traveled about Germany, and these healings are well documented, with times, places, and the names of witnesses recorded."[20]

18. MacNutt, *Healing Reawakening*, 86.

19. MacNutt, *Healing Reawakening*, 86.

20. Stafford, *Miracles*, 125–126.

REFORMATION ERA: FULL CESSATIONISM

The Early Reformers: Soft and Concentric Cessationism

While the early reformers such as Luther and Calvin did reject the ongoing miracles within the Roman Catholic Church, it would be wrong to call them full cessationists. Rather, Luther and Calvin are usually labeled as either soft cessationists (most miracles have stopped) or concentric cessationists—miracles could still occur in unevangelized areas as a means of spreading the gospel.[21] However, their views were not always uniform and did change over time and depended upon the particular context of the miracle. Also, as Ruthven notes, full cessationism did not arise as a fully formed doctrine until after the first Reformers: it was largely a post-Calvin phenomenon.[22] Leading Reformers such as Luther, Calvin, and Knox all believed in contemporaneous miracles and prayed for and attempted to perform such miracles.[23]

Luther

According to Eddie Hyatt, Luther is often falsely labeled as a cessationist. This label largely arose because he challenged many of the miracles claimed by the Roman Catholic Church. "Secondly, he opposed certain Anabaptists who claimed the direct leading of the Spirit for their bizarre teaching and actions."[24] However, even a cursory view of Luther's writings and sermons will show that the cessationist label is in error.

For instance, Luther said in his Ascension Day sermon (1522), "Where there is a Christian, there is still power to work these signs if it is necessary."[25] He did state that miracles were less common where the gospel had already been spread (concentric cessationism). However, if the Gospel faces opposition, then ". . .we verily should have to employ wonder-working rather than permit the Gospel to be derided and suppressed."[26] One year later, he stated his belief in contemporary miracles even more strongly: "Therefore, we must allow these words to remain and not gloss them away, as some have done who said that these signs were manifestations of the Spirit in

---

21. Ruthven, *Cessation of the Charismata*, 23.

22. Ruthven, *Cessation of the Charismata*, 7.

23. See Hyatt, *2000 Years*, 73–75.

24. Hyatt, *The Charismatic Luther*, 30.

25. Oss, "A Pentecostal Response," loc. 2888–2898 of 6641.

26. Oss, "A Pentecostal Response," loc. 2888–2898 of 6641.

the beginning of the Christian era and that now they have ceased. That is not right; for the same power is in the church still. And though it is not exercised, that does not matter; we still have the power to do such signs."[27]

Luther's belief in miracles was more than just intellectual; he actively sought to heal others. According to Hyatt, "Luther regularly prayed for the sick, and even composed a divine healing service for Lutheran congregations. He is quoted as saying, 'Often has it happened, and still does, that devils have been driven out in the name of Christ; also by calling on His name and prayer, the sick have been healed.'"[28]

Finally, it is believed that Luther personally performed miracles. For instance, when his close friend Philip Melanchthon was extremely ill and near-death Luther said: "Be of good courage, Philip, you shall not die." Melanchthon immediately revived and soon regained his health. He later said, "I should have been a dead man had I not been recalled from death itself by the coming of Luther."[29]

Calvin

Calvin is usually labeled a soft cessationist, meaning that he believed that the gifts of the Spirit had ceased in general—with rare exception(s). According to Douglas Oss:

> In his commentary on 1 Corinthians 12–14, he vaguely allowed that "it is difficult to make up one's mind about gifts and offices, of which the church has been deprived for so long, except for mere traces or shades of them, which are still to be found." Calvin allowed for the extraordinary gifts "as the need of the times demands" and wrote, "This class does not exist today or is less commonly seen.[30]

Therefore, Calvin allowed that the various gifts of the Spirit would still manifest on occasion: for a particular need. However, Calvin's adherents, within a few generations, transformed this weak cessationism into full cessationism. In the late nineteenth-century United States, Benjamin Warfield's Calvinist beliefs would become the foundation for his full-blown cessationist

27. Oss, "A Pentecostal Response," loc. 2888–2898 of 6641.

28. Hyatt, *The Charismatic Luther*, 32.

29. Hyatt, *The Charismatic Luther*, 32.

30. Oss, "A Pentecostal Response," loc. 2902–2906 of 6641.

polemic, *Counterfeit Miracles* (1918),[31] which became cessationism's authoritative text.

Full Cessationism—The Polemic against Catholicism

> The Protestant view changed little from that of Aquinas, except that it became a tool to attack the authority of the Roman Catholic Church, based on claims of miracles among their saints and shrines.[32] —William Dryness

> The miracles that happen in these places prove nothing, for the evil spirit can also work miracles, as Christ has told us in Matt. 24:24."[33] —Martin Luther

The Reformation brought many changes to how post -biblical signs and wonders were viewed. The original Reformers such as Martin Luther (1483–1546) and John Calvin (1509–1564) held to concentric cessationism (i.e., the belief that miracles still occurred in unevangelized areas to aid in the spread of the gospel).[34] However, in time, the various denominations founded in the Reformation came to embrace full-blown cessationism. This occurred largely to facilitate an attack on the authority and the ongoing signs and wonders in the Roman Catholic Church.[35] According to Calvin, those miracles still occurring within the Roman Catholic Church were satanic in nature:

> You can't establish the truth simply by pointing to miracles, he said, because not all miracles come from God. "We must remember that Satan has his miracles, too," Calvin wrote. (For example, Pharaoh's magicians did miracles [Exod 7: 11–12]; the slave girl in Acts 16: 16 could predict the future by a spirit that possessed her; and Jesus warned in Matthew 7: 22–23 that many people in the Last Judgment would protest that they did many miracles, only to be told by Jesus, "I never knew you!") Miracles associated with relics and shrines, Calvin asserted, linked to a false gospel of superstition and human attempts to please God by our own efforts. They were false miracles accrediting a false gospel. Furthermore, Calvin said, the Reformation churches did

31. Ruthven, *Cessation of the Charismata*, 41.

32. Ruthven, "Miracle," 547.

33. Hyatt, *The Charismatic Luther*, 36.

34. Ruthven, *Cessation of the Charismata*, 21–23.

35. For a fuller discussion of this see Ruthven, *Cessationism of the Charismata*, 21–22.

have accrediting miracles: Jesus' miracles and the apostles' miracles. Those were enough. They had accredited the true gospel of the Protestant churches—the gospel found in the Scriptures.[36]

Additionally, according to Jon Ruthven, the Reformers' emphasis on *sola scriptura* caused them to deny revelatory spiritual gifts (e.g., prophecy) as well as the ongoing miracles within Catholicism and the "Radical Reformation."[37] This denial gave birth to "Protestant Scholasticism,"[38] which held that the authority claimed by the Roman Catholic church, and the roles of its traditions and creeds, were irrelevant to biblical interpretation. Ruthven summarizes:

> We've now seen how the doctrine of cessationism was resurrected by Protestants—I say "resurrected," because this doctrine was invented a few centuries before by pagan Greeks and Jews who hassled each other and especially Christians over reports of miracles among them. This doctrine of cessationism paradoxically co-existed with all kinds of reports of miracles and prophecies throughout church history up to the reformation era. Why? Well, if you are defending your doctrines, the last thing you want to do is concede miracle-working among your opponents. It makes you look bad. This happened over and over again when some Christians took the New Testament seriously and started praying for sick people or started receiving revelatory dreams or messages; jealous church officials typically banned the practice. Or if they did it themselves it was cool. Saints Augustine, Gregory VI, and even some writers of the Westminster Confession both denied and affirmed revelation and miracles![39]

Within Catholicism, ongoing miracles were used as both an apologetic and a polemic to attack the Reformation. The Catholics argued that since no miracles were occurring within the Protestant church, that the church lacked God's stamp of approval.[40] Due to the Reformation, the church did begin a more formalized process to both authenticate miracles as well the Canonization of Saints. The process of miracle authentication used the

---

36. Stafford, *Miracles*, 125–126.

37. The Radical Reformation was a sixteenth century movement which began in Switzerland. Specific groups included the Anabaptists and Mennonites. Adherents rejected the ecclesiastical authority of the Catholic and Lutheran churches. Heavy emphasis was placed upon the invisible church of believers.

38. Ruthven, *Protestant Theology*, 3.

39. Ruthven, *Protestant Theology*, 23.

40. Stafford, *Miracles*, 125–26.

three-degree classification system which had existed since the early Middle Ages:

1. First degree: Miracles against nature (e.g. Moses parting the Red Sea)

2. Second degree: Miracles exercised over nature (e.g. Jesus resurrecting Lazarus)

3. Third degree: Miracles beyond nature (e.g. Jesus healing the blind)[41]

The Canonization process consisted of a series of seventeen trials covering the life, work, and possible miracles of each candidate.[42] The paths towards sainthood were different depending upon the era of the saint. The lowest status (venerable), could be awarded simply by the petition of local authorities. However, moving to the next statuses (blessed or saint) required two miracles performed in front of eyewitnesses, three if there were no witnesses, and four if the case was not contemporary.[43]

Previous to this process, there were many local saints whose miracles lacked the Vatican's authentication. That did not necessarily mean that their miracles did not occur, but rather that the Vatican chose to remain silent on the matter due to a lack of evidence. While miracles and saints did help to bolster the faith of many Catholics, the church remained very guarded against false claims of miracles, and miracles which lacked authentication. As Parigi notes:

> Because of the pressures that local communities exerted on the Congregatio, particularly before 1642, few cases moved through all the steps in either process. Of the 348 cases that the Congregatio considered in the period from 1588 to 1751, almost 43 percent remain venerable today, that is, they sit at the lowest rung of the Congregatio's holy ladder (ASV Fondo Processi, 1147). More interestingly, 96 percent of all cases during this period moved less than one step. Besides the 108 cases that were made venerable and remain so to this day, there were also eleven contemporary candidates who were declared saints "on the spot."[44]

41. Parigi, *Rationalization*, 37–38.

42. Parigi, *Rationalization*, 34.

43. Parigi, *Rationalization*, 36.

44. Parigi, *Rationalization*, 37.

Anti-Supernaturalism and the Rise of Historical Criticism

> The misuse of historical criticism has undermined many people's faith in God's word and in the church's teaching about scripture.[45] —Scott Hahn

Eventually, many Protestant scholars came not only to reject the on-going miracles within Roman Catholicism and elsewhere; but, the very concept of miracles themselves—including biblical miracles. This rejection came with the development of the historical-critical method of biblical interpretation. While this school has presented itself as being value-neutral and scientific, it has always had ulterior political motivations. Additionally, it contains numerous philosophical and theological presuppositions. Its effect was a rejection of the authority of Scripture and, subsequently, of the church. Its presuppositions required a rejection of any supernatural elements, such as miracles, as well. The resultsof this school of thought are still strongly felt today.

Understanding the historical development of historical criticism is important to this discussion. According to Scott Hahn, it was the historical-critical method that first began to undermine confidence in Scripture within Christendom. While undermining Scripture was concomitant an attack on miracles and God's interaction in the world was a necessary consequence as well. While most scholars trace historical criticism back to the eighteenth century, Hahn sees the roots of criticism going back to William of Ockham (1285–1348) and Averroes (1126–1198). Tracing the lineage through the ages, Hahn concludes that Benedict Spinoza, Richard Simon, and Thomas Hobbes were the three founding fathers of historical criticism—with Spinoza being the most important. All three men were either excommunicated or condemned as heretics by their church bodies.[46]

Political Motivations

Hahn believes that the methods of historical criticism (the analytical tools) are, in and of themselves, value-neutral. However, since their inception, these tools have been used for ulterior political and secular motivations. As Hahn states: "Because, at root historical criticism is grounded in a hermeneutic of suspicion—a basic distrust of tradition—and this was self-conscious on the

---

45. Keating, "The Bible Politicized," lines 422–444.
46. Keating, "The Bible Politicized," lines 45–49.

part of those who developed the methods and of the early practitioners of them in Germany and England and throughout the world."[47]

What the practitioners of historical criticism were attempting to do was to shift authority from the priesthood (and the church), over to the secular. Hahn states: "In regard to political liberalism, as we recall, a common feature running from Marsillius through Hobbes, Spinoza, and Tolland was the denigration of the priesthood because the primacy of the priesthood implied a primacy of the sacred over the secular, the priest over the king."[48] This motivation, however, was not shared by the original Reformers such as Luther and Calvin who desired to reform the Catholic Church, not splinter from it. As Hahn notes: "Luther and Calvin despite all their zeal, and for all of their concern for reform in the church and for all of their pride, didn't really believe that what they were doing was going to represent a permanent fragmentation of Christendom."[49]

Philosophical Presuppositions

It is the misuse of the historical-critical method which has caused many scholars—and the laity—to lose their faith in the authority of Scripture, the role of tradition, and ultimately to adopt a secular worldview. Despite the claims of scholars such as Wellhausen, the historical-critical method always proceded from various philosophical underpinnings.[50] Almost always, the methods were abused for secular and political purposes.[51]

Hahn's analysis is of importance as Hume's critique is rooted in the same philosophical tradition of the Enlightenment, which gave rise to the fullest expression of the historical-critical method. Many Christian scholars who became proponents of historical criticism adopted deistic and anti-supernatural worldviews. Subsequently, these scholars also became skeptics of 'Special Divine Action.' This phenomenon continues today, and many scholars who do not hold to historical-critical "orthodoxy" find themselves marginalized and blackballed. Karl Keating states: "Cutting-edge scholars who question these things are marginalized. Their books don't get reviewed, they don't get promoted, and the centers of this scholarship—certain universities—invite onto their staff only people who already agree with the

---

47. Keating, "The Bible Politicized," lines 21–23.
48. Hahn, *Politicizing the Bible*, 562.
49. Keating, "The Bible Politicized," lines 28–31.
50. Hahn, *Politicizing the Bible*, 8–9.
51. Hahn, *Politicizing the Bible*, 8–9.

majority opinion. It seems as if they're more concerned with maintaining this dike against leaks than in seeing whether there's some substance."[52]

Hahn's analysis of the contention between critical and conservative scholars is similar to Karl Keating's. Hahn states:

> This phenomenon is especially prevalent in American Catholic scholarly circles. But you seem to find many more Jewish and Protestant scholars doing what Cardinal Ratzinger called for in his 1988 Erasmus Lecture, that is, a "criticism of the critics"—and their misuse of historical-critical methods. And you don't need to look very far to find their vested interests and ulterior motives, their hidden agendas beyond their hypothetical reconstructions, and why these tenuous theories catch fire and become the rage of the day. But in Catholic circles you don't find the same sort of thing, at least in North America. Yet Ratzinger's lecture was a clarion call to do precisely this, to recognize the real but limited value of historical criticism: limited uses, but almost unlimited abuses.[53]

Hahn's Conclusion

The adoption of the historical-critical method—over the biblical worldview—by many biblical scholars, amounts to subornation of divine revelation to philosophy and reason. According to Hahn, this trend began with Spinoza:

> He tried to create a natural civil religion by subordinating theological method and religious truth claims to the categories of philosophy. It wasn't simply the elevation of reason over revelation. It was a pitting of reason *against* faith. This marriage which has endured for many centuries throughout Europe—the marriage of reason and faith based upon divine revelation—was split, seemingly forever.[54]

Moreover, while proponents of this worldview believe it to be value-neutral, this is far from the truth. The adoption of a secular worldview requires numerous philosophical presuppositions. As Hahn notes: "If our own lengthy analysis has established anything, it is that philosophy did precede

---

52. Keating, "The Bible Politicized," lines 169–173.
53. Keating, "The Bible Politicized," lines 174–183.
54. Keating, "The Bible Politicized," lines 61–65.

biblical criticism."[55] This philosophical worldview is typically at odds with what Scripture states.

The solutions for these dilemmas, according to Hahn, are twofold:

1. Not to discard completelythe entire artifice of historical criticism; instead, studies of "significantly more politicizing aspects of nineteenth-century scriptural scholarship are called for, and only such studies can hope to disentangle the legitimate tools of the historical critical method from the various political and secular aims."[56]

2. In terms of worldview, Christians should return to the classical Christian worldview, as exemplified in the *Via Antiqua* (e.g. Augustine, Aquinas, pre-modernism). In a word, this worldview could be described as philosophical *realism*. Seeing a timeless transcendence to the Christian faith, which crosses all epochs and geographical boundaries, is one of the implications of this worldview. Having some access to an actual reality, which actually exists, is another. Understanding that reason and logic have limits, that there are ineffable truths, but that these truths are not irrational, but rather are *suprarational*, would be a third implication.

As Hahn concludes:

> It is hard to define, but what I mean by "historical criticism" needs to be understood in two ways. First, the methods are analytical tools, and in and of themselves can be considered neutral. They can be used positively, and they can be used negatively. Second, the actual circumstances in which these tools were developed gives us another and a clearer understanding of what historical criticism is, because at root historical criticism is grounded in a hermeneutic of suspicion—a basic distrust of tradition—and this was self-conscious on the part of those who developed the methods and of the early practitioners of them in Germany and England and throughout the world.[57]

55. Hahn, *Politicizing the Bible*, 561.
56. Hahn, *Politicizing the Bible*, 566.
57. Keating, "The Bible Politicized," lines 16–23.

Ruthven's Conclusion

The doctrine of cessationism did not originate from a careful
study of the Scriptures. The doctrine of cessationism originated
in experience."[58] —Jack Deere

Protestantism—true to its name—eventually became a protest of everything Catholic. In doing so, it came to neglect many things that were
biblical in order to reject Catholicism. Miracles played a vital role not just
in aiding in the spread of Christianity, but in allowing God to interact with
his creation.

The cessationist view of the *charismata* reached its fullest expression
in the Post Calvin era. Most Protestant denominations embraced full-blown
cessationism at the expense of the plain record and meaning of Scripture.[59]
This radical sub-biblicism was—according to Ruthven—due to a complete
rejection of Catholicism by later Protestants who sought to completely protest everything Catholic—often at the expense of the biblical text itself.[60] Additionally, the later Reformers came to reject or ignore the soft or concentric
cessationism of Luther and Calvin, in preference for this full cessationism.

Ruthven, in *What's Wrong with Protestant Theology* (2013), concludes
that this rejection of the miraculous is ultimately based upon a fundamental misunderstanding of Scripture.[61] Ruthven argues that Scripture is the
means through which God communicates and delivers direct divine revelation—the prophetic word.[62] All are called to be prophetic. All are called to
listen and obey God.[63]

Sola Scriptura

Perhaps more than any of the other Reformation maxims (the five solas),
sola scriptura caused the later adoption of cessationism. Most of Luther's
references to contemporary miracles see them as a means of authenticating
the gospel. His view foreshadowed the same belief held by modern cessationists—that miracles served only an evidentiary function. That function
alone, of course, is not entirely descriptive of Luther's views or those of the
early Reformers. Rather, the early Reformers relied on *sola scriptura* plus

58. Oss, "A Pentecostal View," loc. 4506–4510 of 6641.

59. Ruthven, *Protestant Theology*, 31.

60. Ruthven, *Protestant Theology*, 31.

61. Ed. The similarity of this presupposition to that of higher criticism is noteworthy.

62. Ruthven, *Protestant Theology*, 115.

63. Ruthven, *Protestant Theology*, 115.

ongoing revelation(s) that were yet subordinate to Scripture.[64] A more appropriate label would be *prima scriptura*—the primacy of scripture. As Gaffin notes: "Presupposing the revelation of himself that God gives in creation (general revelation), does Scripture in fact teach not, as the Reformers were convinced, 'Scripture alone' but a 'Scripture plus' principle of revelation?"[65]

According to Oss, this principle of Scripture plus revelation can be seen in the Westminster Confession of Faith. Within that document, several passages support the view that special revelation was ongoing. He argues that references "in chapter 1 to 'new revelations of the Spirit' (sec. 6) and 'private spirits' (sec. 10) do suggest that that document is at least open to the view that revelations, subordinate to Scripture, continue today."[66]

Luther sought Scripture as the foundation for belief. He believed that the role of miracles was to authenticate the gospel. However, he did not reject contemporary miracles that served this function, and he did believe in ongoing revelation and prophecy. However, Luther's and Calvin's primacy of Scripture became distorted by later generations and became an argument in favor of cessationism. Luther's *sola scriptura* is much to blame for this phenomenon. Later generations also took Luther's words against the Catholics and Anabaptists out of context and essentially "proof-texted" Luther to justify their doctrines of cessationism. This dynamic occurred among the successors of Calvin, as well. As Hyatt notes:

> Miracles, he [Calvin] argued, were particularly suited to the apostolic age and were no longer necessary to vindicate the authority of the one who stands on the side of Scripture. Interestingly, Luther presented the same Catholic demand to certain Anabaptists who, in his opinion, maintained an undue reliance on visions and miracles, and neglected the study of the word of God. Sadly, his remarks were taken out of context by later theologians and codified into a legal system resulting in Lutheran and Reformed churches harboring a distinct bias against the possibility of present-day miracles.[67]

64. Gaffin, "Concluding Statement," loc. 5958–5963 of 6641.
65. Gaffin, "Concluding Statement," loc. 5958–5963 of 6641.
66. Gaffin, "Concluding Statement," loc. 5963–5967 of 6641.
67. Hyatt, *The Charismatic Luther*, 34.

The Great Debate: Enlightenment Philosophy vs. Miracles (David Hume's Polemic)

The logical end of cessationism—coupled with the Enlightenment worldview—was deism. God, the great clockmaker, did not interact with his universe. This lack of interaction made miracles impossible. It was in this context—"The Great Debate"—that Hume formulated his attack on miracles. Hume's critique of miracles is still cited today by most skeptics of the miraculous. As Craig Keener notes, "Hume is generally regarded today as the starting point for modern discussion of miracles. Hume provided the basis for most Enlightenment arguments against apologetic use of miracle reports, and many modern arguments simply restate Hume's earlier claims."[68] Hume made three primary arguments against miracles:

1. Miracles are a violation of a law of nature.

2. The laws of nature are based upon very high probabilities.

3. Miracles lack credible witnesses.[69]

Hume's argument(s) give a robust philosophical challenge to any account of the supernatural, based upon the limits of human knowledge. In essence, Hume is stating that an apparent supernatural event cannot be labeled as such since the laws of nature are based upon probabilities. The apparent causality of the laws of nature is just an inference based upon past events. Therefore, we cannot know the future laws of nature nor causality. Thus, there are no events that could ever appropriately be labeled as miraculous.

The numerous philosophical presuppositions contained in this argument are based upon the Enlightenment philosophies of empiricism, materialism, and reductionism. Just as in the case of the historical-critical method, supernatural causation is eliminated *a priori*. Miracles are impossible as they violate all the key presuppositions of the Enlightenment. Hume's skepticism—along with historical criticism—helped to dismiss belief in the miraculous for many Protestant denominations. Meanwhile, the cessationist tendencies of the Reformation caused unbelief in others. This combination of disparate factors led to Protestantism's nearly ubiquitous cessationist position for three hundred years—previous to the twentieth-century revivals.[70]

---

68. Keener, *Miracles*, 119–120.

69. Hume, *An Inquiry*, 50–54.

70. Stafford, *Miracles*, 127–28.

THE RENEWAL MOVEMENT: TWENTIETH/ TWENTY-FIRST CENTURY MIRACLES

> Jesus' teaching was demonstrated by His action: He had the authority to back it up. This is the basic teaching of the Gospel, which we have largely lost: The Kingdom of God is here; the kingdom of Satan is being destroyed.[71] —Francis MacNutt

The Enlightenment view against Special Divine Action still holds sway today in many areas of the academy, including those more liberal streams of theological and biblical studies that still embrace historical criticism. This tendency is especially true in western academia. As Dryness states: "The topic of miracle shows a clash of cultures between traditional Christian theology and human experience worldwide. This is especially true for most non-Western societies, but increasingly, in the postmodern Western world as well, where, for example, 89% of Americans believe that even today, God performs miracles by his power."[72] The belief in and occurrences of Special Divine Action are even stronger outside the west. According to Walton and Keener, millions of conversions that have occurred in China are the result of healing experiences. In India, one survey showed that more than ten percent of non-Christians claimed to be cured by Christians praying for them in the name of Jesus.[73]

While Catholics continued to believe in miracles and the ongoing work of the Holy Spirit after the Reformation, it is arguable that the influence of Thomistic theology did encourage a lesser form of continuationism. This diminution occurred because Aquinas limited the performance of miracles, as gifts of the Holy Spirit, only to believers of great sanctity.[74] Such belief took miracles outside the reach of the ordinary laity and priesthood. It was not until the Catholic Charismatic Revival began in the late 1960s that a large segment of Catholics began to operate in the special gifts of the Holy Spirit and engage in miraculous healings. Spirit baptism came to be seen as an experience and resource available to all believers, not just to those of great sanctity and the saints. The widespread experience and influence of this movement did much to overthrow the limiting views of Aquinas in this area, which had held primacy for centuries. As Ruthven states:

> According to Aquinas, the central function of miracles was to serve as a *signum sensibile*, a *testimonium* to guarantee the

---

71. MacNutt, *Healing*, 56.

72. Ruthven, "Miracle," 546–47.

73. Walton, *Cultural Backgrounds Study Bible*, loc. 215398–215402 of 350904.

74. Ruthven, *Cessation of the Charismata*, 23.

divine source and truth of Christian doctrines, particularly the deity of Christ. To explain the lack of visible miracles in his day, Aquinas asserted that Christ and his disciples had worked miracles sufficient to prove the faith once and for all; this having been done, no further miraculous proof of doctrines could be required. In a number of other places, however, he vitiates this position by maintaining that miracles can recur if they aid in confirmation of preaching and bringing mankind to salvation. But even beyond this, Aquinas suggested that believers of great sanctity may exhibit miraculous gifts of the Spirit, a doctrine that strengthened the veneration of shrines and canonization of saints via miracles. A widespread belief in these last two exceptions, which essentially contradicted cessationism, resulted in the excesses surrounding miracles which precipitated the Reformation.[75]

Beginning in the early twentieth century, many miracles began to occur at various Protestant revivals. While initially mainstream Protestants and fundamentalists continued to hold to cessationism, by the end of the twentieth century, various forms of continuationism had become dominant. Today, cessationism is widely seen as a theology in retreat.[76] According to Grudem, the largest group of evangelicals do not fit within either cessationist or continuationist camps, but rather can be described as "open but cautious."[77] Due to this openness toward miracles, there are now hundreds of millions of testimonies of miracles within Protestantism.[78]

CONCLUSION

Unless we share in Jesus' ministry of healing the sick and casting out evil spirits, our preaching about the Kingdom of God being here among us is simply an empty promise.[79] —Francis MacNutt

While it is debatable if charismatic gifts and miraculous healings were less frequent in previous eras, it is beyond debate that we are living in a time

75. Ruthven, *Cessation of the Charismata*, 23.

76. Grudem provides an in-depth discussion about the various views. He labels the "open but cautious" position as the largest group amongst evangelicals in America today. See: Grudem, "Preface" loc. 91 of 6641.

77. Grudem, Preface. *Miraculous Gifts*, loc. 91 of 6641.

78. Keener, *Miracles*, 762.

79. Keener, *Miracles*, 762.

of great healing worldwide. The last century has simultaneously (and not coincidentally) seen both the birth of the global Pentecostal revival and the Charismatic Renewal Movement, as well as the spread of the Gospel into more unevangelized areas than in any previous era.

Previous to the Renewal Movement, the Reformation had an overall negative effect on the frequency of Special Divine Action due to the belief in cessationism by many Protestant denominations.[80] Meanwhile, within Catholicism, there was an undeniable belief in Special Divine Action as a special grace, accomplished either via intercessory prayer or directly by God. However, the Catholic Charismatic Revival took the frequency of Special Divine Action to a higher level with its rejection of Thomistic theology in that area.

This chapter has shown that healing miracles have existed throughout both biblical and church history. The healing miracles occurring today are no different from ones that have occurred throughout history. What is different today is that medicine and science have advanced to a stage where they are better able either to authenticate healings as miraculous or dismiss them to naturalistic causes. Thus, we are living in an unprecedented time for the evaluation—and confirmation—of miracles.

BIBLIOGRAPHY

Augustine, St. *The City of God*. New York: Catholic Way, 2015.
———. *Revisions*. Vols. 1 and 2. Translated by Boniface Ramsey. Hyde Park, NY: New City, 2010.
Driscoll, John T. "Miracle." In *The Catholic Encyclopedia*, edited by Charles G. Herbermann et al., loc. 436954–437542 of 700382. New York: Catholic Way, 2014. Kindle edition.
Gaffin, Richard B., Jr.. "Concluding Statement." In *Are Miraculous Gifts for Today? Four Views*, edited by Richard B. Gaffin and Wayne Grudem, loc. 5901–6009 of 6641. Counterpoints. Grand Rapids: Zondervan.
Gaffin, Richard B., Jr. et al., eds. *Are Miraculous Gifts for Today? Four Views*. Counterpoints. Grand Rapids: Zondervan, 2011. Kindle edition.
Grudem, Wayne. "Preface." In *Are Miraculous Gifts for Today? Four Views*, edited by Richard B. Gaffin Jr. et al., loc. 34–236 of 6641. Counterpoints. Grand Rapids: Zondervan. Kindle edition.
Hahn, Scott, and Benjamin Winker. *Politicizing the Bible: The Roots of Historical Criticism and the Secularization of Scripture 1300–1700*. New York: Crossroads, 2013.
Hume, David. *An Inquiry Concerning Human Understanding*. Oxford: Clarendon, 1902.
Hyatt, Eddie. *2000 Years of Charismatic Christianity*. Lake Mary, FL: Charisma House, 2002.

80. Ruthven, *Protestant Theology*, 23.

———. *The Charismatic Luther: Healings, Miracles & Spiritual Gifts in the Life and Ministry of the Great Reformers.* Grapevine, TX: Hyatt.

Keating, Karl. "Scott Hahn on the Politicized Bible." https://www.catholic.com/magazine/print-edition/scott-hahn-on-the-politicized-bible.

Keener, Craig. *Miracles: The Credibility of the New Testament Accounts.* Grand Rapids: Baker, 2011.

Kreeft, Peter, and Dave Nevins. *Charisms: Visions, Tongues, Healing, etc.* Pennsauken, NJ: BookBaby, 2013.

MacNutt, Francis. *The Healing Reawakening: Reclaiming Our Lost Inheritance.* Grand Rapids: Chosen Books, 2006.

Oss, Douglas A. "A Pentecostal/Charismatic View." In *Are Miraculous Gifts for Today? Four Views,* edited by Stanley N. Gundry and Wayne A, Grudem, loc. 4161–5077 of 6641. Grand Rapids: Zondervan, 1996. Kindle edition.

———. "A Pentecostal Response." In *Are Miraculous Gifts for Today? Four Views,* edited by Stanley N. Gundry and Wayne A. Grudem, loc. 2844–2988 of 6641. Grand Rapids: Zondervan, 1996. Kindle edition.

Parigi, Paolo. *The Rationalization of Miracles.* New York: Cambridge University Press, 2012.

Ruthven, Jon Mark. "Miracles." In *Global Dictionary of Theology: A Resource for the World-wide Church,* edited by William A.Dyrness et al., 546–50. Downers Grove, IL: InterVarsity, 2008.

———. *On the Cessation of the Charismata: The Protestant Polemic on Post-Biblical Miracles.* Rev. ed. Word & Spirit Monograpah Series 1. Tulsa: Word & Spirit, 2012.

———. *What's Wrong with Protestant Theology? Tradition vs. Biblical Emphasis.* Tulsa: Word & Spirit, 2013.

Stafford, Timothy. *Miracles: A Journalist Looks at Modern Day Experiences of God's Power.* Bloomington, MN: Bethany House, 2012.

Walton, John H., and Craig Keener eds. *NIV Cultural Backgrounds Study Bible.* Grand Rapids: Zondervan, 2016. Kindle edition

Wilson, Christopher J. "Modern Miracles as the Foundation for a Renewal Apologetic." PhD diss., Regent University, 2017.

12

Justification and Transformation as a Better Model Than *Theōsis*

JAMES M. HENDERSON

INTRODUCTION

ON THIS 500TH ANNIVERSARY of Luther's nailing of his ninety–five theses on the church door, some Lutherans are reevaluating Luther's soteriology. Did Luther, in fact, teach a view that was similar to *theōsis*, a kind of "divinization" or "deification"? In this same vein, Pentecostals such as Veli-Matti Kärkkäinen and Frank Macchia have argued that Pentecostals should abandon "forensic" justification as an empty and theologically bankrupt "point-event" view of justification and adopt a model of justification by the process of *theōsis* as a more biblical and pneumatologically rich understanding of salvation. This chapter shall first describe their idea of *theōsis* as a justifying process in the context of the Finnish School of Luther studies. Second, it shall evaluate the idea of *theōsis* in contrast to the idea of forensic justification and transformation in Lutheran thought. It shall then show that a forensic model of justification is compatible with and presupposes the idea of the transformation of the human soul by the work of the indwelling Holy Spirit. The conclusion will show that the model of forensic justification, with a concomitant transformation of the soul by the indwelling Holy Spirit, is a better model for understanding justification than a process of *theōsis*.

JUSTIFICATION AS THEŌSIS IN RECENT PENTECOSTAL THOUGHT

The Finnish Pentecostal theologian Veli-Matti Kärkkäinen and the American Pentecostal theologian Frank Macchia have called for Pentecostals to abandon the Reformation formulation of forensic justification, or "justification by faith," for a model that sees justification as a process which, while it includes a declaration of pardon, is not completed without sanctification and good works.[1] Both theologians cite the influence of the Finnish School of Luther studies headed by the Finnish historical theologian Tuomo Mannermaa for turning their thinking toward the idea of "union with Christ" or "participation in God" —ideas that they say are very similar to the Eastern Orthodox idea of *theōsis*—as models of justification more appropriate to Pentecostal theology.[2]

Kärkkäinen paints the picture of two "dominant approaches" to justification in Protestant theology in general and in Lutheranism in particular. The first is the idea of "union (with Christ)" which the Finnish School and Kärkkäinen cite as very close to Orthodox theology's idea of *theōsis*, and which both insist is more characteristic of Luther's theology. The second, forensic justification that "sets the doctrine of justification in antithesis to the Orthodox idea of union,"[3] is the "official confessional standpoint of Lutheranism" and so not authentically Luther's thought. According to Kärkkäinen, this makes for justification without transformation. He asserts that the idea of *theōsis*, or "divinization" is "equally meaningful" with justification as a metaphor for salvation and is necessary for a proper view of salvation.[4]

"EMPTY" JUSTIFICATION

Reformed, Baptist, and Finished-Work Pentecostal thinkers have tended to avoid any talk of transformation in their discussion of justification in order to avoid any hint that justification is based on a meritorious work, or even a meritorious being in the sense of ontological good in the Christian or the

---

1. Kärkkäinen, *Spirit and Salvation*, 312–367; Kärkkäinen, *One with God*, 55–58, 65, 98, 125; Macchia, "Justification through New Creation," 205–11; Macchia, *Baptized in the Spirit*, 129–140; Macchia, *Justified in the Spirit*, 5–14, 293–312.

2. For recent works on Eastern Orthodox thought on *theōsis* and its engagement in Western theology, see the extensive discussion in Kärkkäinen, *One with God, passim*.

3. Kärkkäinen, *One with God*, 97.

4. Kärkkäinen, *Spirit and Salvation*, 338.

Christian's nature. Justification is primarily the product of a kind of (intellectual) knowledge or apprehension of God. Reformed theologians strongly assert that the "declaration of justification itself does not have a transformative power."[5] This categorization is primarily a matter of language, an attempt to avoid any usage that includes works of love or merits contributing to justification, rather than a denial of transformation, but Maachia and Kärkkäinen would disagree.

Frank Macchia

Because of the view of justification cited above, Macchia has charged that the Reformed view of forensic justification is "empty" and meaningless.[6] He argues that the Reformation understanding of forensic justification is culturally conditioned (by Roman "distributive justice") and "theologically bankrupt," because Reformation theology had no place for the role of the Holy Spirit in justification.[7] Macchia asserts the early church centered its thought on the work of the Holy Spirit in raising Christ from the dead, but the Reformation lost this insight and centered on the work of the cross alone.[8] The Bible "clearly makes Jesus' resurrection by the Spirit of God the very basis of our justification."[9] Macchia equates the idea of Christ's resurrection to the believer's "new creation" or "life in the Spirit" as the "locus of God's saving righteousness."[10] Although he states (along with Mannermaa) that there is yet a place for forensic justification,[11] Macchia wishes to find the center of justification in the process of transformation and not in imputation of an outside or alien righteousness. Macchia attributes this process

5. Strobel, "By Word and Spirit," 58.

6. Macchia *Baptized in the* Spirit, 137; Macchia, *Justified in the Spirit*, 59–60, 72. Anderson sets out the positions of both Macchia and Kärkkäinen in "Justification as the Speech of the Spirit," 145–188, and in "The Holy Spirit and Justification: A Pneumatological and Trinitarian Approach to Justification, 292–93. In both, Anderson develops an alternative to *theōsis* based on the idea of the Holy Spirit as the Father's creative speech-act.

7. Macchia, "Justification and the Spirit," 4, 7; see also Macchia, "Justification through New Creation," 202, 205.

8. Macchia, "Justification and the Spirit," 8–9; Macchia, "Justification through New Creation," 209. Macchia has lost the sharpness of this language about forensic justification in his monograph, *Justified in the Spirit*. I include Macchia's earlier language because I believe it explains well his motive for opposing the language of forensic justification. ""

9. Macchia, "Justification and the Spirit," 9–10.

10. Macchia, "Justification and the Spirit," 11.

11. Macchia, "Justification through New Creation," 204.

to the reality of the indwelling Holy Spirit. Human cooperation is primarily through participation in the Holy Spirit's interior work, as part of being caught up in "one's participation in the triune life."[12] All this is contrary to forensic justification.

Veli-Matti Kärkkäinen

Kärkkäinen considers the "Protestant" (forensic) doctrine of justification to be the child of medieval feudalism, although the idea of *theōsis* remained in Western thought until the Reformation completely separated the two.[13] He argues that the Reformation idea of "justification by faith" as a rubric covering all aspects of the saving relationship to God "cannot be established biblically" nor historically before the Reformation.[14] A forensic view neglects the full scope of biblical data and falls short of being fully "Christian" in the wider sense of what the church has always believed. Perhaps worst, "a forensic view of justification, at its best, makes good works more or less optional."[15] For Kärkkäinen, this is no justification at all, since "the indwelling of God is not that righteousness through faith by which we are declared righteous. The indwelling of God, rather, follows the antecedent justification by faith. This means that God is not really present in the Christian when declaring her righteous through faith for Christ's sake."[16] Against such an idea, Kärkkäinen argues from an ecumenical point of view. He notes with implied disapproval that, while Western theology has made the doctrine of justification the "hinge on which all true religion turned,"[17] early church fathers such as Irenaeus, Athanasius, and the Cappadocian fathers asserted that *theōsis* is the original Christian doctrine of salvation.[18]

Kärkkäinen stresses that both Eastern Orthodox and Pentecostal thought "emphasize that to be a Christian is to experience Christ and his Holy Spirit, not only at conversion but throughout one's Christian life."[19] A forensic view of justification is not adequate for this because, "like the Orthodox, Wesley and Pentecostals are deeply concerned with what happens in

---

12. Macchia, *Justified in the Spirit*, 25.

13. Kärkkäinen, *Spirit and Salvation*, 313, 316.

14. Kärkkäinen, *Spirit and Salvation*, 312, 340.

15. Kärkkäinen, *One with God*, 116, 125.

16. Kärkkäinen, *One with God*, 56.

17. Kärkkäinen, *One with God*, 6.

18. Kärkkäinen, *One with God*, 24–27.

19. Kärkkäinen, *One with God*, 110.

the Christian, and not just what happens for the Christian."[20] Kärkkäinen's desire to advocate for a more "Wesleyan" theology—which magnifies the requirement for transformation in the believer's life and leaves more room for the willing response of the believer as the believer's own response, unforced by divine sovereignty—drives, in part, both his denigration of forensic justification and his desire for the adoption of the idea of *theōsis*, He also wishes to affirm the *Joint Declaration on the Doctrine of Justification* published by World Lutheran bodies and the Roman Catholic Church.[21]

THEŌSIS AS A PROCESS OF JUSTIFICATION

Macchia and Kärkkäinen reject forensic justification partially because, in itself, it is said to have no transforming power. What is unstated but important is that both Macchia and Kärkkäinen wish to promote a view of salvation that is primarily the result of a process of (subjective) sanctification. For Macchia, a proper view of justification is the idea of *theōsis,* a growing participation in God's goodness, particularly as the "Finnish School" following Mannermaa understands *theōsis,* and as Kärkkäinen works out *theōsis* for a Pentecostal context.

For these thinkers, justification requires active human participation and effort. Justification cannot be a fiat pronounced from just one side. Justification takes work as one grows in Christlikeness, as one participates in the life of Christ and is transformed in a synergistic effort. "Justification as a *relational dynamic* is thus essentially transformative."[22] In part, Macchia sees this as a return to a proper soteriology that is brought about by the work of the Holy Spirit. For Macchia justification and sanctification cannot be distinguished, even "logically," "from involving the life of the Spirit and the new creation to come." This view not only accentuates the Spirit's role in justification, but also motivates Macchia's emphasis on the unity of justification and sanctification in one Spirit-empowered process which reaches beyond the believer to embrace all of society.[23]

Kärkkäinen also accepts Mannermaa's thesis and extends the idea of *theōsis* as a work of the Holy Spirit. "Charismatic theologians" teach that forgiveness and imputation "cannot be separated from *unio* with Christ," Christ as gift living in the believer, where justification and sanctification

---

20. Kärkkäinen, *One with God*, 111. Kärkkäinen here thinks primarily of Pentecostals who embrace a Wesleyan-Holiness theology.

21. Karkkainen, *Spirit and Salvation*, 349.

22. Kärkkäinen, *Spirit and Salvation*, 70, emphasis mine. See also 50–55.

23. Macchia, "Justification through New Creation," 213, 214–17.

"occur alongside each other and happen simultaneously."[24] He cites Pannenberg in arguing that Jesus' words of forgiveness, found in Mark 2:5 and Luke 7:48, demonstrate the claim of God's righteous demand (that we live according to his righteous rule) and the pronouncement of forgiveness.[25] Kärkkäinen links Mannermaa's thesis on Luther's theology to the work of E. P. Sanders, James D. G. Dunn, N. T. Wright, and others and cites this scholarship in support of the idea that *theōsis* as a better understanding of salvation than the "one-sided" and "perhaps misguided" doctrine of justification by imputation.[26] Kärkkäinen will soften his view somewhat, critiquing Mannermaa's view in his later work, *Spirit and Salvation*, advocating that justification as favor should be more robustly highlighted, but, again, never separated from participation.[27]

What is clear is that the view of *theōsis* that Macchia and Kärkkäinen have adopted from the Finnish School presses toward synergism. Salvation must include the work of God, plus the work of the human who is being saved. For example, Simo Peura, a Finnish School theologian, asserts that God enters into union only with those "who in Christ fight against sin."[28] The Christian is protected by grace only "in so far as the gift is realized" in moral renewal. "In this sense, we could say that the Christian's renewal is the necessary condition for grace and staying under Christ's protection."[29] While attempting to eschew synergism, the way Peura uses this idea of participation is to call the Christian to greater effort in sanctification. The believer must not be satisfied with any righteousness already given but must move "ever more deeply toward" Christ. Only as the Christian experiences "continuous change into the form of Christ" and "deepening enclosure in Christ and his righteousness" is the believer secure, since "grace and gift presuppose each other."[30] Despite the nod to the idea that God's grace does all, this seems much more a Roman Catholic idea of justification as a life-long gradual process and goal than the Reformed idea of a presently-enjoyed justification by an act or declaration of God in Christ. The next section shall demonstrate that an "effective" model of sanctification appears to be what Macchia and Kärkkäinen offer to Pentecostals and Evangelicals alike in place of forensic justification. In contrast to the idea that only a view

---

24. Kärkkäinen, *One with God*, 65.
25. Kärkkäinen, *Spirit and Salvation*, 333.
26. Kärkkäinen, *One with God*, 11.
27. Kärkkäinen, *Spirit and Salvation*, 350.
28. Peura, "Christ as Favor and Gift," 57.
29. Peura, "Christ as Favor and Gift," 57, 58.
30. Peura, "Christ as Favor and Gift," 61, 62.

of justification as *theōsis* is valid, the next section will show that transformation through union with Christ through the Holy Spirit is a vital part of Luther's and Reformed thought.

THEŌSIS VERSUS JUSTIFICATION IN LUTHER AND LUTHERAN THOUGHT

We have seen that Macchia and Kärkkäinen, in line with the Finnish School of Lutheran studies, understand Luther to have taught a doctrine very similar to *theōsis*, speaking of the Christian's "union" with Christ. This section shall examine other thinkers who agree with the Finnish School, then critique the argument.

On this 500th anniversary of Luther's nailing of his ninety–five theses on the church door, some Lutherans are reevaluating Luther's soteriology. Did Luther teach a view that was similar to *theōsis*, a kind of "divinization" or "deification"? Or, was Luther expressing what might be called a Reformed view of sanctification following justification? We shall first examine the view of the Finnish School as explicated by Mannermaa and supported by other scholars, then survey several authors who critique the Finnish School.

The Case for Theōsis as Luther's View of Justification

Tuomo Mannermaa examined the theology of justification developed by Martin Luther and concluded that it differs significantly from the theology of the later Lutheran theologians. For Mannermaa, Luther taught an idea of "participation" in the divine life (*inhabitatio Dei*) that comes very close to the Eastern Orthodox view of *theōsis* or "divinization."[31] The evidence for this is capsulated in Luther's phrase "Christ is present in faith" (*in ipse fide Christus adest*)[32]. When the believer is baptized, he receives the actual presence of the person of Christ and not just the favor of God. Christ is both the favor of God (*favor*) and the gift of God (*donum*), and to receive Christ is to receive both. This presence is in itself "the righteousness of faith." Thus the believer receives "real righteousness," meaning more than imputed righteousness in a forensic transaction. The believer herself is changed, and a new being is created (Mannermaa scrupulously avoids the term "infused") in justification rather than "merely" gaining a change of status *coram Deo*. Mannermaa considers this understanding to be the "underlying structure"

31. Mannermaa, *Christ Present in Faith*, 3.
32. Mannermaa, "Why Is Luther?," 2–6.

of all of Luther's theology.[33] In recognizing this center of Luther's theology, "the Lutheran tradition is born anew."[34]

According to Mannermaa, the essence of God for Luther is the divine properties, or "names," that God gives. First, God makes us "nothing," meaning that he demonstrates to us that we cannot become good by our effort. This realization creates a vacuum and so makes us *capax Dei;* God then gives us himself.[35] His self-giving results in participation in the divine life, which is similar to the Orthodox idea of *theōsis*.

Luther's concept of faith was based on the Christology of the early church wherein Christ takes on actual human nature. In faith, humans "*really* participate in the person of Christ," in whom there is no sin, death, or curse. The core of Luther's concept of participation is the "happy exchange" in which Christ "takes upon himself the sinful person of a human being and bestows his own righteousness on him or her." This process results in a kind of communication of attributes (Mannermaa seems to refer to the *communicatio idomatum* here) in which Christ gives us "divine righteousness" and "absorbs" our death and curse,[36] resulting in the believer really participating in the essence of God. Thus, Christ is more than the favor of God; he is also the gift through which this participation in the divine nature takes place.[37]

For Mannermaa, this progression is only understood in the context of Luther's theology of the cross. Luther did not distinguish between the person of Christ and his work. Since Christ is both the favor of God (in the sense of forgiveness of sins, atonement, and the abolition of wrath) and the gift of God, then God himself is present in the believer through faith in Christ. The core of God's being is relational, and so this self-giving has the character of essence (*esse*). Luther thought of Christ as being really present in and through the believer's faith in somewhat the same way as Christ was present in, under, and around the bread of the Eucharist.[38] Thus the divine nature is joined to the believer in Christ.[39] Such faith grants justification because it takes hold of and possesses the treasure, which is Christ's own person being present. Christ is *ontologically* present, and that presence is

33. Mannermaa, "Why Is Luther?," 6, 17.

34. Mannermaa, "Justification and *Theōsis*," 25.

35. Mannermaa, "Justification and *Theōsis*," 39.

36. Mannermaa, *Christ Present*, 13–16, 17.

37. Mannermaa, *Christ Present*, 19–21.

38. Mannermaa, *Christ Present*, 2.

39. Mannermaa, "Why Is Luther?," 12–14.

righteousness, and so the believer participates in an ontological reality.[40] "*In ipsa fide Christus adest*: in faith itself Christ is present, and so the whole of salvation."[41] This understanding is seen as the "key to the fundamental structure of the Reformer's thinking."[42] If Christ is not present, then there is no righteousness conferred. Christ is then "the *forma* that makes faith real" and not human *charitas* as the Schoolmen supposed. God's *agape* brings us a share in Christ, and therefore "the believer partakes in the properties of God's being" or the "names, treasures, and goods of the divine nature."[43] Mannermaa asserts that Luther goes so far as to speak of Christ and the believer as "one person" because of this participation.[44] This union does not result in a loss of the human nature. The believer has "two natures" in the sense that Christ is the believer's "divine nature" even while the believer remains human.[45] However, the human being becomes "God" through this participation, and the oneness gained in participation "must not be divided; what is at stake here is salvation, or the loss of it."[46]

According to Mannermaa, although Luther did not use the terms of *theōsis* often, there are many points of contact between Luther and the Orthodox view of salvation.[47] The Christian becomes a "completely divine person," in a manner like that of the hypostatic union of the divine and human seen in Christ. Christ becomes "incarnate" in the believer.[48] This union is distinct from the incarnation in that the nature of the believer remains *homoiousios* rather than precisely the same divine nature. Nevertheless, the human has always been destined to "assimilate" the "divine dignity for which he was created." As with Irenaeus and Athanasius, this participation does not result in a change of substance; the human remains human and does not become a "little God" in the sense of a being with creative power. Those deified "retain their own identity" since *theōsis* is a relative transformation rather than absolute: our humanity is not diminished, nor

---

40. Mannermaa, *Christ Present*, 37. The emphasis is mine.

41. Mannermaa, "Why Is Luther?," 15, Mannermaa, *Christ Present*, 26.

42. Mannermaa, *Christ Present*, 55.

43. Mannermaa, "Why Is Luther?," 16, 19.

44. Mannermaa, *Christ Present*, 39.

45. Mannermaa, "Why Is Luther?," 17. See also Peura, "What God Gives Man Receives," 88.

46. Mannermaa, *Christ Present*, 42.

47. See Kärkkäinen's discussion of the Eastern Orthodox position in *One with God*, 17–36.

48. Mannermaa, *Christ Present*, 43, 46.

do we share in an identity of *ousios* with God.[49] It results in a "community of being."[50] This ontological relationship gives form to the ethical relationship.

According to Mannermaa, the early church did not make a hard distinction between ontology and ethics. There is still a sense in which justification is forensic in Luther, because faith—though it is real righteousness—is "weak" and there is still some of the "old Adam" in the believer. Thus, an imputed righteousness is necessary to the believer. This imputation "perfects" the Christian as long as one lives in this age as a person who is "partly righteous" and partly a sinner.[51]

This focus on ethics is advanced in the work of Simo Peura and it is in fact the classical problem of love—of how one can fulfill the commandment to perfectly love God and one's neighbor—that Peura sees as the essential question in Luther's theology and *not* the question of how one can find a merciful God. In Luther's thought the Christian is not only joined with Christ but is transformed by a process which "creates in the Christian the same form (*forma*) as Christ.[52] Christians receive the "form (*forma*) and likeness (*similitudo*) of God." "A new person bearing good fruit is created in 'faith.'"[53] Peura argues that this "effective" aspect of justification is crucial to Lutheran identity, and any attempt to restrict justification to a forensic understanding will cause "great difficulties" for Lutherans. "God becomes present and begins to live in us at the moment he creates true faith in us. Therefore, faith always results in union with God." This is why a doctrine of justification as declared righteousness does not grasp the whole intent of Luther's doctrine.[54]

I noted above that Peura goes on to describe salvation in an almost synergistic way. God enters into union only with those "who in Christ fight against sin," etc. Peura asserts that this is not really synergism because it all comes from the work of Christ in his union with the believer and is based on Christ's righteousness and not any self-righteousness.[55] However, Peura seems to want to lock the barn door after he has ridden off on the synergistic horse. This tension is unresolved. On the one hand, Saarinen notes the caution of the Evangelical Lutheran Church in America in this area. In

---

49. Kärkkäinen, *One with God*, 20, 21, 27, 31.

50. Mannermaa, "Justification and *Theōsis*," 26; Mannermaa, "Why Is Luther?," 10, 11.

51. Mannermaa, *Christ Present*, 2, 55, 63–65.

52. Peura, "God Gives Man Receives," 76, 60.

53. Mannermaa, *Christ Present*, 44, 52.

54. Peura, "Christ as Favor and Gift," 42 especially note 1, 86, 76.

55. Peura, "Christ as Favor and Gift," 57–59.

its *Common Statement* with the Orthodox churches, the ELCA is careful to affirm justification and sanctification as distinct categories, with justification consisting of a declared righteousness.[56] On the other, Dean Zweck would not allow such a distinction. He asserts that the orthodox Lutheran statement of concord (which emphasizes forensic justification) "with its singular emphasis on imputed righteousness, [has] a tendency on the one hand to separate Christ from his work and benefits, and on the other hand Christ from the believer. It is not just Christ's obedience, atonement for sin, and righteousness that faith appropriates, but Christ himself."[57] In my view, Zweck misunderstands Luther, especially in light of what Luther says about "forms."[58]

Kärkkäinen concurs with Peura and presses the idea of moral transformation. He states that Luther's discovery of a gracious God is actually a rediscovery of the greatest commandment, to love. Luther did not largely endorse the view of justification as forensic declaration: "for him Christ's presence and union are linked not only, or even primarily, with declaration, but also with continuous change of life."[59] "If so, it is not the doctrine of justification that is the key to Luther's theology, even though it is a central theme, but rather his theology of love. Indeed, Luther is first and foremost a theologian of love." Luther "usually prefers terms like 'presence of Christ in faith', 'participation in God', 'union with God', and other terms that highlight the motif of deification and so "Christ's real presence in a believer is the leading motif in Luther's soteriology." "The idea of union and the consequent divinization becomes understandable also from the perspective of love."[60] Although Kärkkäinen admits a place for forensic justification as forgiveness (favor) in Luther's thought, it must always be amplified by the idea of participation in Christ.[61] This participation creates an ontological change in the believer. "God changes the sinner ontologically in the sense that he or she participates in God and in his divine nature, being make righteous and 'a god'," bestowing on the believer "God's essential properties."[62]

56. Saarinen, "Salvation," 176, 77.

57. Zweck, "Union with Christ," 158, citing Luther's *Lectures on* Galatians, 167.

58. For Luther on "forms," see *Lectures on Galatians,* 88, 234.

59. Kärkkäinen, *Spirit and Salvation,* 321.

60. Kärkkäinen, *One with God,* 40, 47, 48.

61. Kärkkäinen, *Spirit and Salvation,* 341.

62. Kärkkäinen, *Spirit and Salvation,* 342.

The Case for Justification with Transformation in Luther's Thought

A number of Lutheran scholars do not accept the conclusions of the Finnish School. Among these, I examine primarily the European Eberhard Jüngel and the American Gerhard O. Forde. There are Evangelical biblical scholars who do engage the Finnish thesis from the biblical perspective, but space forbids me to consider the large body of discussion in biblical circles that revolves around the "new perspective" on Paul.

Perhaps the leading critic of the Finnish School in Europe is the German theologian Eberhard Jüngel. Jüngel engages the Finnish School positively, giving credit to Mannermaa at one point and suggesting ways in which *theōsis* might be understood which would not violate the historic Protestant view of justification. But, Jüngel sharply criticizes the Finnish School as well and offers an understanding of justification that meets some of the objections raised; namely that forensic justification is an empty, merely mental, and Spiritless theological concept.[63]

Jüngel also criticizes the Finnish reading of Luther as out of context. For example, the "joyous exchange" (the "happy exchange" upon which Mannermaa lays great weight) is not an ontological exchange. The context of Luther's passage will not allow it. Rather, it is a *relational* category. Jüngel places this in the "new being" that he discusses.[64] He also criticizes the entire ecumenical movement for its handling of the relationship of Luther to the *Formula of Concord* with "duplicity" and for avoiding intellectual honesty in regard to questions raised against it.[65]

In place of *theōsis*, Jüngel offers an understanding of justification which is both forensic and effective in the sense that it is Word-centered and realized in the death and resurrection of the believer in Christ. Righteousness in human beings (according to the Formula) is similar to "covenant faithfulness" (what Aristotle called "justice") and is a "power that creates and maintains life" because it first has to do with being acknowledged by God as his people.[66] The pardon received in justification creates a "word-shaped structure" in the believer.[67] This word is the creative Word, which calls into existence what was not. So, the forensic act *is* the effective act of "making the ungodly righteous" because what God declares comes to be. This Word

---

63. Jüngel, *Justification the Heart of the Christian Faith*, 199 n.21, 212.

64. Jüngel, *Justification the Heart of the Christian Faith*, 88.

65. Jüngel, *Justification the Heart of the Christian Faith*, 207 n. 136.

66. Jüngel, *Justification the Heart of the Christian Faith*, 62.

67. Jüngel, *Justification the Heart of the Christian Faith*, 199.

remakes our existence by relating us to Christ and bringing us "outside of ourselves" in order to find our true existence in Christ. We are "given a role in Jesus' story," particularly in his death and resurrection, which then brings death to the old person and brings into being a "new person" through a "thoroughgoing renewal" which means that righteousness is imputed and imparted to the believer through her being in Christ.[68]

Only the Word can both pronounce and make righteous. Jüngel stresses this and the idea that such righteous comes to us "outside of ourselves" (*extra nos*) because then it can never become our possession, our own righteousness independent of (or even congruent with) the power of God in the Word. This disallows any notion of justification as a process of maturation or something either earned or maintained by human effort. But if so, if justification is all pronouncement and remains external, then how can we take it seriously? We can do so because of who God is; because God sees the end from the beginning and so sees the sinner becoming righteous; and because the judgment he makes in forensic justification has the creative power to make it so.[69] Because of this, the creative Word does not remain external, but penetrates deeply and "touches us more closely than we can touch ourselves" and becomes "more inward than our innermost being."[70]

I find support for Jüngel's position in Luther's own *Lectures on Galatians: Chapters 1–4*. Luther chides the "sophists," among whom he might number some modern Lutherans. "Therefore this is a marvelous definition of Christian righteousness: it is a divine imputation or reckoning as righteousness or to righteousness, for the sake of our faith in Christ or for the sake of Christ. When the sophists hear this definition, they laugh: for they suppose that righteousness has a certain quality that is first infused into the soul and then distributed through all the members."[71] To dismiss imputation is, for Luther, to "extinguish the Spirit."[72] Luther is quite explicit on the need for and benefits of the imputation that occurs in justification, which does not include any works of love on the Christian's part. After discussing how God has imputed our sins to Christ, or "wrapped" Christ in our sins, Luther says that a faith "formed by love" would unclothe Christ from our sins, making him useless and ourselves overwhelmed and unjustified.[73]

---

68. Jüngel, *Justification the Heart of the Christian Faith*, 210, (cf. 11), 213, 214.

69. Jüngel, *Justification the Heart of the Christian Faith*, 204, 205–06, 208–11.

70. Jüngel, *Justification the Heart of the Christian Faith*, 212.

71. Luther, *Lectures on Galatians*, 233.

72. Luther, *Lectures on Galatians*, 217.

73. Luther, *Lectures on Galatians*, 279.

The American Lutheran Gerhard O. Forde makes a similar argument in some ways and is perhaps more forceful in what he offers as an alternative. Forde acknowledges that there is some validity to complaints about how the idea of forensic justification has been framed. He opines that the doctrine "has indeed been tied to modes of thinking and systematic structures that are too parochial."[74] According to Forde, the legal metaphor alone will not do, and gets us in trouble if extended too far. It makes salvation a "repair job," even when one speaks of transformation. It disallows the countering of the charge of "cheap grace" except by the illegitimate piling on of qualifications for "real" faith (as if sincerity could purchase grace). Or, if we attempt to combine grace with an empirical legal scheme such as the movement conceived by Aquinas, we always end by depending on the person's ability to *do*, to accomplish what is commanded ourselves, no matter how much one talks about grace.[75]

But where the legal metaphor runs out, the powerful truth of our death and resurrection in Christ takes over. We become simultaneously alive and dead. This links with the legal metaphor. Luther emphasized that the judgment of the law had been executed in the death of the sinner, and that God had raised up a new person in Christ apart from the consideration of any human performance.[76] This death and resurrection is not a legal metaphor nor is it some kind of imitation of Christ in the sense of "mortifying" our members.[77] Forde adduces Luther's commentary on Romans to show that the true enemy of grace is not the "godless sinner" but the "righteous who think in terms of legal process, an 'intrinsic' moral process which renders grace fictional and gradually unnecessary."[78]

This "biblical and Reformation understanding of death and life," added to our legal metaphor, will make the doctrine of justification "both radicalized and found more satisfying and universal."[79] Though forgotten historically,[80] this understanding of "death and new life in the crucified and risen Christ" was for Luther the "full and complete justification which resulted "new creation, regeneration, (and) spiritual birth," not symbolically or allegorically but in reality. The righteousness granted in this death and life is eschatological as "the totality of the Kingdom of God moving in upon

---

74. Forde, *Justification by Faith*, vii.

75. Forde, *Justification by Faith*, 10, 17, 25–27.

76. Kolb, "Human Performance," 133.

77. Forde, *Justification by Faith*, 35–37.

78. Forde, *Justification by Faith*, 31

79. Forde, *Justification by Faith*, viii, 10.

80. Forde, *Justification by Faith*, 3

us." As such, it is a "complete" sanctification which is not the goal of good works, but the very fountain of good works.[81]

This is a powerful concept, made more powerful because Forde actually describes how this sanctification works. Rather than changing our human nature into something else (even morally) this death and resurrection changes the affections of the heart. By the action of the Holy Spirit, the believer is now able to love God and hate sin. This change of what the heart loves is real, and not just a theological abstraction. Thus, good works flow from the believer spontaneously because the heart has been changed. Any process or growth is now the making of this new heart visible by doing good works as the Spirit moves. Thus, sanctification is spontaneous love and not moral slogging. There is neither merit nor possession ascribed to good works. The human person does not own this sanctification, even though he experiences it and grows with it. Living out the commandments is the opposite of the quest for personal holiness. It is the incarnation into one's world of what God has already accomplished.[82] If the Father credits the Christian with "passive obedience" because the obedience of Christ is credited to him,[83] this obedience becomes active in an incarnational way as the work of the Holy Spirit expressing itself in and through the believer.

A Reformed thinker, Carl R. Trueman of Westminster Theological Seminary, notes the positive contribution made by the Finnish School (particularly in pointing out the anti-metaphysical influence of neo-Kantian philosophy).[84] He then questions whether the Finnish School has represented Luther fairly, or has engaged in an over-harmonization of Luther. Trueman notes the absence of any interaction with the "thoroughly documented and tightly argued secondary scholarship" on Luther.[85] He argues that some of the ideas presented by the Finnish School are on shaky historical ground. He suggests that the idea of "union" as participation in God is not appropriate for Luther's thought. The passage in the Romans commentary that discusses the "joyful exchange" (what the English edition of Mannermaa calls the "happy exchange;" see above) does not discuss the idea of ontological union at all and its use represents "a clear misappropriation and misapplication of the passage." Although his argument does not depend on this passage, Mannermaa also may not be able to adduce the other terms which he says speak of ontological union. For example, he does

---

81. Forde, *Justification by Faith*, 51.
82. Forde, *Justification by Faith*, 53, 54, 59.
83. Kolb, "Human Performance," 130, cf. 133.
84. Trueman, "Is the Finnish Line a New Beginning?," 232.
85. Trueman, "Is the Finnish Line a New Beginning?," 133, 34, 36, 243, cf. 33.

not explore the meaning of "gift" in reference to Christ in the context of historical discussion, even though several contemporaries in dialogue with Luther used the term.[86]

According to Trueman, Mannermaa does not take the theological context of Luther's *Commentary on Galatians* into account. The realist language used by Luther here does not require an ontological reading, and Luther's understanding of the Eucharist argues against it. For Luther, there is a very real presence of Christ in the Eucharist, but no ontological change occurs in the bread and wine. Rather, such "ontological" presence is described by Luther in terms of its effects upon the human, rather than describing it as divinization.[87] Dennis Bielfeldt, who analyzes Luther's thought in the context of the medieval quadriga, supports this view. For Bielfeldt, Luther's hermeneutic is primarily tropological, and Luther understands in this manner that Christ's second coming (*adventus*) is to the soul as a result of preaching. But, does this "advent" work an ontological change in the Christian? Bielfeldt notes that Peura finds a number of images in the *Dictata*, such as believers are "made heavenly" by Christ coming in faith.[88] Yet, *Luther always contrasts this with Christ's future presence.*[89] His presence in us now is dim and shadowy and will be made full only in the future. At present, Christ is "hidden" from us. Biefeldt cites Lutheran language of the presence in the bread and wine and concludes that there is no ontological change expected through the sacraments.[90]

Justification with Transformation in Reformed Thought

There is a deep and lively appreciation for the idea of transformation by the work of the Holy Spirit in the Reformed thought of John Calvin and Jonathan Edwards that I do not have space to investigate here. Suffice to say that, for Edwards, the Holy Spirit unites the Christian to Christ in regeneration and "infuses" the soul with grace, which alters the saint's nature and gives to the Christian a love for God and holiness. Rather than being an "empty" declaration, forensic justification is part of a supernatural and transformative event that alters or restores the human soul." Touched, then, by the light of the sun, the saint's nature is changed and becomes a little sun. However, this is not a divinization of the human, but a communication of

86. Trueman, "Is the Finnish Line a New Beginning?," 237, 135–37, quote page 37.

87. Trueman, "Is the Finnish Line a New Beginning?," 239.

88. Bielfeldt, "Deification as a Motif," 408–410.

89. Emphasis mine.

90. Bielfeldt, "Deification as a Motif," 411, 414.

divine moral attributes. The divine "nature" spoken of in 2 Peter is not God's essence, but his moral qualities. These are "communicable" attributes, qualities that God may share with the believer. Slater asserts that the union that the believer has with Christ is primarily his union with his human nature.

It is therefore a mistake to see the Reformed/Lutheran doctrine of justification as "empty" since justification never occurs without a concomitant regeneration. Justification is one event in a series of saving acts of God, a series that begins with a gift of grace that regenerates the soul and culminates in the declaration of "not guilty."[91] This gift of grace is a double imputation of the gift of righteousness and the presence of the Holy Spirit himself.[92] "Moreover, both the "promise of the Spirit" and the "gift of righteousness" are thoroughly interwoven together in Paul's thought. . . . For it seems the apostle wants us to understand the blessing of Abraham as *both* the gift of righteousness *and* the gift of the Spirit. This appears to be Luther's conclusion as well."[93] The Holy Spirit is the Father's agent in bringing righteousness to the believer. Regeneration, which can be distinguished but not separated from justification,[94] is the inward work of the indwelling Holy Spirit, which transforms the affections—the loves, loyalties, and commitments—of the soul. Regeneration accomplishes transformation alongside justification, but it is not the same as the long process of becoming conformed to the image of Christ that is usually called "sanctification." Justification, therefore, accompanies a transformation but is never a *process* of transformation, whether ontological or moral.

CONCLUSION: JUSTIFICATION WITH TRANSFORMATION IS A BETTER MODEL THAN THEŌSIS

Kärkkäinen and Macchia depict a tension in the Western church between an empty and theologically bankrupt "point-event" justification and a more biblical and pneumatologically rich process of justification through transformation. They see the standard Reformation doctrine of justification as a purely intellectual or rational view of justification that anticipates no conversion or change in the moral affection or behavior of the believer. Any "change" in the believer is purely mental, the result of a change in knowledge.

---

91. Moody, "Introduction," 13; Anderson, "Holy Spirit and Justification," 298–99.

92. Anderson, *Justification,* 440.

93. Anderson, *Justification,* 448.

94. Anderson, "Holy Spirit and Justification," 299; *Justification,* 62–63, 441–451.

This leaves any moral transformation to "sanctification," which seems often again to be intellectual in the sense that it is the product of Bible study or understanding theological propositions. The work of the Holy Spirit is disregarded except as it illuminates the Word. None of this makes for real believers or authentic Christianity.

Against this, they set a view of justification that in some way sees the Holy Spirit and the believer working to accomplish justification. The Holy Spirit motivates and empowers us to be holy, and we are obedient to God over a long period of discipleship. This they aver to be substantially the same as the Eastern Orthodox idea of *theōsis*, becoming like God in a moral and perhaps even an ontological sense. While it is notable that both Pentecostal authors profess their intention to retain the idea of a declaration of pardon, the Orthodox idea of *theōsis* does not include a forensic declaration of righteousness but understands disciplined obedience to God as the only way to become righteous.

Neither of the views set out by Kärkkäinen and Macchia seem sound or "healthy" in a spiritual or theological sense. While it does seem that a rationalistic "spirituality" of the Western church—that calls us to believe without power from the Holy Spirit for inward transformation—has resulted in a near collapse of Christianity in the West, both Jüngel and Forde demonstrate that such a barren view of justification only results if one ignores the very Pauline idea of the believer's death and resurrection by participation in the death and resurrection of Christ.

Justification is one aspect of salvation that always includes the concomitant idea of the believer's participation in the death and resurrection of Christ. This truth opens the way to understand how the power of the Holy Spirit is involved in justification. Our union with Christ that is forged by the Holy Spirit not merely attaches us to Christ but transforms our affections in the sense of changing the architecture of the soul. This augments the declarative character of forensic justification and makes the forensic declaration part of a transformative event in the sense that we cannot think of one without immediately including the other. If this change comes about by the power of the Holy Spirit, who communicates to us the resurrection life of Christ, then the basis or substructure of ongoing sanctification becomes the event of justification rather than sanctification becoming the ground of justification. We have no need to think of justification as a process. Justification is neither linked to the believer's performance, the utilization of divine grace (which should be seen as the power of God and not merely an attitude in God), nor the "cooperation" of the will of the believer with the will of God. "Process" is placed *after* "proclamation," and so we avoid the danger of the proclamation being swallowed by the process.

By this, we are encouraged to overcome sin daily by considering ourselves dead to sin and alive to God. In my own view I believe that this cuts away all pride and all anxiety or hopelessness. We must first adopt a "kenotic" spirituality by acknowledging our emptiness and dependence on grace. We then participate in resurrection life by asking God to fill this emptiness with the life of Christ through the power of the Holy Spirit. All life and growth in us, from the initial faith to the final glorification, comes from God by the work of Christ through the power of the Holy Spirit. A "kenotic" spirituality enables us to maintain a charismatic and powerful daily spiritual walk without the pride of ascribing glory and power to ourselves.

At the same time, we must also have assurance that we are justified and will be saved. Assurance in salvation prevents us from continually having to do over our "first works," and so never gaining maturity in the faith. Assurance in faith is profoundly necessary for the Christian and comes primarily from the idea that we are (forensically) justified by Christ's work alone. With this Kärkkäinen agrees. "Trust in the reliability and faithfulness of the promissory God rather than in one's own resources laid the basis for assurance."[95]

Only (forensic) justification by faith grants us a firm basis for seeking greater maturity. We can risk following the Spirit's call to progress to a greater level of godliness and receive the grace to go "higher up and further in" as the Holy Spirit works to transform our character into Christ-likeness, which is our calling and destiny (Rom 8:28–30). Each time we receive such transforming grace, we find our passion is to come to a place where our ability to walk in his will and ways by the Holy Spirit grows and we please our Father continually.

In this sense I would argue that all proper spirituality is "kenotic." I do not believe that any of us can accomplish this walk by the Spirit without the constant empowerment of the Spirit. We cannot take pride in an "imparted" or "infused" righteousness, but instead must empty ourselves of all pride in our so-called accomplishments, confess our disability, and receive daily the ability of the Spirit. We must hold to a view of justification which provides the foundation for sanctification—indeed demands growth in Christ-likeness as we exercise daily choices—yet grounds itself in the decree of God that we are "not guilty" in Christ and so are already covenant children. We are already sons by faith—adopted, cleansed, and empowered—and so both our calling and our pursuit are effective by the working of the Holy Spirit. For these reasons, the adoption of the concept of *theōsis* or divinization into Pentecostal theology seems unwarranted We already have a model of

95. Kärkkäinen, *Spirit and Salvation,* 348.

justification which provides both the firm ground of the forensic declaration and the open horizon of continual growth in holiness by our participation in the death and resurrection of Christ through the power of the Holy Spirit.

BIBLIOGRAPHY

Anderson, Jeffrey K. "Justification as the Speech of the Spirit." PhD diss., Regent University, 2015.

——. "The Holy Spirit and Justification: A Pneumatological and Trinitarian Approach to Justification." *Evangelical Review of Theology* 32 (2008) 292–305.

Bielfeldt, Dennis. "Deification as a Motif in Luther's *Dictata Super Psalterium*." *Sixteenth Century Journal* 28 (1997) 408–10.

Forde, Gerhard O. *Justification by Faith—A Matter of Death and Life.* 1982. Reprint, Eugene, OR: Wipf & Stock, 2012.

Henderson, James M. "Transformation by the Spirit in Justification and Sanctification." In *From Northampton to Azusa: Pentecostals and the Theology of Jonathan Edwards*, edited by Amos Yong and Steven M. Studebaker, 127–49. Systematic Pentecostal Charismatic Theology. London: Bloomsbury, forthcoming.

Husbands, Mark, and Daniel J. Treier. eds. *Justification: What's at Stake in the Current Debates.* Downers Grove, IL: InterVarsity, 2004.

Jüngel, Eberhard. *Justification the Heart of the Christian Faith: A Theological Study with an Ecumenical Purpose.* Translated by Jeffrey F. Cayzer. Edinburgh: T. & T. Clark, 2001.

Kärkkäinen, Veli-Matti. *One with God: Salvation as Deification and Justification.* Collegeville, MN: Liturgical, 2004.

——. *Spirit and Salvation.* A Constructive Christian Theology for the Pluralistic World 4. Grand Rapids: Eerdmans, 2016.

Kolb, Robert. "Human Performance and the Righteousness of Faith: Martin Chemnitz's Anti-Roman Polemic in Formula of Concord III." In *By Faith Alone: Essays on Justification in Honor of Gerhard O. Forde*, edited by Joseph A. Burgess and Marc Kolden, 125–39. Grand Rapids: Eerdmans, 2004.

Luther, Martin. *Lectures on Galatians 1535, Chapters 1–4.* Luther's Works 26. Edited by Jaroslav Pelikan. St. Louis: Concordia, 1963.

Macchia, Frank D. *Baptized in the Spirit: A Global Pentecostal Theology.* Grand Rapids: Zondervan, 2006.

——. 2000. "Justification and the Spirit: A Pentecostal Reflection on the Doctrine by Which the Church Stands or Falls," *Pneuma* 22 (2000) 3–21.

——. "Justification through New Creation: the Holy Spirit and the doctrine by which the church stands or falls," *Theology Today* 58 (2001) 202–17.

——. *Justified in the Spirit: Creation, Redemption, and the Triune God.* Grand Rapids: Eerdmans, 2010.

Mannermaa, Tuomo ed. *Christ Present in Faith: Luther's View of Justification.* Translated and edited by Kirsi Irmeli Stjerna Minneapolis: Fortress, 2005.

——. "Justification and Theōsis in Lutheran-Orthodox Perspective." In *Union with Christ: The New Finnish Interpretation of Luther*, edited by Carl E. Braaten and Robert W. Jenson, 25–41. Grand Rapids: Eerdmans, 1998.

————. "Why Is Luther so Fascinating? Modern Finnish Luther Research." In *Union with Christ: The New Finnish Interpretation of Luther*, edited by Carl E. Braaten and Robert W. Jenson, 1–20. Grand Rapids: Eerdmans, 1998.

Moody, Josh. "Introduction." In *Jonathan Edwards and Justification,* edited by Josh Moody and Douglas A. Sweeney, 11–16. Wheaton, IL: Crossway, 2012.

Peura, Simo. "Christ as Favor and Gift: The Challenge of Luther's Understanding of Justification." In *Union with Christ: The New Finnish Interpretation of Luther*, edited by Carl E. Braaten and Robert W. Jenson, 42–69. Grand Rapids: Eerdmans, 1998.

————. "What God Gives Man Receives: Luther on Salvation." In *Union with Christ: The New Finnish Interpretation of Luther*, edited by Carl E. Braaten and Robert W. Jenson, 76–95. Grand Rapids: Eerdmans, 1998.

Piper, John. *Counted Righteous in Christ: Should We Abandon the Imputation of Christ's Righteousness?* Wheaton, IL: Crossway, 2002.

Saarinen, Risto. "Salvation in the Lutheran-Orthodox Dialogue: A Comparative Perspective." In *Union with Christ: The New Finnish Interpretation of Luther*. Edited by Carl E. Braaten and Robert W. Jenson, 167–81. Grand Rapids: Eerdmans, 1998.

Strobel, Kyle. "By Word and Spirit: Jonathan Edwards on Redemption, Justification, and Regeneration," In *Jonathan Edwards and Justification,* edited by Josh Moody, 45–70. Wheaton, IL: Crossway, 2012.

Trueman, Carl R. "Is the Finnish Line a New Beginning? A Critical Assessment of the Reading of Luther Offered by the Helsinki Circle." *Westminster Theological Journal* 65 (2003) 231–44.

Zweck, Dean. "Union with Christ: Understanding Justification from the Perspective of Christ's Real Presence." *Lutheran Theological Journal* 45 (2011) 156–66.

13

The Reformation, World-Changing, and the Thesis of James Davison Hunter

Jan B. Drayer

INTRODUCTION

How *does the world* ultimately change? By what processes does comprehensive cultural transformation principally take place? More specifically, when we consider epoch-transforming events such as Luther's Reformation in sixteenth-century Germany, what can we discern to be the prevalent factors involved in such a change? In the opinion of James Davison Hunter, the LaBrosse-Levinson Distinguished Professor of Religion, Culture, and Social Theory at the University of Virginia, such world-changing most consistently commences by a nuanced set of interconnected sociological realities, which are set in motion by human agents in concert with God's providence.

In his provocative 2010 text, *To Change the World: The Irony, Tragedy & Possibility of Christianity in the Late Modern World*, Hunter passionately appeals to the American Christian community to consider, concerning culture transformation, the subtleties of social change theory as opposed to the machinations of contemporary populist theology. The text's subtitle reveals the author's hopefulness for Christian participation in repairing American culture while simultaneously recognizing the presence of ambivalence and error in the applications of Christian-induced cultural change. Important to

248

our focus on the 500th anniversary celebration of the Reformation, Hunter, in Essay One of his text, utilizes the Reformation as a historical backstop for his argument regarding the sociological realities of cultural change. He observes that while the changes emerging from the Reformation had roots in a quest for spiritual and theological "purity and . . . truthfulness" their success was dependent on other issues, including the formation of an alternative elite outside of the Roman Catholic Church which intersected with the resources of other leaders: "intellectual, institutional, administrative, financial, and political—all in common cause." These interlocking realities were, in the opinion of Hunter, "nothing short of decisive."[1]

James R. Payton, Professor Emeritus of History at Redeemer University College, concurs with Hunter's basic premise stating (contrary to some popularly-held myths in Protestantism) that the Reformation did not simply drop down from Heaven, but arose "on the ground,"[2] having historical, social, cultural *and* doctrinal antecedents attached to its genesis.

If Hunter is correct in his sociological propositions, then academics *and* practitioners do well to heed this counsel. One could argue that the ongoing mandate from the Lord to reach our generation, appied to the contemporary challenges that uniquely face the American church, demands that we explore all avenues of academic research, not simply imbibing and replicating transformational schemes derived from multitudinous theological echo-chambers. To this point, Greg Forster wrote presciently (responding to criticism of his assessment of Hunter's text): "The various social sciences all have to listen to one another; social scientists and theologians need to listen to one another; scholars, integrators and practitioners need to listen to one another. We all know things the others need to know, and we won't learn anything if we only listen to people who are like us."[3]

Crucial to our task is to discern the role of the Holy Spirit in the framework of Luther's Reformation, and also, moving forward, in public theologies of change. When considering pneumatology, the contexts of Luther's era and the twenty-first century are quite different. Nevertheless, the same Spirit that moved providentially in Luther's Germany moves still in this era to revive, renew, and reform the global Church. Thus, the purpose here is to explore Hunter's sociological propositions on world-changing in *To Change the World*, and the juxtaposition of Luther's Reformation as historical proof

---

1. Hunter, *To Change the World*, 70.

2. Payton. *Getting the Reformation* Wrong, 23

3. First Things. "Revisiting 'Revisiting Faithful Presence.'" https://www.firstthings.com/blogs/firstthoughts/2016/01/revisiting-revisiting-faithful-presence [Accessed October 13, 2017].

of those propositions, while taking some space to consider the pneumatological realities implicit in Luther's and Hunter's writings.

"TO CHANGE THE WORLD"

To Change the World is Hunter's sociological/theological critique on the strategy of cultural transformation utilized by the American church's various denominational components and movements. The text is made up of three intertwined essays, each building upon the other; the final portion being the formulation of Hunter's paradigm of Christian cultural influence called "faithful presence." Essay I burrows deep into the various strategies toward cultural transformation, which crowd the American Christian topography at the outset of the twentieth century. In Hunter's estimation, there is much by which we can be encouraged in the American church's pursuit of the Creation Mandate[4] and Great Commission[5] while there is also much that needs realignment toward a more holistic construal of world-changing. Thus, Hunter's text began a robust and necessary conversation[6] within the American church community on the merits of Christian cultural transformation—which continues heatedly to this day.[7] Hunter contends that American Christians of the last generation have vied to change the culture through the infusion of better ideas, which he calls the "common view of culture." Hunter defines the "common view" as being the content found in the hearts and minds of individuals, specifically values which guide our moral preferences and that which we distinguish as being preferable, right and accurate. Culture, for example, is what the majority of people feel is the best way to pursue life whether it be child raising, marriage or worship.[8] He critiques this view of culture, held by conservative Christian thinkers (such as the late Charles Colson) who, along with other "cultural warriors," insist that deeper knowledge of the world and a more dedicated application of the Christian worldview would change the world from the bottom up, one person at a time. In other words, better values advanced by faithfulness

---

4. All Scripture references are from the NIV unless otherwise noted. Gen 1:28; 2:15.

5. Matt 28:18–20.

6. Indeed, Hunter hoped for this very thing. "The three interconnected essays. . .are an attempt to make sense of these bewildering realities that, I hope, will contribute to scholarship" (*To Change the World*, ix).

7. See for example, Strange, "Faithful Presence: A Theology for the Trenches?" loc649–766.

8. Hunter, *To Change the World*, 7.

to the Christian worldview would mean better choices, which would auto-matically equate to a better culture.

Hunter's critique of the contemporary, commonly held view of culture is scathing: "I contend that the dominant ways of thinking about culture and cultural change are flawed, for they are based on both specious social science and problematic theology. In brief, the model on which various strategies are based not only does not work, *but it cannot work*" [emphasis author]. Hunter concedes that culture and cultural realities comprise a "knotty, dif-ficult, complex, perhaps impossible puzzle,"[9] while insisting that changing culture through the winning of hearts and minds to an ideal is not plausible.

While Hunter generally agrees with University of Chicago professor Richard Weaver's famous quote, "Ideas have consequences," he thinks that one is on safer ground to affirm that *not all ideas have consequences* [empha-sis author]. Better yet, writes Hunter, one is on far more solid sociological ground to say, "Under certain specific conditions and circumstances ideas have consequences."[10] In other words, when the conditions are right, ideas have the capacity to inspire "greatness, creativity, sacrifice, and human flourishing." It is not, Hunter clarifies, as if evangelism, political activity, and social reform are wrong or ineffective in themselves, but they form an incomplete philosophy and praxis for deep and lasting cultural change.

World-changing, says Hunter, is principally the work of elites whom he describes as "gatekeepers who provide creative direction and manage-ment within the spheres of social life."[11] Hunter further observes that while it is sometimes true that economic revolts, social movements, and political movements led by common people can have tremendous influence, they are most often short-lived and limited in effect. Deep cultural changes, he states, result from theorists generating ideas and knowledge, which then move on to educators who convey these ideas forward. From the educators they then transition to the popularizers who simplify the ideas, who pass it forward to the practitioners who put the ideas in motion in the marketplace. Hunter, at this point, leaves us with this sociological morsel, "Cultural change is most enduring when it penetrates the structure of our imagination, frameworks of knowledge and discussion, and the perception of everyday reality."[12] He further stresses that it is primarily networks of elites acting together in common purpose and with shared ends that have the greatest possibility of world-changing. When resources of cultural, social, economic, and political

9. Hunter, *To Change the World*, 40.

10. Hunter, *To Change the World*, 41.

11. Hunter, *To Change the World*, 41.

12. Hunter, *To Change the World*, 42.

capital overlap one another over a period greater than three to five years, the world, writes Hunter, "indeed changes."[13] As we will see, Hunter's thoughts have a tremendous impact on the commonly held perceptions of Luther's Reformation.

Hunter's Critique of the Common View of Culture

Hunter critiques the common view of culture's foundational tenet that the essence of culture is found in the hearts and minds of individuals, i.e. the moral values they adhere to and the worldview they hold. It is thought that the transformation of the habits and mindsets of ordinary people will shift the balance of culture toward a decidedly more Christian change.

American Christians, under the influence of this common view of culture, have focused on three basic strategies of cultural transformation.[14] First, the values and the tactic of evangelism, where the primary focus is praying and fasting for revival and individual soul winning—the hope being that a spiritually-transformed people will change the culture. Second, the values and the tactic of political action. In other words, more Bible-based laws and more ethical politicians will turn the tide in America toward positive cultural change. Throughout his text, Hunter shows particular concern regarding Christian political advocacy, noting in his first essay that the dominant public witness of the Christian churches of America since the 1980s has been a political one.[15] This political witness, he emphasizes, has had decidedly mixed bag results—mostly negative. Third, Hunter critiques the values and the tactic of social reforms noting that its adherents have sought to transform society through the reforming of schools, the family and other civic associations.

Hunter notes three assumptions implied by the purveyors of the common view of culture. First, the common view's purveyors adopt the notion that real cultural change happens individually through personal transformation, as has been already noted. Second, that cultural change can be willed into being. Third, that change to the culture can happen in a bottom-up, democratic-style order in which ordinary people carry the day. While all of this activity is helpful and even needed, Hunter explains that sociological realities weigh-in negatively with respect to these attempts at actual, long-lasting and deep transformation. He further locates the overriding error of the common view perspective by its adoption of a kind of

13. Hunter, *To Change the World*, 43.

14. Hunter, *To Change the World*, 43.

15. Hunter, *To Change the World*, 12.

Hegelian idealism. This idealism, adds Hunter, is also fueled by the unique brand of American/Protestant individualism, as well as pietistic tendencies at work in the contemporary American church.

This particular form of idealism, writes Hunter, leads people off the path of real cultural transformation in five ways:[16]

1. It misconstrues agency, implying an ability to bring change where there may be none.

2. It underplays the importance of history and its forces.

3. It ignores the way culture is generated, coordinated, and organized. Thus, it underplays the difficulties of cultural change.

4. It imputes logic and rationality to culture where such does not always exist.

5. It communicates that if Christians try harder, learn more, and embrace the right worldview formulation, the culture will change.

"In sum," observes Hunter, "idealism leads to naiveté about the nature of culture and its dynamics that is, in the end, fatal."[17]

Hunter's Propositions on Culture and Cultural Change

Hunter counters the common view's philosophy of cultural transformation with eleven propositions of his own about culture. Seven of the propositions describe definitions of culture proper, and the remaining four convey the ways in which cultures are actually changed. For the purposes here, and in light of our focus on the Reformation, we shall note two of the important propositions on culture and include Hunter's four propositions dealing with cultural transformation.

Proposition Three on culture states that "culture is intrinsically dialectical."[18] Here, Hunter underlines two important points, first a relationship between ideas and institutions, that is, ideas generate more traction through the influence of the institution from which they spring. Second is the relationship between individuals and institutions; namely, individuals act while an institution provides a framework for that activity, thus, giving more influence to the individual. Also noteworthy in our context

---

16. Hunter, *To Change the World*, 26–27.

17. Hunter, *To Change the World*, 27.

18. Hunter, *To Change the World*, 34.

is Proposition Six: "culture is generated within networks."[19] To this point, Hunter importantly addresses the "great man" view of history which states that culture change comes on the backs of the leadership of outstanding men and women throughout history. Here, Hunter stresses that it is not just individual genius, but also the networks within which these persons co-labor, that combine into an influence-multiplier. In other words, for Hunter, ideas (such as Luther's) have consequences under specific sociological conditions and circumstances.

From Hunter's propositions on culture spring his four propositions on sociological cultural transformation. First, "cultures change from the top down, rarely ever from the bottom up."[20] While Hunter acknowledges that the mobilization of "ordinary" people does change culture, he emphasizes that the most deep-rooted cultural alterations begin with elites whose capacity to bring about change is greater than that of those outside of the upper strata of sociological influence. Second, "change is typically initiated by elites who are outside of the centermost positions of prestige."[21] Hunter here illustrates the point of center and periphery by comparing the influence of two newspapers. For example, the Boston Globe's influence is noteworthy, but that pales in comparison with the reach of the New York Times. Therefore, the New York Times occupies the center while the Boston Globe the periphery. In a similar vein, Regent University is prestigious, but Harvard is arguably the most influential academic institution in the United States. In this proposition, Hunter recognizes that "Innovation. . .generally moves not from the elites and the institutions they lead to the general population but among elites who do not necessarily occupy the highest echelons of prestige."[22] Third, "world-changing is most concentrated when the networks of elites and the institutions they lead overlap."[23] When elites from transecting spheres of social life share resources and act together there is a powerful catalyst for profound cultural change.

Hunter's last proposition states, "Cultures change, but rarely without a fight." Conflict is one of the constants of social transformation. Institutions and their agents will protect their turf when innovation attempts to stir the status quo. Hunter encapsulates these four propositions of cultural change by asserting that "Overlapping networks of leaders and overlapping resources, all operating near or in the center institutions and in common

19. Hunter, *To Change the World*, 37.
20. Hunter, *To Change the World*, 41.
21. Hunter, *To Change the World*, 42.
22. Hunter, *To Change the World*, 42.
23. Hunter, *To Change the World*, 43.

purpose are some of the practical dynamics within which world-changing occurs."[24] In *these* sociological settings, Hunter affirms, ideas will have consequences.

Hunter on the Reformation

In his first essay of *To Change the World* Hunter recognizes at least nine social, political, economic, and theological conditions that allowed Luther's Reformation to flourish. These, he postulates, were critical to the effectiveness of the German Reformation's success where other medieval reform movements failed to have the same success. While self-admittedly limited and dependent on the scholarship of others when speaking to historical issues, Hunter nevertheless sees his sociological propositions on cultural transformation as being illustrated by the Reformation.[25]

Hunter begins by noting that the Holy Roman Empire was not largely centralized, politically nor administratively, at the time of Luther's Reformation.[26] Central Europe was a collection of more than two hundred somewhat self-governing principalities and cities, overseen by the Emperor Charles V. Preoccupation with internal disputes, political conflicts, and growing discontent among the common people wanting more freedoms made governing difficult to balance. The specter of the mounting threat from the Ottoman Empire also weighed heavily on the relative attention that could to be paid to rising internal issues. Thus, Luther and his followers were the beneficiaries of imperial and papal distractions at that moment in European history. Second, there were changes in the late medieval economy that were favorable to the Reformation.[27] The growing wealth from international commerce, trade and export began to trickle down to a new class of merchants and entrepreneurs. This new economic power brought not only prosperity to them but also a desire to protect their growing political and religious autonomy. Third, the leading reformers were scholars of distinction, masters of medieval and classical thought as well as experts in the language arts.[28] This gave the Reformation a depth and breadth of rigorous academic erudition which greatly aided the movement. Fourth, foundational to the

24. Hunter, *To Change the World*, 44.

25. Hunter also utilizes other Christian historical epochs as sociological evidence of cultural transformation.
See *To Change the World*, 48–78.

26. Hunter, *To Change the World*, 65.

27. Hunter, *To Change the World*, 65.

28. Hunter, *To Change the World*, 66.

Reformation's success was its inspiration and strategic alliance[29] with the Humanist movement.[30] Erasmus' vast influence in a network of German, Swiss and Austrian universities proved helpful in preparing the ground culturally and intellectually for the Reformation. Fifth, Luther received much attention and support from a wide network of other scholars sensitive to Reformation ideas.[31] These alliances proved to be valuable in the spread of the movement. Sixth, the Reformation created a vast number of political refugees that were exiled from their Catholic homelands, which became a favorable yet unexpected consequence to the movement.[32] Reformation ideas spread as the hot winds of persecution carried them. Seven, the Reformation was bolstered by universities located in urban centers that were also located along prominent trade routes. Merchants and traders within these large municipalities became valuable allies in the spread of the Reformation message.[33] Eight, the new technology of the printing press allowed Reformation theology to flourish in these urban areas.[34] Finally, the success of the Reformation was also aided by the protection of regional nobility.[35] Though other reformers and reform activities before Luther had suffered severe persecution, he was the recipient of the protection of Fredrick the Wise, which gave him and other reformers space to more diligently attend to their labors.

A survey of some modern church historians' observations about the Reformation seems generally favorable toward Hunter's statements on the same. The observations of Cairns,[36] Gonzalez,[37] Hsia,[38] MacCullough,[39] and McGrath[40] comprise a sampling of general agreement with the majority of Hunter's historical reflections. Social historians, including Grimm[41] and Holt,[42] also appear to be in general agreement with Hunter's sociological

29. Although Luther and Erasmus later had a major falling out. See, Cairns. *Christianity*, 286.

30. Cairns. *Christianity*, 286.

31. Cairns. *Christianity*, 66–68.

32. Cairns. *Christianity*, 68.

33. Cairns. *Christianity*, 68–69.

34. Cairns. *Christianity*, 69.

35. Cairns. *Christianity*, 69.

36. Cairns. *Christianity*, 272–77.

37. Gonzalez. *The Story of Christianity*, 9.

38. Hendrix. "Martin Luther," 3–19.

39. MacCullough. *Reformation*, 77–129.

40. McGrath. *Reformation Thought*, 1–31.

41. Grimm. "Social Forces," 3–13.

42. Holt. "The Social History," 133–144.

assessments regarding the Reformation. Grimm, for example, adds three reasons for Germany's unrest against the Church in Rome. First, the lack of political unity in Germany allowed Rome to exert greater influence upon the German people, and to impose "financial extractions" that enflamed resentment.[43] Second, the age-old question "How can I be saved?" was stronger in Germany at this time than elsewhere. The people, Grimm states, were largely dissatisfied with the answers coming from the Catholic Church. Third, Germany had high numbers of wealthy, educated people who chafed under the restraints that certain institutions (especially the Roman Catholic Church) laid upon them. In sum, Hunter appears to be on solid ground using the Reformation as a means to verify his sociological propositions on cultural change.

LUTHER, THE HOLY SPIRIT, AND THE REFORMATION

However, even as we have seen Hunter so thoroughly explain these very human, socially-ordered elements and processes (being played out on many different levels), we also realize that it was almost certainly the Holy Spirit who orchestrated the broader strokes of this movement that so shook sixteenth-century Europe. The Holy Spirit was at work in the life of Luther molding him both personally and in the course of his theological constructs. Here we must revisit and take into account Hunter's critique of the "great man theory" of culture change as well as the slight tweaking of Weaver's axiom,[44] "Under specific conditions and circumstances ideas can have consequences."[45] We account for the inimitable person of Luther and the vast reach of his "idea." Of Luther's unique character, Grimm wrote humorously,

> There is no doubt that Luther was a passionate, impulsive man which felt his theology before he began with logical questions and answers about God . . . which resulted in a theology full of paradoxes or downright contradictions . . . In any century in which he was born, Luther would have guaranteed a richly memorable night out, whether hilariously entertaining or infuriatingly quarrelsome.[46]

---

43. Grimm, *The Reformation Era*, 75.

44. "Ideas have consequences." Hunter, *To Change the World*, 40–41.

45. Hunter, *To Change the World*, 41.

46. Grimm, *The Reformation Era*, 112.

To the point of Luther's uniquely-suited temperament and character, one must ask, what is it that *forms* a reformer? Also, what is it that forms a reformation? Can a reformation be fashioned by human hands alone, or is it all of God? In Luther's case, was his formation a result of the type-A fathering that he received in his youth? A thunderstorm?[47] The cloistered life? Was it his smitten conscience, or was it the later caress of a heavenly grace? Was it an outcome of a visitation of the Holy Spirit, or was it the wounds of excommunication that drove him to his convictions?

Looking deeper into Luther's life, we find it somewhat unremarkable in its initial stages. Born into a middle-class family, Luther's father, Hans, was involved in the mining industry, which necessitated the elder Luther to encourage his son toward a degree in law. Everything seemed to be on a trajectory of normalcy until young Luther was caught in a blasting thunderstorm that so terrified him that he called upon St. Anne to grant him safety. In return, Luther vowed that he would enter the priesthood, which he did in 1505, becoming a member of the Erfurt house of the Augustinian Eremites.[48]

Observing that Luther had a definite gift for learning, the leadership of Erfurt house encouraged him to pursue his education, which Luther did with good results, paving the way for him to be installed as a teaching monk at the University of Wittenberg in 1511.[49] Prior to Wittenberg, Luther had an opportunity to travel to Rome in 1510 as a delegate for a consortium of Saxon Augustinian monasteries.[50] While in Rome, Luther was awed by the majesty of the Vatican but thoroughly dismayed by the corruption. These contradictions likely had some cumulative effect on Luther's later choices, particularly with respect to taking a stand against the extremes he saw in the sale of indulgences,[51] begun under the direction of Pope Leo X as a way to financially support the rebuilding of the basilica of St. Peter.

Luther both taught and preached to great effect while at Wittenberg. He began his study and lectures on books of the Bible (including Genesis, Psalms, Romans, Galatians, and Hebrews) beginning in 1513. Between 1515 and 1519, while preparing for his lectures, he had a dramatic spiritual encounter, which he called his *Turmerlebnis* ("tower experience"). It was at this time that Luther was deeply struck and challenged by the shared words of Hab 2:4 and Rom 1:17—"The righteous will live by faith." "Righteousness,"

---

47. MacCullough, *Reformation*, 112.

48. MacCullough, *Reformation*, 112.

49. MacCullough, *Reformation*, 112.

50. MacCullough, *Reformation*, 112.

51. Cairns, *Christianity*, 282.

or "righteous," translated from the Latin *justia/justus*, became the foundation of Luther's doctrine of justification by faith in which a person is "declared righteous by God who imputes the merits of Christ, through his grace which is received by faith."[52] For Luther, this revelation was personally life-altering as he had struggled for long years with feelings of guilt over sin and fear of a righteous and wrathful God. Reflecting on his experience, Luther wrote, "At this I felt myself straightway born afresh and to have entered through the open gates into paradise itself."[53] Little did Luther then know of the gate of persecution that he had also opened through his innocent, Spirit-directed study of the Scripture.

On October 31, 1517, in response to Johann Tetzel's sale of indulgences at Jutterbock near Wittenberg, Luther nailed his ninety-five theses to the door of the Castle Church.[54] Luther condemned the exploitive sale of indulgences and challenged the theological structure on which they were based, calling for a debate on the matter.[55] It was not then Luther's desire to separate from Rome, but to defend his newfound convictions of New Testament soteriology, and, on a pastoral level, to protect his parishioners against a pope-sanctioned fleecing. In response, Tetzel attempted to silence the "rebel" monk by way of his stature in the Dominican Order. Luther was ordered to Heidelberg in 1518 to debate the issue, which led instead to more support of Luther's idea.[56] Luther was beginning to lean more upon the authority of the Scriptures than upon the authority of the Church. What followed was a rise in the temperature of the tactics of Luther's interlocutors to the point where, as Cairns notes, that by the fall of 1518, Luther insisted that his sole authority in the pending dispute was to be the Bible alone, rather than the Church's teaching, or the pope. Further, Fredrick of Saxony promised his support for the reformer against the pressure of the Dominicans.[57] What followed was popular backing of Luther by the German people and other allies; and near-constant persecution by the Church authorities that sought to stamp out the fledgling movement.

Luther's timely, world-changing idea, which eventually found a deep resonance in the hearts and minds of many in sixteenth-century Northern Europe, had an important and noteworthy theological antecedent—the writings of Augustine of Hippo. As an Augustinian monk Luther was deeply

52. MacCullough, *Reformation*, 115–16.
53. MacCullough, *Reformation*, 116.
54. Cairns, *Christianity*, 282–3.
55. Cairns, *Christianity*, 283.
56. Cairns, *Christianity*, 283.
57. Cairns, *Christianity*, 283.

immersed in and influenced by Augustine's teachings. Through Augustine's theology, Luther was confronted with and inspired by the Bible, which became the foundation of his pneumatological deliberations. Of the influence of Augustine on the Reformation, MacCullough declared, "It is essential to grasp the contours of Augustine's soteriology because otherwise it is impossible to understand why the Reformation happened or the profound nature of the issues at stake."[58] B.B. Warfield also noted Augustine's vast impact on the Reformation stating, "The Reformation, inwardly considered, was just the ultimate triumph of Augustine's doctrine of grace over Augustine's doctrine of the Church."[59]

We note that Augustine's influence on Reformation thinking was not just upon German Augustinian monks, nor solely upon Luther himself. Around Luther's time, other scholars were coming to the same conclusions relative to justification via their own interactions with Augustine's writings. For example, in 1506, Johann Amerbach, from Basel, published a scholarly edition of all of Augustine's works.[60] In 1521 French theologian Jacques Lefevre d' Etaples wrote and published commentaries on Paul's epistles, which were influenced by Augustine's view of the irrelevance of human works in salvation.[61] Augustine's theology crashed with much power upon the shoreline of the common humanist impulse in Europe, displacing theological, philosophical, and social norms in its wake.[62]

As we turn to consider Luther's pneumatology, we must observe that Luther would have been considered very much orthodox with regards to the teachings of his time before his "tower experience." Luther lived in a time when Scholasticism heavily influenced the Church's pneumatology, i.e., grace was available to the believer through the Holy Spirit's work, which was infused in the sacraments. While Luther, early in his career, was fully orthodox with regards to that era's pneumatological formulations, his own salvation experience seemed to aid him in forming a fresher understanding of the Spirit's work. Grimm notes that Luther, both experientially and also academically discovered something unconventional for his day with regards to the workings of the Holy Spirit in the believer's life:

> Luther . . . developed a new conception of grace that, he believed, did not operate magically or mechanically through the sacraments, but directly, as a constant, dynamic, ethical force

---

58. MacCullough, *Reformation,* 107.
59. MacCullough, *Refomration,* 108.
60. MacCullough, *Reformation,* 108.
61. MacCullough, *Reformation,* 108.
62. MacCullough, *Reformation,* 108–9.

in the individual, enabling him to combat sin—which is always present until death—and to fulfill the law, which requires righteousness. God had made this possible by sacrificing Christ on the cross.[63]

Lutheran theologian Arnold E. Carlson's article, "Luther and the Doctrine of the Holy Spirit,"[64] notes the difficulty in nailing down Luther's pneumatology because it is nowhere systematized. However, at a very foundational level of Luther's pneumatology, there is an inextricable connection in Christians between the work of Scripture and the work of the Spirit. Martin E. Marty, commenting on Luther's sermon on Luke 1:39–56, quotes Luther, "The Word must be used (the sword does nothing unless taken in hand) to be creative; but its creativity, changing the whole of man, depends on the Spirit."[65] Luther's insistence upon the Scriptures for pnuematological clarity was in full use on two fronts as his theological context was not without rival thoughts about the work and person of the Holy Spirit. Prevalent in Luther's immediate context were, of course, the teachings of the Church that understood the Spirit being "channeled to the believer exclusively through the sacramental structures of the church,"[66] and the Enthusiasts,[67] "who claimed the direct inspiration of the Holy Spirit, irrespective of what Scripture might teach through the Word and Sacraments."[68]

Carlson, along with Regin Prenter, disagreed with the common view that Luther minimized the work of the Holy Spirit.[69] Citing Prenter, Carlson sees Luther's pneumatological center affirming six tenets: 1) justification by faith, 2) his doctrine of grace, 3) *Anfechtung*, or inner conflict,[70] 4) *simul justus et peccator* ("at the same time righteous and a sinner"), 5) the theology of the cross over the theology of glory, and, 6) the whole concept of vocation. Carlson, agreeing with Prenter's view of Luther's pneumatology, notes that "the work of the Spirit is to conform man to Christ. This is accomplished by conforming man to Christ's death and resurrection."[71] This conforming is

---

63. Grimm, *The Reformation Era*, 86.

64. Carlson. "Luther and the Holy Spirit," 135.

65. Marty. "Preaching on the Holy Spirit," 429.

66. Carlson, *Luther and the Holy Spirit*, 136.

67. Whose leading voices included Andreas Carlstadt, Thomas Müntzer, Nicholas Storch, Thomas Dreschal and Markus Stubner. See Thiselton. *The Holy Spirit*, 259.

68. Thiselton, *The Holy Spirit*, 259.

69. See Carlson, "Luther and the Holy Spirit," 137, and, Thiselton, *The Holy Spirit*, 257.

70. "In which the believer is corrected of sin and his or her self-confidence is done away (cf. John 16:8)." Thiselton, *The Holy Spirit*, 258.

71. Carlson, "Luther and the Holy Spirit," 137.

to be distinguished from Scholasticism's concept of the imitation of Christ[72] in which Christ remains a distant ideal that humanity, in its own strength, must strive toward. Rather, explains Carlson of Luther's thought, "God, through his Holy Spirit, is actively struggling for man's redemption. He is stripping us of every false confidence that we may solely rely upon his divine mercy. It is God's 'foreign work' preparing us for his 'proper work.'"[73] Thus, Luther held fast, against many foes, to a robust biblical view of the Spirit. This grand idea sparked a spiritual and social revolution that shook the edifices of power in his day.

"TO CHANGE THE WORLD" AND THE HOLY SPIRIT

Hunter's observations on the Reformation, relative to his social change theories that emphasize top-down social change activated by networks of cultural elites, chafes against what many American Pentecostals might intuitively understand or champion. After all, it could be reasoned, was it not the human foundation of the Church, established predominantly through common people who were empowered by the Spirit, that changed the Roman world? Do not the gospels, the book of Acts, and the testimony of the early Church inform us of this? Does it not say in the King James Version of Acts 17:6 that the Thessalonian mob accused the apostles of "turning the world upside down. . .?" Do not the kingdom parables of Jesus inform us that humble and seemingly powerless entities have the greatest possibility of advancing God's cause in the earth? Was not Martin Luther himself a simple believer like us who had an extraordinary encounter with the word of God illumined by the Spirit?

Nevertheless, Hunter's argument does bear further scrutiny in light of his idea of moving toward spiritually healthy cultural change. Hunter spends an entire chapter warning Christians against three potentially harmful paradigms of engagement with culture. First, a "defense against" culture in which the Christian attempts to maintain Christian distinctiveness against "the assault of secular modernity."[74] The Christian response to the incursions of the secular is to evangelize and to advocate, in all of the social spheres, for the Christian worldview. The second paradigm is the engagement of "relevance to" the culture. Hunter sees the "seeker movement" and the "emergent church" movement as exemplifying this model.[75] In short,

---

72. Carlson, "Luther and the Holy Spirit," 137.

73. Carlson, "Luther and the Holy Spirit," 139.

74. Hunter, *To Change the World*, 214.

75. Hunter, *To Change the World*, 215.

this is the attempt to show that the Church is not a stodgy, dusty repository of old ideas and old people, but a place where the ancient truths of the
Christian faith have consequence in the twenty-first century. Unfortunately,
some wrong-headed notions of relevance have marred the message, distinctiveness, and holiness of Christianity. Third, "purity from" culture, which is
somewhat similar to the "defense against" stance. Hunter explains the difference as being that those of this view see that "there is very little that can be
done for the world because, in its fallen state, the world is irredeemable this
side of Christ's return. The church has been compromised by its complicity
with the world's sinfulness."[76] In this view, the Church is to "extricate itself
from the contaminating forces of the world."[77] As that extrication is undertaken, the Church will return to its pristine purity and power.

Hunter dedicates an entire essay to promoting his vision of world-
changing, which he calls "Faithful Presence." Hunter describes this as, first,
"[Christians who] are . . . fully present to each other within the community
of faith and fully present to those who are not."[78] Hunter reasons that if
believers cannot extend grace to one another, how are we to touch others
outside of the church walls? To be present faithfully is also to "welcome
the stranger—those outside of the community of faith. . .Believer or non-
believer, attractive or unattractive, admirable or disreputable, upstanding or
vile—the stranger is marked by the image of God."[79] Second, faithful presence needs to be seen in our tasks and vocations. Our lives must not be lived
from a compartmentalized view of spirituality, but with commitment to
work for the glory of God in *all* that we do.[80] Third, to be present faithfully
necessitates Christians being "fully present and committed in their spheres
of social influence, whatever they may be: their families, neighborhoods,
voluntary activities, and places of work."[81] Here Hunter stresses that believers must use caution in the use of power given to them in relationships,
institutions, and organizations of which they are a part.[82] Where power is
given, the believer is to exercise it by the example of Jesus, whose use of
power was ". . .Rooted in intimacy with the Father, rejecting the privileges
of status, oriented by a self-giving compassion for the needs of the other,

76. Hunter, *To Change the World*, 218.

77. Hunter, *To Change the World*, 218.

78. Hunter, *To Change the World*, 244.

79. Hunter, *To Change the World*, 245.

80. Hunter, *To Change the World*, 246–47.

81. Hunter, *To Change the World*, 247.

82. Hunter, *To Change the World*, 247.

and not only non-coercive toward those outside of the community of faith, but committed indiscriminately to the good of all."[83] In sum, Hunter states:

> A theology of faithful presence obligates us to do what we are able, under the sovereignty of God, to shape the patterns of life and work and relationship—that is, the institutions of which our lives are constituted—toward a shalom that seeks the welfare not only of those of the household of God but of all. That power will be wielded is inevitable. But the *means of influence* and the *ends of influence* must conform to the exercise of power modeled by Christ.[84] (emphasis Hunter)

Hunter's pneumatological element in faithful presence is somewhat hard to completely discern, due to the paucity of direct mentions of the Holy Spirit in *To Change the World*. Where Hunter does use Spirit language, he does so broadly, yet effectively, by focusing the Church's prophetic witness through an incarnational stance. Hunter summarizes a theology of faithful presence by incarnation in two "essential lessons." The first is that Christians living incarnationally will be the best possible answer to those who have experienced dissolution in the Church and the world. From this follows the second lesson: "it is the way the Word became incarnate in Jesus Christ and the purposes to which the incarnation was directed that are the only adequate reply to challenge of difference."[85] Hunter asserts that the Christian must embody God's word of love if human flourishing is to occur. Trust is forged when the words we speak cohere with actions of love.[86]

Finally, it is important for Hunter that the believer realize first that God is faithfully present to us and for us, and that we return that grace by being faithfully present to him. We, his Church, are faithfully present to him when we comprise a worshipping community. As Hunter so beautifully states, "Only by being fully present to God as a worshipping community and as adoring followers can we be faithfully present in the world."[87]

PENTECOSTALS AND WORLD-CHANGING

Pentecostals have at times looked suspiciously at academia generally, and sociological ideas specifically, yet Hunter's sociological premises here seem

83. Hunter, *To Change the World*, 247.
84. Hunter, *To Change the World*, 254.
85. Hunter, *To Change the World*, 241.
86. Hunter, *To Change the World*, 241.
87. Hunter, *To Change the World*, 244.

unassailable. We would thus do well to consider all of the data regarding cultural transformation, and to remember that the Holy Spirit is active in all of society—whether the Church recognizes this immediately or not. Keith Warrington, a New Testament scholar from the UK, bemoaned the fact that Pentecostals "have tended to view the work of the Spirit in empowering the Church to evangelize the world and not considered his role in socially transforming it."[88]

Further, irrespective of purely sociological propositions—important as they are—it seems that awakenings, renewals, revivals, and reformations are the operations of the Spirit that uncover a part of God's character, as well as his will and purposes that have become obscured, clouded, or suppressed by human failures. God will not be mocked by foe, nor will he long be mischaracterized by friend. Rather, he has been clearly revealed in Reformation history and the five hundred years since—even when the Church's uncharitable dealings with others have besmirched the reputation of our compassionate and generous God. Luther himself sometimes stumbled badly within the context of the Reformation he largely initiated. His influence on the Peasant War and his irritated dealings with the Jews, among other things, cast long shadows over the Germany he loved. The best intentions of God's people can sometimes overshadow his glory, for instance, when they do not fully realize his ways or do not immediately recognize his work at the moment. Thus, reformation, revival, and the like are God's revealing of an important and necessary aspect of the Kingdom, on earth as it is in heaven. Humans yearn to be free, to live under God's blue sky unbound by the coercions, repressions, and the evils that ail our race. In Jesus, humanity has found a mighty liberator, and from time to time men and women of faith, fitted with a fiery passion and holy anointing, join him as co-liberators.

CONCLUSION

Hunter's sociological foundation stones, expressed in *To Change the World*, appear to be, first, his attempt to coax Christians into not wounding either themselves *or* demurring unbelievers in the pursuit of a more Christianly-influenced America. The inculcation of more Christian values to the American populace via the common view of cultural change's three main tactics—evangelism, political action, and social reform—are all good, fruitful, and helpful; however, Hunter finds that most Christian strategies for cultural transformation are largely wanting. This is not for the lack of resources invested in the process, nor negligence in application, but by a

88. Warrington. "Social Transformation," 21.

fundamental misunderstanding of the sociological processes by which lasting cultural changes take place.

True and lasting Christian transformation, according to Hunter, will not occur through the force of better ideas, nor necessarily through careful articulation of an alternative worldview, nor even by earnest attempts to will cultural change, but *primarily* through a complex of divine sovereignty, historical serendipity, sociological facts, and human contingency. Thus, we as theologians and practitioners would do well to take heed of Hunter, and to other voices different from our respective academic disciplines, who might inform us of our intellectual and moral blind spots. As we have seen above, it is also of the utmost importance that room is made within the disciplines of social change for the influence of the Holy Spirit, without whom we are left to our shallow inspiration, myopic guidance, and frail power.

BIBLIOGRAPHY

Benedetto, Robert, gen. ed. *The New SCM Dictionary of Church History*. Vol. 1: *From the Early Church to 1700*. London: SCM, 2008.

Cairns, Earle E. *Christianity through the Centuries: A History of the Christian Church*. Grand Rapids: Zondervan, 1996.

Carlson, Arnold E. "Luther and the Doctrine of the Holy Spirit." *Lutheran Quarterly* 11 (1959) 135–46.

Cameron, Euan. *Interpreting Christian History: The Challenge of the Churches' Past*. Malden, MA: Blackwell, 2005.

Glouse, Robert G., Richard V. Pierard, and Edwin M. Yamauchi. *Two Kingdoms: The Church and Culture through the Ages*. Chicago: Moody, 1993.

Douglass, Jane Dempsey. "The Lively Work of the Spirit in the Reformation." The 2002– 2003 Word & World Lecture. *Word & World* 23 (2003) 121–33.

Gonzalez, Justo L. *The Story of Christianity: The Early Church to the Present Day*. Peabody, MA: Prince Press, 1999.

Grimm, Harold J. *The Reformation Era 1500—1650*. New York: Macmillan, 1973.

Hendrix, Scott. "Martin Luther, Reformer." In *The Cambridge History of Christianity: Reform and Expansion*, edited by R. Po-Chia Hsia, 3–19. Cambridge: Cambridge University Press, 2007.

Hunter, James Davison. *To Change the World: The Irony, Tragedy, & Possibility of Christianity in the Late Modern World*. New York: Oxford University Press, 2010.

Holt, Mack P. "The Social History of the Reformation: Recent Trends and Future Agendas." *Journal of Social History* 37 (2003) 133–44.

MacCullough, Diarmaid. *A History of Christianity: The First Three Thousand Years*. London: Penguin, 2009.

————. *Reformation: Europe's House 1490—1700*. London: Penguin, 2003.

Marty, Martin E. "Preaching on the Holy Spirit: A Study of Luther's Sermons on the Evangelical Pericopes." *Concordia Theological Monthly* 26 (1955) 423–41.

McGrath, Alister E. *Reformation Thought: An Introduction*. 4th ed. Chichester, UK: Wiley–Blackwell, 2012.

———. *Roots that Refresh: A Celebration of Reformation Spirituality.* London: Hodder & Stoughton, 1991.

Oberman, Heiko A. *The Reformation: Roots and Ramifications.* Edinburgh: T. & T. Clark, 1994.

Payton, James R. *Getting the Reformation Wrong: Correcting Some Misunderstandings.* Downer's Grove, IL: IVP Academic, 2010. eBook version.

Ryrie, Alex. *Protestants: The Radicals Who Made the Modern World.* London: Collins, 2017.

Strange, Daniel. "Faithful Presence: A Theology for the Trenches?" In *Revisiting 'Faithful Presence': To Change the World Five Years Later,* edited by Colin Hansen, 47–56. Deerfield, IL: Gospel Coalition, 2015. Kindle edition.

Thiselton, Anthony C. *The Holy Spirit—In Biblical Teaching, through the Centuries, and Today.* Eerdmans: Grand Rapids, 2013.

Vondey, Wolfgang. "Pentecostalism and the Reformation: Toward a Joint Ecumenical Commemoration." *Journal of the European Pentecostal Theological Association* 37 (2017) 110–22.

Warrington, Keith. "Social Transformation in the Missions of Pentecostals: A Priority or a Bonus?" *Journal of the European Pentecostal Theological Association* 31 (2011) 17–35.

Made in the USA
Coppell, TX
20 April 2021

54093143R00164